T
=

LECTURES ON THE HISTORY OF
MORAL AND POLITICAL PHILOSOPHY

LECTURES ON THE HISTORY OF MORAL AND POLITICAL PHILOSOPHY

G. A. Cohen

EDITED BY JONATHAN WOLFF

PRINCETON UNIVERSITY PRESS

Princeton and Oxford

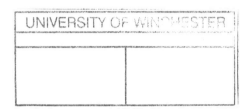

Copyright © 2014 by Princeton University Press
Published by Princeton University Press, 41 William Street, Princeton, New Jersey 08540
In the United Kingdom: Princeton University Press, 6 Oxford Street, Woodstock, Oxfordshire OX20 1TW

press.princeton.edu

Jacket photograph: Owl standing right, head facing. Reverse of a silver tetradrachm from Athens, ca. 480–420 BC. Photo: Marie-Lan Nguyen. Location: Museum of Fine Arts of Lyon, France.

Library of Congress Cataloging-in-Publication Data

Cohen, G. A. (Gerald Allan), 1941-2009.
  Lectures on the history of moral and political philosophy / G. A. Cohen ; edited by Jonathan Wolff.
    pages cm
  Includes bibliographical references and index.
  ISBN 978-0-691-14900-4 (alk. paper)
  1. Ethics—History. 2. Political science—Philosophy—History. I. Title.
  BJ71.C64 2013
  170—dc23
    2013000199

British Library Cataloging-in-Publication Data is available

This book has been composed in Sabon

Printed on acid-free paper. ∞

Printed in the United States of America

10 9 8 7 6 5 4 3 2 1

Contents

————

Editor's Preface

———————

> I think I may try to publish a book of wholly unpublished
> material, consisting of my lectures, or some of them, on political
> (and some moral) philosophy, with chapters on Plato, Hobbes,
> Locke, Hume, Kant, Hegel, Marx and maybe Nietzsche. The
> good thing about the project is that the lectures are, if I may say
> so, stimulating and interesting. The bad thing is that they don't
> refer at all to recent scholarly literature on their subjects.
>
> —JERRY COHEN, EMAIL (JUNE 14, 2007)

Shortly before his tragic and untimely death, Cohen discussed with Michael Otsuka his plans for producing volumes of his then-uncollected papers. They also considered how to bring that work to completion if he did not live to finish the task—a conversation that was sadly prophetic. Two volumes of his papers are now published, under Mike's superb editorship. It was suggested that I might edit a third volume, and I was honored to take on this task.

Cohen's writings in this volume fall into two parts. The main section contains Cohen's previously unpublished lectures on the history of moral and political philosophy. The second part reprints some writings bearing on the history of political philosophy and ethics that have not previously been included in collections of Cohen's work. The third part contains a memoir of Cohen that I wrote for the *Proceedings of the British Academy*, and sets out an account of Cohen's remarkable life and work.

One surprise for many readers will be that this volume does not include lectures on Marx. However, some of Cohen's lectures on Hegel and Marx were reprinted as chapters 3 to 5 of *If You're an Egalitarian, How Come You're So Rich?*, and little remaining material was found. That book, therefore, should be regarded as an essential companion to this one, as well as a brilliant work in its own right. Earlier lectures and papers on Marx led to Cohen's *Karl Marx's Theory of History: A Defence*, and the papers in *History, Labour, and Freedom*, the most important of which were included in the second edition of *Karl Marx's Theory of History*. Hence most of Cohen's writings on Marx are already widely available, with the exception of those now reprinted here. Their contents will be explored below.

Of the chapters in Part One, many are based on lectures first given in the 1960s and then subsequently revised. Several, although not all, were still undergoing revision for delivery in Oxford even toward the end of Cohen's career there, and have final revision dates of between 1999 and 2004.

Taking the chapters in the chronological order in which they appear in this book, the first chapter, on Plato, is based on Cohen's lectures for a course titled Classical Political Thought. From correspondence between Cohen and Richard Wollheim, his head of department at University College London, where he had started lecturing in 1963, it appears that these lectures were first delivered when Cohen was visiting McGill in 1965–66, where he gave two lecture courses, each requiring three lectures a week. Classical Political Thought was one of these, and Hegel and Marx the other. It appears that he also gave them on his return to UCL. Cohen seems not to have lectured on Plato in the 1970s and 1980s, although he did teach this material in tutorials. However, in 1990 Cohen and Mark Philp together revived an earlier lecture course, Plato to Rousseau, that had previously been offered by Charles Taylor. This took place every second year. The Plato lectures were revised then, for that purpose, and Cohen continued to work on them. Normally Cohen lectured on Plato, Hobbes, Locke, and Hume, with Philp lecturing on Aristotle, Natural Law thinking, Aquinas, Machiavelli, Montaigne, Pascal, Montesquieu, and Rousseau, although in some years some lectures were given by others.

The central focus of Cohen's lectures on Plato is the nature/convention distinction, and how it is taken up by the pre-Socratics, and treated in more critical fashion by Plato. The lectures also contain material on Aristotle. This was not revised from the earliest version, although from the notes on the lectures it seems that Cohen did sometimes include this material in his later lectures, or at least make provision to do so.

The next three chapters, on Hobbes, Locke, and Hume, are based on Cohen's lectures at Oxford. On taking on the Chichele Chair in Social and Political Theory at Oxford, Cohen agreed to gives lectures on the history of political thought, and this lecture course was devised to meet that commitment. They were certainly given in 1988–89. Shortly afterward they were incorporated into the course taught with Mark Philp mentioned above. Although Cohen lectured on Locke earlier at UCL, there his focus was private property in the context of explaining and criticizing Robert Nozick's view. This material made its way into print as part of Cohen's 1985 British Academy lecture, "Marx and Locke on Land and Labour," reprinted in Cohen's collection *Self-Ownership, Freedom, and Equality*. The lectures on Locke included here, with their greater focus on political obligation, form a natural complement to the preceding chapter on Hobbes and to the succeeding chapter on Hume on the social contract. What appear here as three separate chapters were written up as a single set of connected lectures, all of which take political obligation as their central focus.

The lectures on Hegel are essentially an account of the master/slave dialectic from the *Phenomenology of Spirit*. These, according to the notes on the lectures, were first written in 1968, then revised in 1998, and "tidied" in 2004. Cohen gave classes at UCL on Hegel for those taking the finals option "Hegel and Marx," which ran until around 1980, at which point it was split into two and Cohen concentrated on Marx. However, he taught Hegel again after his return to Oxford in 1985, and continued to run graduate classes, often cotaught with Michael Rosen.

The lectures on Kant's ethics were typed up in 1999, but almost certainly date back to the beginnings of Cohen's teaching career, perhaps as early as 1963. Cohen was engaged to lecture on ethics at UCL, and he is very likely to have included lectures on Kant at this time, as well as lectures on contemporary themes in ethics. He lectured on ethics in London on his return from McGill in 1966, and probably until the early 1970s, but not again after that as his teaching turned to political philosophy and Marxism. The lectures on Kant fall into two parts; the first is a rather general account of Kant's moral philosophy, exploring in particular Kant's account of reason. The second part is a tour de force in which Cohen identifies twelve different distinctions made by Kant, which Kant needs to be coexistensive, and documents some of the most significant ways in which Kant fails to achieve his aims.

For those familiar with Cohen's work the Nietzsche lectures are the most unexpected discovery. They were given at McGill in the academic year 1965–66, and the first third or so of the material was retyped in revised form in 1970, a version that also includes later handwritten annotations. These then formed part of Cohen's early lectures on ethics at UCL. It seems unlikely that they were given again after the early 1970s. Here Cohen's task is primarily to explain Nietzsche's approach to morality, and although some important criticisms are registered, they are not pursued in detail. These are perhaps the most straightforwardly expository of Cohen's lectures, and many will benefit from reading them even now. They are remarkable for their time, especially considering that Cohen was in his midtwenties when he first wrote them.

The volume ends with a selection of previously published material, although none of the essays have been included in Cohen's other collections. The first, "Bourgeois and Proletariats," was published in the *Journal of the History of Ideas*, and reprinted in *Marx's Socialism*, edited by Shlomo Avineri. It addresses the still-neglected question of the nature of the alienation of the bourgeoisie under capitalism. The second paper, "The Workers and the Word," is included at the suggestion of Paula Casal. It was published in the important Yugoslavian journal *Praxis*, but as a result has been virtually unobtainable in recent years. It explores the vital question of why Marx's arguments against ideological illusion do not undermine his own theory. The third paper, "Reply to Elster on 'Marxism, Functionalism, and Game

Theory,'" responds to Jon Elster's criticism of Cohen's use of functional explanation in his presentation of historical materialism. It is, perhaps, the clearest defense against some trenchant criticisms, registering some dissatisfactions of its own. The fourth paper, a short review of Allen Wood's book *Karl Marx*, is included as it contains the first published statement by Cohen of his view of Marx's thinking about justice. The final paper, a response to Christine Korsgaard's Tanner Lectures, takes up in more detail some of the arguments made in the lecture on Hobbes, applying them also to Kant and to Korsgaard's own views.

The chapters present the manuscripts as they were found in the latest edition, sometimes including some handwritten or typed additional notes, often marked "not for lecture" or the like. Most of these additional notes have been included in the text, as that was clearly Cohen's intention. In some cases a chapter is clearly unfinished, but rather than try to guess what Cohen would have liked to include, I have generally included all available material.

Corrections have been very few: the very rare occasional typo has been corrected where spotted. Wherever possible, the original source of quotations has been used, and references found. This sometimes means that more than one translation of a text is cited in a single chapter. Cohen sometimes referred to a marked passage in his copy of a text rather than type it out. In almost all cases these have been found.

Inevitably these lectures will be compared to John Rawls's *Lectures on the History of Moral Philosophy* and *Lectures on the History of Political Philosophy*. However, the enterprises, like their authors, are very different. Rawls aims to give a fair and complete overview of the figures he discusses, identifying their strengths, and, regretfully, pointing out their limitations, though generally assuming that great philosophers do not make obvious mistakes, and so reinterpretation is called for. Cohen, in contrast, essentially discusses those things that interest him. Cohen records, in his lectures, his engagement with the figures he discusses. Yet in doing so he locates, and provides his unique perspective on, some of the central concerns in the thought of the philosophers he engages with, almost all of whom can be convicted of mistaken arguments or positions that are flawed in particular ways. Rawls talks of reverence for the texts he discusses, trying to understand the thinker in his historical context, where history includes political history as well history of ideas. Cohen shows a different sort of reverence: for him to respect a thinker is to engage with the arguments, following the logic wherever it leads. In this Cohen shows greater affinity with his teacher Gilbert Ryle than with his teacher Isaiah Berlin. Yet Cohen always seems to go to the heart of the issue. Whether you agree or disagree with the criticisms he makes, you see more in a philosopher than you had noticed before. More than anything, Cohen always makes you think.

Acknowledgments

I would particularly like to thank the Cohen family for having the confidence in me to allow me to take on this project. Many people have given up time and effort to help bring this book to completion. For help in various forms I would like to thank Chris Bertram, Chris Brooke, Myles Burnyeat, Paula Casal, Matthew Clayton, Maggie Cohen, Michèle Cohen, Miriam Cohen Christofidis, Max Collins Wolff, Cécile Fabre, Sebastian Gardner, Marcus Giaquinto, Keith Graham, George Hull, Edmund Hussey, Fiona Leigh, Brian Leiter, Peter Millican, Martin O'Neill, Michael Otsuka, David Owen, Mark Philp, Barnaby Raine, Michael Rosen, Seana Shiffrin, Andrew Williams, and Arnold Zuboff. I'd also like to thank Lauren Lepow for expert copyediting and for making the production process so painless (for me at least), and also Ed Lamb for his excellent work in preparing the index.

The papers in Parts Two and Three are reprinted with the following permissions:

8. "Bourgeois and Proletarians." © 1968 *Journal of the History of Ideas Inc*. Reprinted with the permission of University of Pennsylvania Press.

9. "The Workers and the Word: Why Marx Had the Right to Think He Was Right." © 1968 *Praxis*. 3/4, 376–90. Reprinted with the permission of the Croatian Philosophical Society.

10. "Reply to Elster on 'Marxism, Functionalism, and Game Theory.'" © 1982 *Theory and Society* 11: 483–95. Reprinted with the permission of Springer.

11. Review of *Karl Marx*, by Allen W. Wood. 1983 © *Mind*, 92, p. 440–45 Reprinted with permission of Oxford University Press on behalf of the Mind Association.

12. "Reason, Humanity, and the Moral Law." © 1996. In Christine Korsgaard, *The Sources of Normativity*, pp. 167–188. Reprinted with permission of Cambridge University Press.

13. "G. A. Cohen: A Memoir." © The British Academy, 2011. Reproduced with permission from *Biographical Memoirs of Fellows, X*, Proceedings of the British Academy volume 172, Oxford: 2011, pp. 49–67.

PART ONE

Lectures

Chapter 1

PLATO AND HIS PREDECESSORS

0. I believe that the philosophically most fundamental motivation of Plato's *Republic* is to reply to a staple proposition of fifth-century Greek thought, a proposition propounded by many of Plato's Sophistic predecessors, and that is the proposition that there is a distinction between nature and convention, *phusis* and *nomos*, and that *nomos*, convention, human law, cannot be derived from nature, and, according to some, though not all, of those who believe all that, even *contradicts* nature. I think Plato was an extreme social conservative who found the line of thought that contrasted nature and convention threatening, and that it is profitable to read the *Republic* as a reply to that threat.

It is true that the threat is not put expressly like that in the *Republic*. But the subversive distinction between nature and convention *is* alive in the challenge that Glaucon lays down to Socrates. Plato's manifest aim, among other things, is to respond to Glaucon, and thereby to refute a contractarian account of justice which debases it by tracing it to individual self-interest. Here's what Glaucon says:

> Well, I promised I'd talk first about the nature and origin of morality, so here goes. The idea is that although it's a fact of nature that doing wrong is good and having wrong done to one is bad, nevertheless the disadvantages of having it done to one outweigh the benefits of doing it. Consequently, once people have experienced both committing wrong *and* being at the receiving end of it, they see that the disadvantages are unavoidable and the benefits are unattainable; so they decide that the most profitable course is for them to enter into a contract with one another, guaranteeing that no wrong will be committed or received. They then set about making laws and decrees, and from then on they use the terms "legal" and "right" to describe anything which is enjoined by their code. So that's the origin and nature of morality, on this [that is, the Sophist] view: it is a compromise between the ideal of doing wrong without having to pay for it, and the worst situation, which is having wrong done to one while lacking the means of exacting compensation. Since morality is a compromise, it is endorsed because, while it may not be good, it does gain value by preventing people from doing wrong. The point is that any real man with the *ability* to do wrong [and get away with it] would never enter into a

3

contract to avoid both wronging and being wronged: he wouldn't be so crazy. Anyway, Socrates, that is what this view has to say about the nature and origin of morality and so on.[1]

Glaucon is saying that morality is not natural to us, like affection or anger, and he is putting a particular individualist spin on that.[2] But in replying to Glaucon Plato goes beyond the contractarian argument to dispute the Sophistic terms in which it is framed.[3] "Glaucon's account resonates with the fifth-century distinction (associated particularly with the sophistic movement) between nature and convention, and the preference for the competitive values of natural law rather than the co-operative values of conventional law."[4]

Accordingly, and in order to expound the doctrine of the *Republic* from the explained angle of vision, that is, within the perspective of the nature/convention contrast, I shall first discuss the contribution of Sophists.

1. In the history of European civilization, the fifth-century traveling teachers known as the Sophists were the first to treat social and political affairs as an *independent* object of study. Now the phrase "independent object" invites the question "independent of" what? And the answer is that they studied society and politics, indeed, humankind itself, as something independent of, or separate from, the world of nonhuman nature: that is the deepest meaning of their famous distinction between nature and convention, between what comes naturally and what comes by human and social contrivance. We may conjecture that, before the Sophists, or at any rate before the Athenian fifth century, there is not a *developed* conception such as we take for granted of the human being as operating differently from beings of nonhuman nature, nor of the individual human being as a being endowed both with *freedom of choice*, and notably with the capacity and the right to govern his or her own life; nor of a human community as having an unambiguous right to make and remake laws which reflect its optional ideals and interests. I do not mean that, before the Sophists, no one has any inkling of these truths, some of which may indeed be truisms, but that, as I put it, there is no integrated *developed* conception answering to them. (It would be as absurd to suppose that, pre-Sophistically, *nomos* and *phusis* were *entirely* confounded as it would be to suppose that there was *no* assimilation that their emphatic distinguishing rejected. Only

1   Plato, *The Republic* (358c–359b), p. 46.

2   Not all contractarian accounts of justice debase it. Rawls's contractarian account notoriously—if that is the right word!—doesn't. But Glaucon's does.

3   He responds to Glaucon as though he's responding to the sharp contrast between nature and convention in Antiphon's poem: see below.

4   Robin Waterfield, commenting on 359b of the *Republic* at p. 386 of his translation.

bores say with special emphasis what everybody knows to be true. When the Sophists contrasted nature and convention, many were shocked as no one could be if anyone happened to say with special emphasis: there's a difference between the dry and the wet.)

The *nomos/phusis* distinction generates a possibility of radical criticism and radical transformation: the space society occupies, when society is conceived in separation from the natural world, is a space of possibility and choice (at *least* relative to natural constraint). Much conservative thought is an attempt to shrink that space, and it is not surprising that there exists a perennial conservative rhetoric in which certain existing institutions are said to be *natural*, which means that they have arisen with some necessity, like a flower from its seed, or that they are natural in that they can be suppressed only at great cost, at the cost, and here again we can use the flower analogy, of distortion, of destruction of natural growth. The Sophist distinction between nature and convention, *phusis* and *nomos*, between what comes of itself and what comes by deliberate contrivance contradicts that particular conservative outlook.

Now, as I said, the Sophist emphasis on the nature/convention distinction proves that in pre-Sophistic thought it was not made, or not with the appropriate and required emphasis: nobody makes a great to-do about a distinction that is entirely familiar. Taking that as a clue, I hypothesize that we encounter in pre-Sophistic thought a conception of humanity in which it is *engulfed*, or sunk, in nature.[5] In this conception humanity is not conceived to be *as* separate from the rest of nature as humanity later came to be conceived to be. And on that hypothesis, it follows that we find in *pre*-Sophistic thought a conceptual predisposition to if not the full doctrinal structure of a conservative social philosophy. (A fully articulated conservative doctrinal structure is, in any case, impossible, until its doctrinal opposite is also possible. You cannot deny that there is a distinction between nature and convention until that distinction is on the table. We can certainly say that the conservative *post*-Sophists, Plato and Aristotle, rejected the distinction that the Sophists made: but the Sophists' predecessors simply *failed* to make it—it was not yet there to be rejected.)

In the lectures that follow, I shall do five things. First, I shall set forth a partly conjectured pre-Sophistic thought pattern, in which humanity is, to a degree, engulfed in nature. Next, I shall describe the Sophistic revolution, or, better, the fifth-century revolution in conception that found a particularly sharp expression in the teaching of some Sophists. (It is not so important for my purposes to credit the Sophists in particular with originality in this respect, by comparison, say, with the Athenian playwrights, of whom I know very little. What matters is that the Sophists

---

5   For that concept of engulfment, see my *History, Labour, and Freedom*, pp. 187–89.

were militant public or semipublic deniers of a traditional thinking that Plato sought to retrieve.) Third, I shall present the political thought of the political reactionary Plato as an attempt to recoup and refashion the subordination of humanity to nature which characterized the pre-Sophistic tradition. Fourth, I shall also say some things about Plato's *Republic* in particular which amplify my principal theme, and then, fifth, some further things that have almost nothing to do with it.

2. I now pursue my hypothesis about pre-Sophistic thought. I cite three indications that it failed thoroughly to distinguish humanity from nature, and, with respect to each indication, the contrast with the Sophists is plain. In summary description, the three are: (1) that *in explanatory theory* humanity is regarded as continuous with nature, as are the Gods and nature, and the Gods, of course, are more or less naive projections of human beings; that human beings are not viewed as free and responsible; or as determining their own history; (2) that they are thought of as dividing naturally into (a) Greeks and barbarians, (b) free persons and slaves, and (c) natural aristocrats and natural hoi polloi; and (3) that there was much reflection at a high intellectual level about cosmology and physics, and, one could say, physical chemistry, but not systematic reflection, just occasional asides, about human society. I must now elaborate and connect these points.

3. (i) As far as fundamental explanations of them are concerned, *humanity and nature are in a relatively undifferentiated continuum*. Indeed, divinity, humanity, and nature are all three assimilated to one another—natural occurrences are explained in the language of justice, a language that later comes to be restricted to the human realm; human beings are understood on the model of other parts of nature; and nature is understood as manifesting divine forces where the divine is itself understood in human terms.

We think of nature as mindless and of ourselves as possessed of consciousness and acting out of deliberation. We think of natural things as lacking in spontaneity and operating *according* to law, and we think of ourselves as, by contrast, spontaneously adopting designs, being *guided* by laws (as atoms are not), and even as *devising* the laws by which we are guided. To be sure, there are materialists among us who are skeptical about the robustness of the distinction that I just drew. They will say that the special powers of humankind are *ultimately* grounded in or reducible to nothing but a complex arrangement of nature, that part of nature which comprises the human cerebrum and nervous system. But, when they are not addressing ultimate questions, which is to say, most of the time, the materialists think the way everybody else does, using contrasts which we all take for granted, whether or not in a philosophical hour we labor to stress the contrast or to reduce its force or even to explain it away.

Since it is obvious for us to make the foregoing distinction between the structures of human and natural agency, we readily distinguish, as I indeed did a moment ago, between the *laws* that human beings make and the laws to which *nature* conforms, so much so that one might claim that the word "law" is now ambiguous across those two contexts.[6] But that distinction between social and natural law was not at all obvious to the early Greeks, one indication of which is the manifest fact that when the Sophists contrasted *nomos* and *phusis* what they said was treated as novel and subversive.[7]

The *nomos/phusis* distinction is absent or slurred in early Greek thought since, for the early Greeks, the human estate is understood in terms of nature *and* the realm of nature is explained by principles that we have learned to restrict to the human realm. When Anaximander of Miletus (610–ca. 547 BC) says, "Things come into existence and perish as it is ordained; for they pay the just penalty and retribution to each other for their injustice, in accordance with the order of time,"[8] and when Heraclitus (of Ephesus ca. 540–ca. 480) echoes, "The sun will not overstep its limits, because if it does the Erinyes [the Furies, handmaidens of justice] will find him out,"[9] they are not, so I think, (consciously) pressing the idea of man-made law into merely metaphorical service as explanatory of natural processes.[10] Rather, it is the same principle of justice which regulates the movements of nature and of humankind. "For all human laws are sustained by one law, which is divine"[11] which also controls nature. Of course, laws were *made*

6   Though I am not myself sure that it actually is: see Roger Wertheimer, *The Significance of Sense*: his case for the univocity of the modal "must" might be extended to the word "law," as designating what *must* happen.

7   The early Greeks, so my colleague Myles Burnyeat says, had no concept of a law of nature as such, but only of natural regularities that reflect justice. [This is the first of a number of footnotes in which Cohen quotes or responds to comments attributed to Myles Burnyeat. Reprinted with kind permission of Myles Burnyeat—Ed.]

8   Quoted in Barnes, *The Presocratic Philosophers*, p. 130. This is Theophrastus reporting Anaximander, and Hussey, *The Presocratics*, p. 23, translates it as follows: "[Anaximander says that] the destruction of things that are [that is, that exist] takes place by their turning back into those things from which they had their origin, *according to necessity*; for they *make requital and recompense* to one another for their injustice, according to the *assessment of Time*." Hussey remarks that "Time" may here refer to "a divine power, namely the Unbounded," which imposes the retributive law. (Ibid., p. 24.)

9   Quoted in Barnes, *The Presocratic Philosphers*, p. 131.

10   See on Anaximander, Irwin, *Classical Thought*, p. 23; on Heraclitus, ibid., pp. 47, 52. And consider Hussey, *The Presocratics*, p. 17: The "easily observable cycles [of nature] must have been the best guarantee for the Milesians of the existence of a controlling law in the universe: the parallel with the periodic rotation of political office necessary among equals was close at hand." See ibid., p. 40, for nuance in the relationship between human and divine law in Heraclitus, and pp. 48–49 on some possible differences between the Anaximanderian and Heraclitean conceptions of natural justice, also discussed by Barnes, *The Presocratic Philosophers*, p. 130.

11   Heraclitus, quoted by Dodds, *The Ancient Concept of Progress*, p. 98.

by human beings and customs were perpetuated because of thousands of daily *decisions* in the times of Anaximander and Heraclitus, just as they are now, but that is not conceived in the theoretical *representation* as a matter of creation and decision in the sense of those terms in which they denote transcendence of the impositions of nature. They conceived the order in social life, the regularity, as more like the order in the movement of the stars or the tides, with the former being a special case of the latter, since society is a part of nature. Let me quote from Dodds's essay, *The Ancient Concept of Progress*, on the Sophistic movement:

> When a Greek of the archaic period spoke of "law", and even when he spoke of "the laws" in the plural, he usually meant not the contents of the statute-book but the entire body of traditional usage which governed the whole of his civic conduct, political, social, and religious. He thought of it, not as something which was liable to be altered next year, but as an accepted inheritance which formed the permanent background of his life. The laws represented the collective wisdom of the past; perhaps they had been codified by some great man, a Lycurgus or a Solon, but they were felt to rest ultimately on an authority higher than that of any individual statesman. Heraclitus made the feeling explicit when he declared that "all human laws are sustained by one law, which is divine."[12]

Here the arrangements that people had made and which they themselves sustained are presented as rooted in nature, and to nature is attributed the principle of justice that is not yet explicitly affirmed as a human cultural artifact.[13]

Now all this was of course the easier to do because of a reciprocal conceptual assimilation: while the human world was, as emphasized, engulfed in nature, the world of nature was interpreted as though it consisted of the doings of human beings. The originating agencies of natural occurrences are Gods, but the character of the Gods is nothing but a reflection of human character. So humanity is permeated by nature, and nature through being divinely run is permeated by humanity. In Anaximander and Heraclitus the principles regulating social existence are read into and made constitutive of nature, and their manifestation in human life is then understood as a reflection of nature itself. This process is what the nineteenth-century thinkers Hegel, Feuerbach, and Marx called a process of *alienation*. Something human is projected into something

---

12   Dodds, *The Ancient Concept of Progress*, pp. 97–98.

13   For an interesting discussion of the texts of Anaximander and Heraclitus used above, see Barnes, *The Presocratic Philosophers*, pp. 129ff. Barnes says on p. 130 that Anaximander was "seduced" by the fact that *nomos* and *dike* applied both to human and to natural law. I think it far more likely that the double application reflected a conceptual assimilation than that it generated it.

nonhuman, and its manifestation in humanity is then regarded as secondary to its manifestation in what is not human.

Nor is the assimilation of the natural to the divine and therefore to the human a feature only of mythological picture-thinking, for the "naturalists in general," that is, the pre-Socratic philosophers, "seem to claim that everything is divine and that the divine order is nothing more than the natural order":[14] they follow Thales, for whom "all things are full of Gods,"[15] so that for Heraclitus, in Hussey's words, "theology and physics are one."[16] As Hussey also emphasizes,[17] in Milesian cosmological speculation the view of the Gods as multiple and disorderly is transcended, and that no doubt means that they are less waywardly *human* than they are in myth. But that does not eliminate the triune continuum, although it does make it less colorful.

The second respect, consequent on the first, in which humanity was in its conception of itself engulfed in nature was that human beings were not in their own cultural self-representation viewed as responsible choosers of their actions.

Over the beating of my heart and the peristaltic movement of my gut I have little or no control: these are natural processes. And if all my functioning is seen as comparably natural, if there is no range of functioning which is set aside as transcending nature, then there is no concept of freedom and there is not *that* concept of responsibility which goes with the concept of freedom of choice. And so, and in this and the next two paragraphs I follow Adkins's book on *Merit and Responsibility* (which, so I must warn you, is highly controversial, most scholars *not* accepting it), it is unsurprising that the early Greeks, engulfed as they were, lacked the elementary moral ideas of choice and guilt, which began to be articulated in the fifth century and which remain with us today, although we are to a degree losing our grip on them precisely to the extent that Darwin and Freud and Pavlov and Crick, Watson, and Wilkins, and their successors purvey theories which tend to restore the continuity of humanity and nature through which the Sophists broke.

The behavior of a character in Homer (ca. 750 BC) divides like anybody's behavior does, into actions which are in and actions which are out of character. The implicit explanatory doctrine for actions in character is that they are due to the character they are in, where that is thought of as a feature of the person on a par with, for example, her height, thought of in a way that is at the opposite extreme from existential notions that we form our character through our choices. Inflammable material tends to

---

14 Irwin, *Classical Thought*, p. 39.
15 Hussey, *The Presocratics*, p. 19.
16 Ibid., p. 47.
17 Ibid., p. 29.

burst into flame and a courageous person tends to behave courageously. When, however, a person departs strikingly from his usual way, when he acts out of character, then that is not thought of as showing his freedom, for it rather tends to be thought that he must have been seized by a God. Neither when acting in character nor when acting out of it are people thought of as *governing* their own behavior.[18]

They consequently cannot be called to account for it in the way that we are. They can be *held* responsible, but only in the way that you hold a dog responsible, without implication that it could have chosen otherwise. People can be praised and admired or condemned and contemned but in the spirit in which natural things are assessed, as you admire a fine horse or throw out a rotten apple with disgust. The vocabulary of evaluation of character, words like *agathos* and *arete* (good, virtue), is applied to animals as it is to people. Dogs can be brave, loyal, charming, elegant, faithful, perhaps ashamed, but not conscientious, guilt-ridden, in moral conflict, saintly, maybe not sensitive, and it is the first range of terms that is applied to people, not the second. What people feel is not guilt but shame which, unlike guilt, does not presuppose morally wrong choice: you can be ashamed of what your father did but not so easily feel guilty about it. You can feel ashamed of but not guilty about a disfigurement. You can be ashamed of what you inescapably are, and people are calumniated for that or even for having the shame of being vehicles of bad Gods-imposed processes.[19]

Now Adkins no doubt exaggerates the position, but we should note that Protagoras, in the Platonic dialogue that bears his name, urges that people should be punished only for those evil features which they can be expected to try to remove, not for those indelibly imposed on them by nature. An elementary reflection, but Vlastos[20] shares Adkins's view in *Merit and Responsibility* that it was original with Protagoras.[21]

3 (ii). The Sophist rejection of the construal of the social as natural was politically explosive in its denial of a natural basis to three distinctions: between Greeks and barbarians, between freemen and slaves, and between the aristocracy, or wellborn, and the mass.

18   [The text at this point has the comment: "[See, however, Hussey's good critique of this]." This refers to a set of notes Edward Hussey gave to Cohen. I thank Edward Hussey for this information.—Ed.]

19   For similar structure of blamability in Confucius, see Gerth and Mills, *Character and Social Structure*, p. 189.

20   Plato, *Protagoras*, introduction.

21   "Sophists, with their practical interest in law-court speeches, were particularly interested in questions of guilt and responsibility, and the cases in which a human agent could claim to have been 'overcome' by some force so that the act in question was not truly his. But the greatest insight into the complexity of human motivation at this time is to be found in the Attic tragedians, and in the delicately clinical analyses of Thucydides" (Hussey, *The Presocratics*, pp. 122–23).

Heraclitus denied that barbarians possessed a developed reasoning faculty.[22] Someone as late as Epicurus (341–271) could still say that only Greeks were able to philosophize: the tradition persists and does not divide from the protest against it in a neatly chronological way.

Now this distinction between Greek and barbarian tends to converge with one between natural master and natural slave: the naturally inferior barbarian is fitted by nature to labor menially for the naturally superior Greek.

These are prejudices that *came* to be adopted. "Came to be," because, unlike the other patterns of thought I have been expounding, they are not visible in Homer. Homer saw the possibilities of human behavior thoroughly constricted by natural gifts, but he did not distribute those gifts in special proportions as between Greeks and barbarians, nor did he connect slavery with naturally inferior character, only with physical inferiority (a more obviously natural dimension).

A history of war and conquest in Greece produced a relationship of mastery and servitude between conqueror and conquered, and poets and pundits were eager to justify the socially durable arrangement in terms of natural endowment. Thus Theognis could write, in the sixth century: "A slave's head is never upright, but always bent and he has a slanting neck. A rose or a hyacinth never comes from a sea-onion: no more does a free child from a slave woman."[23] Like Theognis (ca. 550–500), Pindar (528–438) and other late sixth- and early fifth-century poets insisted on the barbarian/Greek and slave/freemen distinctions, and also found a basis in nature for the division between[24] the aristocracy and hoi polloi, the many.

The aristocratic social orders of the seventh and sixth centuries claimed a natural superiority. That natural superiority proposition it sustained in certain near-equivalences of meaning in common language that I shall presently mention[25] as well as in the explicit teachings of poets like Theognis and Pindar.

A term like "good" (*agathos*) served to denote *both* goodness taken generally as belonging to anything that is superior in value *and* good birth and good breeding in particular, rather like the outmoded English term "quality," which once meant the quality, people of quality, as well as enjoying its wider meaning in which it denotes value as such. The

22   Myles Burnyeat says that this attribution misuses the text, which says that "[e]yes and ears are poor witnesses for men, if they have barbarian souls" (Fragment 107, Diels-Kanz), and that in *this* sense he would have said that most Greeks had barbarian souls. But (1) how does Burnyeat know the latter? and (2) there would still be *a* link to *ethnic* barbarian-ness. (Consider "goyishe kop" [Yiddish for "gentile head," a remark indicating that gentiles are not as clever as Jews.—Ed.]).

23   Quoted by Williams, *Shame and Necessity*, p. 114.

24   See Schlaifer, "Greek Theories of Slavery from Homer to Aristotle."

25   [A note in the text at this point says: "The development of this claim below needs wholesale clarification."—Ed.]

aristocracy are best born, best by origin and therefore by nature, so they are the best. (Cf. "good family": we haven't quite given up saying things like "she comes from a good family," and that doesn't mean that they're morally good. It means they're rich but un-merely-recently rich. Cf. "nice people," "Schöne Leute haben schöne Sachen."[26])

Once such linguistic joints have developed, it is very difficult to fracture them. It can be more difficult to say that ordinary people are good, have value, than it is to mock the desirability of being "good" altogether. That is, it can be easier for anti-aristocrats to debase the term "good" than to claim goodness for the demos.

This is so because aristocracy thrives on the idea of (natural) *distinction*, and a resonance of such distinction gets built into the terms of positive appraisal. (When, by the way, Robert Burns says, "the rank is but the guinea stamp, a man's a man for a' that,"[27] he is saying that distinction of rank is purely conventional, a guinea stamp, marked on nothing *naturally* more valuable. He is making a radical nature/convention point. The poem is great, and its datedness shows there was a thought-structure that has now gone.) And since the term is redolent of distinction, it is difficult to claim that everyone satisfies it. So it takes time for epithets like "Monsieur" and "Sir" and "gentleman" and "esquire" to be universally usable. When "gentleman" means that not everyone is a gentleman, it cannot mean what it comes to mean when everyone is.

Because these terms denote *both* something distinguishingly honorific *and* value in general, it can be difficult, as I said, to disparage the social property that they properly denote in their aristocratic application without appearing to be a moral or value nihilist. So democratic ideology faces a difficult linguistic task: it appears possible neither to generalize the honorific terms, since that violates the redolence of distinction in them, nor to disparage those to whom they apply. (The words "bad" and "wicked," which mean "good" and "understood," are no doubt *used* at Eton, but they were more likely to have been invented in some American ghetto.) You can't call *all* men *gentle*men and you can't say gentlemen aren't really gentle.

Poets like Pindar and Theognis affirm tenets in the pre-Sophistic thought pattern. A major and interesting claim they made is that virtue could not be taught, that one was either born with it or fated never to have it. The question "Can virtue be taught?" came to have a complex epistemological

---

26   ["Beautiful people have beautiful things," or, alternatively, "Nice people have nice things."—Ed.]

27   [This is a slightly inaccurate account of two lines from the poem "Is There for Honest Poverty," also known as "A Man's a Man for A' That." The correct couplet is this:

The rank is but the guinea's stamp,
The Man's the gowd for a' that.
—Burns, *Selected Poems*, p. 181.—Ed.]

significance in Socrates and Plato. But in the tradition and in the Sophist reaction against it, it was simply an early version of the issue dividing democrats and antidemocrats in the nineteenth and twentieth centuries: can environment improve character? It is in the interest of those born in more congenial environments to deny that environment can do that. And this interest is sponsored by Theognis, who repeatedly urges that training will have but negligible effect on character. And by Pindar too, who claims for inborn goodness a superiority over that acquired by training, thereby drawing the snob's line between the truly wellborn, the effortlessly superior, on the one hand, and the *parvenu* on the other.[28]

Thus aristocrats are divided from the people by distinctions of nature, and it is revolutionary and progressive of the Sophists to maintain that virtue *can* be taught, and not only to maintain the principle, but also to offer to teach it to anyone who sought to regulate his life effectively. Of course, only the wealthy could pay, but maybe that's how things have to go in the beginning of an anti-aristocratic democratic revolution. The first innings are for the radical rich, whether they be disaffected sons of the aristocracy or of more *parvenu* origin. The sans-culottes come later. The two mistakes to avoid are to see *nothing* revolutionary in the anti-aristocratic bourgeois moment and to see *everything* revolutionary there.

3 (iii). Earlier I cited passages in Anaximander and Heraclitus in which they use something like the concept of justice to explain the realm of nature. They, and the other so-called pre-Socratics, dealt energetically and extensively with cosmological questions, developing a kind of proto-physics, but there was no proto-sociology alongside it.[29] The Sophists, and in this respect they were followed by Socrates, professed skepticism about and/or disdain toward natural-scientific studies, and directed attention to the study of humanity. This change of focus constitutes a recognition of the distinctive character of human society and thereby asserts an emancipation from the comparative engulfment in nature, in which people lack articulate awareness of their capacity to arrange their social affairs themselves, an engulfment which gave aristocratic ideology comfort and support. Before I address the Sophists' contribution, let me briefly summarize what I have said about pre-Sophistic thought.

To sum up: I have spoken of an early, that is, pre-fifth-century, Greek conception in which humanity in its self-representation is engulfed in

---

28   Myles Burnyeat admonishes: But Pindar also said—laws differ from state to state, and each praises their own. Pindar is singing to tyrants, who aren't ruling because that's how it's always been, they seized power. See also the different poet Simonides, near beginning of *Protagoras*. So some say this, some say the other, and so the *contrast* is OK, but not the *temporal* contrast.

29   On the comparative neglect of ethics in pre-Socratic philosophy, see Barnes, *The Presocratic Philosophers*, pp. 121–22.

nature, and I described three indexes of that engulfment: (1) Divinity, humanity, and nature are all three assimilated to one another—natural occurrences are explained by a principle of justice that we would restrict to the human realm; human beings are understood on the model of other parts of nature and nature is understood as manifesting divine forces where the divine is itself understood in human terms; (2) They are imagined as divided into natural subspecies, Greek and barbarian, free and slave, aristocracy and hoi polloi; and (3) There is a lot of proto-physics and proto-chemistry but not much proto-sociology.

Let us now turn to the Sophists, who participated in an entire change of conception.

THE HISTORICAL CONTEXT OF SOPHISM

4. The Sophists enjoyed prominence in the fifth century BC, principally in Athens, to which most of them flocked and where they set themselves up as teachers. They came to Athens, because Athens was an intellectual center: "with her maritime empire and commerce she was now the wealthiest Greek city and a natural centre of communications. The democracy [moreover], under Pericles, prided itself on its tolerance and its openness to new ideas,"[30] and, because the Assembly played a large role in public life, the Sophists could find in Athens an audience for their teachings, in the young men who sought to dominate the Assembly through the exercise of rhetoric and the display of political knowledge. And I say that the Sophists *came* to Athens because, apart from, among prominent ones, Antiphon, they were not themselves born in Athens. They hailed from many different parts of Hellas (the Greek-speaking world), and this is a significant fact about them, because it helps to explain why they so readily embraced the view that all human beings were by nature the same and why they resisted the tradition which maintained natural distinctions.[31] They were themselves cosmopolitans and they lived, moreover, in a century which had seen a "widening of the Greek horizon . . . The inquisitive Greek traveller in foreign lands could not fail to observe that different peoples have different . . . laws and customs: the classic example is the symposium in Herodotus on the right way to dispose of a deceased parent, cannibalism [which was practiced by some inhabitants of India] versus cremation [which was practiced by Greeks]."[32]

---

30   Hussey, *The Presocratics*, p. 116.

31   [A footnote here says: "Myles: there are only two relevant texts: Antiphon, whom I quote later, and Hippias in the Gorgias [CHECK]."—Ed.]

32   Dodds, *The Ancient Concept of Progress*, p. 98. Dodds reflects on the significance of this: "We can see why Plato, like the Nazis and the Russians, wished to restrict the opportunities of foreign travel. (He would forbid it to persons under forty: an experience so

Now the fifth century began with the war against the Persians, and ended with the Peloponnesian war, the war between Athens and Sparta, each aided by allies. It was therefore a century of great strain and turmoil, which are conditions that make a revolution in humanity's attitude to itself easier to perpetrate. We may conjecture that unreflective conceptions of the naturalness of ancient customs, of the superiority of Greek to barbarian and of aristocrat to commoner, lost their hold in a society rent by civil war, foreign attack, and plague within the city.

A final point is that a growing complexity of social and economic structure in the fifth century necessitated the formation of a great deal of *new* law, and that undermined the authority of the received *nomos*.[33] The new laws lacked traditional sanction and they were constantly altered, so it became patently clear that law was a human contrivance.

THE HISTORICAL SIGNIFICANCE OF SOPHISM

5. The *historical* importance of the Sophists cannot be reckoned on the narrow basis of what their contribution was to the civic life of Athens, a contribution which was often venal in inspiration: they were private tutors trying to make money. But their historical importance is that they expressly rejected the tradition that I have described. They severed the cord that tied humanity to nature and thereby asserted humanity's freedom. The celebrated distinction between nature and convention,[34] which they might not have invented but which was deep in their outlook, declared that human beings were not destined to be unreflective slaves of inherited custom and law: these were *human* creations, not products of natural processes. People therefore had authority over them, not they over people. And if it is no longer satisfactory for people to obey rules conceived as externally imposed necessities, if they have to recognize the laws as *their* laws, then they must convince themselves of the validity of what they bind themselves to. They must guide their social relations rationally, not through unthinkingly accepted custom, or what purports to be oracular inspiration. In this manner, then, we can count the Sophists as the founders of social and political theory as a self-consciously practiced subject. At least they asked the questions.

---

unsettling is only safe when middle age has fortified the mind against the infiltration of new ideas; and even then he would put the returned traveller into a sort of intellectual quarantine until he has been pronounced free from germs of dangerous thought.") See Plato *Laws*, 950d, 952b–d. Also the permitted travel would only be on public duty, "as a herald or on an embassy, or on a sacred mission" (Plato, *Laws* 950d, p. 461).

33   Dodds, *The Ancient Concept of Progress*, p. 98.

34   For ambiguities in that distinction, on which at least some Sophists played, see Hussey, *The Presocratics*, pp. 123–25.

To repeat what has been said at the start of these lectures, it is not as though their predecessors *denied* the distinction they made between *phusis* and *nomos*: there is a difference between denying it and not making it. And there is also a difference between making it in practice (of course the predecessors did that) and recognizing it in theory (which they did not).

USES TO WHICH THE NATURE/CONVENTION DISTINCTION CAN BE PUT

6. Merely to distinguish between that which exists by nature and that which comes from human contrivance is not yet to say what consequences ensue from the distinction. Different Sophists drew very different, even, in an important sense, opposite, conclusions from it.[35]

In a widespread traditional representation, the Sophists are thinkers who said that instead of restricting himself by obeying the laws of his city, a man should satisfy his natural appetites through self-seeking. But this characterization is defective in two ways. First, since it does not mention the humanity/nature continuum through which the Sophists broke, it fails to identify what was intelligent in the egoism that it attributes to them, to wit, its premise, which is to say the nature/convention distinction. But, second, it is simply false that the Sophists were, as such, egoists, that they all drew egoistic or nihilistic consequences from that premise, that is, from the contrast between *phusis* and *nomos*.[36]

---

35   "It may not be superfluous to point out that thinking in these terms could lead to widely different conclusions according to the meaning you assigned to the terms themselves. *Nomos* could stand for the Conglomerate, conceived as the inherited burden of irrational custom; or it could stand for an arbitrary rule consciously imposed by certain classes in their own interest; or it could stand for a rational system of State law, the achievement which distinguished Greeks from barbarians. Similarly *Physis* could represent an unwritten, unconditionally valid 'natural law,' against the particularism of local custom; or it could represent the 'natural rights' of the individual, against the arbitrary requirements of the State; and this in turn could pass—as always happens when rights are asserted without a corresponding recognition of duties—into a pure anarchic immoralism, the 'natural right of the stronger' as expounded by the Athenians in the Melian Dialogue and by Callicles in the *Gorgias*. It is not surprising that an antithesis whose terms were so ambiguous led to a vast amount of argument at cross-purposes. But through the fog of confused and for us fragmentary controversy we can dimly perceive two great issues being fought out. One is the ethical question concerning the source and the validity of moral and political obligation. The other is the psychological question concerning the springs of human conduct—why do men behave as they do, and how can they be induced to behave better?" Dodds, *The Greeks and the Irrational*, pp. 182–83.

36   [A footnote appears here: "Myles [Burnyeat]: indeed, maybe none did, because Thrasymachus is merely descriptive. He doesn't appeal to nature, Callicles isn't a Sophist, and Antiphon . . . might just have been describing the difference between nature and law, as Barnes says. . . . Is this consistent with the Antiphon text, whose translation Myles does not impugn?"—Ed.]

Thus, for example, Protagoras (ca. 485–ca. 415)[37] concluded that, the laws being a human creation, they should be embraced as such, tended to, and, where desirable and possible, improved upon. His famous statement that "Man is the measure of all things," the sole surviving fragment of his essay "On Truth," had an epistemological significance explored in Plato's dialogue the *Theaetetus*, but we can conjecture that for social theory its message was that institutions are the responsibility of those whose institutions they are and that they should criticize their traditions and modernize the laws so that human life might be improved.[38]

In the view of Protagoras, "the laws of any state are valid for that state for so long as that state affirms them":[39] his was a tolerant relativism.[40] The view of Hippias was different. He regarded some laws as binding and

37 "When law and human nature conflict, which ought we to follow? Is the social restraint which law imposes on nature a good or a bad thing? For the Sophists that was the grand question. They did not all answer it in the same way. Protagoras' view of the matter, as represented by Plato, is much like that of Herodotus (who may well have been influenced by him). There are better and worse laws, but the laws of any state are valid for that state for so long as the people believe in them. It is the business of a wise man to get the laws improved by peaceful propaganda. But laws there must be: without *diké* and *aidos*, respect for the legal and moral rights of others, there can be no civilization; life in the state of nature is poor, nasty, brutish, and short. Protagoras himself drafted a legal code for the new colony at Thurii, and since he did so as the trusted friend of Pericles we can infer that he was considered a sound democrat. He belonged to the optimistic generation which grew up immediately after the Persian Wars, the generation which gave currency to the idea of progress." Dodds, *The Ancient Concept of Progress*, p. 99.

38 (1) The promise of improvement was a potentially dangerous one. According to Irwin (*Classical Thought*, p. 63), "The sophists aroused both enthusiasm and suspicion. They claimed to add something useful to the gentleman's traditional upbringing, based on Homer, the poets, and the laws of the city. Their claims aroused suspicion that their teaching would be subversive. Many sophists fully accepted conventional norms and moral beliefs; and to this extent suspicion was unjustified. But the claim to improve traditional education implied scope for criticism; and to this extent social and political conservatives were right to be suspicious."

(2) Hussey describes the "prevailing spirit of optimism" characterizing "the older generation of Sophists: . . . Protagoras, Gorgias, and Hippias. It merged with the scepticism of the age to produce a cheerfully pragmatic attitude towards life, and a conviction that the proper study of mankind was man. The irreducible variety of human behaviour and character was accepted, and above all there was a faith in the ability of the human mind to surmount almost all obstacles by intelligence, especially when intelligence was accumulated and organised as a body of skill and knowledge, as a *techne*. The concept of *techne* had long been present in the Greek language, but at this time it was sharpened and made more significant. It came to suggest not simply a traditional skill or craft but a clearly articulated system of theoretical or practical knowledge, organised according to the nature of the subject—in other words, it took on much of the sense of the word 'science' at the present day. It is as professors of a newly self-conscious *techne*, the 'science of speaking,' that the Sophists must be seen" (*The Presocratics*, p. 114).

39 Dodds, *The Ancient Concept of Progress*, p. 99.

40 [The text here contains a comment attributed to Myles Burnyeat: "Text Dodds bases this on is in Plato's *Protagoras*, where justice and piety are relative, but goodness and advantage are not. So you *can* ask whether a community's laws are *advantageous* to

others not: he recognized the validity of only those laws whose universality showed them to be of divine origin.[41] Some nations practice incest, so it is not a natural prohibition. All nations enjoin respect for parents, so it has natural/divine standing.

If for Protagoras law is valid, as long as it is accepted, and regardless of variations across Polities, while for Hippias some law is valid and some not, for others, like Antiphon (ca. 480–411) and Thrasymachus, whom we meet in Plato's *Republic*, all submission to law derogates from intelligent self-seeking, which they conceived to be the only natural thing. Not believing that anything in nature bound people to cooperate self-denyingly with others, they thought people were fools unless they strove to satisfy self-interest, and that they should follow nature *rather* than convention. Antiphon wrote: "The requirements of the laws are most of them at war with nature; they have made rules for our eyes, to tell them what to see; for our ears, to tell them what to hear; for our tongues, what to say; for our hands, what to do; for our feet, where to go; for our minds, what they shall desire."[42] For Antiphon, *nomos* is a set of "fetters binding nature."[43]

---

it. The utilitarian philosophy requires the nature/convention distinction. (This supports my position.)"—Ed.]

41   [The text here contains a comment attributed to Myles Burnyeat: "it's Guthrie who says this, but he doesn't support it well."—Ed.]

42   Quoted in Dodds, *The Ancient Concept of Progress*, p. 101. Dodds comments interestingly on Sophistic antimoralism:

A liberalism which is merely individualist, which does not take the community as its moral unit, is always in danger of giving birth to its opposite, an individualism which is the reverse of liberal. The idea of nature was a critical weapon with two edges. Nature assures us that distinctions of birth and blood rest on arbitrary convention—man was created free. And liberalism welcomes the assurance. But suppose nature whispers that democratic justice and obedience to the will of the people are also an arbitrary convention, that man was created free to be himself and push the weak to the wall? So long as it treats the individual as an ultimate moral unit liberalism has no effective answer to Callicles. And Callicles is in a sense its child. Certainly he was no Sophist: he represents himself as a practical man who despises Sophists. And certainly Plato was right in making Gorgias shrink from Calliclean conclusions: the older Sophists were as anxious as Jeremy Bentham to fit their individualism into the framework of traditional ethical teaching. Yet it was they or their pupils who furnished Callicles with his intellectual weapons. *Phusis* became the slogan of the robber-individual and the robber-society, as "the survival of the fittest" was in the later nineteenth century and as "realism" is today. (*The Ancient Concept of Progress*, pp. 103–4)

43   Quoted in Irwin, *Classical Thought*, p. 57; I think Jonathan Barnes's unwillingness to agree that Antiphon attacks *nomos* here is perverse: see *The Presocratic Philosophers*, pp. 513ff. On pp. 513–14 Barnes writes: "Antiphon does not say 'Follow nature when you can get away with it'; he asserts, as a statement of fact and not a suggestion for action, that if you do follow nature and get away with it you will act in your own interests."

Antiphon says:

Justice, then, consists in not transgressing the laws and customs of the city of which one is a citizen. It follows that the way for a man to be just with most advantage to

7. Now the slogan "Follow Nature, Not Convention," the slogan of the antisocial Sophists, might seem to contradict my central thesis that they *rescued* humanity from nature. In fact, it illustrates it, for what the rescue thesis, spelled out a bit more, says is that they rescued human culture from the illusion that society is part of nature. For, in the Sophist view, Greeks were *not* following nature but following custom, the established social order with its naturally sanctified class and power distinctions, *and* misrepresenting all that to themselves *as* nature. They were not following nature conceived as *opposed* to custom, for they did not conceive of that opposition. To say "Follow Nature, Not Convention" is to presuppose that social rules are not natural by their very nature. And the nature which people were being counseled to follow was, of course, *human* nature, not external nature (as such).

My principal point about the Sophists is that they discovered that human law transcends nature, even if, like Protagoras, they favored loyalty to the laws. And their development of the contrast between nature and convention was, as I have said elsewhere,[44] the foundation of all social criticism. Criticism compares reality with a standard that it fails to meet. Only with the distinction of nature from convention can the satisfaction of *human* nature and *human* interests be employed *as* a standard, as a criterion for evaluating *social* institutions. There was no criterion before, because the social was treated as natural, which is fetishism, in

---

himself is for him to respect the laws when in presence of witnesses, but when he is alone and unwitnessed to respect the commands of nature. What the laws command is an extraneous imposition; what nature commands is a constraint that is part of our very being. The law is an artificial convention, not a natural growth; but nature is natural not conventional. If, then, you transgress the laws, you are free from shame and from penalty—provided that those who participate in the convention do not know, but not otherwise; whereas if you seek to repress, beyond the bounds of possibility, what inheres in your nature, the resulting damage to you cannot be any the less for being kept private, nor any the greater for being made public, because the damage is caused not by what people think but by what actually happens.

The point to which these considerations are leading is this: *that many duties imposed by law are hostile to nature.* Laws have been made for the eyes, to tell them what they shall and shall not see; for the tongue, what it shall and shall not say; for the hands, what they shall and shall not do; for the feet, where they shall and shall not go; for the mind, what it shall and shall not desire. Can it really be that what the laws forbid men is no less repugnant and alien to nature than what they command?

. . . If, then, we consider rightly, it is not true that what is painful benefits nature more than what is pleasant; and it is not true either that what is in man's interest is the painful rather than the pleasant things. What is truly good for a man must benefit him, not damage him. (Quoted from Hussey, *The Presocratics*, pp. 124–25)

Myles thinks it's not perverse: that Antiphon just contrasts *nomos* and *phusis*, but doesn't say what to do about it. I think that mistakes the tone of the text.

44   See my *Karl Marx's Theory of History: A Defence*, p. 107.

the Marxist sense of the word.[45] The Sophists made the criterion possible. Some used it antisocially, and others did not.

SOPHISTIC UNIVERSALISM

8. At least some Sophists had corrosive things to say about the traditionally pseudonatural distinctions between Greek and barbarian, freeman and slave, and aristocrat and commoner. They asserted a form of natural equality of humankind. Antiphon claimed for barbarians a humanity equal to that of Greeks in the following partly quaint assertion:

> The laws of our neighbours [from context that must be "cocitizens"] we know and revere: the laws of those who live afar we neither know nor revere. Thus in this we have been made foreigners with regard to one another. [But] For *by nature* we are all in all respects similarly endowed to be foreign or Greek. [That is, upbringing could have made anybody either.] One may consider those natural facts which are necessary in all men and provided for all in virtue of the same faculties—and in these very matters none of us is separated off as a foreigner or as a Greek. For we all breathe into the air by way of our mouths and noses, we laugh when we are happy in our minds and we cry when we are in pain, we receive sounds by way of our hearing and we see with our eyes by light, we work with our hands and we walk on our feet.[46]

The Sophist Lycophron also denied the validity of distinctions of birth, and Alcidamas, a Sophist pupil of the Sophist Gorgias, possesses the honor of having attributed to him the first known explicit condemnation of slavery, his statement being: "God has left all men free; Nature has made none a slave."[47] To be sure, Alcidamas is speaking of cities, not individuals, but the terms of the denial give it broad reach. I do not think he could have added: except in the case of *individual* slaves.

The Sophists also rejected the natural superiority of aristocracy in their contention, which was shared by Athenians of the day, that virtue could be taught, for they thereby rejected the natural union of virtue and aristocracy claimed by Theognis and Pindar. And they also *offered* to teach anyone skill in social affairs, and, in particular, the art of rhetoric.

Now it might seem a trivial matter, the art of rhetoric, but in the context of aristocratic beliefs it had a special importance. For, in the old

---

45 See, again, ibid., chap. 4, sec. 4, "Revolutionary Value of the Distinction" (between the matter and the form of society), pp. 195–98.

46 Translation from Barnes, "New Light on Antiphon," p. 5.

47 Dodds, *The Ancient Concept of Progress*, p. 101.

tradition, the many did not have the right to speak. When Thersites[48] opens his mouth in Homer's *Iliad* and complains of the hardships of the Trojan War, Odysseus descends on him and pummels him, and everyone is scandalized that a commoner should make bold to express his opinion. Pindar says, "[T]he vulgar will say anything.[49] They clatter vainly like crows."[50] In the *Gorgias* Socrates, opponent of the democracy, puts forward as one of his criticisms of Pericles the fact that he encouraged the *ordinary* people to engage in discussions, and in the *Persae* of Aeschylus, it is said that now that the Persians have been repelled, "uncurbed the common tongue shall prate of freedom."[51] The privileged disfavored elementary self-expression on the part of the masses.[52]

The Sophist offer to teach rhetoric to anyone constituted an opposition to this tendency. Of course the Sophists in fact taught only the rich, who could pay them. But, as I said before, their historical significance transcended their particular political involvements: the theory they evolved to justify their practice made claims about the right of all people to speak out on matters affecting them. This was not the last time that a rising class or generation in challenging the established order made claims on behalf of humanity as such. Practice and precept in the French Revolution bear an analogous relationship. In each case, we must distinguish the immediate parochial contributions of thinkers from their place in the larger context of humanity's reflection on itself. And we should not

---

48   Irwin, *Classical Thought*, p.13:

Homer largely ignores the effects of the observance of Homeric morality on the non-heroic classes who are its victims. He attends to them in just one episode in the *Iliad*. Thersites—a brash, obstreperous, and (for good measure) ugly rabble-rouser, corresponding to some people's prejudices about trade-union leaders—presents a good argument against the kings and their outlook, denouncing them as selfish parasites wasting the resources of the community. He is answered by the skilful debater Odysseus; this time, however, Odysseus relies not on his debating skill, but on forcible suppression. Homer is not the last conservative to approve of this treatment of subversive arguments presented by unmannerly people who do not know their place. Nor is he the last to represent the lower classes as agreeing with such treatment for those who complain about their betters.

49   Myles: But in Plato's dialogues, so do Protagoras and Hippias.
50   Pindar, *The Odes of Pindar*, "Olympia 2," p. 8.
51   Aeschylus, *The Persians*, p. 139.
52   [At this point, there is a comment: "Not for lecture: Aristotle *Politics* Bk IV, Ch XIII, para 8 is amusing in the present connection. For a perhaps exaggerated presentation of the significance of the offer to teach effective speech, see Hussey, *The Pre-Socratics*, p. 115." The intended passage from Aristotle is probably this: "The poor will keep quiet even without sharing in the honours, provided no one outrages them or takes away any of their property. (This, however, is not easy; for those who have a part in the government do not always happen to be courteous.)" Aristotle, *Politics: Books III and IV*, p. 108.—Ed.]

go along with any one-sided methodological insistence that tells us to *choose* between those two ways, microhistorical and macrohistorical, of looking at the great episodes in the history of political theory.[53]

SOCRATES[54]

9. I now turn to Socrates, who responded to the Sophists. There is an interesting contrast between them and him. I said that the Sophists' immediate interests tended to be mundane or even venal, but that they have a long-range significance for political philosophy and democratic theory which far transcends the significance of their thought and speech for *their* immediate interests. With Socrates, by contrast, the transcendent comes first, as far as his own immediate interests were concerned. He was primarily concerned in a politically unprejudiced way with deep philosophical questions, yet the current of his thought ran in an aristocratic direction, and that tendency was made explicit and developed further by his follower, Plato. The Sophists' parochial affiliations led them to devise theories of general range and radical import. With the Sophists, one can say, practice led theory. With Socrates, theory is original and dominant, but the way Socrates theorized and the theories he advanced connected him, at *least* in the democratic mind, to the aristocratic party.

As to the way Socrates theorized, the first thing to say is that he did not, like the Sophists, offer lectures in exchange for drachmas. And he did not claim that his teaching would endow young men with the wherewithal for political success. Instead, he sought to engage people (mostly men) in dialogue, to question the notions they took for granted, to ask them what they meant when they spoke of virtue and justice and courage. Now the associates Socrates attracted were, of course, those who had both the

---

53   More on the Sophists as teachers, from Dodds, *The Ancient Concept of Progress*, p. 103.

True, the Sophists were not required to teach a particular official doctrine, as many European professors are today; but neither were they free, like English professors, to inflict what they pleased on their pupils. They depended for a livelihood on their fees, as we do not; we can bore our pupils with impunity, they could not. Hence demand exercised a dangerous control over supply. What such men as Protagoras would have liked to teach, if I understand them rightly, was simply the art of citizenship; what the discontented young aristocrats of Athens required them to teach was something more specific—the art of acquiring personal power in a democratic society. If the seed of the new learning produced a strange crop, we must remember that Alcibiades was a pupil of Socrates, and blame the soil before we blame the seed.

54   [There is a footnote at this point that reads: "See, now, NB—Burnyeat, 'The Impiety of Socrates'." Presumably Cohen intended to revisit this section in the light of Burnyeat's paper, published in 1997.—Ed.]

leisure and the inclination to talk to him. So far as I know, he did not venture into the Attic countryside to debate with the poor Athenian farmer, still less with any of the seven thousand slave miners in the Laurion silver mines. The only people who had the leisure necessary to enable them to discourse with Socrates were the established landed aristocracy, who actually resided in the city, and the rising sons of the middle class. But the middle class was concerned, as always, to get *on*, to increase their influence in the *polis*. The aristocrats were already perched at the top, so they could more comfortably devote time and energy to dispassionate argument.

It thus transpired that Socrates developed connections which were to lead to his execution by the democrats in 399 BC. From 431 to 404 Athens had been at war with Sparta and her allies. During that period the Athenian aristocrats betrayed the cause of their own city on several occasions. One case hard to be sure about was that of Alcibiades, a student and affectionate devotee of Socrates, who at least objectively speaking *harmed* the city by encouraging it to institute a naval campaign against Syracuse, then an ally of Sparta. This ended in disaster for the Athenian fleet, and it was thought, probably rightly, that he was well aware of what the upshot would be of the expedition that he had proposed. Also, he fled to Sparta instead of presenting himself at Athens when the Assembly had summoned him to account for his earlier behavior (not in the matter of the Syracusan expedition but in the matter of mutilation of the herms).

When Socrates was later accused of corrupting the youth, it was people like Alcibiades that the jury might have had in mind, for Alcibiades had once been a favorite of the people, and they saw Socrates as having molded him into a traitor. In this they were wrong. But they were not wrong in thinking that Socrates had *some* kind of connection with the thirty aristocratic Tyrants who ruled Athens terroristically for eight months in 404 BC, having been installed by Lysander, the victorious Spartan general. Charmides and Critias, relatives of Plato, were prominent among them, and Socrates fraternized with them. I am assured by scholarly Socrates-lovers that it is certain that he did not actually approve of the thirty Tyrants' more violent measures; but when the democrats, having recaptured the city, sought to punish the aristocrats, there were reasons why the old philosopher was unpopular which had nothing to do with the annoyance of his always asking philosophical questions. The idea that he was executed because he was an intellectual gadfly, or nudnik, is a philosophers' myth. ("When you say. . . .") And the reason why he was accused of impiety is that a postwar amnesty forbade charging him with wartime misdeeds.

10. Socrates was stimulated by the Sophists' controversial ideas. He took them seriously, but criticized them sharply, notably for using terms like virtue and justice without proper attention to what they meant by them.

He also thought, and considered this a related fact, that political life in Athens suffered from a failure to grasp essential principles. The concern, he thought, was too much with the particular requirements of particular situations. Socrates by contrast enjoined his interlocutors to look to the fundamental ideas endowing political activity with whatever value it could claim to have, and to analyze them through the give-and-take of debate.

I said earlier that the Sophists turned intellectual focus away from natural science or cosmology, study of how the *world* is, to the study of the practices and conventions of human beings. They speculated about the springs of human action and taught the art of influencing people. Socrates, too, abjured cosmological speculation, but he took a large step beyond the Sophists in a humanistic direction. It is not enough to observe the behavior of people around you, or even to *observe* their behavior and your own: there is a stance different from that third-person stance, namely, the first-person stance, and it must always have the last word, in the sense of the title of Tom Nagel's brilliant book, which is a wonderful defense of the autonomy of philosophy.[55]

Let me give an illustration of the Nagel point: see the second paragraph of the flyleaf of his book.

> In *The Last Word*, Thomas Nagel, one of the most influential philosophers writing in English, presents a sustained defense of reason against the attacks of subjectivism, delivering systematic rebuttals of relativistic claims with respect to language, logic, science and ethics. He shows that the last word in disputes about objective validity of any form of thought must lie in some unqualified thoughts about how things are—thoughts that we cannot regard from outside as mere psychological dispositions. His work sets a new standard in the debate on this crucially important question and should generate intense interest both within and outside the philosophical community.

First, consider Quine's plea for a naturalization of epistemology. He said, contemplating the historic disagreements regarding criteria of knowledge and rational belief: "Why not settle for psychology?" But how do we get a psychology save by practicing science under canons of right reasoning on whose rightness science is impotent to comment? It is our criteria that endow science with its warrant. Science could thus never impugn our status as normative, warrant-giving, creatures. It is thus important to know ourselves, as producers of criteria of validity. "Know thyself" was Socrates's watchword, and, for him, the pursuit of this knowledge was closely connected with the analysis of key ideas such as

55   Nagel, *The Last Word*.

those of virtue and justice. (He did not mean "know thyself" in a psychological sense: Socrates never talks about what Socrates is really like, deep down.) For to analyze such ideas is to ask ourselves what *we* mean by them, and we cannot reach an understanding of what we mean without a revelation of self. Philosophy is an essentially first-person activity—though not necessarily first-person *singular*.[56]

To furnish an understanding of justice, it does not suffice to cite an example, or a string of examples, of just dealing or just institutions. No such list can show what we *mean* by calling the dealings and institutions just. An understanding of the concept requires a characterization of it in general terms; we are looking for what *our* criteria are for its application. This was a methodological claim for Socrates, but, I speculate, perhaps it could be thought to have had a political color. Perhaps it could have been thought to embody a disparagement of the actual institutions of democratic Athens. It could also have been thought to involve an assertion of intellectual superiority consonant with an antidemocratic attitude, as we shall see in Section 12 below.

PLATO

11. Plato was Socrates's student. Himself an aristocrat (that is, a man of wealth from a family perceived as possessed of a noble lineage and raised in a milieu where there was much cultured leisure), he was shocked as a young man of twenty-eight, when the democracy murdered his teacher. His lifework was a homage to and continuation of the Socratic achievement. In his early dialogues he exhibits Socrates in debate with Sophists and others, and probably with large elements of reportage in the dialogue. In his middle and later dialogues, Plato uses the figure of Socrates as an expositor of his own views. The *Republic* is generally accounted to be a middle dialogue.

Plato differed from Socrates in that he wrote down his teachings, for there is obviously a huge difference between *engaging* in a dialogue and writing one down on papyrus. More importantly for our purposes, Plato differed from Socrates in the breadth of his intellectual interest. While retaining the fifth-century enthusiasm for social and political questions, he also returned to the older cosmological issues, and he wove a unified theory of divinity, humanity, and nature, and reestablished in a more sophisticated form the continuum of the three that had been a feature of

---

56 [The text at this point includes an aside: "Possibly: excursus on the nature of ordinary language philosophy, and why, *pace* Arne Naess, it doesn't do surveys of how people speak. See Cavell, *Must We Mean What We Say?*."—Ed.]

the pre-Sophistic tradition. The category of purpose was read back into nature itself. The observable world is as it is, insofar as it possesses reality and is not mere illusion, because and to the extent that it participates in the goal-imposing order of the suprasensible Forms, which themselves culminate in the idea of the Good.[57] The material world *strives* toward exemplification of the world of Forms, and shows its deficiency in its failure to do so fully. So the ultimate explanatory category is, once again, as in Anaximander and Heraclitus, an evaluative category, in Plato's case, the Idea of the Good. Value inheres in external reality itself, is indeed the supreme reality. And a right ordering of society depends on perception of that *super*natural order of value. Of course value is not natural in the sense of made of natural stuff, but it is natural in the sense of independent of humanity, and it asserts its right governance over humanity. Plato was in a certain fashion restoring the pre-Sophistic subordination and engulfment.

12. The idea of an order of value which is independent of social and human construction, of what people *will*, is a *potentially* antidemocratic idea, and it becomes actually antidemocratic when the principle is added that social construction is illegitimate when it does not imitate that independent order of value. The democratic idea is that you legislate what the people will, not something of independent value *whether or not there exists an independent order of value.*[58] So you *can*, like Ronald Dworkin, affirm an independent order of value and still be a democrat, but nevertheless try to resist any antidemocratic inferences from acknowledgment of its existence. An *easy* way to be a democrat is to deny an independent order of value. A harder way is to acknowledge it but, like Dworkin, and me too, and, more or less, Rawls, deny its sovereignty over the polity. Plato affirmed it *and* affirmed its sovereignty over the polity. (This is a case of the familiar competing "obviousnesses" structure of philosophical debate. It seems obvious that government should be at least influenced by what's good *and* that it should not go against the will of the people. Liberals and perfectionists respond differentially to the incompatible obviousnesses.)

So note that the cobbler/shoes, captain/ship analogies are profoundly antidemocratic, *but* also motivated by an important idea—the objectivity of value, of right and wrong.

---

57 [The text at this point includes the comment "(Santayana on the *Timaeus*)." It is not clear what this refers to, although Santayana's marginal notes on the *Timaeus* have now been published. See Santayana, *Marginalia, Book Two*.—Ed.]

58 In representative democracy, on the Burke/Mill view, you could *want* your representative to make the decision, e.g. because you think he's good at telling what the order of value is.

13. The denial, by most Sophists (for a possible exception see the discussion of Hippias in Section 6), that there is an independent order of value and that the laws have natural sanction often went with what after the seventeenth century has been called the contract theory of morality, of the state, and such a theory is advanced with lucidity and economy by Glaucon in book 2 of Plato's *Republic*.

Indeed, the contract theory is, more than anything else, *the* theory which the *Republic* opposes, at the level of *political* philosophy. (For you could say that the *Republic* opposes the social contract theory in political philosophy and ethical egoism in moral philosophy, which is connected with the contract theory, as Glaucon expounds that: ethical egoism is the view that each person is morally entitled to seek his own good only.)

In the relevant contract theory social arrangements and laws reflect a human agreement to accept certain restraints in order to acquire certain benefits, on the part of such persons. They would rather have the benefits without the restraints, but they know that no such deal is available. As Glaucon says, and as I quoted him at the beginning of the first lecture:

> So that's the origin and nature of morality, on this [that is, the Sophist] view: it is a compromise between the ideal of doing wrong without having to pay for it, and the worst situation, which is having wrong done to one while lacking the means of exacting compensation. Since morality is a compromise, it is endorsed because, while it may not be good, it does gain value by preventing people from doing wrong. The point is that any real man with the *ability* to do wrong [and get away with it] would never enter into a contract to avoid both wronging and being wronged: he wouldn't be so crazy. (358e–359b)[59]

Gauthier agrees.

Now, this view offers what can seem only a precarious justification of authority, and of morality, because, much as it justifies authority and morality as long as the promised benefits are forthcoming, it also justifies resistance to authority by individuals and groups who judge that authority is not serving their interests (hence Locke on right of rebellion). It is therefore a theory which conservatives oppose, which is not to say that that is their only reason for opposing it. For *they also have this better reason*: they deny, Plato denied, and so did Aristotle, and so, profoundly developing this insight, did Hegel, that the social contract theory reveals the point of society. Society has a prior purpose, one that is *necessarily* prior to that of satisfying human demands, for it has the purpose of forming human beings in the first place, of shaping and *educating* human beings. A person nurtured within a community receives from it not only material benefits but her very character, and the absurdity of the contract theory, in

---

59 Plato *Republic*, p. 46.

the conservative critique, lies in its treatment of individuals as possessed of determinate character and a set of demands independently of the institutions that shape them. (In calling that a *better* reason for rejecting the contract theory than the reason which consists in fear of its consequences, I am *not* thereby endorsing *anything* in the conservative critique.)

14. Instead of asking, at the outset of our evaluation of a polity, whether it, that polity, is satisfactory with respect to the interests of the human beings living in it, we must ask, this is the first thing to ask, whether the polity produces satisfactory human beings, human beings with the right *sorts* of interests. And now I can say how the familiar social structure of Plato's *Republic* displays rejection of the *nomos/phusis* distinction and reversion to a new domination by nature. For in order to ensure that the right sorts of human beings are produced, it is necessary for society to be ruled by people of innately superior nature who are trained to an insight into what is highest in nonhuman nature, to wit, the universal Forms radiating out of the Idea of the Good.

The state is to be ruled by those who are blessed from birth with natures of a higher grade than others have, where the criterion for evaluating a person's nature is how capable of wisdom and therefore of justice it is, and where justice is, in the first and generative instance, a matter of a psychological harmony of which people are not equally capable, rather than of just dealing or just conduct or just laws. Indeed laws are only required where people's *natures* are defective, which is a weirdly unsociological idea, because of coordination problems.

The top-quality specimens are educated to a perception of the Good, and they impose the wisdom that results from their encounter with the idea of the Good on a society which possesses two other grades of humanity. The hierarchy of roles assigned to people of different nature is justified through propagation of a myth which says that some are of a golden, others of a silver, and still others of a bronze, nature. The golden ones supervise the breeding of everyone else, and it *is* conceived on the model of breeding; the "one thing that's important" (423e) is their "education and upbringing . . . a good educational system, if maintained, engenders people of good character; and then people of good character, if they in their turn receive the benefits of an education of this kind, become even better than their predecessors in every respect, but especially—as is the case with other creatures too—in that they produce better children (424a–b)."[60] Here and elsewhere the animal analogy is used,[61] in consonance with the return to nature which I say the Platonic political philosophy betokens.

60   Ibid., p. 128.
61   See, further, ibid. (451d), p. 162; Adkins, *Merit and Responsibility*, p. 300; Annas, *An Introduction to Plato's Republic*, pp. 80–81.

15. The *Republic* is usually said to have three classes: the guardians, the auxiliaries, and the producers. But that is misleading. To be sure, there clearly are those three grades, but there are also slaves, who are mentioned in passing, like part of the furniture of the landscape. But if we set aside the slaves, who are a nuisance,[62] it is really a two-class society in which some members of the upper class are selected at the age of twenty for special training that will eventually make them rulers from the age of fifty. (The *Republic* is only a three-class society if you think there is a hierarchical class division between those Etonians who go to Sandhurst and become military officers and those who go to Oxbridge and end up as civil service mandarins and cabinet ministers.) To be sure, there are three types of *humanity*, but the silver and gold are collected together in terms of social structure and only differentiated with respect to a subset of one age-group. Otherwise they live in community under an abolition of the family and private property. Those in the silver mass serve the golden leaders as a militia used to repel foreign enemies and to keep order within the city. The nonclass distinction between these auxiliaries and the guardian-rulers is confirmed by the isomorphism between the structure of the state and the structure of the soul: in that isomorphism, or parallel, the guardians correspond to reason, the auxiliaries to spirit or passion, and the producers to bodily appetite. But the spirited element, which corresponds to the auxiliaries, is by its nature an ally and support of reason, whenever reason and appetite are in conflict with one another (440e):[63] so the auxiliaries stack up with the guardians, in class terms. (After all, they're all *related*.)

The (politically) subordinate class is engaged in productive work, and, so far as I can see, Plato does not seek to make their life very different from what it was in his contemporary Athens, except that they are deprived of political rights and that extremes of wealth and poverty are forbidden. And although he claims that he is constructing a state in which all souls may achieve virtue, his rather benign neglect of the condition of the many, about which I shall say a lot more in Sections 19 to 21, reflects a belief that the scope for development in their case is highly restricted.

So the state has an educative role: its prime function is the benign shaping of human beings, and that serves as a refutation of the contractarian philosophy, which sees the state as the result of a compact among magically preformed beings. But this state activity of nurture is not something from which all can benefit as much as some can. There

---

62 They are a nuisance philosophically. I rather doubt, for example, that they constitute a fourth grade of person. They're probably just enslaved conquered people, of different flavors. That is, they're not slaves *because* of their low-grade flavor. It is, however, of immense historical and ideological interest that Plato mentions them in this throwaway fashion: that I do not doubt.

63 Plato, *Republic*, pp. 151–52.

is a division not only in Plato but also in Aristotle between those who undergo spiritual and moral growth and those whose energies are absorbed in providing material necessities not only for themselves but for the higher types. Economic activity is the substructure of culture, of the pursuit of virtue and philosophy. The purpose of production is consumption, and the chief value of manual labor is the instrumental one that it supports the leisure in which culture is possible. With that assessment of the relationship between labor and culture democrats, and even many Marxists, might agree. But Plato and Aristotle, arming themselves with a biological story, draw the antidemocratic and illiberal conclusion that some are by nature suited to devoting themselves to self-cultivation and being free of the burden of labor, while those onto whose backs that burden is to be shifted are unsuited to a life of leisure and culture. This class division among *people* can follow from the distinction between *activities* only when people are regarded as so different by *nature* that activities of radically different grades of value are suitable for them. Otherwise we could share the task of baking the bread and cultivating the garden, and we could then share the bread and roses together.

16. So whereas Plato agrees with the Sophists that political arrangements as they exist do not follow natural principles, he believes, in contradistinction to at any rate most of the Sophists, that there *exist* natural principles to which the polity *ought* to be made to conform. But these natural principles will not be found by observing the movements of natural things in the physical world. This world of experience is a defective copy of a higher realm of nature, a realm of universal ideas, and it is into this that the guardians are to achieve insight, discovering justice in the ultimate nature of things. They can then strive to make this world as natural as possible in that higher sense of nature, nature as something *not* derived from an independently understood human interest and human will and to which human interest may be shown to conform, and to which human will must therefore be *made* to conform. In this manner Plato's aristocratic identification induced him to retrieve and refashion elements in the old tradition and thereby arrest the development of democratic ideas.

Strong confirmation of this interpretation of Plato as a reactionary comes from a passage in the *Laws*, part of which I shall quote. The passage shows that Plato was a reactionary in a rigorous sense of the term, in a sense of the term in which, so the text to be exhibited shows, he could have agreed that he was one. For he could have agreed that he wanted to turn the clock back. He more or less says so himself, in the *Laws*.

In the *Laws*, the Athenian stranger laments the breakdown, under Sophist and other onslaught, of the pre-Sophistic thought-world, and Cleinias tells him what the remedy is, a remedy which will reward close scrutiny. Here is the Athenian stranger's lament about the loss of the old values that we took for granted in the good old days:

> In the first place, my dear friend, these people would say that the Gods exist not by nature, but by art, and by the laws of states, which are different in different places, according to the agreement of those who make them; and that the honourable is one thing by nature and another thing by law, and that the principles of justice have no existence at all in nature, but that mankind are always disputing about them and altering them; and that the alterations which are made by art and by law have no basis in nature, but are of authority [only] for the moment and at the time at which they are made. — These, my friends, are the sayings of wise men, poets and prose writers, which find a way into the minds of youth. They are told by them that the highest right is might, and in this way the young fall into impieties, under the idea that the Gods are not such as the law bids them imagine; and hence arise factions, these philosophers inviting them to lead a true life according to nature, that is, to live in real dominion over others, and not in legal subjection to them.

Cleinias and the Athenian stranger then proceed to agree that it would be regrettable to have to use brute force to resuscitate the old ideology, and Cleinias suggests that

> if . . . persuasion be at all possible, then a legislator who has anything in him ought never to weary of persuading men; he ought to leave nothing unsaid in support of *the ancient opinion* that there are Gods, and of all those other truths which you were just now mentioning; he ought to support the law and also art, and acknowledge that both alike exist by nature, and no less than nature, if they are the creations of mind in accordance with right reason.[64]

Now what interests me in Cleinias's response is his statement that law exists by nature if it is a creation of mind in accordance with right reason, the right reason, we can add, which is written into the objective order of things. A partly "persuasive redefinition" (in Stevenson's technical sense)[65] of "nature" is occurring here, in response to the following threatening iconoclastic argument, which was promoted by the more destructive Sophists:

Laws have authority only if they derive from nature
But: Laws do not derive from nature
So: Laws have no authority.

---

64 Plato, *Laws* (888–89), pp. 631–32.
65 Stevenson, "Persuasive Definitions."

To resist this argument, you can deny its first premise, and, indeed, as we have seen, Protagoras, in effect did so. He affirmed the second premise but rejected the first, and was therefore not committed to the conclusion. He rejected the first by saying that Laws are indeed not derived from nature, *Nomos isn't Phusis*, but they nevertheless have authority, *human* authority: man is the measure of all things. But the *Laws* passage suggests that Plato did not want to quarrel with the first premise and therefore could resist the conclusion only by denying the second premise, and, in order to do that, he had to redefine "nature," so that, to repeat, it would suffice for the laws to count as existing by nature if they were creations of mind in accordance with right reason. That is one way in which the "order of value" of which I spoke in Section 12 might be thought to count as natural.

AUTHORITARIANISM, TOTALITARIANISM, AND THE PRODUCING CLASS

17. A favorite exam question on Plato is: was he a totalitarian? It is the contention of Karl Popper that he was, but a class analysis of his ideal city satisfies me that he was not. I shall try to persuade you of that conclusion, and, as prelude to that task, it is appropriate to make the point that it is a *sine qua non* of the justice of Plato's just state that not too many golden individuals be born. Plato *has* to suppose that the mass of the people who are born in his society are of the bronze nature: otherwise there will not be enough people who are suited to nonintellectual work, and it is a prime aspect of Platonic justice that people's callings be suited to their natural grades. Such suiting would be inconsistent with the material requirements of society if inferior natures were scarce. Thus a state can only be just if most people in it are by nature inferior, and, therefore, comparatively unjust, for it is only the souls of the guardians that attain completely to justice.

Now this would not sound as paradoxical to Plato's contemporaries as it does to us, because we all believe, or at least *affirm*, certain egalitarian presuppositions. Contemporary meat-eaters might say that it would be a bad thing if no more animals, that is, animals inferior to human animals, were born, but what contemporary political reactionary would *say* that it would be a bad thing if people inferior by nature were no longer born, if all human beings born from now on were of sterling quality? "It would be very nice, if everybody were clever, but fortunately, I mean, unfortunately, most people are stupid." (They might *think* that it's fortunate because they might realize how hard it would be to get decent help if the rabble didn't keep getting reproduced, but they won't say it.) I suggest that Plato's contemporary audience could think of inferior people *some-what* analogously to the way meat-eaters think of nonhuman animals: useful that they should keep on being produced.

Another apparent and surprising precondition of the *Republic*'s ideal city is that it looks as though Plato's just state can exist only if there exists in it an unjustly intemperate desire for luxury. To see why that seems so, observe that the genesis of the ideal state is as follows. In response to the case for *in*justice presented by Glaucon and Adeimantus, the case for injustice as a feature of persons, Socrates proposes to look at what justice means in a society (368e) because there justice will be on a larger scale and therefore "easier to discern."[66] He then proceeds to describe an austere society in which people are so temperate in their desires that they are satisfied by and with a life without luxury. It is only when Glaucon protests that life in what Socrates calls the healthy society is too frugal that Socrates allows for luxury. But then, once luxury is introduced, the society will need more territory, hence will be in military competition with other societies, and will also be vulnerable to attack from without. So it will need a class of guardians, whose first function, the very reason why they are introduced, is defense of the city.

So we now have two respects in which the supremely just state cannot exist unless there is a certain amount of injustice around. The first respect was (1) that plenty of bronze individuals must keep on being born. The second is this: since the supremely just state requires guardians, and guardians come in only because of intemperate desire which leads to the danger of war, (2) justice requires the intemperate desire for luxury, which is unjust, as is shown by the fact that it is not a desire that the guardians themselves will have.[67] If all states were, like the one Plato goes on to describe, just, then there could be no war, and, therefore, no role for the guardians (as a whole class) that each such state requires in order to be just!

Socrates himself says:

"All right . . . I see. We're not just investigating the origins of a community, apparently, but of an indulgent community. Well, that may not be wrong: if we extend our enquiry like that, we might perhaps see how morality and immorality take root in communities. Now, I think that the true community—the one in a healthy condition, as it were—is the one we've described; but if you want us to inspect an inflamed community as well, so be it."[68]

66 Plato, *Republic*, p. 58.
67 Ibid. (419a), p. 122.
68 Ibid. (372e), p. 64.

Robin Waterfield remarks, "[S]ince morality is going to be found, by the end of Chapter 6, to be the control of desire and passion by reason, Plato needs to imagine a community where desires tend towards excess and therefore need controlling."[69] Well, maybe Plato needs to proceed in that way, but does that make his proceedings consistent?

18. I haven't worked out everything that I think about that, but I do not believe that Plato really thought that only states with injustice in them could become just. We may take his story of the *genesis* of the ideal state as a narrative device. The *real* point of introducing the guardians, as opposed to the pretext for doing so, is not for defense, but so that the city will be graced by philosophy. Indeed, I would go so far as to say that the main purpose of Plato's ideal city is to make the philosophical life possible, and that means the aristocratic life, but the truly aristocratic life, the life that is truly best. Plato's dearest interest is not in how an ideal ruling class, or aristocracy, can make a *state* ideal but in how an ideal state can make an ideal aristocracy possible. We must bear that in mind when we try to answer the question whether Plato's state is a totalitarian one. (See 496c–497a, on how bad things are for philosophers *outside* the Republic, in actual states.)[70]

19. Now when Plato speaks in a general way about the state he is constructing, he says that in his state each human being will develop to as high a pitch of virtue as is possible for him. But in fact I do not think he cares very much about the condition with respect to virtue or lack of it in the members of his lower class. I think his true view is that, as far as they are concerned, virtue is a hopeless cause. For otherwise, so it seems to me, he would want to intervene *more* than he proposes to do in their lives. In fact the only social reform proposal he makes is that extremes of wealth and poverty be eliminated, which is not very extensive by comparison with the communism he imposes on auxiliaries and guardians. The other change is the political one that members of the lower class are not to deliberate on public issues. But whereas this might be justified by the sorts of characters they have, it can scarcely be represented as a means whereby they develop and exercise virtue. It is just a means of not letting their comparative virtuelessness harm the state.

For Plato, a just person devotes himself or herself wholeheartedly to his particular function. So at one point he endorses the "idea that a person who has been equipped by nature to be a shoemaker or a joiner or

69   Ibid., p. 389.
70   Ibid., 218–19.

whatever should make shoes or do joinery or whatever" (443c).[71] And at 370c he explains that "productivity is increased, the quality of the products is improved, and the process is simplified when an individual sets aside his other pursuits, does the one thing for which he is naturally suited."[72] And he also says that "ours is the only kind of community where we'll find a shoemaker who is a shoemaker and not a ship's captain as well, and a farmer who is a farmer and not a judge as well, and a soldier who is a soldier and not a businessman as well, and so on" (397e).[73] And also:

> [W]e prohibited a shoemaker from simultaneously undertaking farming or weaving or building, but had him concentrating exclusively on shoemaking, to ensure quality achievements in shoemaking; and we similarly allotted every single person just one job—the one for which he was naturally suited, and which he was to work at all his life, setting aside his other pursuits, so as not to miss the opportunities which are critical for quality achievement.[74]

Yet despite *all* those declarations, and in partial contradiction of them, what Plato *really* cares about, in his application of the division of labor idea to the lower orders, is that they be prevented from entering on the territory of auxiliaries or guardians. He does not mind much what in particular a producer *does* as long as he keeps to his own sphere; his *status*, not his last, is what the cobbler must stick to. The illustrations in 397 (just quoted) are consistent with that,[75] and 434a–b cannot be read in any other way:

> "See if you agree with me on this as well: if a joiner tried to do a shoemaker's job, or a shoemaker a carpenter's, or if they swapped tools or status, or even if the same person tried to do both jobs, with all the tools and so on of both jobs switched around, do you think that much harm would come to the community?"
>
> "Not really," he said.
>
> "On the other hand, when someone whom nature has equipped to be an artisan or to work for money in some capacity or other gets so puffed up by his wealth or popularity or strength or some such factor that he tries to enter the military class, or when a member of the militia tries to enter the class of policy-makers and guardians when he's not qualified to do so, and they swap

71   Ibid., p. 155.
72   Ibid., p. 60.
73   Ibid., p. 94.
74   Ibid. (374c), p. 65.
75   [At this point the text contains the note: "[explain]."—Ed.]

tools and status, or when a single person tries to do all these jobs simultaneously, then I'm sure you'll agree that these interchanges and intrusions are disastrous for the community."[76]

So much for the principle that the born shoemaker or carpenter must stick to his trade (443c):[77] the *real* point is not that the cobbler becomes a supreme cobbler through dedication to his task, but that the lower orders should not "butt in" when it comes to ruling. The important specialization is into classes. So, to repeat: what goes on within the lower class is not of great interest to Plato.

20. I shall say more about the essential virtuelessness of the lower class in a moment. But first I want to draw some consequences, with respect to whether the *Republic* is totalitarian, of what has been said so far. The main point is that Plato's state is not totalitarian precisely because of the dim view Plato takes of the quality of the mass of its citizens. Because they are pretty hopeless, the state will not intrude enough into their lives to qualify as totalitarian, as far as they are concerned. Vis-à-vis the masses, Plato's state is untotalitarian, not because he respects them and therefore grants them liberty but because he disrespects them and therefore sees no point in extensive intervention in their lives. The purpose of Plato's state is to mold souls: It is not its project to conquer the world, for racism or for communism. It has no other project than to mold souls. And not much molding of low-grade souls is possible.

Those who think Plato's state totalitarian either read the *Republic* carelessly *or* concern themselves only with the governing class *or* do not know what the word "totalitarian" means. For what one *can* say, using the relevant words with proper discrimination, is that the *Republic* is a combination of totalitarianism for the guardians and authoritarianism for the masses. Totalitarianism and authoritarianism are distinct concepts, as may be brought out by considering what their opposites are. The opposite of authoritarianism is democracy, and of totalitarianism is liberalism. The authoritarianism-democracy continuum is a matter of who rules over whom, while the totalitarianism-liberalism continuum is a matter of what aspects of life come *under* political rule. Marks of totalitarianism are the Hitler Youth and the Soviet Young Pioneers, organizations that recruit private life to political goals, and note that they

---

76   Plato, *Republic*, p. 142. Myles Burnyeat comments: Plato's audience would have realised that this was a very important boundary line. If they could butt into fighting, they could butt into ruling. Ordinary folk could man the triremes, but hoplites needed potatoes to arm themselves, and cavalry need to be able to afford horses.

77   Ibid., p. 155.

both un-Platonically presuppose that ordinary people can be heroes and heroines. You can have totalitarian democracy, where such institutions enjoy popular support, and you can have liberal authoritarianism, where the rulers allow the people extensive freedom in their private lives: they are denied political rights, but their private lives are entirely their own. What Plato prescribes, you might now agree, is totalitarianism for and within the ruling class and an authoritarian relationship between the rulers and the ruled.[78]

21. Now you might think that my description of the lower orders as virtueless is contradicted by Plato's assignment to them of the particular virtue of temperance. In the standard presentation, the guardians have wisdom, courage, and temperance, or self-mastery, the auxiliaries have courage and temperance, and the producers have only temperance, but they *do have* it, they do have that one virtue. But I now want to show, on the basis of what Plato himself says, that the producers cannot be credited, unequivocally, with even so much as the virtue of temperance. Plato's dim view of the capacities of the producers means that he does not really apply his doctrines of function and virtue to them.

(a) First, consider function. We have already seen that Plato slides away from his insistence that each producer be wholeheartedly committed to the activity which constitutes his contribution to the city, but here I have a further point in mind. The function a group performs in the city is supposed to be one they are particularly good at performing, given which of the three elements, reason, spirit (or self-assertiveness), and bodily desire, is dominant in their members. And this works tolerably well for the two upper orders: where reason predominates, as it does in the guardians, the virtue of wisdom flourishes, but good rule requires wisdom, so the souls of the guardians make them good at carrying out the ruling function. Once again, when spirit dominates, as it does in the souls of auxiliaries, then courage flourishes. But good soldiering requires courage, so the souls of the auxiliaries make them good at fulfilling the function of defense. Notice, now, that this formula cannot be carried through for the ordinary people, in whom carnality or bodily desire is dominant. For dominance of bodily desire does not fit a person particularly well to the

---

78 We can represent the matter in a 2-by-2 matrix:

	Liberal	Totalitarian
Democratic	liberal democracy	Chinese cultural revolution (in its self-description)
Authoritarian	some enlightened despotisms	Saddam Hussein

function of producing material means of life that satisfy bodily desire. Being dominated by a desire for material things does not generate special competence at creating them. Indeed, the best businesspeople and workers are often the most ascetic ones, *least* taken up with their *own* bodily satisfactions.

That carnality dominates in the bronze folk might well mean that it would be *better* for everybody if the bronzies are producers rather than soldiers or, God forbid, rulers. But it does not follow that they will produce *better* than people of a different mettle would. In fact, Plato tends in the *Republic* at various points to conflate two or more of the following three questions: (1) What can X do better than anyone else can? (2) What can X do better than anything else X can do?[79] (3) What is it best that X do, given what there is to do and who there is to do it? Undoubtedly where X = a bronze person, the answer to (3), on Plato's premises, is "produce," and pretty clearly the answer to (1) is nothing, and the answer to (2) is unclear: they might make *better* soldiers than producers (though not as good soldiers as the silver folk can be) yet it might be better that they be producers.

(b) Now, I said that the best businessmen and workers are often the most ascetic ones, least dominated by bodily desire. And it is a reasonable thought that being a good producer requires self-control, self-discipline, self-mastery, or what Plato calls temperance. And it is indeed true that Plato puts temperance or self-mastery as the virtue of the lower classes, not, of course, as a virtue exclusive to them, but as a virtue which not only guardians and auxiliaries but they *too* have. Yet we can argue that temperance, unlike courage and wisdom, which *are* properties of the souls of the superior, is not a property of the souls of the producers.

The supporting stretch of text here, from which I'll quote more than one bit, is 430–32. Note first that (431c–d) temperance, or self-mastery, obtains in the state only because "the desires of the common majority are controlled by the desires and the intelligence of the minority of better men."[80] If that is so, then the members of the inferior multitude do not control their *own* desires and therefore *lack* the *virtue* of self-mastery.[81] If they *behave* temperately, that is a feature not of their souls but of their situation, perhaps a result of sumptuary legislation, although no such

---

79 For bald confusion of (1) with (2), see 370a et circa, Plato, *Republic*, p. 60. He confuses justification of the division of labor on grounds of efficiency with justifying it on the grounds that people have different aptitudes.

80 Ibid., p. 138.

81 One may go further, and ask whether the auxiliaries, for their part, are truly courageous. For the *Laches* teaches that *real* courage requires wisdom, and the auxiliaries are merely indoctrinated. They indeed hold fast to what courage requires, but, as book 4 says, they act according to what their *rulers* say is or is not to be feared.

thing is mentioned. The point is confirmed by Plato's analysis of self-mastery at 430e–431a:

> "Isn't the phrase 'self-mastery' absurd? I mean, anyone who is his own master is also his own slave, of course, and vice versa, since it's the same person who is the subject in all these expressions."
>
> "Of course."
>
> "What this expression means, I think," I continued, "is that there are better and worse elements in a person's mind, and when the part which is naturally better is in control of the worse part, then we use this phrase 'self-mastery' . . ."[82]

Recall, now, how temperance in the state is characterized (see beginning of this paragraph): it is the circumstance that the better part of the state is controlling the worse. Since, in an inferior person, the part better by nature *lacks* the power to control the worse—otherwise temperance in the *commonwealth* would not have to be characterized as I just reported—it follows that the members of the multitude lack the virtue of temperance. And we are indeed told that their souls display a riot of desire, "whereas simple and moderate [forms of desire] which are guided by the rational mind with its intelligence and true beliefs, are encountered only in those few people who have been endowed with excellence by their nature and their education" (431c).[83]

It might be suggested, in mitigation of my charge that even if they *behave* temperately the people do not possess the virtue of *temperance*, that they are *themselves* temperate at least insofar as they *accept* their guardians' control over them. Perhaps that does modify my claim. But, even so, it remains true that the people are able to be temperate only when in a relationship with higher others in the community. As Plato himself says: "unlike courage and wisdom, both of which imbued the community with their respective qualities while being properties of only a part of the community, self-discipline literally spans the whole octaval spread of the community. . . . we couldn't go wrong if we claimed that self-discipline was this unanimity, a harmony between the naturally worse and naturally better elements of society as to which of them should rule both in a community and in every individual" (431e–432a).[84] My point can be put thus: there is temperance, so characterized, in Plato's state only because there cannot be temperance, so characterized, in the inferior members of it. If they had *self*-control, they would not need to be controlled by their

82   Ibid., p. 138.
83   Ibid.
84   Ibid., p. 139.

governors.[85] A man cannot be his *own* master if he needs to be under another's mastery.[86]

22. Low-grade people are in every sense incapable of virtue except when they are appropriately related to people of a different grade. But something like the opposite might *seem* to be true of those possessed of golden nature, that is, it might seem that commerce with people of other grades *detracts* from, or threatens, the virtue of the guardians. To be sure, the guardians require a community with low-grade people in it in order to be *formed* into virtuous people, if only because even guardians need to eat and someone has to produce the food: and, since they also need to keep on eating once their studies are consummated and they are ready to embark on the supremely just life, the life most in contact with justice, the life of philosophy, they need a wider supporting community even then. But this doesn't mean that they need a wider community to be virtuous as such. As far as what they need is concerned, they just need a community to stay alive, and they only need a wider community to be virtuous because they can't be virtuous if they aren't alive, and the wider community is needed for being alive. It is not because of the nature of their souls that they need a wider-than-guardian community to be virtuous, but because of the nature of their perishable bodies, while it *is* because of the nature of their souls that the lower orders need people of other grades to be around. They need them to keep them in order. (Deliver us from temptation!)

85   (1) For difficulties in Plato's account of temperance, and their possible resolution, see Irwin, *Plato's Moral Theory*, chap. 7, sec. 7.6, and his reference ahead.
　　(2) For an excellent account of the relations between justice and the other virtues, including temperance, see Irwin, ibid., pp. 206–7.
　　(3) [The note at this point contains the remark "For doubt that the auxiliaries *really* possess the virtue of courage, see 311 notes, pp. 47–8." The "311 notes" originally written in 1965, contain at that point the following paragraph:

So the lowest class, I am maintaining, and shall return to this point under heading (3) and finally prove it, lack a characteristic virtue. But even the second class, the auxiliaries, lack a virtue they can call pre-eminently their own. The excellence allocated to them is courage. But courage for Plato is not fearlessness, for this can be foolhardy, but an ability to distinguish between situations and encounters which are dangerous and those which are safe. Now this ability can be based on knowledge or on right opinion. When it is based on knowledge it is more solidly grounded, and hence only then does the virtue flourish fully. But only the Guardians have this sort of courage. The auxiliaries whose development is arrested at the stage of right opinion do not have it. In the fullest sense then, the lowest class has no virtue, the second class only a very inferior sort, and the highest class enjoy a near-monopoly.—Ed.]

86   On the virtuelessness of the lower orders, see, further, Williams, *Shame and Necessity*, p. 99, and his "The Analogy of Soul and State in Plato."

But I said not only that the guardians don't need other people for virtue as such, but that their case *seems* to be the *opposite*, in this respect, of the producers, and I meant by that something stronger than what I have said thus far. I meant not merely that the guardians do not *need* the others but that their very virtue would *flourish* with less restriction only if there *were* no others: not only do they not *need* to have other people around, for the sake of the stability of their virtue, but they need *not* to have other people around, for their virtue to flourish maximally.

The thought justifying that more extreme claim is that, insofar as the guardians turn away from the Forms and relate to other people, which they must do *because* they have to rule, then that must *derogate* from their virtue. How can it not spoil their justice, at least a little, to be in the company of the less than fully just, on the Platonic view, so strongly and repeatedly stated in the exposition of the guardians' educational regimen, that people tend to take on the character of, or be affected by, what is in their vicinity? That's the premise for all those cultural regulations about banning various forms of poetry and so on. (See 401c–d for future development of this theme: note "salubrious" at 401c.)[87] How can they not become less just when they turn from contemplating the Forms and their fellow Forms-contemplators to contemplating the *canaille*? At 412d Plato says that the ruling guardians will "devote their lives to wholeheartedly doing what they regard as advantageous to the community."[88] But is such zeal truly consistent with having to look away from the Forms and take up the toils of ruling that they face when they return to the cave? Plato expressly says, and even hopes, that the guardians will *not* regard ruling as a "desirable thing to do" (520d).[89] He wants rulers who don't want to rule so that their relationship to power will not be a corrupt one. But is that consistent with the zeal that he attributes to the ruling guardians at 412d?[90] How can they devote themselves *whole*heartedly to what they find undesirable? See how Plato describes their burden at 540b:

> [T]hey spend most of their time doing philosophy, but when their turn comes, then for the community's sake they become involved in its affairs and slog away at them as rulers. This is something they do as an obligation, not as a privilege. Because they have this attitude, they're constantly training others to follow suit.[91]

---

87   Plato, *Republic*, pp. 99–100.
88   Ibid., p. 116.
89   Ibid., p. 248.
90   Ibid., p. 116.
91   Ibid., p. 275.

Which is to say that they won't monopolize power, because they don't like exercising it.

A major question about the *Republic* is whether Plato succeeds in showing that a just life is a happy life. I have raised a further question: suppose Plato *does* show that a just life, a life of contemplation of the Forms, is a happy one, because one in which the soul is supremely well ordered. Does not the requirement that these contemplators turn from contemplation to the job of *ruling* then mean that they have to sacrifice not only happiness but also justice?[92] Isn't Plato asking the rulers to be unjust, or anyway less just than they could be, when he asks them to look away from the Forms? I shall first deal with that question and then address the separate "happiness" challenge.

One might think that Plato is only in trouble if one of the challenges succeeds and the other fails, since, if *both* succeed, if the guardians are neither just *nor* happy, then they are not a counterexample to Plato's proposition that the just are happy. But Plato seeks not only to clear that proposition, that the just are happy, against a counterexample of the contemplated kind but to substantiate it, and he fails to do that if the guardians fail to illustrate both justice and happiness.

To be sure, Plato himself says that it is an entirely *just* demand that each guardian should do his bit of ruling: he owes that to his country. Here is Hussey's translation of the relevant passage:

> "Well then, Glaucon," I said, "consider that we shall not then be committing any *injustice* against those philosophers who appear in our city. What we shall say to them will be *just*, when we impose on them the extra necessity of taking care of the others and guarding them. We shall say that it is reasonable, that those who in other cities turn out to be such do not take a share of the labours in those cities, since they grow up in them spontaneously, against the wishes of the constitutions of any of those cities, and it is fair that what is self-sown, since it is not dependent on anyone for being brought up, should not be willing to pay anyone the dues required for upbringing." (520a–b) (The italicized words translate the Greek *adikḗsomen* (to do something unjust) and *dikaia* respectively, both rooted in *dikḕ*, the root for justice.)[93]

But our philosophers, so Plato says, cannot say that. In all justice, they should discharge an obligation which they have to the city.

---

92 Adkins, whose pp. 290–92 of *Merit and Responsibility* make the case I am expounding, calls this "scandalous."

93 [This translation was provided by Edward Hussey at Cohen's request in 2004. Used by kind permission of Edward Hussey.—Ed.]

That may sound plausible to our modern ears, but *wait a minute!* Justice is *supposed* to be psychic harmony, and, if it is, then it is quite unclear that it would be *unjust* for the guardians not to engage in government. For if justice is psychic harmony, then the guardians are characterized by the highest form of justice only when they are doing philosophy. Plato nowhere suggests, after all, that an interest in philosophy and contemplation can be too strong in a person, and that interest is, surely, sacrificed when they step out of the ivory tower and return to the cave, or city hall, and he seems to more or less say so himself. Plato seems to need an *un*Platonic concept of justice to defend his injunction that the philosophers are obliged to rule, an *un*Platonic concept of justice which, moreover, in this context, recommends a course which diminishes the justice of the guardians, in the Platonic sense of "justice." The uses of "injustice" and "just" in the passage seem to have nothing to do with justice as it is expounded in the *Republic*. One might conjecture that Plato thinks that those who have observed with the eye of the intellect what justice is will see that what he says in the passage is endorsed by justice, but we would simply have to take Plato's *word* for that. There is no argument to substantiate it in the *Republic* (or elsewhere in Plato).

Let me separate two problems here. The first problem is that there is an apparently *un*Platonic conception of "justice," justice as reciprocity, at work in the 520a–b passage: Plato seems to need, and to use, an *un*Platonic concept of justice to defend his injunction that philosophers are obliged to rule, and one, *moreover*—this is the second problem—which recommends a course which is *anti-* the Platonic conception of justice. The second problem is how the guardians can fail to be departing from justice in *Plato*'s sense when they turn to ruling.

About the first problem I can only say what I did in the penultimate sentence of the paragraph two paragraphs back. But about the second problem I suggest the following elements of a solution. The solution says that engagement in ruling does not make them less just but simply diminishes their opportunity to *exercise* that virtue. Their virtuous character is acquired and sustained through Forms-contemplation, but their virtue is not so precarious that it begins to decay as soon as they do something else. And that seems to me a good line of defense. It might still be true that the rulers are not as *happy* as they would be if all they did was contemplate the Forms: we'll come to the happiness problem in a moment. But it works against the charge that they are less just than they would be if all they did was contemplate the Forms.

To this one might add that, while Forms-contemplation is the highest activity, it might nevertheless be an activity which can indeed reach saturation point (as just mentioned): beyond a certain amount in a given stretch of time, further Forms-contemplation could be pointless (genug shoin!).[94] Just as, beyond a certain point, further weight lifting is point-less, and you should go forth and use your muscles, not build them up further. And that would mean that there could be scope for other activity, hence, in principle, for ruling, in a life that was thoroughly just.

23. I turn to the happiness charge. Here is how Glaucon formulates it at 519c–d:

> "Our job as founders, then," I said, "is to make sure that the best people come to that fundamental field of study (as we called it earlier): we must have them make the ascent we've been talking about and see goodness. And afterwards, once they've been up there and had a good look, we mustn't let them get away with what they do at the moment."
>
> "Which is what?"
>
> "Staying there," I replied, "and refusing to come back down again to those prisoners, to share their work and their rewards, no matter whether those rewards are trivial or significant."
>
> "But in that case," he protested, "we'll be wronging them: we'll be making the quality of their lives worse and denying them the better life they could be living, won't we?"[95]

But, so one might remind Glaucon, Plato is not committed to the proposition that his rulers' interests are *entirely* in conformity with the interests of their community, and, therefore, entirely satisfied. All that Socrates has to show is that the justest people are also the happiest, that you are happier if you are just than if you are unjust, not that the just are in no way unhappy. If Plato can show that the just man is happier than anyone else, he has met the challenge at the beginning of the *Republic*, which was to show that the just man is happier than the unjust man. To show *that* he need not show that the perfectly just man is perfectly happy or even that the juster you are the happier you are, and vice versa. Even his heady claim that

> [t]he happiness which people attribute to Olympic victors is due to a tiny fraction of what our guardians have. The guardians' victory is more splendid, and their upkeep by the general populace is more thorough-going. The fruit of their victory is the preservation of the whole community, their prize the maintenance of themselves and their children with food and all of life's essentials. During their lifetimes they are honoured by their community, and when they die they are buried in high style. (465d–e)[96]

---

94   [A Yiddish expression: "enough is enough!"—Ed.]

95   Plato, *Republic*, p. 247.

96   Ibid., p. 181.

does not imply that everything in their lives is a blessing, that there is nothing they are obliged to do that conflicts with something else that they would prefer to do. Olympic victors didn't lead perfect lives. Nobody ever promised anybody a rose garden.

24. My answer to the two charges runs, thus far, as follows. Engagement in ruling might count as diminishing the *exercise* of justice, but that does not mean that it diminishes the volume and purity of that virtue in the guardians' souls. And while such engagement might indeed diminish the happiness of the guardians, they could remain happier, because just, than anyone else.

Let me now strengthen this defense of Plato further by expounding a view which says that, among nonphilosophical activity, ruling is, for Plato, a particularly apt way of completing a life *both* of justice *and* of happiness, because if you are just then you will indeed have an actual *desire* to rule, that will make you happy when it's satisfied. But what would make the just have such a desire?

Following Richard Kraut,[97] Irwin suggests that Plato's theory of love explains why the philosopher-guardians have an actual *desire* to carry out what 520 lays on them as a reasonable and fair obligation.[98] According to that theory, which is expounded in the *Symposium*, we want to augment and propagate what we love, and, since the philosophers love justice or psychic harmony, they will want so far as they can to implant it in the members of the city's other orders. So on this view, and contrary to my first excessively modest defense (see 22 above), it *is* a special *exercise* of the very virtue of justice that is involved when the guardians rule. This would mean that it is false that they rule simply to make sure that they are not themselves ruled by unjust people who would deprive them of their permanent semisabbatical. It may indeed be an unavoidable necessity (521),[99] without detracting from their possession and exercise of justice.[100] On this view, one might say, they do not turn their backs on the Forms when they rule: they simply apply them *in practice*.

(Finally, can one reconcile the Kraut/Irwin view with *Republic* 520d, which suggests—see above, 22—that ruling will not be "highly desirable" for the guardians? Yes, because you can have higher and lower desires.

97   Kraut, "Egoism, Love and Political Office in Plato," an admirably clear but implausible article, yet one well used by Irwin.

98   Irwin, *Classical Thought*, pp. 105–6.

99   Plato, *Republic*, pp. 248–49.

100   On the foregoing theme I recommend Adkins, *Merit and Responsibility*, pp. 290–92; Irwin, *Classical Thought*, pp. 105–6; Irwin, *Plato's Moral Theory*, pp. 239–40, 241–43, 257–59; and Kraut, "Egoism, Love and Political Office in Plato."

Parents who seek with enormous desire to have babies might still find it a drag to have to get up at night.)

ARISTOTLE

Aristotle, a student of Plato, also identified himself with the aristocratic cause, but he did not appeal to a realm of nature that transcended the nature of everyday experience, and he criticized Plato's project of constructing an ideal state, charging it with an unrealistic idealism. Aristotle claimed that various provisions of the *Republic* were unworkable because against the grain of human nature. In particular, Plato strips the guardian class members of personal property and family ties, in the conviction that a communism of material goods and personal relations alike would bind people together. For Plato, family and private property derogate from wholehearted service to the state: they generate attachments which conflict with loyalty to the community. But Aristotle judged that without nuclear family affection and some private property an individual would not be fully formed, and that it was only on the basis of such particularist formation that a person could extend himself or herself to wider social involvement.

A word in defense of Plato here. At the end of the first paragraph of book 2 of the *Politics*, the book which reviews ideal states, Aristotle offers a methodological admonition which is clearly (from the context) meant to apply against Plato. He says that

> when we proceed to seek for something different from the forms of government we have investigated, we shall not be thought to belong to the class of thinkers who desire at all costs to show their own ingenuity, but rather to have adopted our method in consequence of the defects we have found in existing forms.[101]

But it begs various questions to imply that Plato was not himself proposing to act as doctor to a deficient actuality. Plato's ideal state promotes those virtues in which, so he believed, Athens was deficient, and there is plenty of reference to existing defects requiring remedy in the *Republic*. Nor is it clearly the case, as Aristotle sometimes suggests, that Plato is willing to legislate only for ideal human raw material, that he does not take people as they actually are. For, first, this characterization cannot be squared with the fact that Plato must suppose that the majority in his city will be made of inferior, bronze, stuff (see above). And second,

---

101   Aristotle, *Politics* (2.1.1), p. 39.

his opinion of the human nature of even the higher citizenry cannot be entirely rosy, for otherwise it would not be necessary to educate them so assiduously over so extended a period.[102]

Like Plato, Aristotle rejected the Sophist opposition between nature and convention. He thought that human society could have, and often did have, a natural form: indeed he thought that all terrestrial things would achieve a perfection appropriate to themselves if allowed to undergo an unobstructed growth. So, unlike Plato, he did not look to an order of nature transcending experience which human society should emulate. The Sophists were wrong to oppose nature and convention not because a higher nature should govern convention but because men are by (ordinary, terrestrial) nature convention-making animals. Under appropriate conditions, a human community achieves a perfection proper to itself: there is no need to intercede and *impose* a form. One must, however, study what the circumstances are in which a harmonious structure is spontaneously achieved.

Aristotle's emphasis in his conception of society and politics on growth and the proper conditions of it is continuous with a teleological biologism pervasive in his view of the world. Everything in nature, including its very elements (earth, air, fire, and water) possesses natural tendencies of development, tendencies which explain observable phenomena, which, consequently, are not to be explained by theories of mechanical interaction.

If you look at Aristotle's *De Anima* (On the Soul) you will not discover a sharp opposition between vital functions such as breathing, digestion, and sleep and conscious mentation. There is not, as in Plato, a gulf between the senses and the mind, connected respectively with lower and higher orders of nature that are hostile to one another. Instead, mind grows out of sensation; the higher functions are developments of the lower ones, not supernatural activities for the time being tied to a material existence. In Plato's supernaturalism humanity is to imitate a nature of a higher order. In Aristotle the human is nature's supreme achievement: human life is not the imprisonment of a supernatural soul in a material body.

The natural state of a thing is its final form, the shape it takes when it is fully grown. Thus the acorn is by nature an oak, and the polis or human society is the natural destiny of the fully developed human being. When Aristotle urges that man is a political animal, that the state exists

---

102   [The text at this point contains the note: "CONTINUE WITH 311, p. 76 WHEN LECTURING ON ARISTOTLE AT GREATER LENGTH." "311" is a reference to the original lecture notes, written in 1965. It is unclear how much of this material was to be included, and so the original pp. 76 to 83, the final page of the original notes, are included as Appendix 2 to this chapter.—Ed.]

by nature, he does not mean that it has an origin connected with primitive impulses, but that it is in the nature of human beings that, when properly developed, they live in polities. Nature is associated with the fully developed rather than the primitive, and the state exists by nature because it fulfills human nature.[103]

There is a connection between Aristotle's view of nature and society and his engagement in the empirical study of politics. A greater respect than Plato had for the observable world went with a greater interest than Plato had in studying it. Aristotle studied the actual conventions or nomoi that people had adopted, connecting their variations with the types of people who had adopted them. He collected 156 constitutions and wrote commentaries on them, but of that, fortunately, only the Constitution of Athens survives. Aristotle thus practiced as a dispassionate political scientist, showing like a physician what sorts of measures could be used to sustain *or* subvert what sorts of constitutions. Though himself favorable to aristocracy, he explained how any government, including aristocracy itself, might be resisted and destroyed by those wishing to do it in.

Plato's temper was, manifestly, more *radical* than Aristotle's. Plato thought that anything *short* of the ideal was not really worth striving for, whereas Aristotle found something of value in virtually any human association. Aristotle was prepared to advise states of all kinds on how best to preserve their stability, because he believed that every human community *must* be realizing some of the goals he hoped to fulfill in his ideal scheme. Aristotle was a physician to actual states, prescribing, with great diagnostic insight, various medicines for various ailments in the social structure. But Plato could never prescribe anything but the most drastic form of surgery. His advice would always be: scrap your existing institutions, recast your city in the mold of the ideal. The poet Ezra Pound wrote, "What thou lovest well remains, the rest is dross."[104] Plato agrees. Aristotle does not. And he is right. For to treat as worthless anything which does not fully embody our highest ideals is to take a dangerous and ultimately self-destructive course, both in politics and in ordinary life.

Because of his focus on the real world, Aristotle can claim the title "father of political science," for he did not restrict himself to the normative questions that were the main preoccupation of his predecessors. But he also displays his preferences, and in his own fashion perpetuates the reversion to pre-Sophistic tradition that Plato had effected. He believes

103   [At this point in the text Cohen includes the remark "(311–p. 66P3 continues here)." Once more it is unclear how much of this material Cohen intended to include, and so Appendix 1 contains the material from p. 66 to p. 76 of the 311 notes, with Appendix 2, as mentioned above, running from p. 76 to the end of the notes.—Ed.]

104   Pound, *The Cantos of Ezra Pound* (Canto 81), pp. 540–41.

in a natural division of mankind into freemen and slaves, a division warranted by the fact that some people possess only an inferior sort of rational capacity (they can carry out but not clearheadedly formulate plans) and are best suited to serve those who are more generously endowed. And he urges that the best possible state is a democracy in *form*, economically based on a class of small farmers. These will be too far from the Assembly, he points out, to visit it very often and disturb its functioning. For Aristotle everything in nature and society has a natural relationship of subordination to something else. The body exists to further the purposes of the soul, the passions exist to further the purposes of intellect and morality, and the lesser classes in the state exist to further the purposes of men of leisure who pursue knowledge and engage in civic life.

Aristotle's preferred community is a small community. He argues for severe restrictions on the size of the polis. The Sophists, Socrates, and Plato also thought in terms of small-scale communities. Aristotle himself was tutor to Alexander the Great, but I do not think he realized that his pupil would bring an end to the context which Aristotle and his predecessors thought necessary for successful politics, through his conquest of Greece and Asia and his synthesis of Greece and the Near East into one vast Hellenistic world.

For Aristotle, man is a political animal, an animal in a polis. This is much less true, in one of the senses that it carries, of Plato, for whom, one might claim, government is a distraction from the highest human fulfillment, in which those capable of that fulfillment, which lies in contemplation of the eternal, engage in order to safeguard their continued contemplation of it. For Plato governing is a burden which people of culture from time to time assume, so that uncultured people will not govern and ruin the city. For Aristotle running the city is a principal way in which a person of culture can be fruitfully exercised, a form of, rather than a distraction from, self-realization. But all that is possible only in a polis, and now the polis disappears, new schools of thought arise stressing a person's link with his fellow human beings, whoever and wherever they may be, Greek or barbarian, free or slave. The development of this theme belongs to Stoicism and to the Christian tradition.

Appendix 1[105]

Now when speaking of the original pre-Sophistic engulfment, I showed how it was associated with an aristocratic ideology. And this association is to be found in Aristotle as well, whose tendencies are no less aristocratic

---

105 [This is the section from the 311 notes, referred to above, starting from p. 66, paragraph 3.—Ed.]

than Plato, but who realizes more than his teacher the natural obstacles to the realization of aristocratic principles, but also that a great deal will take care of itself as long as a polity is functioning naturally. Thus he argues forcibly for the old doctrine of the natural division of mankind into slave and free, and identifies this with the division between barbarian and Greek. The barbarian is by nature suited to serve the Greek, because of the barbarian's inferior rationality. He develops himself to the full only when under the instruction and dominion of another: thus slavery is his natural estate. Again, most Greeks are by nature unsuited to the deliberation required in political life; they are suited to manual toil, and form the basis of the state, from whose citizenship they are excluded in Aristotle's ideal picture. They are the matter underlying the state; its form is provided by those of a higher nature. (More on matter/form soon.)

Whereas the Sophists took law to be conventional, to be conscious human edict, and hence urged that it be changed if necessary, avoided if undesirable, Aristotle assimilates law to nature by conceiving of it as custom which develops with the development of the state. As I argued earlier, this makes law a matter of habit, of arrangements naturally adopted. Thus there is no legislature in Aristotle, as there is none in the *Laws*. But whereas Plato's Laws derive from heaven, the laws in Aristotle are the outgrowth of human life on earth.

Aristotle also has arguments against the contract theory. (Arguments later lifted by Hegel in his contrast between civil society and the state.) Certain institutions in society *are* regulated by agreement, by contract, certain economic activities and social pastimes.[106] But such contractual arrangements only form the basis on which the state, not itself contractual, grows. For the community within which they are made is not itself contracted into, either in fact or in principle. The law of the community is not, as the Sophist Lycophron[107] suggested, a "guarantor of men's rights against one another." Its purpose is loftier: the encouragement of virtue in human beings so that they develop as far as their natures are capable of doing.

Now, Aristotle is often spoken of as the father of political science, a field distinguished from political philosophy through its more empirical character. I have reserved this point until now because I want to connect it with the view of nature which he held and which I have now outlined. Again, the Sophists had opposed nature and convention; and Aristotle's response can be phrased thus: man is by nature a convention-making, i.e. law-adopting animal, and the laws men live by and through which they realize themselves can be traced to their nature-given characters, and are not a result of will (pure free choice). This view provoked him to

106   Aristotle, *Politics* (3.9.13), p. 120.
107   Ibid. (3.9.8), p. 119.

study the actual conventions men had adopted, the actual legal systems which grew naturally among them.[108] And so he, assisted by students, collected 156 constitutions, and wrote commentaries on them thereby practicing as a dispassionate political scientist. Sadly, only the Constitution of Athens survives. He appreciated the variety of human institutions and showed how different kinds of political societies could be kept stable according to their own principles in the beyond. More on this when I contrast Aristotle with Plato.

Matter and Form

Aristotle's optimistic approach to nature is evident in his theory of matter and form, a theory which applies to all things in the universe, and whose influence can be identified in many of his formulations in the *Politics*. Everything is divided into matter and form. But of everything we can ask—what is its matter, what is its form? We can define the matter of a thing as that out of which it has been made, the stuff it is made of, and the form is that into which it has been made, the shape it has assumed at the end of its development. Matter and form are relative terms, for the same thing can be form relative to one thing and matter relative to another. It will be form relative to something lower than it in the scale of development, matter relative to something higher than it in that scale. Thus earth (cold and dry), air (hot and wet), fire (dry and hot), and water (wet and cold) are form relative to primary matter; but matter relative to substances like copper and brass and human flesh which are formed out of them. Again, copper and brass will be matter relative to bronze, a form of copper and brass; bronze will be matter relative to a statue of Venus. Human flesh will be matter relative to the bodily form of a human being, and the same body will be matter when compared to the human soul, the principle which unites and gives shape and purpose and structure to the activity of the body. Thus the master/slave relation of which I spoke before is a totality of which the master is the formative principle, the source of direction, and the slave provides the material basis for achieving things.

The passage from matter to form is the actualization of a potentiality. The copper and brass are *potentially* bronze; physical flesh is *potentially ensouled*; the Greek and barbarian are *potentially* master and slave, in a relation which assumes the form proper to their respective substance or matter. And what is superior over potentiality is actuality, which is another way of asserting the superiority of form over matter. The movement we observe in the world is everywhere a striving toward form, a tendency on the part of things to embody shape and structure. Now we know Plato also made the Forms or principles superior to matter; but he placed them

108   Ibid. (3.17.1), pp. 149–50.

in a suprasensible world, and the wise philosopher king had to try to realize them on earth. For Aristotle, Forms exist in the world itself; they are what explains what takes place within it.

Forms exist in the world. What are the consequences of this? Well, Aristotle becomes the first patron of the *concrete universal* (Hegel's term). Socrates sought for a universal justice, etc., apart from particular right usages. Aristotle is concerned to find justice embedded in right usages, concerned to discover the universal in the particular: there is no abstract universal, only concrete universals. So you will not find in Aristotle the type of Socratic reasoning we found so unsatisfactory: A is B, C is B, but A is B through being D, so C must also be D. Aristotle is concerned with how the universal embodies itself differently in each particular. So Aristotle resists the idea that justice in the state must mirror justice in the individual. The general law of principle operates in several spheres, its embodiment varying according to the matter it is shaping. Again, separate kinds of goodness belong to man, woman, child, slave; separate goodnesses to ruler of a family, of a slave, of a state, because the material context of rule differs. Barker contrasts Aristotle's view of affectional connections with Plato's:

> The argument implied by Aristotle is that the ordinary system of the family and of family relationship (1) enables A, B, and the rest to feel to a man, in their different ways and from different angles, "that keen sense of something *idion* [i.e. of personal interest] which the change proposed by Plato would take away or seriously diminish" (Newman's note), and (2) enriches the man himself, who is placed in these different and individual relations to A,B, and the rest, by giving him, as it were, a number of facets, which would be absent on the Platonic plan, and the absence of which would leave him one plain, dull, and unrelieved surface.[109]

The point is that the universal relation of human affection is not and cannot be made a monochrome thing, but differentiates itself into specific forms for differently related people. "It is as if you were to turn harmony into mere unison, or to reduce a theme to a single beat."[110]

Morals and Politics

In a short section in the *Ethics*, quoted by Barker,[111] Aristotle states his view of the relation between ethics and politics, and we may profitably

---

109   Ibid., p. 45n. The reference to Newman is to the editor of the Greek edition of the *Politics*, of which Barker made his translation.

110   Ibid. (2.5.14), p. 51.

111   Ibid., pp. 354–55. The sections quoted are bk. 1, chaps. 1 and 2.

examine this before passing to book 1 of the *Politics*. He represents human spheres of activity as a hierarchy, in which the community is the highest, because most comprehensive, and he maintains that the social good is the supreme good to which other goods must be subordinated, into which they must be integrated. This means that for Aristotle there can never be more than a superficial conflict between what is morally required and what is politically good. Where what I feel it right to do appears to conflict with the general advantage, I must be confused. Thus he says that the goodness of the man and the goodness of the citizen co-incide in the well-ordered state.

Today I submit we must find this doctrine hard to accept, principally because our concepts of morality and politics have changed. For Aristotle a man's end is to develop a good character, and this is associated with being happy. To be moral is to have a good character, fine dispositions, noble desires. And the end of the community is to develop such good characters in its members. But today we do not tend, in the West anyway, to allocate such a function to the community, or at any rate to govern-ment. In fact, the community of course "socializes" us, but (a) we sharply distinguish community and government, whereas Aristotle makes gov-ernment an ineliminable aspect of community, and (b) this socialization is more making us feel bad if we don't follow social rules, rather than implanting a healthy character in us. Where a government, like the Soviet one, explicitly states as one of its aims the education of the character of the people, we find this totalitarian. We think there are ends in politics, but we conceive of them as the production of welfare and opportunities for people, not the shaping of their characters.

And we also do not have Aristotle's concept of morals, which we do not link so indissolubly with the virtuous man, the man who has been trained to do what is best. Aristotle's ethics is to be contrasted with that of Kant, and we are not as far away from Kant as Aristotle is. While for Aristotle the good man is he who has good desires, for Kant the good man is he who can suppress and restrain his desires and do the right thing. Being moral in Kant is not behaving according to the dictates of a finely ordered nature, but cleaving to principle, often in defiance of the proddings of our nature. And so whereas Aristotle associates good character and happiness, we find no such association in Kant. For Kant the best man is he who has the most strength to suppress wickedness, for Aristotle he who is devoid of wickedness, who functions harmoniously.

So we do not see the good man as he who has developed a good char-acter and we do not see the good state as that which develops good char-acters. So we do not share Aristotle's conviction of the compatibility of moral and political values, and with us there are often conflicts between moral and political values. Conscientious objection does not arise as a problem for Aristotle. There are different forms of conscientious objection. There is the form where the objector wishes to lay a moral condemnation against the state. He does not experience a conflict between moral and political values, but simply sees the state as immoral. But there can be another form of conscientious objection, where the objector accepts the legitimacy of the state's aims, say the destruction of fascism, and acknowledges only war can do this, but declares himself morally repelled by the prospect of killing another man. In such a case, unlike in my first case, a man experiences a conflict between the demands of morality and the demands of politics. And it is such a conflict which Aristotle's philosophy does not countenance.

I now want to look at book 1 of the *Politics*. There is a good deal about slavery in it, and I have already spoken of that. Most of the book is fairly straightforward, and I do not propose in lectures to summarize what is straightforward in Aristotle. What I want to talk about in book 1 is Aristotle's economic theory, because it reflects his aristocratic antibourgeois biases, and because it is historically very important. In his book *Religion and the Rise of Capitalism*, R. H. Tawney made a statement which has been cited many times since: "The last of the schoolmen was Karl Marx."[112] By the schoolmen he meant the scholastic philosophers, primary among whom was St. Thomas Aquinas. And Aquinas borrowed most of his philosophy, including his economic doctrines, from Aristotle. So the suggestion is that there are Aristotelian roots for some of Marx's basic concepts and judgments. And they agree in both opposing the principles of capitalist society, Marx as a socialist, Aristotle as an aristocrat. I shall show how this Aristotelian anticipation of Marx is to be found in book 1.

A key distinction in Marx's economics is that between use-value and exchange-value. The use-value of a product is determined by the extent to which it satisfies human needs. Its exchange-value is determined by the number of products or the amount of money it will command on the market. Now capitalist society is a society whose principle is production for exchange. The worker produces products which he does not use: they are appropriated by the capitalist who does not use them either, but exchanges them on the market, so that he can buy more means of production, wherewith to produce more products to buy more means of production . . . So the whole society is geared to more and more production, not to more and more satisfaction of human needs. The use-value of a product is secondary for capitalism, whose energies are directed to producing more and more, without limit; to accumulating exchange-value, rather than enjoying the wealth produced: thus "Accumulate, accumulate, that is Moses and the prophets."[113] The system is condemned by

---

112 Tawney, *Religion and the Rise of Capitalism*, p. 48.
113 Marx, *Capital*, vol. 1 (Penguin), p. 742.

Marx who looks forward to the era of socialism, when production will be determined by use, directed to satisfying human requirements.

Now the distinction between use- and exchange-value can be found in Aristotle, and also the Marxian attitude of friendliness toward use-value and hostility toward exchange-value. Aristotle expresses the distinction as that between household management, which seeks to satisfy the needs of the members of a family or society, and the unlimited art of acquisition, whose aim is the unlimited accumulation of wealth, undirected to satisfying needs. Aristotle favors the feudal principle in which a body of men produce their needs, part of the product being allocated for the needs of the lord, to whom men have a certain loyalty, transcending economic bonds. He speaks of *the exchange* of a product as a perversion of its natural function. To take, for example, a shoe to market in the hope of selling it for gain is disparaged: "Since the shoe has not been made for the purpose of being exchanged the use which is being made of it is not its proper and peculiar use."[114] This must be read in conjunction with "[Nature] makes each separate thing for a separate end; and she does so because each instrument has the finest finish when it serves a single purpose and not a variety of purposes."[115] Thus the merchant who uses the shoe only to exchange it is misusing it. Like Marx, Aristotle fulminates against the unlimited desire for wealth, dissociated from the needs it is the purpose of wealth to satisfy, the worship of accumulation as such. Again, Marx had said that man's products should satisfy his needs so that he can exercise his skills, release his potentialities, in emancipation from economics. When all human talents are harnessed to economic life, man is a degraded being. We find the same feeling in Aristotle.

> [Those engaging in the art of acquisition use] each and every capacity in a way not consonant with its nature. The proper function of courage, for example, is not to produce money, but to give confidence. The same is true of military and medical ability; neither has the function of producing money: the one has the function of producing victory, and the other that of producing health. But those of whom we are speaking turn all such capacities into forms of the art of acquisition, as though to make money were the one aim and everything else must contribute to that aim.[116]

Of course Aristotle is not a socialist, because he believes in production for use within a hierarchy, rather than in an egalitarian community. But the comparison just shows how much feudalism, which capitalism destroyed, and socialism, which seeks to replace capitalism, have in

114   Aristotle, *Politics* (1.9.3), p. 23.
115   Ibid. (1.2.3), p. 3.
116   Ibid. (1.9.17), pp. 26–27.

common. There are expressly feudal elements in Aristotle to which Marx would not subscribe. The art of war is represented as a natural way of gaining commodities-for-use.[117] We know how this art was glorified in the Middle Ages. That it is feudal in character is urged by Schumpeter, the theorist of capitalism, who sees wars in the capitalist era as atavistic reversions, leftovers from precapitalist societies. The idea is that the merchant, the bourgeois man, wants peace between states, for the purpose of carrying out world trade. World trade is not something to which aristocrats, against trade as such, incline.[118] This puts Aristotle in touch with the Old Oligarch, a pre-Sophistic defender of aristocracy against the rising bourgeoisie who would have razed the Piraeus to the ground as the source of degeneration in Athens.[119]

Aristotle also anticipates another element in Marxism, the idea that the nature of a state, the form of a government, is largely determined by the class composition of its members, and that a change in political life is a direct consequence of a change in the socioeconomic fundament of politics. It is in book 4, chapter 3,[120] that the first thesis is explicitly stated. And the second can be found in book 5, chapter 2, paragraph 6, where a disproportionate increase in the power of a class is presented as an occasion of revolution.[121]

Aristotle as Follower and Critic of Plato

I have already spoken of the temperamental difference between Plato and Aristotle, and have suggested the difference in tone in their response to the Sophists. If we want to employ labels, we can call Aristotle a conservative and Plato a reactionary. A reactionary is a radical conservative. He wants to use every means to instate a hierarchical government, and eliminate the power the people have won for themselves. A conservative seeks what is good in what exists, and reflects wisely that popular power is only apparent. More generally, apart from the common right-wing political allegiance, a radical hopes to change the world; a conservative subscribes to Bradley's statement that "[t]he wish to be better than the world is already to be on the threshold of immorality."[122] The wish to propose principles to the world of politics which develops its own principles is a futile and dangerous wish. So everywhere in Aristotle we find expressions of what might be called good Tory sense: let's not rock the boat, let's enjoy what we can by keeping things as they are.

117   Ibid. (1.8.12), p. 21.
118   Ibid. (7.6.4), p. 294.
119   On Pireaus see ibid. (5.3.15), p. 211. On Aristotle as anticipating historical materialism, see (1.8.5–8), p. 20, and the next two references.
120   Ibid. (4.3), pp. 160–62
121   Ibid. (5.2.6), p. 207.
122   Bradley, "My Station and Its Duties," p. 199.

But while these arguments go to show that in *some* cases, and at *some* times, law ought to be changed, there is another point of view from which it would appear that change is a matter which needs great caution. When we reflect that the improvement likely to be effected may be small, and that it is a bad thing to accustom men to abrogate laws light-heartedly, it becomes clear that there are some defects, both in legislation and in government, which had better be left untouched. The benefit of change will be less than the loss which is likely to result if men fall into the habit of disobeying the government.[123]

Now let us look more particularly at Aristotle's differences from and agreements with Plato. First I shall treat book 2, where he criticizes Plato's *Republic* explicitly. Then I shall show that throughout Aristotle there are echoes of Plato's teaching. Finally I shall indicate a further difference not found in book 2.

At the beginning of book 2, in chapter 1, paragraph 1, Aristotle seeks to distinguish himself from proponents of ideal states, Plato included.

When we proceed to seek for something different from the forms of government we have investigated, we shall not be thought to belong to the class of thinkers who desire at all costs to show their own ingenuity, but rather to have adopted our method in consequence of the defects we have found in existing forms.[124]

But is Plato's procedure really any different? Implied throughout the *Republic* is a criticism of Athens, and what Plato sponsors in his ideal state is precisely those virtues in which, according to Plato, Athens was deficient. The Republic may be unworkable, but it seems to be inspired by what Aristotle here anyway treats as legitimate, the desire to remedy existing defects. Again, it is not the case as Aristotle often suggests that Plato is interested in legislating only for ideal human raw material, and does not take men as they really are. For how does this attribution square with the fact that most of Plato's men are men of bronze. Plato has a none-too-optimistic opinion of the human nature of the members of the Republic: that's why even for those of higher nature he proposes such extensive education, decades long.

Appendix 2[125]

Indeed, the factor of education in the *Republic* seems to be what Aristotle fails to notice, and this tends to vitiate his criticisms of Plato's

---

123   Aristotle, *Politics* (2.8.22–23), p. 73.

124   Ibid. (2.1.1), p. 39.

125   [Although Cohen indicates that this material is to be inserted earlier in the lectures, it is placed here as in the original 311 notes it runs on directly from the previous appendix, as will be evident from the text.—Ed.]

communism. He uses common sense about common men to show that they will not willingly bend to the system of communist living, but his reflections, a Platonist could argue, will not apply to the men who are educated according to the *Republic*'s scheme. Thus he speaks of problems of assault, unnatural affection, and homicide arising out of Plato's scheme,[126] but why should men whose souls are educated to harmony be drawn to such crimes? He speaks of discontent and dissension being bred among the auxiliaries,[127] but these men are supposed by Plato to be *trained*, like certain fierce dogs, to accept proper authority. Aristotle says that the evils Plato wishes to expel are not due to the absence of communism, but to wickedness in human nature, wickedness which he no doubt thought an educational system could not eliminate.[128] But he never argues that it can't. And so he does not properly meet Plato's challenge.

Aristotle also gives an absurd moral argument against communism, to the effect that, even if it succeeds, it will so unify the men in the ruling class in the *Republic* that they will have no chance to exercise charity and benevolence toward one another.[129] This argument is on a level with that given by some Christians in the nineteeth century against relief of the poor—that it destroys the possibility of the virtue of charity; or public education—it eradicates the virtue of responsibility in fathers. Whether you find such an argument compelling depends on whether you see being moral as something necessary to keep society together, or as something valuable in itself, such that something of value would be lost if society could be kept together without it. I incline to the former view. Being moral serves a certain function. This is its justification. Where that function is otherwise served, morality loses its value.

But the gist of Aristotle's attack is his inability to believe that a man can sustain affection and concern for hundreds of people in an intense way.[130] He would thus have to accuse the poet John Donne of speaking senselessly when he asserts his sense of connection with all mankind. Now I think a deep feeling of affection for many many people can exist when people are thrown together in a political movement, inspired by ideals. Anyone who knows what relations between people can sometimes be like within a communist movement knows this. And Plato's rulers are like people bound to one another through the ideals of a movement to which they all belong. Plato thought the feeling of affection could be generated in his communism because he had an insight into the nature of totalitarian culture, an insight Aristotle lacked.

---

126   Aristotle, *Politics* (2.4.10) p. 47.
127   Ibid. (2.5.25), p. 54.
128   Ibid. (2.5.12), p. 50.
129   Ibid. (2.5.10), p. 50.
130   Ibid. (2.4.8), p. 47.

Finally, Aristotle claims that the farmers and artisans in Plato's state will be rebellious, will resent supporting the guardians.[131] But he does not show why Plato is wrong in thinking that they will in fact give their allegiance because they will benefit from the settled order Guardian rule brings to a community, which, according to Plato, men would cling to if they ever experienced it.

Let me now point out echoes of Plato in Aristotle's political theory, some of a general kind, some on points of detail. I shall instance four interesting ones, then go on to some contrasts.

(1) There is a point which Aristotle recurrently makes, advancing it for the first time in book 1.2.8. This is his claim that although the human association comes into being in order to sustain people in existence, its ultimate raison d'être is to provide opportunity for the good life.[132] I want to suggest that there is nothing distinctively Aristotelian about this point. It is unquestionably implied in Plato's *Republic*, which explains the origin of the state in human needs which require a social division of labor for their satisfaction, which Plato delineates as the "healthy state," but which also sees the end of the state as the nurture of souls into harmony and justice. The same is true of the origin and value of guardians. They are introduced to protect the (now luxurious) state, but the ultimate value of having them is so that philosophy may be instantiated in the world.

So they agree, in a broad sense, on the origin and end of the state, but probably Plato thought that its proper end was never truly catered for in actual states, whereas Aristotle probably identified some *good, something* of value in social life as such, even in deficient states. And in Plato society is more or less a launching pad for individual virtue, the harmony in the soul; whereas in Aristotle individual virtue is to a much greater extent realized in and through social relations. The good ruler in Aristotle, unlike in Plato, is not submitting to the burdens of living in a cave, but is fully content as a ruler, shows his full development in his relations with other men.[133]

(2) Now just as the state, for both, has the *original* purpose of sustaining material needs and the *ultimate* purpose of catering for the needs of the soul, so, for both, there are members of the state occupied with the primitive purpose and others with the more lofty one. For Plato's third estate provides for the physical needs of everyone, including the guardians, but is not invited to enjoy the pleasures of philosophy. And for Aristotle, farmers and artisans are not or should not, properly speaking, be a part of the state, but only its necessary condition. They ought not to share in that citizenship, that knowledge of how to rule and how to obey, which is

131   Ibid. (2.5.22), p. 53.
132   Ibid. (1.2.8), pp. 4–5.
133   Cf. ibid (7.3), pp. 287–89, which tends against this thesis.

so essential in Aristotle's view of human virtue, the knowledge, in brief, of how to behave in the most excellent way toward your fellow men. This is reserved for a small class who do not engage in physical labor.

Of course, there is once again a difference to be noted. For while Aristotle would wish the working class out of civil life, he feels it would be folly to exclude them utterly. And so he says:

> It may be also be argued, from another point of view, that there is serious risk in not letting them have *some* share in the enjoyment of power; for a state with a body of disenfranchised citizens who are numerous and poor must necessarily be a state full of enemies.[134]

And he decides they may be given certain limited civic rights and powers, large enough to satisfy them, too little to create problems. Again we can think of him saying to Plato, "Look, friend, don't worry. You are too frightened of giving a sop to the masses."

> Any craving which the masses may feel for position and power will be satisfied if they are given the right of electing magistrates and calling them to account. Indeed there are instances which show that the masses will be contented with a still smaller measure of power.[135]

(3) Both think in medicinal terms about the state, speak of its health, trace its characteristic illnesses, its pathology (Plato in book 9, Aristotle throughout the work). But the difference between the two is the difference between the pure diagnostician and the healer. For Aristotle seeks to show states, any kind of states including tyranny, how they can repair and avoid damage to their particular bodies politic. He lists numerous devices whereby power can be consolidated, order restored or preserved. Plato only shows how order breaks down. And the reason why he doesn't attempt what Aristotle does is not because Aristotle is a Machiavellian prepared to suggest devices even to bad states, whereas Plato is more pure, but because Plato firmly believes that once the rot has set in, there is nothing for it; there is no returning to a healthier condition. He does not believe that diseases in society can be halted so that any society can be improved. The only thing you can do to secure social order is to raze everything to the ground, expel all those over ten, and build afresh on new principles. Ezra Pound said, "What thou lovest well, remains; the rest is dross."[136] Plato agrees. Aristotle doesn't. This is the difference between an uncompromising radical and a mellow conservative.

---

134   Ibid. (3.11.7), pp. 124–25.
135   Ibid. (6.4.4), p. 263.
136   Pound, *The Cantos of Ezra Pound* (Canto 81), pp. 540–41.

(4) Finally there is an echo in Aristotle of Plato's strictures on extreme democracy. Remember Plato's account of the life led by the democratic man, "He spends his hours pursuing the pleasure of the moment."[137] Plato's disapproval of this disorderliness is repeated in Aristotle:

> The democratic . . . ends with the view that "liberty and equality" consist in "doing what one likes." The result of such a view is that, in these extreme democracies, each may live as he likes—or as Euripides says, "For any end he chances to desire."[138]

In both, there is drawn an antithesis between democracy and good order. And Aristotle also accepts Plato's idea that order is secured when each man sticks to one function.[139] In particular, he believes in a rotation of power among the citizens, obeying and ruling in turn, learning how to rule by learning how to obey, and vice versa.

So these are four similarities, though not complete similarities. I now pass on to three decisive differences, in addition to those which arose in book 2.

(1)[140] Whereas both want to give office to the best and wisest men, the men whom we many call men of merit (and Aristotle uses this term), they offer very different reasons for doing so, reasons connected with their differing evaluations of the happiness to be derived from ruling. For whereas Plato wishes to install men of merit because in that way the state will be best served, Aristotle assigns power to men of merit because this is a reward for their excellence. Power is a prize in Aristotle, and the best man or men deserve to have it. For Plato, he should be given it because he will make best use of it. Indeed, for Plato, political power is no reward for the man who has become a philosopher. It is a burden he has to assume.

This difference is connected with their different concepts of justice. Each believes it is just to give power to men of merit, Plato because they are best suited to this *function*, Aristotle because they most deserve this *reward*. For Aristotle justice consists in the distribution of goods and positions to men according to a principle of equality. For Plato it is the distribution of men into positions according to the functions that have to be fulfilled in society. And Aristotle distinguishes two notions of equality, arithmetical, or numerical, and geometric, or proportional. The first is the democratic notion which he rejects, and consists in giving each man the

---

137 [It is not clear which translation Cohen is using here, but the text is Plato, *Republic* (561d), p. 301.—Ed.]

138 Aristotle, *Politics* (5.9.15–16), p. 234.

139 Ibid. (2.9.13), p. 86.

140 [A note in the manuscript in handwriting reads: "Robinson's comment p. 31 in his edition of Books III and IV dubifies much of what I say here." Aristotle, *Politics Books III and IV.*—Ed.]

same amount of everything, including the same chance at political office; the second, more aristocratic notion, is the distribution of gifts to men in proportion to merit, though Aristotle sometimes slips into saying in proportion to merit and wealth, although he does connect the two: "Nobility of birth . . . simply consists in an inherited mixture of wealth and merit."[141] "It may be remarked that while oligarchy is characterized by good birth, wealth and culture, the attributes of democracy would appear to be the very opposite—low birth, poverty, and vulgarity."[142]

This idea of geometric equality was not original with Aristotle. It dates from the aristocratic Pythagoreans of the fifth century, and can be found in Plato too, but again, tied to the idea of function, rather than reward. In sum Plato's justice distributes duties according to capacity, Aristotle's according to desert.[143]

(2) The next difference emerges in Aristotle's critique of Plato's healthy state. You remember that Plato introduces no government in that state. A governing authority is only required, in the form of guardians, once we pass beyond it into the luxurious state. Aristotle objects that even the primitive state must have a government:

> He begins by stating that the four most necessary elements for the constitution of a state are weavers, farmers, shoemakers and builders. . . . as though a state merely existed for the supply of necessities, and not rather to achieve the Good . . . The four original parts—or whatever may be the number of the elements forming the association—will require some authority to dispense justice and to determine what is just.[144]

Now we can take Plato as saying: if men were restrained in their desires, they could live in a primitive healthy anarchic community, without a government. Once appetite asserts itself more strongly, once we cater to Glaucon's demands for luxury, a government becomes necessary; we need a political life in addition to economic and social life. But once we have political life, we can develop a spiritual life for the guardians, which transcends political life. For Aristotle you cannot conceive of society, even a primitive one, without government (this is the force of his criticism at 4.4.13 just cited) and also, as I said before, political life is in itself valuable for in governing and being governed men can express their highest faculties and abilities.

141   Ibid. (4.8.9), p. 176.
142   Ibid. (6.2.7), p. 259.
143   Ibid. (7.9.6), p. 302.
144   Ibid. (4.4.13), p. 165.

(3) Finally, Plato and Aristotle have divergent assessments on what to expect of the judgment of a group of men collected together. Aristotle has faith in it; Plato distrusts it. Aristotle says,

> Just as a feast to which many people contribute is better than one provided by a single person, so, and for the same reason, the masses can come to a better decision in many matters, than any one individual. Again a numerous body is less likely to be corrupted. A large body of water is not so liable to contamination as a small; and the people is not so liable to corruption as the few. The judgement of a single man is bound to be corrupted when he is overpowered by anger, or by any other similar emotion; but it is not so easy for all to get angry and go wrong simultaneously.[145]

Let me immediately say that Aristotle is speaking only of citizens here, in his restricted sense: he is not propounding democratic ideology. Plato would raise his eyebrows at all this talk about the incorruptibility of a group of men. He had more insight into mob psychology, into how emotion could more easily sway a man when he was in a group. And once again I want to say he appreciated, what Aristotle didn't, the culture of totalitarianism, a point I made in connection with his belief, attacked by Aristotle, that universal affection might prevail among the guardians, and a point equally applicable here.

If we now turn our attention away from the specific lines of Aristotle's thought, and the question how he answers the Sophists, and how he echoes and also differs from Plato, we can safely make the general statement, that the political thought of Aristotle, like that of his predecessors, is firmly fixed on the conception of man living in a small community, to which the term "polis" referred. The questions of politics were framed in terms of such a small-scale social unit, however divergent the answers given by the Sophists, Socrates, Plato, and Aristotle, and when Aristotle argues for the interdependence of man and society, for the fact that man can only fulfill himself in community and does so fully in community, he has in mind a community of the shape and size of the Greek city-state. In states beyond that size, the values derived from social living are not to be had.[146] But while Aristotle is committing his thoughts to paper, the death-knell of the civilization he is extolling is being sounded. Macedonia is ending the possibility of society on a small scale, through her conquest of Greece and Asia, her synthesis of Hellenes and Barbarians into one Hellenistic world. The political thought of this world does not respect the walls of the polis, and in a way, it does not respect politics itself. It is

145 Ibid. (3.15.7, 8), p. 142.
146 He urges this strongly in ibid. (7.4.7–14), pp. 291–92.

apolitical in force, urging men to find salvation in private life. Man has not found it possible to enjoy the values the polis brought in the huge states which succeed the polis. The Christianity of Augustine enforces this disposition. The Civitas Terrena is an inferior order; the true social order is the Civitas Dei, beyond this world. Only in the modern era do thinkers again seek to weld individual and society together in harmonious union, do they try to revivify the legacy of Greece. For this is the aspiration of Rousseau, Hegel, and Marx. But Rousseau realizes that the satisfactions to be gained from political life are difficult to attain in a large country like France. He becomes a tragic proponent of decentralization, conscious of the futility of his own proposals. Hegel does not oppose the large modern state but deceives himself into thinking that it can weld individual to community just as the polis did. Each man can fulfill himself freely and fully by performing his social duties, concentrating on the activities proper to his station. Marx's thought takes a different turn. If Rousseau recognized that classical values could not be realized in the modern state, and Hegel pretended they could, Marx demanded that the state be abolished and the values be realized in stateless community. Where Hegel falsified reality and thus came to terms with it, Marx saw the reality and refused to make his peace with it. The modern world, dominated by the hopes of these thinkers, is also not at peace with itself.

Chapter 2

HOBBES

———

1. The principal claims of Hobbes's *Leviathan* are deliverances of a thought experiment in which we imagine away the existence of governmental authority and ask what the human condition would be like without it. We suppose, that is, that a state of nature obtains among people, as we *know* them, as they *actually* are, and we ask what its character must be. Notice that the qualification that the state of nature concerns people as we know them is extremely important. We are not thinking about pre-socialized people who are deprived of their political and, perhaps, social institutions. Hobbes must mean the state of nature in this wise, since his mission is to rescue *us* from its dangers, and they must therefore be the dangers that *we* would face, not what primitives faced. Why should we care about them?[1]

Now, the state of nature is a relational concept. The relation it signifies obtains between two people if and only if neither has authority over the other and there is no third person who has authority over both. By extension, a state of nature prevails among a *set* of people if the stated relation holds between all pairs within the set. So, once again, a state of nature doesn't have to be like the Flintstones; it can be like the Simpsons, minus TV. Think of it negatively—no one has authority over anyone else. Notice that the state of nature, so conceived, is a perfectly possible state of affairs: there is nothing mythical about it. Exercise of *this* concept of the state of nature involves no affirmation of any pseudohistory.

Now, everyone agrees that (i) Hobbes's state of nature is a state of war. As he says in *De Cive*, where two people are such that neither rules the other and they are not jointly subject to a third, the two people are "enemies."[2] Everyone also agrees that (ii) the fact that the state of nature is a state of war is supposed to prove the legitimacy of governmental authority, and, indeed, of absolute, unlimited government authority.

But those agreements leave open two questions, on which there is *disagreement*. The disagreement corresponds, naturally enough, to obscurity in Hobbes, not in the sense of obscure sentences or paragraphs: he is a

---

1 See Vallentyne, "Review of Kraus," p. 193.
2 Hobbes, *De Cive*, 1.14, p. 30.

marvelously clear sentence writer; but in the sense that what appear to be distinct and uncombinable doctrines sometimes seem to be on offer in his text.

The first question is: why *is* the state of nature, the state of no governmental authority, a state of war? And the second is: *how* does the fact that the state of nature is a state of war justify governmental authority?

2. I deal with the second question at Nos. 15–21 below. Here I turn to the first question.

Every answer to the first question must begin by acknowledging that the state of nature is a state of war *because* a struggle for power pervades it, and that a struggle for power pervades it because there exists, as "a generall inclination of all mankind, a perpetuall and restlesse desire of Power after power, that ceaseth onely in Death."[3] Disagreement begins when we ask *why* Hobbes attributes to people so relentless a pursuit of power.

3. Now Hobbes defines power, reasonably enough, at the opening of chapter 10, as the "present means to obtain some future apparent Good."[4] So you might think that the question why, for Hobbes, people seek power resolves itself into: what good do they seek to use it to obtain? But that inference is mistaken. For the fact that something is by definition a means does not imply that when it is wanted it is wanted *as* a means, *because*, that is, it is the means that it is. Money is by definition a means of purchase, of storing value, etc., but it does not follow, and it is not true, that whoever wants money wants it because she wants to buy things, store value, etc. Some people want money so as to be admired or envied for having it, or for having succeeded in acquiring it. And the same goes for power, of which money, on Hobbes's definition of power is, as Hobbes realized, a species.[5] "Instrumentall are those Powers, which . . . are means and Instruments to acquire more: as Riches, Reputation, Friends, and the secret workings of God, which men call good Luck."[6] Money is, indeed, as Karl Marx said, social power in the form of a thing. And power too, in both its money and nonmoney forms, can be wanted other than as a means to achieve what it is by definition a means to achieve. So can any functionally defined thing: a car, a knife, a knitting needle, etc.

Now this is not *just* an interesting, or boring, *conceptual* point. That is, it is very important sociologically that this means power need not be desired exclusively *as* a means. And we can tell a number of

---

3   Hobbes, *Leviathan*, p. 161.
4   Ibid., p. 150.
5   See ibid., p. 161.
6   Ibid., p. 150.

Hobbesian-seeming stories about why Hobbesian men—and it is, indeed, within Hobbes, for reasons I'll give later, men, as heads of families, that we're talking about—seek power, and in some of the stories they do not want it principally to use it to acquire things, or, better, in some of the stories it is not *that* reason for wanting power which makes the state of nature a state of war. In some Hobbesian stories war supervenes because men want power in order to shine, in order to relish the glory of being superior to others. They want honor, which is other people believing in and deferring to your power, and glory, which is your own awareness of your power.[7] Indeed, *that* Hobbesian story goes with the traditional sobriquet, or nickname, of the sovereign Leviathan—King of the Proud. According to that sobriquet, it's because people are proud that they need to be subdued by Leviathan.

4. There is an extensive debate about whether Hobbes is a psychological egoist, that is, whether his men are other than merely *self*-interested, whether they care about anything beyond their own welfare. The answer to that question obviously bears on the first question at the end of 1. above (that is, why is the state of nature a state of war?). Chapter 2 of Gregory Kavka's book has an excellent discussion of that question.[8] Let us suppose, at least for the moment, that Hobbes indeed is a psychological egoist.

But there is a further question about which there has been less debate than there ought to have been, given the interest and importance of the answer to this further question for answering Q 1 in 1.[9] This further question is: suppose that Hobbesian men are egoists who seek what they conceive to be their own good only. Does that good, as they conceive it, encompass what I shall call underivative other-regarding elements? Let me explain "underivative" and "other-regarding." An *underivative* element is one that is not derived from some other element: a desideratum is derivative if and only if it is wanted for the sake of some further one, either as a *means* of getting or as a *way* of getting that further one. My desire to walk to Sainsbury's is derivative on my desire to buy orange juice, which is derivative on my desire to obtain nourishment and sensory enjoyment, which may be derivative on nothing, hence, underivative. Or I may desire to walk to Sainsbury's just as a *way* of satisfying my desire to take a walk. Then it's not a (causal) means since it logically *entails* walking, rather than causally bringing it about, but it's still derivative.

---

7   Ibid., pp. 152–53.

8   Kavka, *Hobbesian Moral and Political Theory.*

9   I do not mean that commentators supply no answer to this question. They supply opposed answers, which each side tends rather to take for granted as true. But there is, as I say, little *debate* about the question.

An other-regarding desideratum is one whose description mentions other people, either referentially (as in I want Sylvia to help me) or existentially (as in I want someone—I don't care who—to help me). Wanting you to get the orange juice for me is other-regarding, but almost certainly derivatively other-regarding: an exception would be where I enjoy the prospect of the irksomeness to you of having to go and buy it, or where I think you'll benefit from the exercise, and that figures in my motivation. Wanting to torture you is other-regarding. That is derivative if it is in order to get information from you. It is underivative if it is to relish your (or somebody's) agony. For then a mention of persons cannot be written out of the fundamental description of what I want.

Do Hobbesian men have underivative other-regarding passions? Or, more germanely, is their possession of such passions central to the genesis of the state of war? We know that Hobbesian men endanger one another, that they are prone to mutual antagonism. Is that because each has a basic desire to put others down? Is it because each basically desires triumph, or only because power over others assures them the security in which to pursue material enjoyment? Hobbes's men undoubtedly want power over others and they want to be honored by others. They compete for position and prestige and rejoice when they reduce others to an inferior position. But do they want prestige and the esteem of others only because that puts them in a secure position with respect to physical safety and material enjoyment? Or do they find it intrinsically satisfying to defeat and dominate other men, so that pride is an underivative passion and prestige is more than instrumentally valuable? More precisely, do such underivative other-regarding passions play a role, whether exclusive, chief, or partial, in generating the state of war?

5. My own view is that there are a variety of Hobbesian stories about how the state of war is generated, in some of which we must suppose men to be egoistic, in some not, and among the egoistic, some involve underivative other-regarding desires, and some not. These stories are all variants of or full or partial combinations of three stories, which I shall name following what Hobbes calls "the three principal causes of quarrel,"[10] which are "competition, diffidence and glory." In the competition story, people are psychological egoists who lack underivative other-regarding passions; in the diffidence story, they are not psychological egoists and they probably have underivative other-regarding passions of a *positive* kind; in the glory story, they are psychological egoists and they have underivative other-regarding passions of a negative kind. The glory story is the most colorful and in *that* sense most interesting, but in another sense,

10   Ibid., p. 185.

which I think deeper, it is least interesting, because it derives the state of war from the strongest of the three sets of premises about human nature in play here. Correspondingly, the diffidence story is in that sense most interesting, because its human nature premises are strikingly weak and unbelligerent.

The first or competition story sits well with Hobbes as someone who was infatuated by Galilean science, the idea, discerned in his work by many commentators, that the aim of each person is to keep on trucking, that is to maintain his vital motion at a decent velocity. The glory story derives more from Hobbes's early classical humanism, his study of ancient texts such as Thucydides and Aristotle which are big on the virtues and vices of humanity. The diffidence story places him on neither side of that Galileo/humanism divide.

6. I begin with the competition story. Hobbes says that because men are effectively equal in ability, they have equal hopes of attaining their ends when they both desire the same things, and they consequently fight over it:

> From this equality of ability, ariseth equality of hope in the attaining of our ends. And therefore if any two men desire the same thing, which nevertheless they cannot both enjoy, they become enemies; and in the way to their end, (which is principally their own conservation, and sometimes their delectation only) endeavour to destroy, or subdue one another.[11]

Compare De Cive, 1.6:

> But the most frequent reason why men desire to hurt each other, ariseth hence, that many men at the same time have an appetite to the same thing; which yet very often they can neither enjoy in common, nor yet divide; whence it follows that the strongest must have it, and who is strongest must be decided by the sword.[12]

Notice that the fact that we both desire the same thing betokens a scarcity, and, moreover, what matters here is scarcity in a necessary good, for we principally desire such a good for "conservation" and only sometimes for "delectation": we're not talking about scarcity in a luxury good where there might be an abundance in the necessities of life. The goods in contention at least include ones which you *have* to get, on pain of death. Now one *might* discern an other-regarding element in the motif in the *Leviathan* passage of *hoping* to win. I'm damned if I'm going to

11 Ibid., p. 184
12 Hobbes, *De Cive*, 1.6, p. 26.

share it with him. Who does he think he is? But the parallel *De Cive* text makes that motif implausible here. It's clear as noonday there that conflict comes from both wanting an indivisible thing.

The competition story unrolls on the assumptions of, first, sufficient equality so that you reckon your chances as good as the next man's; second, scarcity, which means it's unwise to forgo the opportunity to grab what's around; and, third, psychological egoism at least to the extent of putting your own survival before everything else. There is here no assumption needed about how you *regard* other people. They could just be like physical forces, merely in the way. You don't care to help them, but you also don't care to hurt them.

To give a rigorous representation to the competition story, suppose that we have a two-person world. That is for simplicity, and the results we get are easily generalized. Let's also suppose—we shall relax this assumption later, in No. 9, and thereby reinforce, not weaken, our conclusion—that there are no opportunities to *produce* anything in this world: the scarce goods are all consumption goods as opposed to raw materials and means of production: the fight is for fallen fruit, or for carcasses of beasts which no person killed. Now we are also supposing that the two people are roughly equal, which means that neither has more reason to think that he'll prevail in the combat than to think that he'll lose. On all those suppositions, a peaceful sharing of the goods, or, where they are, as Hobbes curiously insists, indivisible, a peaceful 50/50 lottery over them has higher (what is called) *expected utility* for each person than fighting for them.

I'll explain what that is in a moment, but first why I say indivisibility is curious. The Hobbesian indivisibility assumption is curious because so few goods are, and because you could take turns, and because you could have a lottery. I think he puts it in to exclude sharing as a way out, but, as just explained, it doesn't plausibly do that. The real reason why, on his other assumptions, they won't share doesn't require his indivisibility assumption, and I'll henceforth drop that assumption.

Now let me explain what expected utility is. The expected utility of a course of action is the sum of the products of the utility and the probability of each of its possible outcomes. Evidently, as you vary probability and utility, the rational course changes.

When I say that there is higher expected utility for Hobbesian agents in sharing or in a lottery, that is under the assumption that two things determine expected utility here: goods bundles and pain and death from fighting. Expected utility must go down on the given assumptions if, instead of sharing, we fight, since that adds a negative quantum to the output bundles without increasing the utility of the goods. So prospects are better for everybody if everybody shares than if everybody adopts an aggressive posture. It is nevertheless arguable that rationality drives the parties to aggression, because of the egoism assumption. For the parties are in what is called a Prisoners' Dilemma.[13]

7. The structure of their situation is called Prisoners' Dilemma because of the example that is usually used to introduce it. The example itself is rather peculiar, but the application of the point it illustrates is very general. It can explain, or contribute to explaining, the existence of the state, of morality, of the need for intervention in markets, for a law imposing a duty to vote, etc.

The example, then. Two persons are caught *in flagrante delicto* of a certain crime. Other things equal, conviction for that crime, which is easy for the prosecution to secure, will send each to jail for five years. But other things are not equal. The prosecution rightly suspects, yet cannot prove, that the two criminals previously committed another crime together. They say to each: if you confess and the other does not to that earlier crime, you'll get four years altogether and he'll get eight; if you both confess you'll both get seven, and if neither of you confesses you'll get five, for the *flagrante delicto* crime. So we get this matrix:

		Prisoner B	
		Confess	Don't Confess
Prisoner A	Confess	−7, −7	−4, −8
	Don't Confess	−8, −4	−5, −5

Each cares only about how many years he gets, so each has this preference ordering:

1. I confess, he doesn't confess.
2. I don't confess, he doesn't confess.
3. I confess, he confesses.
4. I don't confess, he confesses.

Each is rational, so each takes the dominant course, which is the course where you're better-off, where you get a better payoff, no matter what the other one does, and therefore each confesses. Consequently, each gets seven years, when each would have got five had neither confessed. *Individual rationality generates a Pareto-suboptimal result*: that is, the feasible set contains a state of affairs in which no one is worse-off and at least one

13 On the Prisoners' Dilemma, see Elster, *Logic and Society*, or McLean, *Public Choice*, chap. 7.

person is better-off: indeed, here, in which both are better-off, but, because they behave rationally, the parties cannot secure that state of affairs.

Notice that:

(i) The unfortunate result does not depend on uncertainty about what the other person will do, since, whatever I suppose he will do, confession remains rational for me (and, *mutatis mutandis*, for him).

(ii) It is of no avail to agree on a strategy in advance, since there will be no motive to keep the agreement. The problem does not depend, as is frequently mistakenly said, on lack of communication. Nor does it depend on lack of trust. There is no motive to keep the agreement, even if you trust the other to do so, or even if you *know* that he will do so.

(iii) Suppose now that each has different motives from those stipulated. Each cares about the other, that is, cares enough so that a year for him is like an extra half year for me, then, with that degree of mutual concern, not confessing becomes dominant, and each will so choose that they both benefit (not only all things, including their mutual concern, considered, but even) from a narrowly selfish point of view, because each will then get only five years:

	Confess	Don't Confess
Confess	−10½, −10½	−8, −10
Don't Confess	−10, −8	−7½, −7½

Note that the same result will ensue if they do not *care* about each other through fellow feeling but believe and act on a morality that dictates that 50 percent way of counting others' interests.

It is not of course always true that mutual concern or morality will make not confessing dominant. That will depend on the extent of the concern or moral conviction and on the alternative sizes of sentences. Sometimes the PD will persist. Sometimes neither confessing nor not confessing will be dominant, and a different decision rule will have to be employed.

(iv) Each is thus better-off from a selfish point of view, because he gets fewer years in jail, only if they each act with regard to the other's condition. If, for each, the only aim is to maximize his own welfare, then the welfare of neither will be maximized.

(v) But to get that private benefit, they really have to *have* the mutual concern or moral conviction. They can't *decide* to care or to be moral in order to get the private benefit. They can't argue: if we were moral, or cared about each other, we'd both be better-off: so let's care, or be moral. For although the premise is true, the inference is absurd. It belongs to the nature of morality that you cannot decide for selfish reasons to be moral. And if you don't *actually* care, you can't simulate caring, for the sake of getting the benefits: that simulation won't change the motivating payoffs.

(vi) Note that the solution of mutual concern and/or morality does not require that each knows or believes that the other has any concern for him.

(vii) One could say that the prisoners have both too many options, and also preferences they have reason to regret having. They have reason to want not to be *able* to confess, and they have reason to prefer *not* to confess, when they *are* able to confess. So, to anticipate, what a Hobbesian sovereign does, conceiving that sovereign within the framework of the competition story, is to perform the service of benignly reducing options by (sometimes) removing the noncooperative option and (more often) degrading it through attaching a penalty to it, and thereby rendering it dispreferred. The sovereign makes some destructive actions impossible but, more often, he makes such actions rationally ineligible.

8. In order to present the Hobbesian state of nature, conceived along the lines of the competition story, as a Prisoners' Dilemma, let us take a representative state of nature situation. Two men are equidistant from a deer carcass and each has the choice of adopting a sharing or a grabbing posture with respect to it. First let's pretend that there is no disutility in pain or in the danger of death. If they both adopt the sharing posture each will get half a deer. If one grabs he'll get all and the other none. If both grab each has a 50/50 chance of getting the carcass, because of their rough equality. So the expected value, in carcass terms, for each if both grab is half a carcass. Each is a totally self-regarding egoist. Consequently each has this preference ordering, if we leave out of account the pain and danger of death:

1. I grab, he shares;
2. = I share, he shares;
2. = I grab, he grabs (half a carcass is worth the same as 50-percent chance of the lot);
4. I share, he grabs.

Still leaving out the pain and danger of death, the payoff matrix is as follows, with payoffs expressed as (expected) amounts of carcass:

		OTHER	
		Grabs	Shares
I	Grabs	.5(exp), .5(exp)	1, 0
	Shares	0, 1	.5, .5

Clearly we will both grab, because that is dominant, but there is as yet an element of Prisoners' Dilemma missing: the outcome is not Pareto suboptimal. So a state of war supervenes, but we lack the basic element in the argument for governmental legitimacy. This state of nature is *not* Pareto suboptimal.[14]

Now add the disvalue of pain and of danger of death, which we'll call $-x$. Enter it in modification of the payoffs in the grab/grab cell, so that they become $.5-x$ in each case. (The remaining payoffs don't change.) What will the parties now do? That depends, of course, on how large x is. To be precise, grabbing remains dominant as long as x is less than $.5$, so that the expectation under joint grabbing remains positive. But now the result is suboptimal, however small x may be, because $.5 - x$, which is what they can expect to get if they both grab, is less than $.5$, which is what they get if they both share.

Of course, the figures won't stack up that way every time. In some encounters the carcass will be very small, or the opponent will be very big, and x, the pain plus death danger, will exceed half the carcass's value. Hobbes doesn't say that every encounter in the state of nature is a battle. (Hence his invocation of the rainy weather analogy.)[15] But x will fall short of $.5$ often enough to make the state of nature a state of war.

9. So much, then, in exposition of the Hobbesian state of nature, under the assumption of universal egoism and no underivative other-regarding interests, the exposition which I call the competition story, and which is structurally a Prisoners' Dilemma.

I turn to the diffidence story, where the prevailing game is not Prisoners' Dilemma but the assurance game. The two games differ in that the order of the top two preferences in the Prisoners' Dilemma is reversed in

---

14   The Prisoners' Dilemma has essentially four characteristics, and the fourth is absent here (source: Schelling, *Strategy of Conflict*, p. 214):

  i.   Each has an *unconditional preference*: the same choice is preferred, irrespective of which choice the other person makes. [Dominance]
  ii. Each has an *unconditional preference* with respect to the *other's choice*: this preference for the other person's action is unaffected by the choice one makes for oneself.
  iii. These two preferences go in *opposite* directions: the choice that each prefers to make is not the choice he prefers the other to make.
  iv. The strengths of these preferences (= the payoffs comparisons) are such that both are better-off making their unpreferred choices than if both make their preferred choices. [Pareto Suboptimality]

15   [This is a reference to Hobbes's contention "For as the nature of Foule weather, lyeth not in a showre or two of rain; but in an inclination thereto of many dayes together: So the nature of War, consisteth not in actuall fighting; but in the known disposition thereto, during all the time there is no assurance to the contrary." Hobbes, *Leviathan*, p. 186.—Ed.]

the assurance game (with the third and fourth preferences unchanged). Thus, for the original story about the prisoners, their game is an assurance game if their preferences are as follows:

1. I don't confess, he doesn't confess
2. I confess, he doesn't confess
3. I confess, he confesses
4. I don't confess, he confesses.

More generally, here is the preference ordering in the assurance game, where "defect" just means "doesn't cooperate":

1. I co-op, he co-ops
2. I defect, he co-ops
3. I defect, he defects
4. I co-op, he defects.

Here I am not (fully) egoistic, since, if I know that he will cooperate, then I will cooperate, even though I would benefit from a selfish point of view from defecting: I wouldn't do that because I have a sense of fair play; I don't want to be a free rider. (Yet it seems a curiously limited one, for why do I prefer exploitation [second preference] to nonproduction? I suppose I would prefer that if the stakes are high enough.) Note that I will not cooperate *no matter what*: if I expect him to defect, then I will defect: my third preference is better than my fourth. I don't want to be a "sucker"; I am not a Kantian who will do whatever I would will all to do regardless of whether I expect others to do it. The Kantian preference orderings:

Sane Kantian	*Insane Kantian*
1. I co-op, he co-ops	1. = I co-op, he co-ops
2. I co-op, he defects	1. = I co-op, he defects
3. I defect, he co-ops	3. = I defect, he co-ops
4. I defect, he defects	3. = I defect, he defects (Insane because *all* I care about is being moral).

But, as an assurance game person, I prefer cooperating to free riding. (Notice that none of the 4 Schelling conditions—footnote 14 above—now hold.)

Now the assurance game is so called because I need to be *assured* that *you* will cooperate for cooperation to be my unambiguously preferred option. If I believe you will, then so will I. If I believe you won't, then I won't. And if I just don't know, then I'm thrown into a quandary; it's hard for me to figure out what to do.

Here, unlike what's true in the Prisoners' Dilemma, trust makes all the difference. It is no longer true that defecting is dominant, regardless of what I think you'll do, for, if I can be assured that you'll cooperate, then so will I. But, according to Hobbes, I cannot be so assured, on a regular basis, in the state of nature. I cannot be sure that you will always be disposed to cooperate even if I do, and the cost of wrongly reckoning on your cooperation is often so great that it would be irrational to gamble on your being cooperative. Accordingly, I will act, often enough, just as I do in Prisoners' Dilemma. I will do the uncooperative thing; I will set myself to grab the carcass, not to share it, and so will you, often enough: we will, that is, do so often enough for the state of nature to degenerate into a state of war even if we relax the egoism assumption and construe the state of nature not as competition Prisoners' Dilemma, but as diffidence assurance game.

That ends my exposition of the second story of breakdown into war, the diffidence story, relying not on a desire to have more than others, but on a desire to have enough to live on, together with diffidence with respect to whether others will allow us that. We don't all have to be rapacious for the diffidence story to work. We only have to be uncertain about others not being rapacious. Or, as one Hobbesian text suggests, we only have to believe that some men go beyond desire for secure competence, and be uncertain who they are:

> [T]here be some, that taking pleasure in contemplating their own power in the acts of conquest, which they pursue further than their security requires; if others, that otherwise would be glad to be at ease within modest bounds, should not by invasion increase their power, they would not be able, long time, by standing only on their defence, to subsist.[16]

Perhaps that text doesn't establish the assurance game as opposed to the Prisoners' Dilemma. Perhaps Rob Shaver is right, in his excellent "Leviathan, King of the Proud." He leaves open the possibility that we might both prefer mutual nonanticipation to anticipation without counteranticipation. He is neutral between supposing that we face a Prisoners' Dilemma or an assurance game. In either case, conflict is likely. And in either case, the rationality of anticipation is founded on the empirical point that, in circumstances of scarcity and equality, offense is the best defense.[17]

I told these stories with respect to the grabbing of a deer carcass. But the war will be worse for the fact that people who have managed to

16   Hobbes, *Leviathan*, pp. 184–85.
17   Shaver, "Leviathan, King of the Proud," p. 58.

secure goods to themselves, who have taken their carcasses home, will have good reason to fear that others will try to wrest them from them. And if we add that in the resulting pervasively uncertain conditions people cannot cooperatively produce anything, any more than they can be confident of retaining anything that they produce individually, then the state of nature is seen to be more parlous still.

Having expounded the competition story, I remarked that the sovereign solves the Prisoners' Dilemma partly by making defection impossible but mainly by attaching such a cost to defection as to make cooperation dominant. To the extent that Hobbes relies not on competition but on diffidence, the role of the sovereign is somewhat different: because I know that he will deter potential offenders, I can behave cooperatively with confidence that others will. The penalty is needed not to deter people whose first preference is predatory, but to assure me that others, whatever their motives may be, will not predate.[18]

10. In the competition story people are egoistic, in the diffidence story they are not, but in neither do they, in the mass,[19] display a lust for power over others as something which they desire as such, as opposed to for reasons of safety and comfort. They have no negative underivative other-regarding passion, which is what a *lust* for power, properly speaking, is. It is a desire to do others down, and oneself up, for no further reason.

The first two stories ignore the picturesque side of Hobbes, his picture of humans as prideful beings bent on honor and glory. Glory is delight in one's own power, and, you will recall, it is the third of the "principal causes of quarrel"[20] after competition and diffidence. I turn now to a story of breakdown into war which turns on the glory motivation.

In a pure glory story, and by pure glory story I mean a glory story bereft of competition and diffidence elements, people fight not for payoffs describable independently of their contest but for the sake of victory as such. In competition and diffidence stories, and mixtures thereof, no one cares about the amount of goods that *others* get, except insofar as that might affect his own power in future contests, and he cares about *that* only because he cares about keeping his goods. There is no *underivative* interest in superiority over others. In pure glory, by contrast, the point of fighting is to achieve and display victory, not to obtain or secure the material spoils of victory, and the chief value of those spoils is that their

---

18   [At this point the text says: [Digression on Rawls and assurance]. No further details are given. Rawls discusses the assurance game as well as the Prisoners' Dilemma in sec. 42 of *A Theory of Justice*, p. 238.—Ed.]

19   See, again, Hobbes *Leviathan*, p.184.

20   Ibid., p. 185.

display is proof of your prowess. (Why would being opulent be something you could show off to others unless it was desirable in itself? How could a palace be valuable *only* as impressing others? Perhaps there's this answer: it's valuable because of the power inter alia to command labor that it betokens, like a pyramid. Anyway, even if it has first to be desirable in itself, that need not falsify the statement about what is its chief value.)

Stylizing things a bit, let us say that in state of nature encounters on pure glory assumptions about motivation each party can either go forth aggressively or stand off. The matrix below gives the four possible upshots of those choices:

		B's posture	
		Aggressive	Evasive
A's Posture	Aggressive	A might win or lose/ B might win or lose	A wins/B loses
	Evasive	A loses/B wins	A neither wins nor loses/B neither wins nor loses

Here, analogously to the competition story where grabbing was dominant, aggressing is dominant: it is better for me to be aggressive whether or not he is. So we get a state of war. But, unlike what's true in the competition story, the structure is not by its very nature Prisoners' Dilemma, since, for Prisoners' Dilemma, the lower right outcome has to be worse for both than the upper left is, and, on the motives we've thus far imputed, we cannot yet say that. Insert now the pain and danger of fighting, as a subtrahend which reduces the expected value to each of the upper left outcome, and, if that reduction is high enough, we *do* get Prisoners' Dilemma and the associated rationale for an omnipotent ruler.

However, and, as we shall see in 12, where I discuss Strauss's Hobbes, some commentators so emphasize the prideful side of Hobbes and so play down fear of death as such and aversion to pain in Hobbesian men that those motives don't amount to enough to make the state of war suboptimal, so that the glory story, in their hands, fails to provide a rationale for a sovereign. In other words: massively glory-oriented people who don't care much about pain and death as such might not welcome the creation of a state and settled society, because, in such a condition, they must rein themselves in, and thereby they lose the opportunity for supreme honor and glory, which for them outweighs any advantages that peace brings. Many Mafia people, at least as they are depicted in the movies, would disprefer peace and legal jobs even with a guarantee of more cash.

It is interesting to note, against the background of the stories of descent into war that I have distinguished, that, in the run-up to the Gulf War, it was said, sometimes by one and the same commentator, that Saddam Hussein would not heed the allies' warnings, he would go to war, because he did not realize that the allies' warnings were serious, *and* because he did not care about, he even relished, destruction. Those were incompatible explanations of his intransigence. If he *relished* combat, he *should* have gone to war *if* and *because* he thought the allies were serious.

I promised an explanation of why I always refer to *men* when expounding Hobbes. That is because in the competition and diffidence stories we're talking about heads of families, providers of deer carcasses, whom Hobbes would certainly regard as men: after all, somebody has to stay home and look after the kids; and in the glory story we're talking about strutting cocks of the walk and women will readily agree that the heads of families must be men.[21]

11. There can, of course, be various kinds of *mixed* stories. There can be a mixture through mere conjunction of motives in every person, so that everyone cares underivatively both about material goods and about honor and reputation, and has *some* sense of fair play, in which case all three stories apply, in different circumstances, or even sometimes in the same circumstances. Or there can be a story with a mixture of *people*, like a polymorphous species, as in Kavka's picture of breakdown into war, according to which some people are what he calls "dominators," and there have to be such people, who relish power over others as such, to get the game-theoretical ball rolling toward war. I don't think Hobbes needs dominators for his competition story, or even (though here it's less clear) for his diffidence story, but he certainly says (as we saw in Section 9 above) that *some* people are dominators,[22] and also see the very population-partitioning *De Cive* 1.4.[23]

There can also be more organic structurings of the elements I've distinguished, such as a Marxoid story in which the desire for glory is superstructural on the security preoccupation—if others acknowledge your power they won't threaten you and you'll be safe. I do not mean that then glory is derivative in the defined sense: the point is not that it's here *wanted just as* a means. Rather, the preoccupation with honor and glory

21 [The text at this point continues: "[OMIT, BECAUSE OF HOBBES'S VIEWS ABOUT THE FAMILY AS SUCH, WHICH I IGNORE: indeed the political philosophy of Hobbes will begin to get into difficulty if we bring women and the family explicitly into the picture. For then we have ties of affection, which could extend, tribally, thereby diminishing the necessity of a sovereign]."—Ed.]

22 Hobbes, *Leviathan*, pp. 184–85, quoted above in Section 9.

23 Hobbes, *De Cive*, 1.4, p. 25.

causally derives, in some subtle way, from material considerations. The person *aims* underivatively at power, but the genesis of the prevalence of such aims is in some way economic. (Think of two quite different reasons why a Mafioso brandishes his power: to impress in order to subdue, where subduing is his conscious aim; and to impress, period, where it's nevertheless plausible that such impressing goes on in some way because of its tendency to subdue: it is, that is to say, functionally explained.)

(I have also already implicitly mentioned a reverse structure, in Section 10, where the struggle to get and keep goods is other-regarding at its root, because it's an insult to your pride if others think you're too weak to secure lots of goods for yourself. Here, unlike above, derivativity, as defined, appears.)

Within these elementary motivational differences, we can set out crucially different views about competitiveness, which is a type of motivation, and competition, which is a process. I call the views *crucially* different because they affect how much an aspiration like socialism is or is not a pipe dream. On a left view, competitive*ness* is superstructural on a competitively structured economy, and an argument against such a structure. On one right view competitiveness is in human nature and unless you allow its expression through a competitive structure, you'll get either anarchy or coercion. (John Major said that capitalism goes with the grain of human nature.) On a different right view, it indeed supervenes on the structure, but, although not innate, it *should* be promoted, because of its productivity.

12. Commentators differ in their interpretations of Hobbes, along the axes that I have distinguished. You might think that, whatever other differences in interpretation are possible, nobody could claim that Hobbes offers a *pure* glory story. Even if you think there's a glory element, glory, you might think, is surely accompanied by one or both of the other elements (since people care re eating and staying alive), even if not actually superstructural on them. But one famous commentator thinks that Hobbes goes all the way with glory. For Strauss, the very fear of death exists only in an other-regarding form. A refutation of his view will provide the occasion for a better understanding of Hobbes.

Strauss disdains the view that Hobbesian men are in combat because of natural scarcity. He thinks men fight in the state of nature because of an underivative desire to excel over one another, and that the reason why the state is necessary is that their pride needs to be subdued. As I said, Strauss explains even the fear of death in an other-regarding way. What men fear, Strauss believes, is not death as such but *violent* death, which is death at the hands of another man, because it is the ultimate insult, indignity, or proof of lack of power. "When he says of an agonizing death that it is the greatest evil, he thinks exclusively of violent death at the hand of other men."[24] "Hobbes reduces man's natural appetite to vanity, he cannot but recognize the fear of a violent death—not the fear of a painful death, and certainly not the striving after self-preservation—as the principle of morality . . . The ever-greater triumph over others . . . is the aim and happiness of natural man."[25] Men fear death only because it is a massive humiliation.[26]

Strauss must be wrong about this. Even if there is *an* underivative lust for honor, it is wholly ridiculous to say that fear of death, as such, that is, non-other-regardingly, does not operate *at all* in Hobbes.

You can see that Strauss is wrong, that men care about things other than avoiding death, let alone just *violent* death, as Strauss interprets that, where violence implies violation, by looking at the most famous passage in *Leviathan*, his description of what's bad about the state of nature:

> In such condition, there is no place for Industry; because the fruit thereof is uncertain: and consequently no Culture of the Earth; no Navigation, nor use of the commodities that may be imported by Sea; no commodious Building; no Instruments of moving, and removing such things as require much force; no knowledge of the face of the Earth; no account of Time; no Arts; no Letters; no Society; and which is worst of all, continuall feare, and danger of violent death; And the life of man, solitary, poore, nasty, brutish, and short.[27]

Locke said that God put men under strong obligations of necessity, convenience, and inclination to drive them into society.[28] By this I take him to have meant, respectively, that men join society because outside it life is precarious (hence "necessity"), lacking in comfort (hence "convenience"), and lacking in fellowship (hence "inclination"). Hobbes's catalog of state of nature infirmities certainly *includes* the danger of death, but it also includes absence of comforts and commodities possession of which cannot naturally here be construed as sought for other-regarding reasons. And if they seek Lockean convenience for self-regarding reasons, it is a fortiori plausible that they non-other-regardingly shun death, simply because it would deprive them of the comforts they seek, and not only because it means humiliation. So Strauss is doubly wrong: avoiding death isn't their only aim, and, to the extent that they do avoid death, it's not just because it's a dishonor.

24   Strauss, *The Political Philosophy of Hobbes*, p. 17.
25   Ibid., p. 18.
26   Ibid., p. 165.
27   Ibid., p. 186.
28   Locke, *Two Treatises of Government*, 2.77, p. 318.

Thus far I've discerned in the famous catalog a non-other-regarding desire for commodities, while allowing an other-regarding element in aversion to insecurity and death. But the catalog seems even to contain something belonging to what Locke called the "inclination" reason for joining society, because one of the things we lack in the state of nature is "society," which, so I take it, means companionship, which you might well think means that people actually *like* each other, unless we interpret *Leviathan* here in the light of *De Cive*, which says that "all society . . . is either for gain, or for glory; that is, not so much for love of our fellows, as for love of ourselves."[29] On that view, society, apart from enabling economies of scale and gains from trade, which is the gain bit, is good because it's a field in which you can show off. (Compare Ambrose Bierce's definition of a "bore," in *The Devil's Dictionary*: someone who speaks when you want him to listen.)[30] But whether or not even Locke's inclination plays a role, and if so, in a friendly form, Hobbes is plainly concerned in his depiction of the lacks in the state of nature not only with the "being" but with the "well-being" of mankind, to use a distinction he himself employs.[31]

Strauss may have been misled, as I am sure other commentators have been, by such statements as that all Sovereignty was ordained for the safety of preserving a man's body.[32] But this needs to be read with the passage which says that "by Safety here, is not meant a bare Preservation, but also all the other Contentments of life."[33] Hobbes is explicit that "the Passions that encline men to Peace are Feare of Death; Desire of such things as are necessary to commodious living; and a hope by their Industry to attain them."[34]

In resisting Strauss, I have not been trying to show that men *lack* underived other-regarding passions, but to cast doubt on his curious idea that they alone explain the impulsion to enter society.[35]

Do underivative other-regarding passions play *any* part in generating war? Clearly honor, pride, glory play a part in generating war, but are they underivative?

Hobbes so emphasizes the desire for honor, for others' having a high opinion of one's power, that one might think it must be underivative. But

---

29   Hobbes, *De Cive*, 1.2, p. 24.
30   Bierce, *The Devil's Dictionary*, p. 28.
31   Hobbes, *Leviathan*, p. 104.
32   Ibid., p. 337.
33   Ibid., p. 376.
34   Ibid., p. 188.
35   See, further, on the desire for glory and the fear of death, Murphy, "Was Hobbes a Legal Positivist?," pp. 866–67. But note his failure to report Strauss correctly in the long footnote. He cites Strauss, p. 15: but see Strauss, pp. 16–17.

there is a rather important passage which points contrariwise. Hobbes speaks of "Desire of Power, of Riches, of Knowledge and of Honour." And then he says: "All which may be reduced to . . . Desire of Power. For Riches Knowledge and Honour are but severall sorts of Power."[36] Now this is an interesting non sequitur. It is a non sequitur because the fact that A is a kind of B does not mean that a desire for A reduces to a desire for B. My desire for a banana does not reduce to a desire for some fruit, as if an apple would also necessarily do. And the non sequitur is interesting because Hobbes's making it strongly suggests the derivativity of honor on power. That is, the best explanation of Hobbes's fallaciously inferring the conclusion is that he believes it, independently. Note the relevant parallel. If I want a banana just *because* it is a piece of fruit, then I want a banana derivatively, after the second form of derivativity distinguished at 4 above, the derivativity of *way*, not *means*.

The passage suggests, then, that men want the kind of power that honor is because they want power as such. How does honor give power? Through a bandwagon effect. Honor is belief in another's power, and "Reputation of power is Power; because it draweth with it the adherence of those that need protection."[37]

13. Strauss is wrong that the desire for power is *wholly* underivatively other-regarding. But is the restless desire for power *at least in part* underivatively other-regarding? That factors into two questions. Is it at all other-regarding? If it is, is it, to any extent, underivatively so?

The first question's answer is clearly yes. To be sure, desire for power is not other-regarding just *as* the desire for present means to future good. But it is other-regarding in that men always want more power than others have and glory in such superiority of power. This is expressed in what indeed looks like an underivative way in the *Elements of Law*, pt. 1, chap. 7, para. 7:

> [A]s men attain to more riches, honours, or other power; so their appetite groweth more and more; and when they are come to the utmost degree of one kind of power, they pursue some other, *as long as in any kind they think themselves behind any other*. (emphasis added)[38]

To put it like that, in terms of growth of appetite, makes it look underivative. But in *Leviathan* there is reason for ceaseless power acquisition which doesn't involve a lust for power as such but relates to the

---

36 Hobbes, *Leviathan*, p. 139.
37 Ibid., p. 150.
38 Hobbes, *The Elements of Law*, p. 30.

precariousness of any accumulation of power in the state of nature. Thus, right before he imputes the perpetual and restless desire of power after power, Hobbes importantly adds: "And the cause of this, is not alwayes that a man hopes for a more intensive delight, than he has already attained to; or that he cannot be content with a moderate power: but because he cannot assure the power and means to live well, which he hath present, without the acquisition of more."[39] There is nothing underivatively other-regarding in that, any more than there is something *under-ivatively* other-regarding in the squirrel's undoubtedly other-regarding heaping up of as many nuts as he can.

The *Leviathan* passage certainly gives the desire for power an extensively if not entirely derivative basis, since power is by implication here seen as a means to live well;[40] here they are never content with what they have *not* because they *cannot* be content with a moderate power but because a moderate amount means possibly less than others have and that means possibly not enough: power differences to a large extent determine net power amounts.

The diagnostic problem I've been discussing is parallel to the problem of diagnosing the motives of capitalists in a highly competitive capitalist economy. Is their unlimited profit drive a discontent with any given mass of profit because they want to be top dog as such, or does it reflect the permanent possibility of being outplayed in the future?

14. In 13 I was showing how other-regarding passions *might* be interpreted as derivative, but I want to close this part of the lectures by showing that they are not always so, even if they are not the central part of the story. I give three text-based arguments to that end.

(i) The first, and perhaps the most interesting one, is in chapter 17, where Hobbes deals with an objection to his claim that men cannot live peaceably save under an awesome power. The objection points out that bees and ants do so and asks why men therefore could not as well. He answers thus:

> First, that men are continually in competition for Honour and Dignity, which these creatures are not; and consequently amongst men there ariseth on that ground, Envy and Hatred, and finally Warre; but amongst these not so.[41]

---

39   Hobbes, *Leviathan*, p. 161.

40   [Here the text adds: [IS THIS RIGHT?: and living well couldn't *here* include wanting more power over others, since then the contrast with "cannot be content with a moderate power" would fail. So]—Ed.]

41   Hobbes, *Leviathan*, pp. 225–26.

This says that we have other-regarding destructive passions which they lack. And the next paragraph makes it seem that it is *only* such passions and no other which govern us:

> Secondly, that amongst these creatures, the Common good differeth not from the Private; and being by nature enclined to their private, they procure thereby the common benefit. But man, whose Joy consisteth in comparing himselfe with other men, can relish nothing but what is eminent [i.e. superior].[42]

This pretty well establishes underivative other-regarding passions as figuring in the breakdown to war. Indeed, he seems to go so far as to suggest that men care about nothing but prevailing against others.

Still, there are two things that might be said by way of an attempt to diminish the force of the reply to the bees problem as evidence that *all* people care about is doing others down and themselves up. The first is to suggest, boringly, that Hobbes is carelessly overreacting to the bees problem. The second and more cunning move is to draw a contrast between, on the one hand, sources of "joy," that is, things we "relish," and other things that we want. We may get no wonderful relishable joy from life and physical comfort, but it doesn't follow that it's false that we want them, and that that desire figures as part of the genesis of war. You might think these diminishing strategies are cast in doubt, however, by two powerful statements in *De Cive*, which are not responses to a bees counterexample and which don't restrict their ambit to special pleasure:

> [A]ll the pleasure and jollity of the mind consists in this, even to get some [people], with whom comparing, it may find somewhat wherein to triumph and vaunt itself. (emphasis added)[43]

> [M]an scarce esteems *anything* good which hath not somewhat of eminence in the enjoyment, more than that which others do possess. (emphasis added)[44]

But again, pleasure and jollity of *mind* may not be *all* that one wants, and the second passage does say "*scarce* esteems anything good."

I have no doubt that there are competition and diffidence elements in Hobbes which do not reduce to glory, for all that he fails to invoke them in his response re the bees. He is an implicit game theorist, but he did not realize that he was. (To use an Althusserian contrast, there is game theory in Hobbes, but in a practical, untheorized, not made explicit state.)

---

42   Ibid., p. 226.
43   Hobbes, *De Cive*, 1.5, p. 26.
44   Ibid., 5.5, p. 66.

He should have said, in addition to invoking pride in rebutting the bees counterexample, that bees collaborate instinctively, whereas our reason makes us prey to Prisoners' Dilemmas and assurance games. He was insufficiently conscious of his own innovation to say *that*, so he sometimes lapses into too heavy a use of the picturesque passions, and he sees men's passions as making them shortsighted, as if the problem were short-term versus long-term interest, rather than the Prisoners' Dilemma or the assurance game. (We shall see that Hume too misrepresents what is in fact a Prisoners' Dilemma problem as a matter of short-term versus long-term interest.)

(ii) Back now to the second text-based argument for saying that the glory-centered other-regarding passions are not derivative.

If desire for honor were derivative, why would it continue so powerfully in a well-ordered state (which has tamed the struggle for power) that it needs to be very nicely regulated. Why must the sovereign bestow titles of honor; why are "Lawes of honour . . . necessary"?[45] And compare *De Cive*: "ambition and greediness of honours cannot be rooted out of the minds of men."[46] This is the unbourgeois side of Hobbes's theory of human nature and political philosophy:

> Of the Passions that most frequently are the causes of Crime, one is Vain-glory, or a foolish over-rating of their own worth; as if difference of worth were an effect of their wit, or riches, or bloud, or some other natural quality, not depending on the Will of those that have the Soveraign Authority. From whence proceedeth a Presumption that the punishments ordained by the Lawes, and extended generally to all Subjects, ought not to be inflicted on them, with the same rigour they are inflicted on poore, obscure, and simple men, comprehended under the name of the Vulgar.[47]

(iii) Finally, he puts Pride first in a summary passage when he says that Man's Pride and other Passions have compelled him to submit himself to government, and he calls that government "Leviathan, King of the Proud."[48] If anything, *De Cive* is gloomier about how much men want to lord it sadistically over others: Hobbes vigorously denies "that man is a creature born fit for society." He denies that "by nature one man . . . love[s] another";[49] he speaks of a "mutual will of hurting,"[50] and of "this

45   Hobbes, *Leviathan*, p. 235.
46   Hobbes, *De Cive*, 13.12, p. 149.
47   Hobbes, *Leviathan*, p. 341.
48   Ibid., p. 362.
49   Hobbes, *De Cive*, 1.2, pp. 21–22.
50   Ibid., 1.3, p. 25.

natural proclivity of men, to hurt each other, which they derive from their passions, but chiefly from a vain esteem of themselves."[51]

The right conclusion is that there are two kinds of stories in Hobbes, competition and diffidence on the one hand, glory on the other, one excluding and the other including antagonistic underivative other-regarding passions, two kinds of stories that he did not disentangle from each other. Hobbes occurs, historically, amid an age of transition from an aristocratic to a bourgeois outlook, and he tells stories reflecting each of them, with little consciousness of his own transitional and therefore ambiguous status.

HOW DOES HOBBES JUSTIFY POLITICAL OBLIGATION?

15. So far I've discussed why the state of nature is a state of war. Now I turn to the second question I promised to address, which (see Section 1) is: *how* does the fact that the state of nature is a state of war justify governmental authority, according to Hobbes? Let me generalize that question a little: how does Hobbes justify governmental authority? The point of the generalization is that there are, as far as I can see, four more or less distinct answers to the more general question, and they do not rely equally on the fact that the state of nature is a state of war. The first two answers clearly do: they are, moreover, quite distinct from each other, and I shall call them the consequentialist and contractarian answers. The third and fourth answers are very closely connected, and not so evidently dependent on the thesis that the state of nature is a state of war. I shall call them the consent and authorization answers.

I'll now expound the four answers, and then comment on the first three of them.

(i) The first answer is consequentialist. Government extinguishes the Prisoners' Dilemmas, and/or renders the assurance game benign, and thereby facilitates peace, cooperation, and industry. The two conditions, of nature and civil society, are compared, and, so it is urged, the condition of society and government being conducive to peace, cooperation, and industry, instead of uncontrolled competition and war, anyone must regard the former as superior, whatever standard for judging conditions he uses. He is driven to that judgment if, in particular, he is an expected

---

51 Ibid., 1.12, p. 29. Yet how do we reconcile those texts with this one from *Leviathan*, which might be thought to reject negative underivative other-regarding passions? "*Contempt*, or little sense of the calamity of others, is that which men call CRUELTY; proceeding from Security of their own fortune. For, that any man should take pleasure in other mens great harmes, without other end of his own, I do not conceive it possible" (p. 126). Yes: reconciliation is available, by insisting that only "*great* harms" are in question.

utility maximizer, or a maximinizer, or what Kavka calls a disaster avoider.[52] A maximinizer says: choose the alternative with the best worst outcome, that is, whose outcome, on a worst-case scenario, is better than the worst outcome of any available alternative. A disaster-avoider chooses the course of action that maximizes the chances of avoiding all disastrous outcomes. An *expected utility maximizer* and a maximinizer will choose B and a disaster-avoider will choose A:

Possible outcomes	A	Probability	B	Probability
	10	.3	10	.266
	8	.3	8	.266
	6	.3	6	.266
	5	Last three together .1	5	Last three together .2
	3		4	
	1		4	

(Note: 5 and below are disasters)

Some say risk-aversion, as counterposed to expected utility maximization, is irrational; others say it is properly expressed in an extremely negative payoff value for the outcome you are averse to.

The Hobbesian claim is that society scores over nature on all these criteria. It is unclear which criterion Hobbes intended to invoke, but he scores on all three, *if*, of course, his description of the contrast between nature and governmental society is correct.

The basic and simple idea is that when there's a state capable of enforcing cooperative behavior, through making defecting behavior impossible or too expensive, then collective action problems are overcome, because it becomes each person's rational self-interest, on any reasonable principle of the latter, to play the sharing, cooperative game. The endless frantic accumulating can stop because you can be sure that the police will protect your stock.

Every man indeed out of the state of civil government hath a most entire, but unfruitful liberty; because that he who by reason of his own liberty acts all at his own will, must also by reason of the same liberty in others suffer all at another's will. But in a constituted city, every subject retains to himself as much freedom as suffices him to live well and quietly, and there is so much taken away from others, as may make them not to be feared. Out of this state, every man has a right to all, as yet he can enjoy nothing; in it, each one securely

52 Kavka, *Hobbesian Moral and Political Theory*, p. 142.

enjoys his limited right. Out of it, any man may rightly spoil or kill another; in it, none but one. Out of it, we are protected by our own forces; in it by the power of all. Out of it, no man is sure of the fruit of his labours; in it, all men are. Lastly, out of it, there is a dominion of passions, war, fear, poverty, slovenliness, solitude, barbarism, ignorance, cruelty; in it, the dominion of reason, peace, security, riches, decency, society, elegancy, science, and benevolence.[53]

Note that this is not a contractarian justification. The idea is not that, the state of nature being so bad, men do or would contract into society under government. It's just that, the state of nature being so bad, men are better-off under government. You can see that it's not contractarian by reflecting that it's consistent with thinking (whether or not this is correct) that the contractarian justification is defeated by the consideration that, however bad the state of nature is, collective action problems would prevent people from contracting out of it. Prisoners' Dilemma and assurance problems, and problems of communication and coordination, are irrelevant to the *comparison* of the two conditions but dead relevant to a claim that people *would* contract out of the worse of the two.[54]

(ii) The second and contractarian justification of obedience says that so parlous is the state of nature that those in it would mutually covenant to surrender themselves to a sovereign and thereby be bound by promise to obey him. But, the question naturally arises, does this justification apply to people who never gave such a promise because they never were in a state of nature? A widely favored Hobbes interpretation says yes, because if you *were* in a state of nature, that's what you'd do.

There's an objection to the logic of this answer which is popular but which I think mistaken. But there's also an objection to it as an interpretation of Hobbes, which I think is correct.

The objection to the logic, raised, for example by Dworkin in his critique of Rawlsian contractarianism, is that a hypothetical contract can't bind: if I *would have paid* you £100 for this, how does that show that I'm committed to doing so?[55] A hypothetical contract, one might say, isn't worth the paper it's not written on. But to that there is a reply. Unlike, for example, the Rawlsian hypothetical contract, the Hobbesian one is one you'd make, if you're rational, in *any* circumstance other than that of the unlimited sovereignty into which you'd then contract yourself. Unlike what holds for the Rawlsian contract, it's not just in *special* circumstances that you'd make it: X and Y will make it whenever neither rules the other

53 Hobbes, *De Cive*, 10.1, p. 114.
54 Compare Joshua Cohen, "Structure, Choice and Legitimacy," pp. 311–12, though note his point is slightly different: see p. 312.
55 Dworkin, *Taking Rights Seriously*, p. 151.

and no Z rules both. To that one might counterreply that it's then hard to see how such a hypothetical contract differs from the first consequentialist justification. But the acid test is how the proponent of the justification would respond to the challenge that collective action problems might stymie a contemplated contract. If she regards them as irrelevant, she is consequentializing. If they worry her, she is contractarianizing. And, anyway, justification by what you would will is not identical with justification by your welfare. Under the best interpretation of Rawls his contract doesn't bind because if you were in the veil of ignorance you'd make it, so you're bound by your hypothetical promise. Rather, his claim is that what folk in the veil of ignorance would choose are principles of justice, so you are bound by what they choose not directly because they choose it but because what they choose must be just.

But however that may be, whatever, that is, you may think the force of the hypothetical contract argument is, and whether or not you think that, if it lacks force, then Hobbes couldn't have intended it, it seems to me a powerful argument against thinking that Hobbes rests justification on such a contract that there is no hint of such a suggestion in the text, and Hobbes is pretty explicit in his claims.

(iii) Now, that skepticism regarding the presence of a hypothetical contract argument in Hobbes makes most interesting the presence in Hobbes of a not much discussed third justification of the state. It's interesting because it looks more needed. And here I mean an argument of *actual* consent. Actual consent is of course present in an actual contract in the state of nature, when a commonwealth is, in Hobbes's terms, *instituted*; but it also figures in the case of submission to a conqueror in what Hobbes calls commonwealth by *acquisition*; and, most interestingly, he construes it as offered in effect by anyone who peaceably goes about his business in ordinary society. (I'll expound this at length in a moment, in Section 16.)

(iv) Finally, there is the motif of *authorization*, connected with but not identical with the actual consent justification. Hobbes argues that "the Subject is Author of every act the Soveraign doth"[56] and it is therefore absurd for him to disobey a law. To oppose the sovereign's law is, absurdly, to complain about what you have yourself authored.[57]

16. More on (iii): Hobbes explains Commonwealth by acquisition, or what he differently calls, in *De Cive*, "natural power"[58] as follows:

---

56   Hobbes, *Leviathan*, p. 265, cf. pp. 221, 232, 276, 388.

57   For a treatment of this justification see below, at 22, and section 1 of my "Reason, Humanity, and the Moral Law," reprinted as Chapter 12 in this volume.

58   Hobbes, *De Cive*, 5.12, pp. 68–69; 8.1, p. 100.

A Common-wealth by Acquisition, is that, where the Soveraign Power is acquired by Force; And it is acquired by force, when men singly, or many together by plurality of voices, for fear of death, or bonds, do authorise all the actions of that Man, or Assembly, that hath their lives and liberty in his Power.[59]

So it's typically a culmination of war. Now Hobbes's rebuttal of the objection that the duress or fear which drives the submitter to his "authorisation" deprives it of validity is extremely important:

And this kind of Dominion, or Soveraignty, differeth from Soveraignty by Institution, onely in this, That men who choose their Soveraign, do it for fear of one another, and not of him who they Institute: But in this case, they subject themselves to him they are afraid of. In both cases they do it for fear: which is to be noted by them, that hold all such Covenants, as proceed from fear of death, or violence, voyd: which if it were true, no man in any kind of Common-wealth, could be obliged to Obedience.[60]

I shall not stop to consider whether Hobbes's rebuttal of the duress objection is telling.[61] What I do want you to note is the closing emphasis of the rebuttal in the passage just quoted. He says that since in both "voluntary" institution and coerced acquisition men submit from fear, if fear voided the submission to coercion in the acquisition case then in no kind of commonwealth could there be an obligation to obey. Notice for Hobbes it is extremely important that, in commonwealth by acquisition, it is his own actual agreement that binds the subject:

Dominion acquired by Conquest, or Victory in war, is that which some Writers call DESPOTICALL . . . and is the Dominion of the Master over his Servant. And this Dominion is then acquired to the Victor, when the Vanquished, to avoyd the present stroke of death, covenanteth either in expresse words, or by other sufficient signes of the Will, that so long as his life, and the liberty of his body is allowed him, the Victor shall have the use thereof, at his pleasure. And after such Covenant made, the Vanquished is a SERVANT, and not before: for

59   Hobbes, *Leviathan*, pp. 251–52.
60   Ibid., p. 252. Cf. *De Cive*, 2.16, pp. 38–39.
61   For critique of the rebuttal, see Kavka, *Hobbesian Moral and Political Theory*, p. 396. "Unfortunately for Hobbes, these arguments fail. To see this, it suffices to distinguish between promises made under two types of duress. A promise is *coerced* when the promisee threatens the promisor with some evil should the promise not be made, with the purpose of obtaining the promise. A promise is *forced*, by contrast, when the promisor enters into it to avoid some evil or danger not created by the promisee, or at least not created by the promisee with the intention of producing the promise. Coerced promised are *not* morally binding. Many, though not all, forced promises *are* morally binding."

by the word *Servant* . . . is not meant a Captive, which is kept in prison, or bonds, till the owner of him that took him, or bought him of one that did, shall consider what to do with him: (for such men (commonly called Slaves,) have no obligation at all; but may break their bonds, or the prison; and kill, or carry away captive their Master justly:) but one, that being taken, hath corporall liberty allowed him; and upon promise not to run away, nor to do violence to his Master, is trusted by him.

It is not therefore the Victory, that giveth the right of Dominion over the Vanquished, but his own Covenant. Nor is he obliged because he is Conqurered; that is to say, beaten, and taken, or put to flight; but because he commeth in, and submitteth to the Victor.[62]

There *is* a contrast, with captive slaves.

The first quoted passage says that that all submission is out of fear, and it *suggests*, *ex silentio*, that commonwealths by institution and by acquisition exhaust the possibilities, a suggestion which is confirmed by *De Cive*, 8.1:[63] the third case, right by generation, isn't exactly a commonwealth. But that raises an acute problem about citizens who neither participated in instituting a commonwealth nor submitted out of fear to a conqueror. The answer, which I shall presently document textually, is that *every* citizen who has not participated in instituting a commonwealth is moved by fear to submit either expressly or tacitly, if not to a conqueror properly so called, then at any rate to a ruler. People divide without remainder into those who submit and a minority who, not doing so, make themselves outlaws, in a state of nature vis-à-vis others, and, consequently, noncitizens without political obligation. Everyone else at least tacitly consents to governmental authority, presumably for fear of being in a state of nature vis-à-vis that authority, and therefore losing its protection against others and possibly also suffering its active enmity. Let me now substantiate this interpretation textually.

Hobbes is anxious to insist that there exist "signs of contract by inference,"[64] where the base of the inference may be not only words but also silence or actions or forbearances, indeed, "whatsoever sufficiently argues the will of the contractor." And other texts show Hobbes exploiting the concept of tacit consent to argue for obedience.

Hobbes says that there is no law over natural fools, children, and madmen, "no more than over brute beasts":[65] vis-à-vis everyone they are in a state of nature. And the reason *why* is that:

---

62   Hobbes, *Leviathan*, pp. 255–56.
63   Hobbes, *De Cive*, 8.1, p. 100.
64   Hobbes, *Leviathan*, pp. 193–94.
65   Ibid., p. 317.

they had never power to make any covenant, or to understand the consequences thereof; and consequently never took upon them to authorise the
actions of any Soveraign, as they must do that make to themselves a Commonwealth.[66]

They are in commonwealth with no one because they have not authorized the actions of any sovereign. That suggests[67] that all others, all those
who are nonfools, nonchildren, and nonmadmen *do* consent to government. And that suggestion is explicit where he says that "[t]he Author, or
Legislator is supposed in *every* Common-wealth to be evident, because
he is the Soveraign, who [has] been Constituted by the consent of every
one" (emphasis added).[68] And what does he think proves or shows that
consent? That each man "hath himself demanded, or [N.B., GAC] wittingly received against others" the Sovereign's "protection."[69]

That "wittingly received" is Lockean tacit consent. And it is further
evident in this passage from the "Review and Conclusion" that Hobbes
relies on tacit consent:

> But this promise may be either Expresse, by Promise: Tacite, by other signes.
> As for example, a man that hath not been called to make such an expresse
> Promise, (because he is one whose power perhaps is not considerable;) yet if
> he live under their Protection openly, hee is understood to submit himselfe to
> the Government.[70]

And the rest of the passage, which you can read for yourself, makes clear
that tacit consent to an established government is equivalent to express
consent to a conqueror, with respect to its obligation-creating significance. And that Hobbes requires actual consent is further confirmed in
De Cive, chap. 14, para. 12:

> The right of making laws could not be conferred on any man without his own
> consent and covenant, either expressed or supposed; expressed, when from the
> beginning the citizens do themselves constitute a form of governing the city,
> or when by promise they submit themselves to the dominion of any one; or
> supposed at least, as when they make use of the benefit of the realm and laws
> for their protection and conservation against others.[71]

---

66   Ibid.
67   No more than that. It certainly doesn't imply it.
68   Hobbes, *Leviathan*, p. 320.
69   Ibid.
70   Ibid., pp. 720–21.
71   Hobbes, *De Cive*, 14.12, p. 162.

17. To summarize the position, as I understand it: Hobbes, in his nonconsequentialist manifestation, goes for sovereignty being justified by covenant and consent, knows full well that in most cases a government enjoys authority over a citizen neither because he participated in its original institution nor because he bowed to it as conqueror (which is commonwealth by acquisition), and he is therefore driven to an anticipation of Locke on tacit consent, because there has to be consent. And, as we shall (retrospectively) see when we come to Locke, Hobbes rests more on tacit consent than Locke does, for in Locke it only binds you for the nonce, whereas in Hobbes it binds no less than express consent does.

Into the bargain Hobbes in effect anticipates and rebuts *one* of the Hume criticisms of tacit consent doctrine, to wit, that you can hardly regard it as consent when it is *forced*.[72] On the contrary, it is precisely the fact that they have no rational choice but to consent, are, that is, forced to, which makes Hobbes sure that in effect they do.

18. As for evaluation of these three lines of justification of obedience, the third (actual consent)—I'll look at in subsequent chapters in the context of Locke and of Hume. I'll say a very little about the first (consequentialist) justification and a bit more about the second (hypothetical contract) justification and the fourth.

A question often raised with respect to the first or consequentialist justification is: how can we be sure that so comprehensive a sovereign will not misuse its power?[73]

An answer imputable to Hobbes is that the sovereign *may* to a degree abuse his power, but, if he is rational, then he will not abuse it so much as to make himself an encumbrance rather than a benefit, for then his subjects would rise, peaceful coexistence would go, and in the ensuing chaos the man or men who constitute *Leviathan* will share in the dire consequences.[74]

Now this is a bit swift, as Kavka shows.[75] But something like it will suffice as an answer to Locke, who, I think, missed the point when he claimed it to be absurd on Hobbes's part to tell men to entrust themselves to lions in order to escape polecats and foxes.[76] For a good Hobbesian

---

72   Hobbes, *Leviathan*, p. 252.

73   Kavka's trimming response is to claim that so comprehensive a sovereign as Hobbes depicts is not required to transcend the state of nature, and that a government with a *balance* of powers and limited (vis-à-vis rights of subjects) power is a better bet. Kavka, *Hobbesian Moral and Political Theory*, pp. 225–31. But is this wrong, on logical grounds? For Hobbes, is it not a matter of logic that sovereignty is undivided and unlimited?

74   See, for extended reasoning to this effect, Hobbes, *De Cive*, 10.2, pp. 114–15.

75   Kavka, *Hobbesian Moral and Political Theory*, pp. 254–66.

76   Locke, *Two Treatises of Government*, 2.93, p. 328.

reply to Locke is that the real choice is between being surrounded by polecats each of whom has reason to be hostile to you and to exert his force against you and submitting to one lion who indeed could finish you off tout de suite but who may reasonably be expected to have better things to do.

19. I think the standard criticism of the second pattern of justification, the multilateral covenant, is pretty compelling. It says, in brief, that if the state of nature is really as bad as Hobbes says, then it cannot be exited from in the way that Hobbes says. The very lack of trust among people which makes the state essential makes forming it impossible. One sees why these men would like to exchange subsequently acted on promises. But, if they can achieve that, why are they in such a mess in the first place? Someone who thinks that world government is necessary because individual states are unrelentingly rapacious thereby concedes that world government is also impossible. He could not expect the states he describes to agree to it, for, if they could, then why could they not agree to lesser restrictions on their rapacity, which would make world government unnecessary? Pressure by citizenries as an alternative is here irrelevant because we're analogizing states with individuals in the state of nature. Anyway, citizenries could also press for reduction in rapacity. In 1961 I heard Otto Nathan, who was secretary to Albert Einstein, say: "All my life I told Einstein: 'World government will only be possible when it is no longer necessary.' But now the situation is so grave that I change my mind."

In Prisoners' Dilemma terms, why should disobedience not remain dominant? Think of the covenant as throwing away one's sword if others do. Then either they will or they won't. If they will I'm better-off keeping mine. If they won't I'd better keep mine. If, being more assurance oriented, I gamble on trusting them, and others are similarly disposed, then why can't we ameliorate the state of nature through bits of trust and wary cooperative behavior? Why do we need a comprehensive Leviathan?

Kavka says that the contractors negotiate under an "awareness that they have a realistic opportunity, if they conduct themselves properly, to trade in the insecurities of the state of nature for the lasting security of civil society."[77] But it's also true that, in the state of nature itself, they'd make big gains if they conducted themselves properly.

> If a Covenant be made, wherein neither of the parties perform presently, but trust one another; in the condition of meer Nature, (which is a condition of Warre of every man against every man,) upon any reasonable suspition, it is Voyd: But if there be a common Power set over them both, with right and

---

77 Kavka, *Hobbesian Moral and Political Theory*, p. 237, and cf. p. 387.

force sufficient to compel performance; it is not Voyd. For he that performeth first, has no assurance the other will performe after; because the bonds of words are too weak to bridle mens ambition, avarice, anger and other Passions, without the feare of some coerceive Power; which in the condition of meer Nature, where all men are equall, and judges of the justnesse of their own fears cannot possibly be supposed. And therefore he which performeth first, does but betray himselfe to his enemy; contrary to the Right (he can never abandon) of defending his life and means of living.[78]

Doesn't that make it impossible to pass *from* "meer Nature" to there being such a "common Power"? Well, you might think you could pass that way through acquisition. But sovereigns by acquisition preexist that acquisition. How, given rough equality, did they get to be sovereigns in the first place? If "the validity of covenants begins not but with the constitution of a civil power, sufficient to compel men to keep them,"[79] how can covenants purportedly *establishing* such a power be valid? Are they validated retroactively? Is making them irrational at the time but rational retroactively?

We can put the problem in yet a different way, drawing on the vocabulary of traditional, i.e., medieval, contract theory. In that tradition there are distinct contracts of society and of government, first a pactum unionis and then a pactum subjectionis. In the first, previously independent people (say peasants) join up in an exchange of promises, perhaps agreeing to common rules for regulating their interactions. In the second the thus united community agrees to submit to a ruler, in exchange for protection: that actually happened in the formation of feudalism. Hobbes wants a kind of pactum subjectionis without a pactum unionis. And, indeed, we can say, given Hobbes's account of what makes a pactum subjectionis necessary, that if a pactum unionis were possible then a pactum subjectionis would not be necessary, would serve no purpose. And yet how *can* there be a pactum subjectionis without a pactum unionis? "If we could suppose a great multitude of men . . . there would be peace without subjection."[80] That is all very well, but, as I said, how *can* there be *anything like* a pactum subjectionis without *some* sort of pactum unionis? I say "anything *like*" a pactum subjectionis because strictly in Hobbes there is no pactum subjectionis either, since the Hobbesian sovereign, unlike the medieval prince, promises nothing. He makes covenants with nobody. Not with the whole multitude, because they have no sort of unity and therefore no capacity for willing a contract that preexists his insti-

78   Hobbes, *Leviathan*, p. 196; cf. Hobbes, *De Cive*, 2.11, pp. 32–33.
79   Hobbes, *Leviathan*, p. 203.
80   Ibid., p. 225.

tution.[81] And not with each man singly, because, if there's a promise, there must be such a thing as breaking it, but anything the sovereign qua sovereign does is authorized by each man and so could not count as the breaking of a promise to any such man.[82] (We'll look at that curious authorization doctrine later.)

To complicate matters further, one might conjecture two stages of contracting from Hobbes:

> A *Common-wealth* is said to be *Instituted*, when a *Multitude* of men do Agree, and *Covenant, every one, with every one*, that to whatsover *Man*, or *Assembly of Men*, shall be given by the major part, the *Right* to *Present* the Person of them all, (that is to say, to be their *Representative;*) every one, as well he that *Voted for it*, as he that *Voted against it*, shall *Authorise* all the Actions and Judgements, of that Man, or Assembly of men, in the same manner, as if they were his own, to the end, to live peaceably amongst themselves, and be protected against other men.[83]

But perhaps he is there misexpressing the logically quite different formulation:

> I Authorise and give up my Right of Governing my selfe, to this Man, or to this Assembly of men, on this condition, that thou give up thy Right to him, and Authorise all his Actions in like manner.[84]

(The big difference is between "*this* man" in the latter passage and "whatsoever man" in the former.)

20. It might be said that the foregoing criticism supposes that Hobbes's construction requires an actual covenanting to institute a sovereign, whereas, in fact, a hypothetical contract will do. I have three replies. (i) Hobbes thinks there have been states of nature from which commonwealths have emerged: "the state of equality is the state of war, and . . . therefore inequality [of sovereign and subject] was introduced by a general consent."[85] And that text suggests that *all* states *start* through contract.[86] (ii) Nor is there any hint of hypothetical contract as a kind of fallback position, as I said before. (iii) And even if there were, or if someone tries so to rehabilitate Hobbes, my argument does not conclude just

---

81   Ibid., p. 230.
82   Ibid.
83   Ibid., pp. 288–89.
84   Ibid., p. 287.
85   Hobbes, *De Cive*, 10.4, p. 117.
86   Cf. the end of ibid., 1.2, p. 24, which suggests the same.

that there was no such contract, but that such a contract is impossible. The hypothetical interpretation says: if you were thus placed, you would submit: therefore you should submit. My argument answers, surely appositely: no, if we were thus placed, we'd have no reason to submit. So, it's false that we *would* contract *if.* . . .

21. Associated with this problem about the rationality of the procedure and the absence of pactum unionis is what is (perhaps only *inter alia*, because also sociological) a legal doctrine about what can constitute unity in multitude. Thus Hobbes says:

> A Multitude of men, are made *One* person, when they are by one man, or one Person, Represented; so that it be done with the consent of every one of that Multitude in particular. For it is the *Unity* of the Representer, not the *Unity* of the Represented, that maketh the Person *One*. And it is the Representer that beareth the Person, and but one Person: And *Unity*, cannot otherwise be understood in Multitude.[87]

And in *De Cive*, he says, "But the people is not in being before the constitution of government, as not being any person, but a multitude of single persons."[88] So, one might say, the pactum unionis is a consequence of, comes pari passu with, the pactum subjectionis: this seems a reasonable gloss on what the people say when they make the covenant,[89] though it is in seeming tension with the two-stage process quoted above concerning the institution of the Common-wealth.[90] It is a curious doctrine because there must be some presovereign instituting coordinative unity if they're to converge on the same sovereign in their individual authorizings.

22.[91] I come now to the fourth justification of obedience, the authorization doctrine, canvassed at length by Gauthier in chapter 4 of his *Logic of Leviathan*.

Hobbes's subjects have no right to disobey a law laid down by their sovereign. They may, it is true, resist arrest, for reasons that I shall not discuss, but that entitlement forms no exception to the above statement: it means, rather, that no law can be made making resisting arrest a crime. By contrast, the sovereign is himself not subject to the law he lays down: he is not obliged to obey it. I now want to suggest that the reason Hobbes gives for the law's failure to bind the sovereign is flatly inconsistent with

---

87   Hobbes, *Leviathan*, p. 220.
88   Hobbes, *De Cive*, 7.7, p. 91.
89   Hobbes, *Leviathan*, p. 227.
90   Ibid., pp. 228–29.
91   [Attached to this section is the comment: "*It probably needs editing down, because of repetition.*" However, the section has been left as it appears in the manuscript.—Ed.]

the fourth reason he gives for the claim that he binds his subjects, a reason to which he attaches great importance.

This fourth reason is tied up with the idea that the sovereign can do no wrong to his subject. One reason why that is so is that the sovereign has covenanted nothing to the subject,[92] and you can do wrong to someone only by breaking faith with him. But the present reason is different. It is that every act of the sovereign is to be regarded as an act of each person, since the sovereign is his representative, and "every man gives their common representer authority from himself in particular; and owning all the actions the representer doth, in case they give him authority without stint,"[93] and there is, of course, no stint in the authority Hobbesian people give their sovereign. Because he is their representative, every act of the sovereign is an act of every one of his subjects. "Of the act of the sovereign every one is author, because he is their representative unlimited."[94] Consider also:

> The law is made by the sovereign power, and all that is done by such power is warranted and owned by every one of the people; and that which every man will have so, no man can say is unjust. It is in the laws of a commonwealth as in the laws of gaming; whatsoever all the gamesters all agree on, is injustice to none of them.[95]

Or again, consider:

> he that doth any thing by authority from another, doth therein no injury to him by whose authority he acteth: But by this institution of a Commonwealth, every particular man is author of all the sovereign doth; and consequently he that complaineth of injury from his sovereign, complaineth of that whereof he is himself author; and therefore ought not to accuse any man but himself; no nor himself of injury, because to do injury to oneself is impossible.[96]

I discern two arguments in these texts, issuing in the same final conclusion:

	What the sovereign does, I do.
But	The sovereign makes the law.
So	I make the law.
Now,	It is absurd to object to what I myself do.
So	I cannot object to the law.
So	I must obey the law (because I made it).

92 Hobbes, *Leviathan*, p. 230.
93 Ibid., p. 221.
94 Ibid., p. 276.
95 Ibid., p. 388.
96 Ibid., p. 232.

In a different version of the argument, which Hobbes also gives, the first premise is, again, that I do whatever the sovereign does, but now the further operative premise is not that I cannot object to what I myself do but that I cannot "injure" (that is, do an injustice to) myself. The argument then runs as follows:

	What the sovereign does, I do.
But,	A man cannot injure himself.
So	The sovereign does not injure me.
So	I cannot object to what the sovereign requires of me.
So	I must obey the sovereign.

In a word, the sovereign has no obligation to the subject, since its acts are their acts. Therefore, when he makes the law, they must obey, since, if they violate the law, they contradict their own will.

In line with this, Hobbes says that "the subject is author of every act the Sovereign doth,"[97] and he here infers that this gives the sovereign the right to put a man to death.[98] He can breach no obligation to the subject when he does so, even if it is a breach of the law of nature, in which case, though not an injury to the man, it is an injury to God, an iniquity, because against the law of nature (the subject then also, presumably, violates, as author of the sovereign's act, the law of nature, but Hobbes doesn't actually draw that ridiculous but required—by his doctrine—conclusion). By contrast, the subject cannot punish the sovereign, nor, a fortiori, put him to death, because "seeing every Subject is the Author of the actions of his Sovereigne; he punisheth another, for the actions committed by himselfe."[99]

Now you might think that, if I am subject to the law *because* I make it, not, albeit, directly, but through my representative, then that representative himself, the sovereign, is equally or even *a fortiori* subject to the law, because *he* makes it, and, indeed, makes it more directly than I do. But that is not Hobbes's inference. Not only does Hobbes not infer, using the same reasoning that he used in the case of the citizen, which should, it seems, also apply to the sovereign, that the latter *is* subject to the law he makes; but Hobbes concludes, oppositely, that the sovereign is *not* subject to the law. And the reason that Hobbes gives for that conclusion is the very same one as the reason that he gives for concluding that the

---

97   Ibid., p. 265.

98   This would seem to have the curious consequence that a man can put himself to death. At ibid., pp. 353–54, by contrast with p. 265, Hobbes flinches from asserting what has that consequence and grounds the sovereign's right to punish not on authorization but on his retaining the one he had in the state of nature. Gauthier notes this lapse from the authorization doctrine: *The Logic of Leviathan*, pp. 146–49, p. 158.

99   Hobbes, *Leviathan*, p. 232.

citizen *is* subject to the law, to wit that he, the sovereign, *makes* the law. Here is what Hobbes says:

> A fourth opinion, repugnant to the nature of a Common-wealth, is this, *That he that hath the Soveraign Power, is subject to the Civill Lawes.* It is true, that Soveraigns are all subjects to the Lawes of Nature; because such lawes be Divine, and cannot by any man, or Common-wealth be abrogated. But to those Lawes which the Soveraign himselfe, that is, which the Common-wealth maketh, he is not subject. For to be subject to Lawes, is to be subject to the Common-wealth, that is to the Soveraign Representative, that is to himselfe; which is not subjection, but freedome from the Lawes.[100]

> The soveraign of a Common-wealth, be it an Assembly, or one Man, is not Subject to the Civill Lawes. For having power to make, and repeale lawes, he may when he pleaseth, free himselfe from that subjection, by repealing those Lawes that trouble him, and making of new; and consequently he was free before. For he is free, that can be free when he will: Nor is it possible for any person to be bound to himselfe; because he that can bind, can release; and therefore he that is bound to himselfe onely, is not bound.[101]

This argument says (in the fuller version of it to be found in the second quoted passage, and very slightly reconstructed):

	The sovereign makes the law.
So	The sovereign can unmake the law.
So	The sovereign is not bound by the law that he makes.

The inconsistency I promised to expose may now be apparent. The subject is bound by the law because he made it. When the citizen violates the law, he contradicts his own will: he, in the person of the sovereign, made the law, and therefore cannot without absurdity violate it. Yet it is precisely because the sovereign makes the law (and, therefore, can unmake it—this lagniappe in the argument occurs within the *second* passage) that he is *not* bound by it: according to Hobbes, it is conceptually impossible for him to violate it.

---

100   Ibid., p. 367.
101   Ibid., p. 313. Or, as Hobbes says at *De Cive*, 12.4, p. 132: "It is evident, that he is not tied to his own laws, because no man is bound to himself." Cf. ibid., 6.14, pp. 79–80: "Neither can any man give somewhat to himself; for he is already supposed to have what he can give himself. Nor can he be obliged to himself; for the same party being both the obliged and the obliger, and the obliger having the power to release the obliged, it were merely in vain for a man to be obliged to himself, because he can release himself at his own pleasure; and he that can do this, is already actually free."

The difficulty is not that two are said to make the one law. Given the authorization doctrine, that is not an inconsistency: one makes as author what the other makes as agent. Nor is the difficulty that of saying both that the people are subject to the law and the sovereign is not: these claims are plainly consistent. The difficulty, the contradiction, is, rather, that it cannot follow from "X makes the law" both that X is subject to it and that X is not subject to it. The conclusions being inconsistent, they cannot both be validly derived. Either the sovereign too is subject to the law, because he made it. Or the subject too is free of it, because he made it, and therefore can unmake it. You cannot say both:

You made the law. Therefore you cannot not obey it.

And:

You made the law. Therefore you need not obey it.

In that pair of arguments mutually contradictory conclusions are drawn from the self-same premise, the premise that you make the law. So at least one of the arguments is invalid. You cannot say both: because you make the law, you must obey it; and: because you make the law, it has no authority over you, so you need not obey it. The inference of the argument about the citizen requires the principle that, if I make the law, then I am bound by it. The inference of the argument about the sovereign requires the principle that, if I make the law, then I am not bound by it. At least one of those principles must be wrong.

Which argument should Hobbes give up? Pretty clearly, the one about the sovereign, since he'll still then have the political obligation he desiderates. And the one about the sovereign is in any case pretty patently invalid. It is true that he can unmake the law, but why should it follow that, before he does so, he is not subject to it? Failing another argument, he should be subject to it, just as citizens are. Hobbes should retain tight authorization, and the doctrine that you cannot resist what you yourself do, and give up the sovereign's freedom from the sway of the law.[102]

---

102   For a fuller assessment of the two arguments, independently of which one Hobbes should stick to, see my "Reason, Humanity, and the Moral Law," pp. 169–70, reprinted as Chapter 12 of this volume.

Chapter 3

LOCKE ON PROPERTY AND POLITICAL OBLIGATION

1. It is a cardinal tenet of liberalism, in one central meaning of that semantically promiscuous term, that each human being is the sovereign owner of her own person, and, consequently, the sole rightful authority over the use of its powers, which means that she may not be required to exercise them on behalf of others, unless she has agreed to do so. Not all those who are now called liberals affirm that tenet, which I call the thesis of self-ownership. John Rawls and Ronald Dworkin, whom it might be paradoxical to call nonliberals, fairly explicitly reject it. For they hold that, since it is a matter of mere luck what powers one is born with, those who are well endowed with talent have enforceable duties toward those with limited powers, duties which are inconsistent with full rights of self-ownership. But others who are eager to call themselves liberals, such as Robert Nozick in the United States and Antony Flew in Britain, deny that such thinkers as Rawls and Dworkin are *true* liberals, precisely because the latter deny the self-ownership thesis. They have, however, abandoned the fight to keep the name, and they now therefore style themselves "libertarians."[1]

Now a thinker who explicitly affirms liberalism in the just-defined sense, and who is, therefore, among other things, the grandfather of libertarianism, is John Locke, but the passages in the *Second Treatise of Government* in which he does so[2] raise two problems for him, and it is his solution to those two problems that I'll discuss in these lectures.

First, the texts that raise the problems, and then a statement of what the problems are.

In paragraph 27 of the *Second Treatise* Locke contrasts the condition of things which aren't human beings with that of things which are, with respect to what sort of rights people have in them. He says that "[t]hough the earth and all inferior creatures be common to all men, yet every man has a property in his own person: this *nobody* has *any* right to

---

1   See Nozick, *Anarchy, State, and Utopia*, p. 172, for Nozick's protest about the name.
2   [At this point the text contains the note: "(I put it that way by design: see next para, re property in common)."—Ed.]

but himself."[3] And the point is repeated at paragraph 44, where he says that "though the things of nature are given in common, yet man [is] master of himself and proprietor of his own person and the actions or labour of it."[4] Again, in paragraph 123 he describes "man in the state of nature" as "absolute Lord of his own person":[5] and see further, paragraph 32 ("which another had no title to"),[6] and paragraph 190.[7]

2. The two problems arise out of Locke's desire to defend the legitimacy of two institutions of the established order, which are private property on the one hand, and legitimate government on the other. To defend private property, he has to show how a person's self-ownership can be expanded to include what is *not* that person. To defend legitimate government, he has to show how self-ownership can be contracted, so that what were rights over myself, for example of self-defense, and of punishing offenders, become rights that government now has, and I have, consequently, a political obligation to government.

(i) This is the first problem: if the earth is given by God in "common to all men," then how may people increase the domain of their ownership so that it extends *beyond* their own persons to include private property in *external* things? Why doesn't private ownership of external things represent an unacceptable *inflation* of self-ownership, given that God gave the earth to us in common? What could justify the extension of ownership beyond the bounds of the self, and how could such an extension, if justified in principle, be justifiably accomplished? The questions I am thereby trying to distinguish can also be distinguished as follows: why should there be some or other legitimate way of forming private property in external things, and, if there should be such a way, what should that way be? This is like Hart's valuable distinction between the general justifying aim (e.g. deterrence) of punishment and its principles of distribution (e.g. that it may only be of offenders).[8] An answer to the question of the general justification of private property might not readily yield an answer to the question of how particular cases of property-ownership may legitimately be established.

Note that one might proceed in two different ways with this first problem. The first is to show that self-ownership, together with other plausible premises, justifies ownership of private property. The second is to justify private property without resting the justification *on* self-ownership,

3   Locke, *Two Treatises of Government*, 2.27, pp. 287–88.
4   Ibid., 2.44, p. 298.
5   Ibid., 2.123, p. 350.
6   Ibid., 2.32, p. 291.
7   Ibid., 2.190, pp. 393–94.
8   Hart, "Prolegomenon to the Principles of Punishment."

though, of course, in a manner consistent with it. I think that there are both kinds of justifications of private property kinds in Locke.

(ii) The second problem is in a way the opposite of the first, although the two problems are not usually recognized as standing in this contrastive relation. This is the second problem: if people own themselves, then with what right are social and political obligations of an *enforceable* kind laid upon them? Why don't such obligations constitute an unacceptable *deflation* of self-ownership? How, to use language drawn from paragraph 123, does a being who is "absolute Lord of his own person" and "subject to no Body" rightly come under the "dominion and control of [an] other power"?[9]

3. Note the emphasis on *enforceability* in the statement of the problem in 2(ii). It needs to be emphasized because moral obligations of an unenforceable kind are clearly consistent with self-ownership. I may be morally obliged to give succor to people in distress, but that is consistent with my self-ownership, since, if I am *merely* morally obliged to do so, so that it would nevertheless violate my rights to force me to do so, then my rights of self-ownership are thus far not abridged: I am *entitled* not to assist them; it's just that it would be morally *wrong* for me not to do so—in not doing so, I should be exercising my right of self-ownership in a morally shameful or shabby way. (Analogously, you do not challenge my ownership right in my land when you claim that I behaved shabbily when I forbade a traveler to sleep on it.)

It is important to bear in mind that only enforceable obligations go against self-ownership when considering the attempt by recent authors, and notably by James Tully,[10] to deny, in effect, though they do not put it that way, that Locke affirms the thesis of self-ownership in his *Two Treatises*. They use, to this end, three arguments: an isolated text in which Locke lays duties of charity on people;[11] the many texts in which he lays on them duties of nonaggression which, as I show elsewhere,[12] they unpardonably assimilate to the first sort of text; and the argument that men *cannot* own themselves because they are owned by God.

(i) The charity passage is the most potent of these three arguments against attributing the thesis of self-ownership to Locke, but even it is somewhat moot with respect to the point in dispute, because Locke does not say—though he also does not deny—that the duty of charity is to be enforced by the state. The text itself is consistent with a distinction

9   Locke, *Two Treatises of Government*, 2.123, p. 350.
10   Tully, *Discourse on Property*.
11   Locke, *Two Treatises of Government*, 1.41–43, pp. 169–71.
12   Cohen, "Marx and Locke on Land and Labour."

between duties of justice and duties of charity, with the latter distinguished from the former in not being coercively enforceable.

> As *Justice* gives every Man a Title to the product of his honest Industry, and the fair Acquisitions of his Ancestors descended to him; so *Charity* gives every Man a Title to so much out of another's Plenty as will keep him from extream want, where he has no means to subsist otherwise; and a Man can no more justly make use of another's necessity, to force him to become his Vassal, by with-holding that Relief, God requires him to afford to the wants of his Brother, than he that has more strength can seize upon a weaker, master him to his Obedience, and with a Dagger at his Throat offer him Death or Slavery.[13]

Now, you might think that Locke *is* speaking of something enforceable here, because of the analogy he draws between retaining resources while another starves and putting a dagger to another's throat: the duty not to do the latter is certainly enforceable. But what's analogous to the dagger is *not* retaining resources, but retaining them *in order to enslave* another. That's what would be punishable, on the dagger analogy.

Setting aside the motif of forcing the indigent to labor for me, exactly what would be enforced if the independent (of that) duty of charity affirmed here is indeed enforceable? I would have to give him extra from my granary, but this does not imply that I am charged with the more severely self-ownership-compromising duty to *labor* for others, to *produce* for them what they cannot produce for themselves.

(ii) By contrast, the duty of nonaggression is certainly enforceable, but, far from being inconsistent with the thesis of self-ownership, it is an immediate entailment of it: it follows from the self-ownership of other people that I may not commit aggression against them. If I own myself and you own yourself, then my right to use my fist as I please stops at the tip of your nose, because of your ownership of your nose. That is why we can deny that there is a right of self-ownership in Hobbes's state of nature: there is no such right precisely because "every man has a right [by which Hobbes means a *liberty*—GAC] to every thing; even to another's body."[14] And it also follows from that universal right that in Hobbes's state of nature, unlike Locke's, there are no private property rights.

(iii) Sometimes, those wishing to deny, in the face of his plain statements of it, that Locke affirmed self-ownership invoke his theology, and, in particular, its principle that we were made by God and therefore belong to *Him*. But the fact that I am subject to God does not mean that

---

13 Locke, *Two Treatises of Government*, 1.42, p. 170.
14 Hobbes, *Leviathan*, p. 190.

anyone else (on *earth*) has the right to tell me what to do. Compare the person who bears Hobbesian sovereignty. He is entirely self-ruling, but he is nevertheless responsible to God. Compare, too, the Christian belief that God assigns to people a dutiful stewardship over external nature. That need not entail less liberal private property laws than what libertarians would affirm. If you have a full private property right, it does not follow that you have no obligations, for example ones laid down by God, about how to use it.

But God forbids suicide, and presumably the state can enforce that, for example, by punishing attempts and/or by forbidding sale of suicide-specific drugs. So the God thing *does* in small measure reduce self-ownership.

4. Locke's answer to the first problem is the doctrine of legitimate private property formation that he lays out in chapter 5 of the *Second Treatise*. His answer to the second problem is the doctrine of contract and consent that he lays out in chapters 7 through 9, where he expounds his doctrine of political obligation.

5. I discern four arguments in justification of private property (of, that is, extending a person's ownership beyond her ownership of herself)[15] in chapter 5. I do not mean that they are presented as four distinct arguments by Locke. They are, rather, lines of justification, sometimes seemingly separate, and sometimes seemingly interlaced. I shall rehearse them very briefly, partly because I've written extensively about some of them, in texts I will refer to below:

(i) *The survival argument.*

Unless what is not privately owned is transformed into private property, people cannot make the use of it, which is indispensable to their survival; and, if you have any rights, you must have the right to do what is necessary for you to survive. Notice that this is not a labor argument for private property. You don't have to think of opening your mouth, chewing, etc., as labor for this argument to go through. Note, also, that it isn't a *good* argument. The mere right to eat is consistent with much less than full private property in the food I eat; for example, *just* a right to eat, but not also to destroy it or give it away, is enough. Basically communal property is consistent with survival. Monasteries are not (necessarily) death camps.[16]

---

15 Note that so construing Locke's purpose is consistent with what David Lloyd Thomas says in *Locke on Government*, pp. 91–93.

16 I discuss the survival argument at pp. 60–67 of "Once More into the Breach of Self-Ownership."

(ii) *The labor argument.*

This is the most famous one, and I won't say anything in evaluation of it. It says: since people own their own labor, they own anything with which they inextricably mix it. Ownership of self can thereby be used to create ownership of what is not self.[17]

(iii) *The proviso argument.*

This says, that if, when privatizing, you leave "enough and as good for others," no one can object, because no one is harmed, and, therefore, no one's rights are violated.

Now, I call this the *proviso* argument because it is usually thought to be a proviso on argument (ii): it would be better to call it the "no harm" argument. Note that, far from being, as Locke thought, a proviso appendable to argument (ii), it is, in fact, inconsistent with that argument: if you own what your labor is in *because* your labor is in it,[18] then it cannot be a condition of your ownership of the thing that you leave enough and as good for others. The *principle* that you own what you've put your labor in provided that you leave enough and as good is consistent, whatever justification it may have or lack. But the *justification* of ownership in terms of owned labor is inconsistent with the proviso. As Lloyd Thomas writes: "If, when you mix what you own with what is in common, you begin an ownership right in the thing previously in common [*because* of that mixing], then that must happen *irrespective* of whether you have left as much and as good for others, and irrespective of whether what you have mixed your labour with will waste uselessly in your possession. For these external circumstances do not affect the suffusing of that which is yours, your labour, with that with which you mix your labour."[19]

But I think (iii) is an extremely powerful argument, indeed the most powerful of the four, when it is used just on its own, as it is *in effect* so used, whatever may have been his intention, by Locke at in paragraph 33:

> Nor was this *appropriation* of any parcel of *Land*, by improving it, any prejudice to any other Man, since there was still enough, and as good left; and more than the yet unprovided could use. So that in effect, there was never the less left for others because of his inclosure for himself. For he that leaves as much as another can make use of, does as good as take nothing at all. No Body could think himself injur'd by the drinking of another Man, though he took a good Draught, who had a whole River of the same Water left him to quench

17   For good criticisms of this argument, see Lloyd Thomas, *Locke on Government*, pp. 108–9.

18   That is: because of that, *tout court*. One might say that one owns it because one's labor is in it and, for example, one therefore deserves to own it. To such *elaborated* forms of the labor-confers-property motif the proviso *is* adjoinable.

19   Lloyd Thomas, *Locke on Government*, p. 109.

his thirst. And the Case of Land and Water, where there is enough for both, is perfectly the same.[20]

Notice, again, that you need not regard opening your mouth and letting the water in as laboring to see the intuitive force of the argument which is simply that, since no one could conceivably have a grievance, the appropriation is unexceptionable. When I say this argument is extremely powerful, I mean that its major premise is. The minor premise will, in all the cases that matter, where anyone has reason to care that anyone has privatized something, be false.

(iv) *The value argument.*

Any useful thing on which labor has been bestowed owes (almost?) all of its value to that labor, and therefore rightly belongs, in the first instance, to whoever bestowed his labor on it, without which labor it would have remained virtually valueless.

Note that this is not the same as the labor argument. As I have written elsewhere:

Note now that the labour mixture argument is different from the argument, whose *conclusion* it shares. The value argument for legitimate appropriation has a different rationale from the argument for labour mixture, although many (and sometimes, perhaps, Locke) are prone to confuse the two. It is easy to confuse them, since it is (at least standardly) by labouring on something that you enhance its value, and perhaps your action on it should count as labour only if it does enhance its value. Nevertheless, in the logic of the labour mixture argument, it is labour itself, and not value-creation, which justifies the claim to private property. If you own what you laboured on because your own labour is in it, then you do not own it because you have enhanced its value, even if nothing deserves to be called "labour" unless it creates value. And, for the value argument, it is the conferring of value as such, not the labour by which it is conferred, that is essential. If you magically enhanced something's value without labouring, but, say, by wishing that it were more valuable, then you would be entitled to whatever the value argument justifies you in having, even though you had not performed any labour.[21] (You could say, in each case—you own it because you've laboured on it, but you have to continue differently: (i) + mixed something you own with it. (ii) + thereby rendered it valuable.)[22]

20 Locke, *Two Treatises of Government*, 2.33, p. 291.

21 Cohen, *Self-Ownership, Freedom, and Equality*, pp. 176–77. (I've assessed the value argument at length in chap. 7 of this book.)

22 See also Lloyd Thomas, *Locke on Government*, p. 106, for a claim that the value argument only justifies property in general, and a speculation that Locke *also* provided the

All of these arguments purport to show how human beings may legitimately extend their sovereignty beyond what they have over themselves, so as to encompass externals under that sovereignty, despite the fact that God gave the world to men in common. The labor argument exploits that initial self-ownership, arguments 1 (survival) and 3 (proviso) add to it without exploiting it, and argument 4 *perhaps* exploits it.

6. I pass to my second theme, which is Locke on political obligation. That problem is: how can the state's commands be legitimate, given that persons are self-owning, and can therefore do with themselves as they please? The short answer is that the state's commands are legitimate in virtue of the particular exercise of self-ownership rights that Locke calls consent, the relevant consent being a voluntary and conditional cession to the state of some of my rights. I shall look closely at consent from Section 11 on. But first, some more general remarks on Locke on the formation of the legitimate polity, and on how his view of that differs from Hobbes's.

7. According to Hobbes, there are no obligations whatsoever in the state of nature. Each is free to do whatsoever he pleases. Or, perhaps, there is one obligation, to wit, to try to exit from the state of nature, provided that others are also trying.

For Locke, even apart from such an obligation, even if it is given that the state of nature will persist, freedom to do as you wish is restricted by the obligations of the law of nature, which every rational creature can discern, and which, importantly, every such creature has *some* greater or lesser disposition to follow. These laws of nature obligations are, as I said (see Section 3 (ii) above) substantially consistent with self-ownership: indeed, they flow largely from the self-ownership of other people. They are largely a matter of obligations of nonaggression against persons and nonviolation of the rights in the property that they legitimately gather or receive. They are obligations to respect what Locke, in a wide use of the term, calls property, that is, my life, my liberty, and my estate, the enjoyments that are *properly* mine. People are, as I said, not only aware of what the law of nature teaches, but also, with, importantly, some people being exceptions, largely disposed to follow it. Since there is no such recognized law in Hobbes's state of nature, and the conditions of physical and human nature ensure[23] that the state of nature is a state of war, it is

---

labor mixture argument in order to justify a tie between particular pieces of property and particular persons.

23   For one or both of two reasons, that is, because of scarcity and lack of assurance, and/or because of passions like pride: see Chapter 2 above.

easy to see why a political state is required for Hobbesian men, what they gain through its formation.

Since Locke's men are in the main cognizant of and responsive to natural obligation, and not overweeningly proud or power-lustful but far more decently bourgeois, his state of nature does not so evidently as Hobbes's take on the quality of a state of war. Yet it is almost certain, so Locke thinks, that it will do so. For not *everyone* is on balance disposed to obey the law of nature, and few (see paragraph 123)[24] are disposed to obey it very *strictly*, and it is, moreover, hard to tell who's a good guy and who's not so good. And even if all were disposed to obey it utterly, three problems would remain, for which see paragraphs 124–26.[25] First, there will be honest disagreement about the terms of the law of nature, in the absence of a legislature to specify them; second, there could be honest dispute about whether and to what extent the terms of the law of nature have been violated, in the absence of a judiciary to decide that; third, there might be no one disposed to enforce the law who has sufficient power to do so. So even Locke's state of nature tends to break down into a state of war.

And to sign on to that story, you needn't think, in the rather archaic way that Locke does, about people trying to discern and apply and enforce a divinely derived natural law. Just think about how people of goodwill who acknowledge morality but without a recognized authority over them would try to behave well but would be quarrelsome because of problems of interpreting what's right and whether what's right has been respected.[26]

That the provisions of the law of nature admit of disagreement is important for explaining why Locke could not accept a justification of state authority which is different from consent, and which it is sometimes thought should be acceptable to him. Why, it might be asked, could the justification of state authority not go like this: the reason why the state has the right to issue commands to self-owning people is that universal self-ownership implies an enforceable obligation against aggression and the state is therefore justified in issuing commands which enforce that obligation. Well, true enough, the state is so justified, just as any individual would be in the absence of the state. But the state also forbids *others* to enforce natural obligations. It claims not just legitimacy for *its* law-of-nature-enforcing violence, which is fair enough, because everyone has *that*, but a *monopoly* on that legitimacy, and that it cannot have save

---

24 Locke, *Two Treatises of Government*, 2.123, p. 350.

25 Ibid., 2.124–26, pp. 350–51.

26 [At this point the text contains the remark: "Illustrate: different interpretations of trespass on legitimate private property."—Ed.]

through consent. There is no obligation without consent to accept another's reading of and enforcement of the law of nature.

8. In fact, Locke gives three bases for the formation of society, when he says, in paragraph 77, that

> God having made man such a creature, that in his own judgment it was not good for him to be alone, put him under strong Obligations of Necessity, Convenience and Inclination to drive him into *Society*.[27]

Locke does not explicate the intriguing trichotomy that he there presents, but I conjecture that the first "obligation" (necessity) is a matter of avoiding the danger of death consequent on the state of war, the second (convenience) a matter of securing the benefits of cooperation that are difficult even in a state of nature that has *not* broken down into outright war, and the third (inclination) a matter of enjoying the fellowship of others as such. Hobbes is often presented as, by contrast, seeing the whole raison d'être of the state as a matter of necessity in the stated sense, but, as I indicated in Section 12 of Chapter 2, in polemic against Strauss, that is clearly a misreading. For if you look at the famous paragraph in *Leviathan* on the infirmities of the state of nature,[28] you will see that convenience, as just glossed, certainly plays a role, and, so I argued in Section 12, so too does inclination. ("No society" suggests reasons of inclination.)

9. By that last remark, I mean that Locke is, in one sense, closer to traditional contract theory than Hobbes is. In traditional contract theory there are two contracts, a contract of society and a contract of government, or, as the medievals put it, a pactum unionis and a pactum subjectionis.[29] In the first previously independent people join up by exchanging promises with one another. In the second the thus united society submits itself to a ruler.[30] Thus Locke distinguishes at paragraph 211, as Hobbes could not, between the dissolution of society and the dissolution of government: one way of getting the second without the first is when a united people rise and overturn a government that has violated the law of nature.[31] You might ask whether paragraph 89 is consistent with 211 in this respect:

---

27 Locke, *Two Treatises of Government*, 2.77, p. 318.
28 Hobbes, *Leviathan*, p. 186.
29 See Chapter 2, Section 19 above.
30 See Gough, *Social Contract*, pp. 2–4, on the early history of these notions.
31 Locke, *Two Treatises of Government*, 2.211, pp. 406–7.

Where-ever therefore any number of Men are so united into one Society, as to quit every one his Executive Power of the Law of Nature, and to resign it to the publick, there and there only is a *Political, or Civil Society*. And this is done, where-ever any number of Men, in the state of Nature, enter into Society to make one People, one Body Politick, under one Supreme Government; or else when any one joyns himself to, and incorporates with any Government already made: for hereby he authorizes the Society, or which is all one, the Legislative thereof, to make Laws for him, as the publick good of the Society shall require; to the Execution whereof, his own assistance (as to his own Decrees) is due. And this *puts Men* out of a State of Nature *into* that of a *Commonwealth*, by setting up a Judge on Earth, with Authority to determine all the Controversies, and redress the Injuries, that may happen to any Member of the Commonwealth; which Judge is the Legislative, or Magistrates appointed by it. And where-ever there are any number of Men, however associated, that have no such decisive power to appeal to, there they are still *in the state of Nature*.[32]

I say that Hobbes cannot have two contracts, and I elaborated that in Section 19 of the previous chapter. He fuses the two, or, rather, there is strictly in Hobbes a pactum unionis fused with universal submission to a prince who grants nothing in return so that what occurs is not a proper pactum subjectionis. So really you have neither in Hobbes.

Still, Locke's story is not without qualification the traditional two-stage one. For he too does not have a contract of government proper, for the relation between people and government lacks the reciprocity requisite for contract. When a community of peasants contract with a prince, they promise support and he promises protection: there are rights on both sides. Locke's government has instead what he calls a fiduciary power: it is *entrusted* by the people with certain functions and they are entitled to remove it when they believe it has violated the trust reposed in it. It has no independent rights of its own: hence the robust right of resistance in Locke. We have here no more than in Hobbes a true pactum subjectionis, but whereas in Hobbes that is because only the ruler has rights, in Locke it is because in an ultimate sense only the people have rights.[33]

10. The functions of government derive from the three defects in the state of nature with respect to perception and enforcement of the law of nature, which I mentioned in Section 8 above. There is lack of a "settled,

32   Ibid., 2.89, p. 325.
33   Yet don't Locke's rulers promise to execute the trust and subjects to obey them as long as they do? For more on Locke on trust, see Hampton, *Hobbes and the Social Contract Tradition*, p. 123.

known law" (paragraph 124),[34] to trump varying interpretations, lack, too, of a "known and indifferent [that is, unbiased] judge" (paragraph 125),[35] and, finally, of "power to back and support the sentence" (paragraph 126).[36]

The provisions of the law of nature being unclear, the function of the *legislature* is to define them. The application of the law of nature to individual cases is hard to determine without bias where your own interests are at stake, whether as defendant or as plaintiff, so the function of the *judiciary* is to eliminate such bias.[37] Finally, individuals with legitimate grievances may lack the power to enforce redress, whence the function of the *executive*.

Note that this account of the functions of government does not justify a separation of powers, in the sense of a division of sovereignty, of the American kind. Such a justification is often carelessly attributed to Locke, but paragraphs 131,[38] 136,[39] and 150[40] make clear that the legislature, as the immediate expression of the popular will, is the supreme power.

11. I turn to the theme of self-ownership and consent.

Locke thinks that it would contradict the natural freedom of persons for government to assert authority over them other than by their consent. He writes, at paragraph 95: "Men being . . . by nature all free, equal and independent, no one can be put out of his Estate, and subjected to the Political Power of another, without his own *Consent*."[41] Note, by the way, that the features of freedom, equality, and independence are identical here. For the equality consists in no one being in a relationship of authority over anyone else, no one "being subjected to the Will or Authority of any other Man" (paragraph 54),[42] and that is exactly the same thing as freedom and independence, as they are to be understood here. Hence Lockean natural equality is identical with universal self-ownership.

Paragraph 95 continues as follows:

The only way whereby any one devests himself of his Natural Liberty, and *puts on the bonds of Civil Society* is by agreeing with other Men to joyn and

---

34   Locke, *Two Treatises of Government*, 2.124, p. 351.
35   Ibid., 2.125, p. 351.
36   Ibid., 2.126, p. 351.
37   Compare Hobbes on this: see Kavka, *Hobbesian Moral and Political Theory*, pp. 245–46.
38   Locke, *Two Treatises of Government*, 2.131, p. 353.
39   Ibid., 2.136, pp. 358–59.
40   Ibid., 2.150, pp. 367–68.
41   Ibid., 2.95, p. 330.
42   Ibid., 2.54, p. 304.

unite into a Community, for their comfortable, safe, and peaceable living one amongst another, in a secure Enjoyment of their Properties, and a greater Security against any that are not of it. This any number of Men may do, because it injures not the Freedom of the rest; they are left as they were in the Liberty of the State of Nature. When any number of Men have so *consented to make one Community* or Government, they are thereby presently incorporated, and make *one Body Politick*, wherein the *Majority* have a Right to act and conclude the rest.[43]

One reason why the majority have that right is that if unanimity were required, there would, in effect, have been no cession of right at all: see paragraph 97.[44] But the argument doesn't show why some qualified majority, like two-thirds or even all minus one, would not suffice for a social union to be created. (The other reason, in paragraph 96,[45] is also not conclusive.)

12. The paragraph I quoted in Section 11, to wit, 95, says that entering the social compact of which it speaks is "the only way by which anyone devests himself of his natural liberty." But Locke also thinks that there is another way of losing *some*, indeed, a great deal, of your natural liberty and falling subject to government. And that is by a consent which is not express, but tacit, and in which an individual adheres to an existing society and government, without, however, fully suspending his natural liberty as express consenters do. That is, and, as we shall see, this is rather curious (see Section 13 below), when the consent is tacit, then *what* you consent to, not just *how* you consent, is different.[46]

There are two distinct bases on which Locke imputes tacit consent, and one seems far more problematic than the other. The first, explained most clearly at paragraphs 73[47] and 120–21[48] has to do with the inheritance of property, and the second, about which I'll say more in Section 13, rests on the much more mere and more questionable basis of enjoyment of security, e.g., on the public highway (paragraphs 119,[49] and 122).[50] Concerning the first: if you accept, as you need not do, an inheritance, then you thereby accept the obligations attaching to it. But the property you inherit was initially, by the social contract, placed under the safety of government protection in exchange for the obedience to it

43 Ibid., 2.95, pp. 330–31. See also 2.54 (p. 304) and 2.123 (p. 350) for similar matter.
44 Ibid., 2.97, p. 332.
45 Ibid., 2.96, pp. 331–32.
46 But this overlooks *express*-consent *adhesion* to an existing government.
47 Ibid., 2.73, pp. 347–48.
48 Ibid., 2.120–21, pp. 348–49.
49 Ibid., 2.119, pp. 347–48.
50 Ibid., 2.112, p. 349.

of its owner. Therefore you, its inheritor, undertake that obedience when you accept the property. Therefore, too, says Locke, the authority of the state over you lasts only so long as you retain the property. If you choose to renounce it, give it away, or sell it, and go abroad, then the state has no authority to prevent that, since it has no authority, just by virtue of your accepting an inheritance, over your person as such.[51] This is by contrast with what Locke curiously says at paragraph 121, that the state does have authority over the person of, and can therefore forbid the emigration of, anyone who has expressly consented to its authority:

> 121. But since the Government has a direct Jurisdiction only over the Land, and reaches the Possessor of it, (before he has actually incorporated himself in the Society) only as he dwells upon, and enjoys that: *The Obligation* any one is under, by Virtue of such Enjoyment, *to submit to the government, begins and ends with the Enjoyment*; so that whenever the Owner, who has given nothing but such a *tacit Consent* to the Government, will, by Donation, Sale, or otherwise, quit the said Possession, he is at liberty to go and incorporate himself into any other Commonwealth; or to agree with others to begin a new one, *in vacuis locis*, in any part of the World, they can find free and unpossessed: Whereas he, that has once, by actual Agreement, and any *express* Declaration, given his *Consent* to be of any Commonweal, is perpetually and indispensably obliged to be, and remain unalterably a Subject to it, and can never be again in the liberty of the state of Nature; unless, by any Calamity, the Government, he was under, comes to be dissolved; or else by some publick Act cuts him off from being any longer a Member of it.

> 122. But submitting to the Laws of any Country, living quietly, and enjoying Privileges and Protection under them, *makes not a Man a Member of that Society*: This is only a local Protection and Homage due to, and from all those, who, not being in a state of War, come within the Territories belonging to any Government, to all parts whereof the force of its Laws extends. But this no more *makes a Man a Member of that Society*, a perpetual Subject of that Commonwealth, than it would make a Man a Subject to another, in whose Family he found it convenient to abide for some time; though, whilst he continued in it, he were obliged to comply with the Laws, and submit to the government he found there. . . . Nothing can make any Man so, but his actually entering into it by positive Engagement, and express Promise and Compact. This is that, which I think, concerning the beginning of Political Societies, and that *Consent which makes any one a Member* of any Commonwealth.[52]

51   Yet paragraph 2.117 (p. 346) seems very much to contradict 2.121 (p. 349) in this respect.

52   Ibid., 2.121–22, p. 349.

So consent is either express, originative of legitimate government, and alienative of rights of exit, or tacit, not originative but adhesive, and not alienative of rights of exit.[53]

13. I now address some puzzles and problems about the distinction between express and tacit consent.

(i) Cases of what Locke calls tacit consent are, as we've seen, less binding, or, rather, they bind to less than do cases of express consent. But tacit consent *should* not be less binding *just* because it is tacit rather than express. If I say, unless you shake your head, I'll take it that you agree, and your head stays still, then you've tacitly agreed, but you've agreed just as consequentially and bindingly as if you've said the words "I agree."

The limitation of what you consent to in Locke's tacit consent cases really comes from the *basis* on which consent is attributed, not the different manner of consenting, as "express" versus "tacit" would imply. The basis in the case of tacit consent excludes the full membership that comes with express consent to full membership. That basis is either inheritance of *private* property or safe enjoyment of *public* property, as when you walk unmolested on the highway. The manner of the consent may be conspicuous but it is surely irrelevant to what sort of obligation is generated. If you actually say, when you inherit the property, "Thank you, Mr. State, I accept your protection of my property and pledge allegiance to you for so long as I retain it," you would not be more bound than you are by just accepting the property and therefore tacitly consenting. Contrariwise, if you simply stay silent and tacitly consent when asked whether you submit yourself to the king, you should be as fully bound to that as though you had physically signed on to it.

(ii) Why should the consent that constitutes the original contract, or an express later adhesion, bind to so much? It clearly cannot be, so we now see, because it is express. And since the lesser thing that is consented to in cases of tacit consent would appear to suffice for social order, that is, it suffices for social order that people obey the state as long as they are within its jurisdiction, then why should they be bound, in their original compact, or by later express adhesion, not to leave it? You might say that only so is a true state, with citizen members, constituted, but that seems, first, false, and secondly, even if true, then the question would be why people have reason to form a true state instead of a looser association.

---

53 Gauthier's quite familiar account of the basis for attributing tacit consent makes that basis weaker than what's available in the inheritance case: see p. 12 of his "David Hume, Contractarian."

(iii) As we have seen, tacit consent is attributed on the basis not only of enjoyment of private property but also of public. As Locke puts it in paragraph 119:

> And to this I say, that every Man, that hath any Possession, or Enjoyment, of any part of the Dominions of any Government, doth thereby give his *tacit Consent*, and is as far forth obliged to Obedience to the Laws of that Government, during such Enjoyment, as any one under it; whether this his Possession be of Land, to him and his Heirs for ever, or a Lodging only for a Week; or whether it be barely travelling freely on the Highway; and in Effect, it reaches as far as the very being of any one within the Territories of that Government.[54]

Now, if you travel freely on the highway, you do not thereby situate yourself on something someone bound themselves and, through inheritance, you, to use in a particular way. It is this public highway bit, not the inheritance bit, that is truly bizarre. For why can the traveler not say, "Look, I don't want your support, MR. STATE, I hereby renounce it, and if a highwayman attacks me, then I do not expect you to come to my aid"? One could not similarly say, "Look MR. STATE, I am withdrawing this property I've inherited from your jurisdiction." For it was placed under state obligation and I have no right to its rights without its obligations.[55]

This highway problem is acute, given Locke's assurance in paragraph 95 (quoted in Section 11 above) that, when any number of men form a state, "it injures not the freedom of the rest: they are left as they were in the liberty of the state of nature."[56] For they do not retain that liberty if they willy-nilly tacitly consent to authority by walking on public land.[57] But why can't the *state* appropriate the land which becomes the highway as long as it leaves enough and as good for others? Public property, we might say, is the state's private property. (But it might not then be leaving enough and as good for others to travel upon.)

(iv) In an excellent article on Locke on tacit consent, John Bennett persuasively argues that suitable signs of tacit consent must satisfy one or other of two conditions, each of which is sufficient: "If I wish to make some action a sign of consent I can do so only if either the action is not of interest to anyone for its own sake or I have a right to prohibit people from making the sign."[58] Thus, I could say to you that, unless you raise

---

54   Locke, *Two Treatises of Government*, 2.119, p. 348.
55   What if what is now the public highway *had been* privately owned? Would the argument work in that case?
56   Locke, *Two Treatises of Government*, 2.95, p. 331.
57   This point is due to M.F.L. Cohen.
58   Bennett, "A Note on Locke's Theory of Tacit Consent," p. 229.

your hand, I'll take you to be consenting to pay me £10, but I couldn't say that, unless you stay here until 1:15 p.m., I'll take you to be consenting to pay me £10, since whether you stay here till 1:15 p.m., unlike, I'm supposing, whether you raise your hand, is, being onerous, something of interest to you for its own sake, and not something which I have a right to forbid you to do, and to your doing of which I can therefore attach a condition.

Since the state has the right to prohibit inheritance of land without undertaking the obligations associated with its ownership, it can treat such inheritance as tacit consent to those obligations: the person has no right to renounce those obligations. But it is not similarly clear how obligations attach as a result of walking on public land. I have an important interest in doing that, and the state can't prohibit me from doing that unless it has the right to govern me, but that's precisely what needs to be established and it therefore cannot be presupposed.[59] [60]

14. A word now about an interesting difference with respect to consent and the state between Locke and his neo-Lockean counterpart Nozick. Just as Nozick makes formation of private property easier than Locke does, by surreptitiously weakening his proviso,[61] so he makes formation of state authority easier than Locke does by contending that non-consensually based obligation is consistent with self-ownership, despite the fact that Nozickian self-ownership is, if anything, more robust than Locke's, since there is no question of there being an enforceable duty of charity, or a prohibition on suicide, in Nozick. For Nozick claims, vastly here to summarize a complex argument, that when people transfer their self-ownership-based rights of self-defense to a dominant protection association, and thereby form an ultraminimal state, they have the right to force independents within its ambit, because of the possible threat that they represent.

But Nozick's argument probably fails.[62] And, if it does fail, then believers in self-ownership must content themselves with the consent doctrine.

---

59 Does this fall to the point made at the end of (iii): public property is the state's private property?

60 Having offered his interesting (partial?) rescue of Locke, Bennett proposes a subtle difficulty in it at pp. 233–34. My hunch is that it can be overcome.

61 [At this point the text contains the remark "Say how and refer to Ch. III of *Self-Ownership.*" Chapter 3 of Cohen's *Self-Ownership, Freedom, and Equality* contains an extended discussion of this point.—Ed.]

62 See Altham, "Reflections on the State of Nature," and Wolff, "Nozick's Derivation of the Minimal State."

Chapter 4

HUME'S CRITIQUE OF LOCKE ON CONTRACT

1. I turn now to Hume's critique of social contract theory, and, more particularly, of the Lockean claim that legitimate government gains its legitimacy from the consent of the governed. The fullest presentation of that critique is in the essay "Of the Original Contract" (published in 1741), but much of what Hume says there is anticipated in book 3, part 2, chapter 8 ("Of the Source of Allegiance") in the *Treatise* (of 1738), to which I shall therefore also have occasion to refer, and some points made in the *Treatise* are not repeated in "Original Contract."

It is clear that Locke is Hume's prime target. He explicitly cites him at the close of the "Original Contract" essay,[1] but, even if he did not, we could be sure that Locke is his target from the language he uses to describe the view he opposes:

> The one party, by tracing up government to the DEITY, endeavoured to render it so sacred and inviolate, that it must be little less than sacrilege, however tyrannical it may become, to touch or invade it, in the smallest article. The other party, by founding government altogether on the consent of the PEOPLE, suppose that there is a kind of *original contract,* by which the subjects have tacitly reserved the power of resisting their sovereign, whenever they find themselves aggrieved by that authority, with which they have, for certain purposes, voluntarily entrusted him.[2]

> They assert, not only that government in its earliest infancy arose from consent or rather the voluntary acquiescence of the people; but also that, even at present when it has attained its full maturity, it rests on no other foundation. They affirm, that all men are still born equal, and owe allegiance to no prince or government, unless bound by the obligation and sanction of a *promise.* And as no man, without some equivalent, would forego the advantages of his native liberty, and subject himself to the will of another; this promise is always understood to be conditional, and imposes on him no obligation, unless he meet with justice and protection from his sovereign. These advantages the

1 Hume, "Of the Original Contract," p. 372.
2 Ibid., p. 356.

sovereign promises him in return; and if he fail in the execution, he has broken, on his part, the articles of engagement, and has thereby freed his subject from all obligations to allegiance. Such, according to these philosophers, is the foundation of authority in every government, and such the right of resistance possessed by every subject.[3]

Yet it is a grave weakness of Hume's critique that he never once addresses the *argument* on which Locke bases his insistence that consent is a necessary and sufficient condition of governmental legitimacy. The premise of that argument is the principle of self-ownership, or, as Locke puts it, the fact that men are born free, equal, and independent.[4] Hume never assesses either that principle itself or Locke's view that it makes consent necessary and sufficient for governmental legitimacy.

To be sure, Hume knows what the argument is: the passage that I just quoted from the "Original Contract" more or less rehearses it. And he also states it succinctly at: "All men, they say, are born free and equal: Government and superiority can only be established by consent."[5] But he never assesses the premise of the argument as such or investigates whether the conclusion follows from it. He only ever contests the conclusion of the quoted train of thought, or, to be more precise, the half of that conclusion which represents consent as *necessary* for legitimacy (for, as we shall see, he does regard consent as sufficient for legitimacy (see 2 and 10 (ii) below) and that is a serious limitation in his treatment of the view he opposes.

2. Many contractarians say that, although there might never have been an actual *historical* contract, legitimacy is *now* sustained by some sort of consent. Interestingly, it is precisely the existence of a historical contract of which Hume has no doubt:

> When we consider how nearly equal all men are in their bodily force, and even in their mental powers and faculties, till cultivated by education; we must necessarily allow, that nothing but their own consent could, at first, associate them together, and subject them to any authority. The people, if we trace government to its first origin in the woods and deserts, are the source of all power and jurisdiction, and voluntarily, for the sake of peace and order, abandoned their native liberty, and received laws from their equal and companion. . . . A man's natural force consists only in the vigour of his limbs, and the firmness of his courage; which could never subject multitudes to the command of one.

3 Ibid., pp. 358–59.
4 Locke, *Two Treatises of Government*, 2.95, p. 330.
5 Hume, *Treatise*, p. 542.

Nothing but their own consent, and their sense of the advantages resulting from peace and order, could have had that influence.

Yet even this consent was long very imperfect, and could not be the basis of a regular administration. The chieftain, who had probably acquired his influence during the continuance of war, ruled more by persuasion than command; and till he could employ force to reduce the refractory and disobedient, the society could scarcely be said to have attained a state of civil government. No compact or agreement, it is evident, was expressly formed for general submission; an idea far beyond the comprehension of savages.[6]

As that text shows, Hume thinks that Hobbesian reasons of rough factual equality among people ensure that authority was *first* established on the basis of agreement.[7] What Hume thinks absurd is the claim that it *now* owes its legitimacy to consent:

> Though the duty of allegiance be first grafted on the obligation of promises, and be for some time supported by that obligation, yet it quickly takes root of itself, and has an original obligation and authority, independent of all contracts.[8]

That authority, the true basis of the duty of obedience in established society, derives, as we shall see, from its consequences, its benefits to the obedient individuals. But first we must examine Hume's criticism of the Lockean view that authority depends on consent.

3. Hume's anti-Lockean polemic is complex, and I divide my presentation of it into three parts. First, there are arguments turning on what princes and subjects actually think and do in the course of practical affairs, and on what people in general and philosophers in particular have thought about political obligation: Sections 4–7; second, Section 8, and somewhat overlapping with the foregoing, there is a presentation of problems peculiar to the idea of *tacit* consent; and finally (Sections 9–11), and of more philosophical interest than the foregoing, there is a claim that reference to consent introduces what is called a needless "circuit,"[9] since consent binds for exactly the same reason that government is, even setting aside consent, legitimate. That is, we are obliged to do what we have consented to do for a reason which is also a reason for obeying government, whether or not we have consented to government. *It follows that you do*

6   Hume, "Of the Original Contract," pp. 357–58.
7   The text just quoted is utterly unambiguous in the stated respect: no other interpretation of it is possible. Yet it is not easy to reconcile with the much more measured concession of historicity to consent at ibid., p. 362.
8   Hume, *Treatise*, p. 542.
9   Hume, "Of the Original Contract," p. 368.

*not understand why promises themselves bind if you think that they are
necessary to justify obedience.*

4. Hume's first species of objection to the claim that legitimate government rests on consent is that people do not think that it does. He makes
this argument first with respect to what people show, in *practice*, what
they think, and then with respect to what their more *theoretical* views are.
    This train of argument begins:

> We find everywhere princes who claim their subjects as their property, and
> assert their independent right of sovereignty from conquest or succession. We
> find also everywhere subjects who acknowledge this right in their prince, and
> suppose themselves born under obligations of obedience to a certain sover-
> eign, as much as under the ties of reverence and duty to certain parents.[10]

But why may one not object that the princes might be making *invalid*
claims, whose invalidity is not removed by the fact that their (perhaps unreflective) subjects accept them? The point is not that that is plainly true,
but that the facts here adduced by Hume are no argument against it, any
more than slavery is shown to be legitimate by the fact that slaveholders
and slaves believe that it is. Suppose one said, plausibly, that slavery is
legitimate only if it is voluntarily undertaken, for example as the result
of a fair gamble. Would the fact that there is plenty of slavery that comes
from taking captives in war, and that such slavery is *regarded* as legitimate, refute that? Only a historian could think so.
    One may respond similarly to Hume's claim that "Henry IV and Henry
VII . . . had really no title to the throne but a parliamentary election; yet
they never would acknowledge it, lest they should thereby weaken their
authority. Strange, if the only real foundation of all authority be consent and promise."[11] Why couldn't Locke reply: of *course* they wouldn't
acknowledge that basis of their legitimacy, since they wouldn't want to
acknowledge the consequent right of rebellion.
    Anyway, Hume *himself* justifies government and obedience to it on
the ground of the self-interest of subjects, yet it is in fact pretty clear
that many subjects regard themselves as bound independent of their
self-interest, and Hume himself says so. So this whole train of argument
against the consent theory (that people don't think consent binds them)
also applies against his own theory (for people do not, on his own account, think the *utility* of obedience is what binds them).

10   Ibid., p. 359.
11   Ibid., p. 362.

Isn't Hume, in the way he phrases these objections, misconstruing Locke as offering nothing but a theory of how political power comes to be, and sustains itself, whereas Locke is actually offering a theory of what renders political power legitimate when it is legitimate? Isn't Hume confusing Locke's normative *explanandum* with a different, factual, *explanandum*? Phrases like "the foundation of authority"[12] nicely cover both issues, thus facilitating their conflation.

For example: Hume speaks of an artful and successful conqueror, who, backed by an army which is just a minority of the population, succeeds in inducing obedience in everyone, because they have difficulty in communicating with each other in the way necessary to resist him. "Even all those who are the instruments of his usurpation," his very army, that is, "may wish his fall; but, their ignorance of each other's intentions keeps them in awe, and is the sole cause of his security."[13] Locke could reply that he is not discussing the *cause* of the security of government but the *warrant* for its legitimacy.

5. In a moment I shall offer a qualified defense of Hume against the charge that he is confusing Locke's "ought" question with a different "is" question. First, though, I report the answer Hume supplies to his opponent in response to his claim that princes do not wait upon consent and subjects do not think they need to give it. He says the opponent might reply that no one is aware of the needed consent because it was given by ancestors a long time ago.[14] He puts the fancied reply aside by remarking first, and correctly, that Lockeans would not want the consent of the fathers to bind the children; and secondly, by noting that most existing governments began in conquest or usurpation.[15] I say, in response, first, that Locke wouldn't have made this reply to the initial objection, for the very reason which is Hume's first one for rejecting it. As for Hume's second reason for rejecting it, it serves to reinforce the suspicion that he is confusing "is" and "ought." Locke has a complex doctrine of the obligations consequent on usurpation, which Hume simply doesn't address.

6. Hume claims that, when, perchance, government is dissolved, no one waits for the people wisely and peaceably to install a new one. Sensible people hope, e.g., for a general who will take control of the headless, directionless multitude.[16] This, together with other remarks on the *unrealism*

---

12   For example, ibid., p. 362.
13   Ibid., p. 360.
14   Ibid., p. 359.
15   Ibid., p. 360.
16   Ibid., p. 361.

of the demand for consent,[17] suggests to me a reply to the objection that Hume confuses the question of how governments *actually* arise with the question of what makes them arise *legitimately*. Perhaps, to express the suggested defense of Hume weakly, he is running two arguments in tight double harness, one of which escapes the charge that he is engaging in an is/ought fallacy. The fallacious argument confuses factual and normative senses of "authority." The nonfallacious argument goes like this:

(i) The power of government is hardly ever *as a matter of fact* based on consent, and it is almost always impossible that it should be so based.

(ii) But government is always necessary: everyone loses from the insecurity attending its absence.

(iii) Anything from which everyone benefits is legitimate.

(iv) Therefore consent is not the (sole) basis of the legitimacy of actual governments.

That is a good challenge to the claim that legitimacy requires consent and, therefore, indirectly, to the principle of self-ownership, which (*pace* Nozick: see Chapter 3, Section 14, above) appears to restrict legitimacy to consent.

7. Hume's final objection of the first sort (objections, that is, based on what people in fact say and think) to the consent doctrine appears at the end of the "Original Contract" and also in the *Treatise*.[18] It is that not only, as he has already urged, do people show in practice that they do not believe it, but that "new discoveries are not to be expected in these matters" and since no one, until "very lately, ever imagined that government was founded on compact, it is certain that it cannot in general have any such foundation."[19] The doctrine goes not only against the general opinion of mankind but against political philosophy through the ages.

I have several objections to this move:

(i) Its minor premise, that no one has, till recently, thought of this particular doctrine, is false. It has an ancient history, one incident in which Hume himself reports when he says that in the *Crito* Socrates forbore to escape from prison "because he had tacitly promised to obey the laws."[20] The clever remark that Socrates thereby "builds a Tory consequence of passive obedience on a Whig foundation of the original contract" does

17 Ibid., p. 362.
18 Ibid., pp. 771–72, Hume, *Treatise*, pp. 546–47.
19 Hume, "Of the Original Contract," p. 372.
20 Ibid., p. 372.

not spoil the counterexample.[21] And the doctrine is strewn about medieval political theory.[22]

(ii) The major premise of Hume's argument is repugnantly conservative. Now Hume was a conservative, so it's not surprising that he expressed a conservative thought. But that particular thought, Hume's major premise—if it's new, it can't be true—is also just plain stupid, so I don't understand how so clever a thinker could have believed it, or, if he did not believe it, why he put it forward.

(iii) I find Hume's major premise especially mysterious in that the self-ownership idea was not entirely foreign to his own convictions. He affirms a version of it himself, *as* something relatively new, in his *History of England*, and even though he does not affirm it, like Locke, as a matter of natural right, and he attaches to its content a curious condition, his proceedings with the idea show awareness that something that's new *can* be true, and, here, something close to the very thing that he says can't be true because it's new.

The context of Hume's affirmation of a quasi-self-ownership principle is an exposition of his views about economic regulation, which incline toward Smithian laissez-faire: and a laissez-faire economy is, of course, usually thought to be what self-ownership justifies, even if laissez-faire can also have other justifications. Hume was a strong critic of government-endowed monopolies, which were prevalent under the Tudors and Stuarts. He regarded them, and also laws setting prices and restricting interest on loans, as unjustifiably "cramping and restraining commerce."[23] That could be a purely consequentialistic critique of them. But he goes beyond such a critique, though not to unrestrained self-ownership, when he adds that, when the bill abolishing them was passed,

> [i]t was there supposed, that every subject of England had entire power to dispose over his own actions, provided that he did no injury to any of his fellow-subjects, and that no prerogative of the king, no power of any magistrate, nothing but the authority alone of laws, could restrain that unlimited freedom.[24]

And he welcomes the forthcoming "full prosecution of this noble principle."

21   Is it, as Hume says, the "only passage in antiquity" where the idea appears? Note that the supremely intelligent formulation of the *social* contract assigned by Plato to Glaucon in the *Republic* lacks the motif of consent. See Dario Castiglione, "History, Reason, and Experience," p. 97.

22   [At this point in the text the comment is added: "The '*tacit*' part? reconsider."—Ed.]

23   Hume, *History of England*, vol. 2, quoted in Miller, *Hume's Political Thought*, p. 128.

24   Hume, *History of England*, vol. 4, quoted in Miller, *Hume's Political Thought*, pp. 128–29.

Now one cannot on this basis pin on Hume a belief in self-ownership pure and entire, not, of course, because of the qualification about not injuring others, but because of his reference to the authority of the laws, whose content is not here specified. But he does applaud "the noble principle" as an innovation, and it was indeed new, and pretty close to Locke's principle. That being so, why should people not in relatively recent times appreciate its truth and its implications in a way that they had not done so before?

(iv) Consider Hume's own main teaching in moral philosophy, which is that virtue "consists altogether in the possession of mental qualities, useful or agreeable to the person himself or to others." He confesses himself surprised that "any man in so late an age, should find it requisite to prove [it], by elaborate reasoning."[25] How does that consort with the major premise of Hume's final objection, that what's new can't be true? Well, he does say, too, that "in common life these principles are [still] implicitly maintained," but the point remains that he does not seem to regard the silence in the history of moral philosophy with respect to his principle as an argument against it.

Then, going beyond the puzzlement he expresses above, there is the curious culmination of part 1 of the *Enquiry*'s conclusion where Hume says that, reflecting on the fact that it took *him* to establish the principle of his moral philosophy, he falls "back into diffidence and skepticism, and suspect[s] that an hypothesis, so obvious, had it been a true one, would, long ere now, have been received by the unanimous suffrage and consent of mankind."[26] If he's being ironical, he is straightforwardly abandoning his major premise in the final anticontract argument. If he's really serious, then he's flirting with abandonment of his own moral philosophy. The major premise of the argument, in each case, says: moral philosophical claims which are new can't be true. If he's being ironical then he doesn't think it follows from the newness of his own claims that they aren't true, and he can't beat Locke on the head with the relevant major premise. If he's seriously worried, then he *can* beat Locke on the head, but he must also shrug off his own moral philosophy.

8. Hume has, by my count, six objections that are targeted specifically against the notion that legitimate government rests on *tacit* consent.[27] Some are variants, of a clever kind, of the already reviewed arguments which confuse "is" and "ought" (unless they can be rescued in the fashion proposed at 6). I'll present these arguments with minimal commentary,

25 Hume, *Enquiries*, p. 268.
26 Ibid., p. 278.
27 As we saw, Locke doesn't actually rest *government* on *tacit* consent, but just a nonmember's obligation to obey it. Where that makes a difference to Hume's critique, I'll point it out.

since I want to pass on to Hume's philosophically most interesting argument against Locke.

The arguments are:

(1) How can we suppose that subjects *have* tacitly consented when they themselves think that they owe allegiance independent of choice?[28]

(2) Even when they expressly consent to a returning good ruler who unseats a usurping tyrant, they consent *because* they think him legitimate, so his legitimacy cannot, in their view, rest on their consent.[29]

(3) In certain cases, e.g. to prevent depopulation (a Berlin Wall case), it is permissible for a prince to *forbid* subjects to leave the kingdom. Hence his rule can't be legitimated by their voluntary consent to submit to him.[30]

I do want to comment on this argument. First, its conclusion doesn't follow from its premise. That the ruler in that way quite "ravishes," as Hume puts it, their freedom of choice, does not show that his doing so cannot follow a prior consent. Second, the objection shows that Hume read Locke carelessly. For Locke believes a ruler has the right to prohibit subjects from leaving only if they have expressly and not merely tacitly consented to his rule (see Chapter 3, Section 12 above). As you will recall, I criticized aspects of that contrast, but that does not excuse Hume's ignorance of it here.[31]

(4) If anyone really does tacitly consent, it is the settling foreigner. Yet his allegiance, though more voluntary, is not therefore legitimately more qualified than that of native subjects, who, Hume must here be supposing, do not, in general, consent.[32]

(5) If tacit consent were necessary for obedience, then, given that it's givable only at majority age, no one could object to someone rebelling immediately he attained his majority.[33]

(6) A John Bennett–like (see Chapter 3, Section 13(iv)) objection is given. It is that it's wildly unrealistic to suppose, with respect to most subjects, that leaving the country is an option for them. The action of staying is overwhelmingly in their interest. Hence it cannot be taken as a sign of consent.[34]

28 Hume, "Of the Original Contract," p. 363.
29 Ibid., p. 365.
30 Ibid., p. 364.
31 See ibid., p. 363—he is going on here re tacit consent.
32 Ibid., p. 364.
33 Hume, *Treatise*, p. 548.
34 Hume, "Of the Original Contract," p. 363. [An addition is included in brackets at this point, prefaced with the word "reconsider": "Note though, that this would apply to the highway basis but not the private property basis (see Chapter 3, Section 12 above) of

Some of this argumentation against the consent doctrine is suasive, although it grossly ignores the detail of Locke on tacit consent: note, once again, that Hume confuses original contract with tacit consent.[35] And also, this being the anti-Hume point with which I began in Section 1, this train of argumentation does not address Locke's *grounds* for putting forward the consent doctrine.

9. I turn now to Hume's philosophically most interesting argument against Locke's doctrine.

It depends on a distinction between two ranges of duties (and associated virtues) which Hume usually denominates as, respectively, natural and artificial. (But he also, confusingly, uses "natural" in a different sense of duties, where the contrast is not "artificial" but "civil," and in the terms of this latter distinction, some of the duties which are artificial according to the former come out as natural.) A duty which is natural in Hume's narrower and philosophically more interesting use, where "natural" is opposed to artificial, is one that runs with the grain of our natural tendencies, such as the duty of benevolence, which matches the propensity to sympathy with others. Artificial duties, by contrast, go against our "primary instincts," so that they are executed "entirely from a sense of obligation, when we consider the necessities of human society."[36] "Original inclination . . . or instinct, is," in their case, "checked or restrained by a subsequent judgment or observation." Examples of artificial duties are respect for property rights, truthfulness, promise keeping, political obligation, and chastity. The corresponding virtues are dispositions which we do not have by nature or instinct, and of which we have no immediate instinctual approval, and which are, consequently, the fruit of artifice and instruction. Artificial virtues are virtues that require cultivation.

In the *Treatise* Hume adds an important nuancing remark on the relation between artificial duties and the passions, when he avers that the "restraint" which the former impose on the latter is not "*contrary* to" the "passions" as such, "for if so, it could never be entered into or maintained: but it is only contrary to their heedless and impetuous movement." When people act from a sense of justice, "the passions are restrained in their partial and contradictory motions."[37] The good that is done by the sense of justice is that it checks and rechannels potentially destructive passion, but that *is not* true of the virtue of benevolence, which is the

---

construing tacit consent. The sovereign has the right to prohibit (see Chapter 3, Section 13 (iv)) the subject from inheriting property and forswearing its obligations, but he could not have the right to prohibit him from leaving the country if his staying is to be a sign of consent. So, as I said, neither Bennett-condition for consent is satisfied there."—Ed.]

35   See ibid., p. 356, the first paragraph of that work.
36   Ibid., p. 367.
37   Hume, *Treatise*, p. 489.

immediate manifestation of a passion, to wit, benevolence. (This suggests, what Hume elsewhere more explicitly says, that, in acting justly, a person sets aside his short-term in favor of his long-term interest. He thereby fails to note that justice, as he himself depicts it, is more a solution to a collective action or free rider problem than it is to a shortsightedness in my pursuit of my self-interest problem. The metaphor of the vault, to which I'll come below, further suggests that it is in my own ultimate interest for me to be just, rather than simply in all our interests for us all to be just. Cf. Chapter 2, Section 14(i) above.)

An example of a *civil* artificial duty is the duty to obey government: all civil duties will involve that duty in one way or another. Examples of natural (as opposed to *civil* duties) are not only benevolence but also the duties to respect property and keep promises, both of which are, as for Locke, antecedent to government.

Because the natural (= nonartificial) duties run with benevolent instinct, each instance of fulfilling one does some good (unless the agent misconceives his situation), which is not to say, and Hume neither says this nor denies it, that it is good-*maximizing*. It could scarcely be the latter, since instinct could not be so perfectly attuned that it induces discriminating maximizing, but it is nevertheless true that the fulfillment of each duty of benevolence benefits someone. (When Goering acted nicely to Hitler, his act was probably not happiness-maximizing. He should have bumped him off.)

By contrast, some instances of fulfilling artificial duties do no one any good at all, such as not trespassing on someone's land when he would not have been aware of your doing so, and some do *only* harm, such as respecting "riches, inherited from a parent," which "are, in a bad man's hand, the instrument of mischief."[38]

What nevertheless makes artificial duties duties is that the regular practice of fulfilling them is massively productive of good, and—this is the kicker—the practice could not be so retailored as to elide from it its unproductive and destructive instances: it's not feasible to have a rule of respecting property rights or keeping promises *only* when the consequences are beneficial. Self-centered bias makes the required judgments of discrimination unlikely to be correct, and those owed promises and respect for their property would lose the security regular fulfillment of the duty affords.

This fact, that single acts of justice (such as promise keeping and respect for property, though sometimes just the latter) often display no convincing rationale, is part of the case for thinking that the virtue of justice must be artificial: there is nothing natural about such a tendency. And, indeed, single acts of justice can be entirely pointless, when considered apart from the general practice of which they are instances.

---

38   Hume, *Enquiries*, p. 304.

Accordingly, Hume uses the following images to distinguish natural and artificial virtues. The product of benevolence is like

> a wall, built by many hands, which still rises by each stone that is heaped upon it, and receives increase proportional to the diligence and care of each workman.

Justice, by contrast, produces its effects in the manner of

> a vault, where each individual stone would, of itself, fall to the ground; nor is the whole fabric supported but by the mutual assistance and combination of its corresponding parts . . . Whatever is advantageous to two or more persons, if all perform their part; but what loses all advantage if only one perform, can arise from no other principle.[39]

The vault/wall contrast enables us to see that Hume's natural/artificial distinction is yet more subtle than I have thus far indicated. For even if no act of fulfilling an artificial duty produced (as some actually do) evil, and no such act produced (as some do) no good, even, that is, if each such act, like each exercise of natural virtue, produced some good, the distinction between the duties, indicated by the images just described, would remain robust, for individual acts of justice produce all of their good *only* through being instances of a systematic structure of such acts, and that is not so for acts of benevolence.[40]

Once again, Hume seems not to notice that justice may be seen as the solution to a collective action problem, where free riding would be possible for a minority. He unrealistically supposes that free riding is against my long-term interest, that the fridge model,[41] where one case of free riding ruins the system, explicates the structure of justice.[42]

---

39   Ibid., pp. 305–6.

40   See the excellent Hume *Enquiries*, pp. 303–4, for future work. See further Mackie, *Hume's Moral Theory*, pp. 81, 84, 91–92. Mackie says that "[w]hereas Hume's explanation of the artificial duties is essentially sociological, his explanation of the natural virtues is essentially psychological" (p. 5) (though see Mackie, pp. 80–82, 123, for doubt that Hume is right about that). One may agree with Mackie that, while *Humean* justice indeed *seems* noninstinctual, the feature that not all just acts are beneficial doesn't show that it is, since natural selection could well have favored the undiscriminating disposition, if it is so overwhelmingly beneficial on the whole. See further Miller, *Hume's Political Thought*, p. 61, for a claim that a truth about artificial duties connected to their noninstinctuality explains why not every instance of fulfilling them is beneficial. But I'm not sure that Miller is right.

41   [The text here adds "expound it." Cohen probably had in mind the example of a fridge in a shared house where if one person takes another's food, then very soon no one will use the shared fridge.—Ed.]

42   [The text here says: "But see *Treatise*, p. 619 (or maybe elsewhere near the end), where he says that the just man might come a cropper, and also see end of essay called 'The Sceptic.'" It is not clear which passage in the *Treatise* Cohen has in mind. I thank Peter

I have noted two distinct senses in which, for Hume, a duty can be natural or not natural. To complicate matters further, he adds a third sense, in which all duties are natural, because it is natural for members of the human species to cultivate them. Note the following passages:

> To avoid giving offence, I must here observe, that when I deny justice to be a natural virtue, I make use of the word *natural*, only as oppos'd to *artificial*. In another sense of the word; as no principle is more natural than a sense of virtue; so no virtue is more natural than justice. Mankind is an inventive species; and where an invention is so obvious and absolutely necessary, it may as properly be said to be natural as any thing that proceeds immediately from original principles, without the intervention of thought or reflexion. Tho' the rules of justice be artificial, they are not arbitrary. Nor is the expression improper to call them Laws of Nature; if by natural we understand what is natural to any species, or even if we confine it to mean what is inseparable from the species.[43]

> The remedy is not deriv'd from nature but from artifice; or more properly speaking, nature provides a remedy in the judgement and understanding for what is irregular and incommodious in the affections.[44]

> The word natural is commonly taken in so many senses and is of so loose a signification, that it seems vain to dispute whether justice be natural or not. If self-love, if benevolence be natural to man; if reason and forethought be also natural; then may the same epithet be applied to justice, order, fidelity, property, society. . . . In so sagacious an animal, what necessarily arises from the exertion of his intellectual faculties may justly be esteemed natural.[45]

> I have never call'd justice unnatural, but only artificial. *Atque ipsa utilitas justi prope mater & aequi.* Says one of the best moralists of antiquity. *Grotius* and *Pufendorf*, to be consistent, must assert the same.[46]

Millican for pointing out that there are similar or related passages in *Treatise*, pp. 497, 548, and 600, as well as a passage very close to the end of the *Enquiry*, pp. 282–83.—Ed.]

43   Hume, *Treatise*, p. 484.

44   Ibid., p. 489. See also pp. 491–92.

45   Hume, *Enquiries*, p. 307.

46   Grieg, *The Letters of David Hume*, 1:33. I am indebted for this reference to Dario Castiglione, who writes: "[C]learly foreseeing the possibility of the 'invidious constructions' which could be made of his theory, he several times insisted that, although he considered justice to be *artificial*, he did not regard it and its rules as *arbitrary*. Justice, property and the 'natural laws' regulating the distribution of property itself were the products of human belief, forethought and action; but, at the same time, the material circumstances in which they arose and the purposes to which they were institutionally directed implied definite and recognizable ('natural' in one specific sense of the word) patterns of behaviour" ("History, Reason, and Experience," pp. 98–99).

From now on, I shall use "natural" in the sense of the first and most theoretical contrast, where the opposite is "artificial."

10. Now Hume classifies the civil duty of allegiance, what we call *political obligation*, among the artificial duties. It therefore has, in his view, the same foundation as the duties of justice and fidelity (i.e. promise keeping). That foundation is utility, and, in particular, that, beyond a rude level of civilization, society cannot possibly be maintained without the authority of magistrates. Hume infers that

> the obligation to allegiance being of like force and authority with the obligation to fidelity, we gain nothing by resolving the one into the other. The general interests or necessities of society are sufficient to establish both.[47]

According to John Locke, the obligation to honor a freely given consent is necessary and sufficient for the legitimacy of government's commands. But Hume says that the reason we have for keeping promises is also a reason for obeying governments: promises should be kept because society collapses when they are not kept, and society also collapses when government does not function. If promises bind, then government commands bind, for exactly the same reason, and independently of whether or not people have promised to obey. Accordingly, if you think political obligation is *founded* on promising, then you don't know why promises themselves bind.

Comments:

(i) To repeat, briefly, my central anti-Humean point: if, as Locke thinks, we are self-owners, then government cannot have rights over us which we do not give to it, and its foundation therefore cannot be utility, for, if that were its foundation, then legitimate government would not require our consent. So, once again, Hume fails to address Locke's fundamental premise.

(ii) Hume's claim that the obligation of obedience is on all fours with the obligation of promise keeping seems inconsistent with this statement from "Of the Original Contract":

> My intention here is not to exclude the consent of the people from being one just foundation of government. Where it has place, it is surely the best and most sacred of any. I only contend that it has very seldom had place in any degree, and never almost in its full extent; and that, therefore, some other foundation of government must also be admitted.[48]

---

47   Hume, "Of the Original Contract," p. 368. Cf. Hume, *Treatise*, pp. 542–43.
48   Hume, "Of the Original Contract," p. 362.

It is very puzzling that Hume should say this. For if the reason for keeping promises is no stronger than the utilitarian reason for obeying government, then why should consent be the best and most sacred foundation of government? Hume could have said, consistently with the "needless circuit" argument, that a government backed by consent is the *best*-founded government, since it then has two grounds of legitimacy, whose distinctness is not defeated by the fact that each is ultimately a matter of utility.[49] This is consistent, because the circuit argument I'm examining doesn't say that promising *adds* nothing, but that "we gain nothing by *resolving* [the obligation to allegiance] into [the obligation to fidelity]."[50] But the passage I quoted that appears to be inconsistent with the circuit argument says not merely that (a) a government with consent is even better founded than one without it, but that (b) the consent foundation is an especially powerful one. So either Hume, in saying (b), is just loosely expressing (a), or he's saying something inconsistent with the criticism of Locke here under examination.

(iii) The institution of promising of course has beneficial effects, and perhaps it is even true that it exists *because* it has those effects, but I do not think that the obligation to keep promises is, or is *entirely*, founded on those effects. How could *my* obligation to keep this promise to *you* be founded on the good effects in general of the institution? Could it be, as has sometimes been suggested, that I must keep it because otherwise I weaken the institution a little? But we could imagine a rogue case in which by breaking it I strengthen the institution. Then, on the suggested view, I would be *as* obliged to break that promise as I am to keep it in normal cases. And in neither instance is there any robust idea of an obligation to *you*, as opposed to an obligation to the community at large.

Consider lying. Truth telling obviously has good effects. People can go astray when they're misled. But it is utterly implausible to locate the whole badness of lying in its effects, so that there is *nothing* wrong with a lie when I know it will have good effects. The something that is wrong even in such a case is that I *mistreat* you, because I break faith with you, when I lie. *The error in pure consequentialism in general is to suppose that the consequences of an act are its only dimension of assessment. For there is also the question of the type of treatment of another person which the act constitutes.*

And as for lying, so, too, for promising. Indeed, I agree with G. Warnock's *Object of Morality*, which represents promise breaking as a *kind* of lying, and as wrong for the reason that lying is;[51] *and* with Judith

49   See Miller, *Hume's Political Thought*, p. 80.
50   Hume, "Of the Original Contract," p. 368.
51   Warnock, *The Object of Morality*, pp. 96ff.

Thomson, whose similar view is that promise breaking is wrong because it is an instance of giving your word that p, where p is false.[52] Her claim is that by giving you my word that p, whether in expressly promising or in another assertion that deserves that description, you acquire a claim against me that p is true.

Still, even if this is so, even if, more strongly, promise keeping is in no way justified by its effects, *if* Hume is right that government has a *sufficient* justification in its utility, then he still has a challenge to Locke's view that consent is necessary. But the challenge loses its interesting ironical turn, for he can then no longer accuse Locke's argument of running in a pointless "circuit."

(iv) It's a mark of the supposed artificiality of the obligation of promise keeping, for Hume, that it rests upon a convention, or a tacit common understanding. But I doubt that. It is of course a convention that in saying, "I promise," I promise, just as it is a convention that, in saying, "There is a cat on the mat," I say that there is a cat on the mat. But I think that, without any conventional device, I can induce you to believe that I will do A, in order to get you to rely on my doing A, and, moreover, at the same time, to believe that I am inducing you to believe that I will do A in order that you should rely on my doing it. All that being so, I culpably break faith with you if I do not then do A.

Two questions now arise. The first, and less important one, is whether the Gricean act just described qualifies as a promise. The second, more important one, is whether the evil you do by not carrying through in the Gricean case is the same as the evil of breaking a promise. I think it *is* the same, and it then seems to me to follow that the duty of promise keeping, as opposed perhaps (if, that is, the answer to the first question is "no") to the existence of promises proper, does not rest on a convention, and is therefore not justified by what justifies such conventions.

So I reject what Hume says in the following:

When a man says *he promises any thing*, he in effect expresses a *resolution* of performing it; and along with that, by making use of this *form of words*, subjects himself to the penalty of never being trusted again in case of failure. A resolution is the natural act of the mind, which promises express: But were there no more than a resolution in the case, promises wou'd only declare our former motives, and wou'd not create any new motive or obligation. They are the conventions of men, which create a new motive, when experience has taught us, that human affairs wou'd be conducted much more for mutual advantage, were there certain *symbols* or *signs* instituted, by which we might give each other security of our conduct in any particular incident. After these

52 Thomson, *The Realm of Rights*, pp. 302ff.

signs are instituted, whoever uses them is immediately bound by his interest to execute his engagements, and must never expect to be trusted any more, if he refuse to perform what he promis'd.[53]

Tertium datur, beyond a mere resolution of the mind and a practice dependent upon an established convention. The heart of promising, so I have argued, is that it deliberately induces reliance on my word: doing so does not essentially require an established convention, and doing so is evidently more than merely reporting an intention.[54] [55]

(v) Finally, and very vaguely, the Humean criticism of the consent doctrine seems to require that consenting is a kind of promising, whereas in fact it seems not to be such. But even if both those things are true, the resulting objection to Hume might not go to the heart of Hume's criticism, as opposed to petty features of its formulation. This is something I haven't had the time to think properly through, but some of you might be able to make something of it.

Consenting isn't promising because I consent to the action of another person, whereas I promise to perform an action of my own. I can't promise that *another* will do A, unless I mean by that that I'll see to it that he does it, or I am using "promise" to mean nothing more than "assure," as in, I promise you the sun will rise tomorrow: I haven't broken a promise if it doesn't. And if I consent to your doing A, then I can withdraw my consent at any time, though I cannot complain of your having done A before I withdrew it. To be sure, I can give you my consent to something you'll do in future, and that implies a promise not to complain *then*, if you do it. It implies a kind of conditional promise. Perhaps it even is such a promise. But Locke's tacit consenter, whether he is a property-holder or a mere highway-user, can, for Locke, hightail it whenever he likes, so it's unclear to me that there is a promise involved in this case.[56]

11. In the *Treatise*, Hume adds a wrinkle to the criticism set out in 10 above.[57] He claims that, far from government being legitimated by promises, people establish it in order that (what are called in the *Treatise*) the three laws of justice, to wit, security of property, of its transfer, and promise keeping will be enforced, since without government men are too unforesightful to stick to them. He says that the "observance" of promising, there-

53   Hume, *Treatise*, p. 522.
54   [The text at this point includes the note: "(correct foregoing along similar lines)."—Ed.]
55   See Hume, *Treatise*, pp. 516ff.; *Enquiries*, p. 199; Scanlon, "Promises and Practices."
56   [At this point the text includes the comment "The foregoing is ill-considered. If you want to salvage it, study Raz, MF, pp. 82–4." MF is *The Morality of Freedom*.—Ed.]
57   Hume, *Treatise*, p. 543.

fore, "is to be considered an effect . . . of government, and not the obedience to government . . . an effect of the obligation of a promise." The Lockean doctrine, as well as offering a needless circuit, gets things backwards.

I have three comments on that. First, notice, as I've emphasized before, that it is not, for Hume, because of collective action problems that government is needed for observance of the laws of justice. Hume notices them no more than Hobbes consciously did, even at points where they would beautifully support Hume's case. He implausibly puts the need for enforcement entirely down to weakness in perception of the future and weakness of will.

Second, there is here, again (see 4 above), a strong whiff of is/ought confusion.

Third, regarding the last quoted statement: if Hume thinks the first effect excludes the second, then he is wrong. We could institute government by promising partly in order to make the fulfillment of promises *more* secure.[58] [59]

---

58   This passage in Castiglione ("History, Reason, and Experience," p. 102) might induce reconsideration of the above, at least partly because of "exact," near the end:

Hume. . . . tended to invert the relationship between private and public law. The moral obligations dictated by the former are indeed established on the basis of 'natural obligations' (i.e. obligations based on 'natural' motives), and perceived more immediately by reflective beings; but the moral and natural obligations of civil justice, although obviously slower to be formed, in so far as they are intended to reinforce private justice, take precedence over the latter, since they are the condition for the 'laws of nature' to be exactly formulated and have proper enforcement. So, in the case of allegiance and promise-keeping, the latter's 'exact observance is to be consider'd as an effect of the institution of government, and not the obedience to government as an effect of the obligation of a promise'. (*Treatise*, p. 543)

59   [It is clear from notes in the text at this point that Cohen wanted to do more work on Hume on justice, and wished in the future to turn to the discussion of James Griffin, *Well-Being*, pp. 285–86 and fns., and Thomas Reid, *Essays on the Active Powers of the Human Mind*, essay 5, chap. 5, "Whether Justice Be a Natural or an Artificial Virtue," which, Cohen notes, attacks Hume. Also Hume's essays "Of the Origin of Government" and "Of Passive Obedience," as well as Jeremy Waldron, "The Advantages and Difficulties of the Humean Theory of Property," on which Cohen remarks: "Ace on Hume on Property."—Ed.]

Chapter 5

KANT'S ETHICS

Thomas Aquinas held that there were two avenues whereby men could come to possess knowledge, the way of reason, and the way of faith, of faith in revelation. These were exhaustive but not exclusive ways of attaining to true propositions. Exhaustive, because no other source of knowledge was entertained; but not exclusive, because there were matters on which both reason and faith were equipped to pronounce. One of these issues was the existence of God. It was guaranteed both by five proofs, devisable by reason, and by the promptings and attractions of revelation, capacity to appreciate which is conferred on us by God's Grace. Certain issues could be settled by reason(-ing) alone: a classification of natural kinds was preeminent among these. And certain things could only be settled by faith. The beginning of the world in time was one of these. That the world has a beginning in time is given in Genesis: reason is impotent to pronounce on the topic—there is no ground either for assuming it or for denying it. It is important that reason does not *deny* that the world has a beginning in time. For reason cannot teach what faith denies, and vice versa. Reason and faith are always at least compatible, and sometimes they pronounce identically: they can never pronounce oppositely. *Credo quia absurdum* ("I believe it because it is absurd") is not a tenet of the Catholic tradition, but "I believe it although I don't know why it is true" is. Faith is not entitled to contradict reason, but it is entitled to assert that for which no reason can be given.

COMPARISON WITH KANT

Now we know that Kant said explicitly that he "found it necessary to deny knowledge in order to make room for faith."[1] It must also be said that he thought this not only necessary, but possible. He was not deliberately engineering a grand confidence trick. But in saying what I just quoted he was permitting himself an uncharacteristic literary extravagance. For he did not accept, with Aquinas, two distinct faculties,

---

1 Kant, *Critique of Pure Reason* Bxxx, p. 29.

which sometimes pronounced univocally on the same subject matter, but a single faculty, reason, which differentiated itself into two employments, a theoretical one and a practical one. The theoretical use enables you to determine what is true; the practical use enables you to decide what to do. And each use has its pure aspect, guaranteeing the truth of what you say or the validity of what you do on a priori grounds alone, without reference to experience.

Kant assimilates pure reason in its practical employment to faith because it is given the office of pronouncing on matters traditionally within faith's purview. More specifically, pure practical reason (which I shall often refer to without the qualification "pure") proves or grounds or necessitates the belief in the objectivity of the moral law, the freedom of the will, the immortality of the soul, and the existence of God. It is with the first two that we shall be concerned in these lectures, as they are treated in the *Groundwork*, the text for these lectures, the *Second Critique* having the other two as part of its burden.

So: unlike Aquinas, Kant entertains not two faculties, but a single faculty in two employments. Also unlike Aquinas, the two employments never conspire to yield the same conclusion: there is no overlap. But like Aquinas, reason theoretic never contradicts reason practical: indeed, when the former presumes to discuss what turns out to be the proper subject matter of practical reason, it falls into contradiction with itself. It produces antinomies, discrepant conclusions by equally cogent arguments, and it is by showing that and how it does so, in the transcendental dialectic, that Kant is denying knowledge and certifying faith.

WHY TWO EMPLOYMENTS OF A SINGLE FACULTY?

The question now arises, what were Kant's motives, and what did he advance as justifications, for treating the sources of knowledge and of moral behavior not as two separate faculties, but as different employments of a single faculty, reason? The question sounds academic, an appeal for a distinction without a difference. It might be argued that faculties are individuated according to what they secure, according to their uses, so that to talk of two different uses of a single faculty is to talk idly, as though one were to say that it's the same ability, but it does not enable the same thing. But Kant himself placed importance on the identity of the faculty, as is manifest in the section entitled by Paton "The aim of the Groundwork."[2]

2   Kant, *Groundwork of the Metaphysic of Morals* (391), p. 59, p. 57. [Cohen has used H. J. Paton's translation from 1947, as revised in 1958, in the Hutchinson hardback edition, reprinted in 1963. The pagination differs from the later Hutchinson paperback version.

So we must try to answer the question, why must it be one and the same faculty which guides us to correct conclusions in theory and moral behavior in practice?

FIRST REASON

We may hazard that the first, seemingly superficial motive, was to arrogate to morality the prestige which attaches to valid reasoning in matters of theory. Faced with the conclusions of Aquinas, a man might accept those which he attributed to reason and, in consistency, deny the precepts required for governing his behavior toward man and God which stem from faith. Such a man might be accused of deficiency of religious appreciation: he could not be accused of contradicting himself. But if the *content* of faith is given not by faith properly so called, but by reason, albeit in a special exercise, then a man who ever exercised and depended on reason, when recognizing its authority in matters of theory, could not consistently disavow its claims in the domain of practice. A man who was theoretically rational, when pressed by a perverse interlocutor who refused to accept his well-grounded conclusions, would eventually have to say to him: you must accept them, since you are a rational being. To such a man Kant could say, in a moral context, you must accept this imperative, since you are a rational being. To put it in another way, theoretical reason provides the grounds or reasons for making assertions; practical reason the grounds or reasons for proper behavior. It is important for Kant that there be no ineradicable equivocation on "grounds" or "reasons" in these statements, for then a man who reasoned theoretically would be under an obligation, as a rational being, to be moral in practice, on pain of inconsistency. And to say that there is no ineradicable equivocation on "reason" here is to say that we have to do with a single faculty in two employments. "Because you are possessed of reason" is the single final answer both to questions like "Why must I assert causes?" and to questions like "Why must I behave morally?"

A PARADOX IN THE ABOVE

Now it must be admitted that there was a ring of peculiarity in the final rejoinder the theoretically reasoning man presented to his recalcitrant opponent. "Because you are a rational being" is an odd-sounding

---

References are given first, in parentheses, to the standard Academy pagination, then to the hardback, then to the paperback.—Ed.]

reminder, and I suggest that its oddness is not a trivial one, a consequence of its infrequent incidence in discourse. Perhaps the oddness lies
in the following: the perverse reasoner has evinced in his refusal to accept the consequences of valid reasoning that he is *not* in fact rational,
or not willing to be so. And so it is futile at this point to tell him that he
is so or has *resolved* to be so. To use a modern jargon, he may be opting
out of the language-game of valid inference. This paradox has its practical counterpart, in the form that it is pointless to point out to a man
that he is a rational agent unless he is striving to be one in the first place.
This paradox is not solved but only expressed in the closing part of the
Grundlegung. For here we learn that we are in reality noumenal beings,
and that our observable characteristics, our desires and inclinations, are
merely phenomenal, possessed of only apparent reality. We are invited
therefore to eschew the latter, since we are fundamentally rational beings. But since we *are* fundamentally rational beings, as free noumena,
there is no point in telling us to overcome desire—the victory of desire
is only the outward show of some secret *noumenal*, and hence moral,
even holy, doing.

Kant wished to establish that men are obliged to obey the moral law.
The instrument for guaranteeing this is the demonstration that they are
in fact noumena: but this proves too much, for it makes it a certain truth
that they *are* doing their duty, and are not merely *obliged* to be.

A SECOND REASON

This reference to the phenomenon/noumenon distinction leads us to another of Kant's motives for fusing knowledge and faith and making of
them two employments of a single faculty. The noumenal world, or the
thing-in-itself, has its existence confirmed by the exercise of theoretical
reason, though the latter cannot pronounce on its character. Theoretical
reason discovers itself to be possessed of synthetic a priori knowledge, in,
for example, the theorems of geometry. It is held that this can only be the
case if the objects of such knowledge are constructed in modes which are
part of the apparatus of cognition, rather than in modes which appertain
inextricably to them as they are in themselves. In the case of geometry,
the relevant nonexperientially dependent furniture of the mind is the a
priori intuition of space. But since we impose forms, alien to it, on the
world, the world as it is in itself must differ from the world as we experience and know it. So the existence of a world possessed of more secure
reality, unconditioned by our modes of cognition, is proved by theoretical
reason. And though it cannot think *about* it, because to think is to apply
categories, and categories are applicable only to our experience, since

they are our categories, it can nevertheless, Kant says, think it; that's to say, so I opine, it can be rationally assured of its existence.

Theoretical reason not only permits morality, but requires it. Theoretical reason finds itself unable to render a consistent account of the world: to complete its work, reason must issue in another employment, without depending on something extraneous and nonrational, operate in a new manner. For if what complemented theoretical reason were not the same thing used differently, but were rather something like Thomist faith, there would be consistency in human knowledge, but the reliability of reason would be weakened since reason would be required to whirl in antinomies forever. Thomist reason did not contradict itself; it was merely silent. So faith *could* supplement it. But reason is doomed to antinomies only if it misuses itself, and does not issue in a practical use. In other words, morality is construed as practical *reason* not only in order to vest *it* with prestige, but also in order to make good theoretical reason's antinomial debts. Knowledge is denied in order to make room for faith, and faith is established in order to complete the canvas of reason, which cannot allow that it contradicts itself, without placing its pretensions as a faculty in direct jeopardy, as it would if it required something alien to itself to take in its dirty laundry.

OBLIGATION AND MOTIVATION

Another reason why morality is to be identified with practical reason (and here I focus on this phrase, not on two *uses*) stems from a general difficulty perennially confronting moral philosophy, the problem of establishing a connection between the recognition of obligation and the disposition to act as one takes oneself to be obliged to.[3] The problem is the following: if moral precepts are the product of ordinary intellection, of what Kant would call reason in its theoretical employment, then it is hard to see why a man who became apprised of them should feel motivated to obey them. If we accept naturalistic reductions of moral statements, which make them truth-valuable, we lose the characteristically moral force of the statements: they fail to impinge on the will. Mrs. Foot makes value certain but irrelevant. The nonnaturalists, like Hare, have no difficulty in showing how we are disposed to follow the moral precepts we recognize: for the test of recognizing them *is* that we follow them. But now when a man "recognizes" a moral precept, he is no longer, as in the first case, coming to appreciate something antecedently valuable: *he* is *valuing* something, making it valuable. There is no *perception* of obligation. The first attaches morality to the intellect, but cannot account for

---

3 See Frankena, "Obligation and Motivation in Recent Moral Philosophy," for an account of recent views of the subject.

the volitional element in it: the second attaches morality to the will, but cannot satisfy the moral philosopher's demand for rationality in ethics. Thus Hare's "arguments" are of a peculiar kind, where reasons have no autonomous force.

Now if it can be shown that the faculty exercise of which constitutes morality is both will and intellect in one, that's to say, is practical reason, then this problem will be solved. For it is neither mere will, which is blind, nor mere intellect, which is impotent, but a practical employment of intellect, that is, intellectual will. Such an employment is *necessary* to solve the riddle of obligation and motivation. This, I think, is the teaching of the first part of the *Grundlegung*. And how such an employment is *possible*, how pure practical reason (or a categorical imperative) is possible, it is the task of the second half to explain.

The duality of obligation and motivation is present in Kant's ethics. Practical reason is that which discerns the validity of the moral law; but it is also that which inclines us to follow it. (Mrs. Foot: reason discovers; not will, but desire, moves, and that means, for Kant, heteronomy. Mr. Hare: will moves; there is no discovery of reason. Kant wants reason both to discover and to move.) I can put this point otherwise by stressing the double-barreled character of "determined" in Kant's use of sentences like: "That action is good which is determined by the moral law." For the determination of the action by the moral law is both efficient *and* formal. It is efficient in that consciousness of the law causes the action, makes it happen, and formal in that the law makes the action a good action: it is because it satisfies the moral law that the action is good: the moral law is the criterion of its goodness. (On formal and efficient causes: Why was it a bad film? Because Fellini directed it. Because it was dull, repetitious, unimaginative—last has Janus-force. The formal cause explains why something comes under a certain description.) The problem for Kant is to show how it is possible that the mere entertaining of the moral law should incline the entertainer to follow it, to show how reverence for the law is, as he puts it, self-wrought by a rational concept, not dependent on desire. Because he believes that every action phenomenally viewed is a result of desire, he needs a noumenal world to make the categorical imperative possible. But once he has generated this world, the categorical imperative becomes not merely possible, but forever actualized, and he winds up proving too much.

THE ARGUMENT FROM ARGUMENT

The *Grundlegung* is an affair of two arguments, the conclusion of the first being the premise of the second. The first argument, which is characterized as analytical, proceeds to establish what the moral law must be like, whether or *not* there is one, and the answer to this is given in the five principal formulae of the categorical imperative. It also involves establishing the necessary and sufficient condition of the validity of this imperative, which is freedom. The synthetical argument proceeds in the reverse manner, proving the legitimacy of assuming what the analytical argument shows to be required, the validity of asserting the freedom it demands, and deriving the actuality of the moral law from that freedom. Kant believes that to show that man is free is to show that he is under the moral law. To be free just is to be under the law and to be under the law just is to be free. Freedom is not freedom to *choose* between this or that course of action, where one course may be that which instantiates the moral law. Freedom is not a matter of choice at all, for the *choice* is *between freedom* and bondage to desire: if your action is not necessitated by the law, then it is contingent on desire, and therefore unfree. We are not free to choose, but we can choose to be free.[4]

(For Kant, in a certain sense, "can" entails "ought." For I can = I am free = I can cause lawfully = I am autonomous = I am moral.)

Kant thinks, then, that if he has freedom, he has all that he wants and needs, namely morality. From the fact that he thinks this, we can perceive another incentive for making morality an affair of practical reason. For in the second part of the "Third Section," entitled "Freedom must be presupposed as property of the will of all rational beings,"[5] the freedom with which practical reason operates is either derived, or made plain to us by analogy, in fact if not in profession, from the freedom with which theoretical reason operates: Kant says, "We cannot possibly conceive a reason *consciously* receiving a bias from any other quarter, with respect to its judgements, for then the subject would ascribe the determination of its judgements not to its own reason, but to an impulse" (emphasis added).[6] If I am engaged in any piece of ratiocination, say in proving the Pythagorean theorem, then I cannot allow that I reached my conclusion as a result of glands or toilet training, but only as a result of the free operation of my intellect, in obeisance to the laws of geometry. My reasoning is most free when these laws necessitate it. The assumption that they do

---

4   [The text at this point includes the comment "(Sorensonization of Kant)." It could possibly be a reference to Søren Kierkegaard.—Ed.]

5   Kant, *Groundwork of the Metaphysic of Morals* (447–48), pp. 115–16, pp. 109–10.

6   [Cohen has quoted Abbott's translation, Kant, *Fundamental Principles of the Metaphysics of Ethics*, p. 81. Paton's translation reads: "But we cannot possibly conceive of a reason as being consciously directed from outside in regard to its judgements; for in that case the subject would attribute the determination of his power of judgement, not to his reason, but to an impulsion." Kant, *Groundwork of the Metaphysic of Morals* (448), p. 116, p. 109.—Ed.]

must be made by reason, and this assumption will establish morality, if freedom establishes morality and morality is a matter of practical reason. We have to treat ourselves as free when we are theorizing, thinking about what to say: we have to treat our assertions as governed, formally and efficiently (the latter to avoid mere orthe doxa, right opinion), by the dictates of reason. Similarly, if the deliberation which precedes action can be called practical *reason*, then we must treat ourselves as free when we are acting by the dictates of the moral law. If there were no laws of Euclidean geometry, or similar ones, then all reasoning about plane figures would be governed by laws of association: reason would suffer from heteronomy.[7] If there were no laws of morality, then all action would be governed by desires and impulses: we would not be free. These statements appear strained, and I suggest they are because they presuppose an *exclusive* and *exhaustive* distinction between motivation by reason and motivation by desire, this being one of the many dichotomies, whose validity is suspect, which Kant uses.

COMPARISON WITH PETERS

Richard Peters believes in a weaker version of this thesis, in his belief that explanation is either by the rule-following model or causal in character. His is weaker because there is no unique set of rules following which emancipates us from the causal nexus. So if we can cast doubt on his position, we shall a fortiori bring into question the stronger position that action is governed either by desire *or* by a single principle, the moral law.[8]

Peters's doctrine is not primarily a theory of the freedom of the will, but rather of the explanation of human behavior. But from it a position on the former can be extracted, insofar as being free involves, as Kant was sure it did, some sort of independence of the causal nexus. But Peters's conviction that actions are uncaused is not founded on a distinction between phenomenon and noumenon, but on a distinction between cases where causal explanations are in order and cases where they are out of order. He works with a model of man as a rule-following animal. Man's capacity to guide his behavior according to precepts differentiates him from the animals, whose behavior, to use Kant's apt language, may operate *according* to law, that is regularly, but not for the sake of law. If a man is engaged in a given purposive activity, then what he does in

---

7 Compare writing down numbers by association and writing down numbers according to a formula.

8 [As becomes clear from a citation below, Cohen is here discussing Peters's *The Concept of Motivation.*—Ed.]

the course of that engagement is explained, for Peters, by citing the rules governing the activity which the man is following. Thus the purposive activity of chess playing, the moves within that game, are explained by the rules of chess and the agonistic aims of the chess-player. These do not explain the movement of the castle causally, because here the explanans entails the explanandum, and this, as Hume showed, does not hold in causal explanations. Given the rules and the aims, the action follows logically; *that* it follows is not guaranteed by past observations, but a priori. Now if a man makes a move in chess which is either contrary to the rules or in manifest contradiction with the project of victory, a causal explanation of his failure is in order, and this explanation may be a neural story. When the rule-following activity is interrupted, the interruption is to be accounted for by generalizations from experience, and psychological theory. If a man adds 7 and 5 and produces 12, there is no demand for a causal explanation; it would serve no function, since the arithmetizing is intelligible on its face, as an instance of rule following. If he gets 11, then a causal explanation of his slip is wanted and sought. But Peters does not say only this. He does not contend merely that in rule-following behavior causal accounts have no point, as many may agree. It is a stronger sense in which they are out of order. It's not true that they are available but pointless; they are even unavailable. This is not to deny that there is a neural tale behind even the effective performance, where error is absent. But, Peters insists, this tale can only provide necessary, never sufficient, conditions of the action while it provides sufficient conditions in the case of faulty behavior. And the reason why it is not sufficient to explain the action is that it is only sufficient to explain bodily movements, and there is no one-one correlation between actions and bodily movements, enabling you to pass from sufficient accounts of the latter to sufficient accounts of the former.

An example he uses is the action of signing a check. The bodily movement involved in spelling out one's name can be accounted for causally. But a full description of the bodily movement falls short of a description of the action: simply scrawling one's name is not signing a contract, unless this is done in the relevant rule-governed context (in the presence of witnesses, etc.). *This* structure which makes the movement of the hand a case of contract signing, cannot, it is held, be explained causally. What is more, many bodily movements would count as the single action of signing a check, given the appropriate context. And, conversely, the same bodily movement might count as a variety of actions, given a differential in the action-making contexts. From this it is supposed to follow that actions are not liable to causal explanation.

Now something in this is undeniable: if we give a causal explanation of the movement of the check-signer's hand, we have not explained it as a case of check signing. But must the fund of relevant explanatory causes stop here, in the physiology of the signer? I suggest not. I do not see why a causal explanation could not be offered for the presence of the context, and for the adherence to the rules which are observed within it. The rules do not explain causally, but the force of appealing to them depends on a causal explanation, not on merely assuming, with Peters, that man is a rule-following animal. This would dispose of the conclusions drawn from the absence of one-one correlations. The action can be causally explicable, fully and completely, if the entire set of factors is taken into account.[9]

Consider, for further clarification of the position and my criticism of it, the following passage in Peters:

> We can ask why Jones is mean or why he eats fish. The way it would be answered would depend on the context. It might be answered in terms of a rule-following type of explanation like "because he is a Scotsman" or "because he is a Roman Catholic." This would assume some *established set of norms* and a system of training for handing them on. It would be radically different from the explanation "because he is an anal character" or "because he is an oral character." For these explanations would presuppose that Jones is in some way a deviant from the norm of the circle in which he had been trained. It would state special conditions in his upbringing which occasioned this deviation.[10]

For various practical reasons we want to understand the people with whom we have to deal in social life. If I know that all or at least most Scotsmen are parsimonious, I no longer find it an intractable and odd fact that Jones is stingy when I am told that he is a Scotsman. I now know how to deal with him, what roles to play, because I know many things about Scottish behavior. For practical purposes, the explanation can stop here, and I shall be quite satisfied: I shall not crave Humean causes. I think, in general, facts of social life like this tend to insinuate themselves into the so-called logic of language, and it is well to be aware of them to separate depth from superficial grammar, for I think that here we have a typical instance of how an unwillingness to sociologize in an elementary manner leads the philosopher astray, tempts him to think he has discovered a "conceptual truth."

For I might not only be a practical man; I might have less limited cognitive aspirations. I might, for example, be a social scientist. The question,

---

9 [At this point the text contains the comment: "(REPHRASE: TWO POINTS ARE BEING MADE—ONE ABOUT DESCRIPTION, ONE ABOUT EXPLANATION (Does 'Man is a rule-following animal' explain?).)"—Ed.]

10 Peters, *The Concept of Motivation*, pp. 16–17.

"But *why* are Scotsmen parsimonious?" though out of place in most ordinary situations (out of place, irrelevant, but not, surely, without sense) is perfectly posable in a scientific context. And it is impossible to rule out a priori that the explanation for the parsimony Scotsmen manifest in their behavior may lie in a general condition of anality that prevails among them. In short, the causal explanation for the deviation from *one* rule-following model, an instrument Peters accepts, may also serve to account sufficiently for the institution of and adherence to another. All that is wanted is a removal of the blinkers which lead us to focus on our immediate needs in immediate situations.

To return to Kant. One of his dichotomies, and he has many, as will emerge later in these lectures, is that between caused behavior and law-obeying behavior. And his law is not multiform, like Peters's, but sole and single, the moral law. There is only *one* emancipating language game. So if I have succeeded in casting doubt on Peters's liberal dichotomy, I have a fortiori made suspect Kant's more rigid one. And he takes himself to need this dichotomy, because it confers freedom, and because without freedom there can be no moral law.

THE FUNCTION OF REASON

This is a very important section, which seems to lie near the beginning of the *Grundlegung* in sovereign independence of the rest of the work. In reality, however, it is indispensable, providing what may be called the teleological linchpin of the whole argument. For Kant has to do two things: he has to show that there is a course of behavior dictated by reason and by reason alone (this being the way of universalizability), and he has to combat a "so what" response to the exhibition of this course. These are two senses in which he has to show how pure reason may be practical: how it can make a recommendation, and how it can incline the will to follow that recommendation. In the section under consideration, he seeks to show that the whole point and purpose of the existence of reason is to produce moral conduct, so that there would be something incoherent about not using it for that end (like using a knife to bang in a nail and a hammer to spread butter). It will be useful to quote a major portion of the passage:

> In the natural constitution of an organic being—that is, of one contrived for the purpose of life—let us take it as a principle that in it no organ is to be found for any end unless it is also the most appropriate to that end and the best fitted for it. Suppose now that for a being possessed of reason and a will the real purpose of nature were his *preservation*, his *welfare*, or in a word his

happiness. In that case nature would have hit on a very bad arrangement by choosing reason in the creature to carry out this purpose. For all the actions he has to perform with this end in view, and the whole rule of behavior, would have been mapped out for him far more surely by instinct and the end in question could have been maintained far more surely by instinct than it ever can be by reason. If reason should have been imparted to this favoured creature as well it would have had to serve him only for contemplating the happy disposition of his nature, for admiring it, for enjoying it, and for being grateful to its beneficent Cause—not for subjecting his power of appetition to such feeble and defective guidance or for meddling incompetently in the purposes of nature. In a word, nature would have prevented reason from striking out into a practical use and from presuming, with its feeble vision, to think out for itself a plan for happiness and for the means to its attainment. Nature would herself have taken over the choice, not only of ends, but also of means, and would with wise precaution have entrusted both to instinct alone.[11]

A series of critical questions must now be posed. First of all, quite apart from the metaphysical premises about teleology that we are invited to accept, we are faced with a factual assumption the validity of which is far from clear. I refer to Kant's conviction that reason is ill-suited to produce happiness. Certainly *bad* reasoning can lead to misery, but is there not a case for saying that the informed exercise of the rational faculty is the best guide to happiness we have? Now this might be so and it might also be so that reason is to be used for morality; why can't the proper purpose of the knife be to cut *and* to spread? For if reason is not the guide to happiness, then what is? And if Kant replies that it is an unwarranted assumption, that something must be the guide to happiness, then why must something be the guide to morality? Anyway he tells us that happiness is *a* purpose of man.[12] At any rate, Kant doesn't tell us what the guide to happiness is: he says that instinct *could have* secured happiness more easily. He puts this in contrary-to-fact terms: could have secured, rather than can secure. Clearly instinct often leads to ruin, and it is reason which can limit it, and at least prevent extremes of unhappiness—for this it seems to be suited. Again, it would seem that any purpose otherwise achieved might be best achieved by an overridingly powerful instinct. Why not morality then?

Well, Kant is probably right when he elsewhere insists that there is a distinction between doing the right thing (e.g., on instinct), and doing the right thing because it is the right thing, the latter alone being conspicuously moral. So instinct cannot be the basis for moral behavior, not because it

---

11 Kant, *Groundwork of the Metaphysic of Morals* (395), pp. 62–63, pp. 60–61.
12 In the section "classification of imperatives," ibid. (414), p. 83, p. 78.

hasn't *in fact* been designed for that end, but because it couldn't have been. Morality involves consciousness of what you are doing. Therefore, although the teleological argument fails, there is, buried obscurely in it, a valid conceptual point about morality, that it necessarily involves reason in the sense of consciousness, or at least consciousness of a certain kind: and reason includes consciousness.[13] But this is not all Kant wants to say: for he wants reason not only to be necessary for morality, but sufficient for it as well. Kant has another reason why instinct cannot lead to moral behavior, a reason which we may feel loath to accept. It is because for him the moral course is necessarily the one which conflicts with inclination, desire, passion, since these are the phenomenal causes of behavior, and morality must be counterphenomenal. This is why Kant believes that he is most morally admirable who has a rotten soul, but acts against its natural dictates. A naturally benevolent man, he feels, lacks all moral worth. This we shall consider later, when we consider his distinctions.

Apart from all this, there is in the passage an attempt to prove two things, which he scarcely differentiates, but which are clearly separate. The first is that the purpose of reason is morality; the second is that morality is man's highest purpose. The two are conflated in the following: "another and much more worthy purpose of existence, for which, and not for happiness, reason is quite properly designed."[14] And while there is a feeble attempt to prove the former, the latter seems merely to be posited, as if it could ride in on the former's coattails.

That reason cannot provide happiness is an essential conviction for Kant: eventually, in the *Critique of Practical Reason*, it is a dogma required for the practical proof of God's existence, as guarantor of the summum bonum, which is a proper proportioning of virtue and joy. And the point is stressed in the section on "How are imperatives possible?,"[15] where he seems to hold with Hobbes that no man can secure to himself happiness by his own efforts.[16]

---

13 [The typescript at this point uses the term "cs-p." It is not entirely clear what is meant, but it has been assumed that it is an abbreviation for "consciousness."—Ed.]

14 Kant, *Groundwork of the Metaphysic of Morals* (396), p. 64, pp. 61–62.

15 Ibid. (417–20), pp. 84–88, pp. 80–83.

16 Hobbes writes:

The Felicity of this life consisteth not in the repose of a mind satisfied. For there is no such *Finis ultimus* (utmost ayme) nor *Summum Bonum* (greatest Good,) as is spoken of in the books of the old Morall Philosophers. Nor can a man any more live, whose Desires are at an end, than he, whose Senses and Imagination are at a stand. Felicity is a continuall progresse of the desire, from one object to another; the attaining of the former, being still but the way to the latter. The cause whereof is, That the object of mans desires, is not to enjoy once onely, and for one instant of time; but to assure for ever, the way of his future desire. And therefore the voluntary actions, and inclinations

The argument may be reconstructed: you cannot, however much you reason and think, produce happiness for yourself, for you cannot divest yourself of unsettling desires. So why not refuse to heed their proddings anyway, and be moral, for this course is far nobler? And I can show you that it is possible to be so, for you are in truth a noumenal being. This teleological argument is odd in many ways, one being this—that pure practical reason is a noumenal affair beyond our natures, but is said here to be authored by nature.[17]

THE TWO USES OF REASON DISTINGUISHED

I opened these lectures by accounting for Kant's insistence on the unity of the rational faculty in its two employments, theoretical and practical. I now want to treat what he considers to be a significant difference between the two uses, apart from the obvious distinction between providing correct knowledge and leading to proper practice.

In sum, the difference is this: whereas in the first critique he is delimiting the capacities and indicating the dangers of the use of human reason, of the cognitive power of flesh-and-blood creatures such as we at least appear to be, he believes that the second stage, the critique of pure practical reason, is concerned not with human reason, but with reason-as-such, and that the moral law it discovers must be valid for all rational beings. It is no part of the doctrine of the first critique that intellection as such requires the use of categories like cause, substance, etc., but only human intellection, connected as it is with the human forms of intuition, space, and time.

Thus he says in the section entitled "Review of conclusions": "to determine the whole faculty of pure practical reason . . . we must not make its

---

of all men, tend, not only to the procuring, but also to the assuring of a contented life; and differ onely in the way: which ariseth partly from the diversity of passions, in divers men; and partly from the difference of the knowledge, or opinion each one has of the causes, which produce the effect desired.

So that in the first place, I put for a generall inclination of all mankind, a perpetuall and restlesse desire of Power after power, that ceaseth onely on Death. (*Leviathan*, pp. 160–61)

17 [The text at this point reads: "(first Sentence—purpose of organic being is life-conflicts with B)." This refers to the text quoted above: "In the natural constitution of an organic being—that is, of one contrived for the purpose of life—let us take it as a principle that in it no organ is to be found for any end unless it is also the most appropriate to that end and the best fitted for it." The suggestion seems to be that this passage contradicts the idea that morality is man's highest purpose (for the passage suggests that the purpose of organic being is life).—Ed.]

principles dependent on the particular nature of human reason, though in speculative philosophy [i.e. critique of theoretical reason—GAC] this may be permitted, or may even at times be necessary."[18] Of course, he does not deny that in the application of the moral law, the nature of the being to whom it is applied must be taken into account—but it must not be taken into account in deriving it. In fact, there can be no categorical *imperative*, unless issued to a being who is not *only* rational in nature: otherwise there is no need of or sense in commanding him to be rational, since nothing obstructs rationality in him: he is a holy will, of which more below. You can't order someone to do something he *is* doing. But note that it does not follow from his not already doing it that he wants *not* to do it. So it doesn't follow from the possibility of an imperative that there is a desire that conflicts with it.

The difference between the two uses can be put strikingly in the following way: it is precisely that with which theoretical reason is not equipped to treat that practical reason is, and vice versa. Theoretical reason must always deal with experience, slips into antinomies when it reaches beyond it; pure practical reason must never deal with experience in the first instance, but only with the noumenal which lies beyond it: if it bases its judgments on experience, it is implicated in what Kant calls the heteronomy of the will. Nothing in experience has any intrinsic worth, but only value conditioned on its being desired. So to find what is of intrinsic worth, flight beyond experience is necessary.

To put the point in yet another way. The function of theoretical reason is to render an account of experience, of the world as it is for us. From this it follows that its starting point must be that world, with its peculiar character as conditioned by our forms of intuition. But the function of practical reason is to render imperatives indicating the moral course in this world of experience. So these imperatives cannot be drawn from it, since so to draw them would involve a passage from "is" to "ought," and such an "ought," since the passage is impossible, will turn out to be a disguised "is," and, what is more, the "is" of some or other sort of desire.

Consider the following parallel. Kant would say that we cannot know about the thing-in-itself, but we can know about the thing as it presents itself to us. So we must content ourselves with the latter. Might one not say, analogously, we cannot know whether or not there is a moral law, but we do know what, terrestrially, things are like; we know that men have certain desires, and seek to satisfy them—in the absence of access to realities transcending those of our acquaintance, we might as well

---

18 Kant, *Groundwork of the Metaphysic of Morals* (411), p. 79, p. 76. [Note that Cohen is quoting from Abbott's translation, which differs in minor ways from Paton's translation. Kant, *Fundamental Principles of the Metaphysics of Ethics*, p. 34.—Ed.]

content ourselves with building our ethic on these facts of human nature. There may be a good beyond desiring. But so what?

Now this is precisely the parallel Kant refuses to recognize. And it seems to me that he is justified in repudiating it. For there do seem to be admissible questions which adherence to it would forbid to be posed, like, for example, what is the dignity or worth of this desire, this need as opposed to that one, etc.? You say that this is good because you desire it, but is it *really* good? In the absence of answers to these questions, we may well wonder with Nietzsche, who was prepared to give up on mankind, whether our conduct, our justifications for it, have any basis at all. True, you can construct analogous questions in the theoretical realm: you say that you know that striking caused the match to burst into flame, but is this really knowledge? And in a sense, Kant would say it isn't, but so what? It is all we require. But can we be similarly satisfied in the practical sphere? Or is there not an irrepressible yearning to do what is right, in an unqualified sense? Moral skepticism has a force which epistemological skepticism lacks.

To put the point otherwise: to the question about the match, one might respond, yes, it is knowledge, in a conditional sense, but knowledge none the less. But if you admit that what you regard as good is only conditionally so, you seem to have given up the claim that it is good, in a way in which you haven't in the parallel case given up the claim to know. "Conditional" is alienans for good, but not for knowledge.

THE DISTINCTIONS

I now want to list and discuss a series of distinctions, made either explicitly or implicitly in the *Grundlegung*, on the validity of which its doctrine depends. There are twelve such distinctions, cutting the moral realm off from the realm of desire. Each pair must exhaust the range of actions and no member of any pair may apply to an action to which the other member applies. Also, each pair of distinctions must be equivalent in extension and division with every other. They must all cover every action and slice them off at the same point. All the distinctions refer to actions or to some construct of actions. If we symbolize them as A-B, A^1-B^1, A^2-B^2 . . . A^{12}-B^{12}, then we can represent the required relations among them as: A ~B1, A^1 > ~B^1 . . . A^{12} > ~B^{12}, which represents the congruency or similar extension and division of the distinctions. From all this there emerge 90 possible errors in Kant: 24 relating to the exhaustivity and exclusivity of each distinction, 66 to the question of congruency. I think Kant fails on about 40 of the counts (one is enough, because of the equivalences) but I do not propose to exhibit all the failures, since very many of them are so close to one another anyway. What I shall do is explicate each distinction, and challenge only some on one or other of the three counts:

	Non- or Immoral	Moral
1	Contingent	Necessary
2	Hypothetical	Categorical
3	Desire	Will
4	Desire	Duty
5	Purpose	Principle
6	Caused	Free
7	Heteronomous	Autonomous
8	Selfish	Selfless
9	Empirical	A priori
10	Empirical	A priori[19]
11	Phenomenal	Noumenal
12	Particular	Universal

1. Every action is governed either by a necessary or by a contingent law, none by both.
2. Every action is obeying either the categorical imperative or a hypothetical imperative.
3. Every action is either the result of will or the result of desire.
4. Every action is either for duty's sake or to satisfy desire.
5. Every action is either governed by a principle or governed by a purpose.
6. Every action is either free or caused.
7. Every action is either autonomous or heteronomous.
8. Every action is either selfless or selfish.
9. The spring of every action is known either a priori or empirically.
10. The spring of every action is known either a priori or empirically.
11. Every action can at one time be viewed either noumenally or phenomenally.
12. Every action is either universal in nature or particular in nature.

(1) Contingent/Necessary. In the section "The need for pure ethics"[20] Kant tells us that for a law to have moral force it must carry with it absolute necessity. This is to say that it cannot apply to this or that rational being only, but to rational beings as such. So there are laws of action which are valid necessarily for rational beings, and laws which are valid, but contingently, given their particular (12) natures, their purposes (11),

---

19 [As will become apparent, this repetition is deliberate.—Ed.]
20 Kant, *Groundwork of the Metaphysic of Morals* (388), p. 56. p. 54.

their desires (3, 4). The moral law is necessary, indefeasible; laws relating to the satisfaction of our desires or needs are contingent: were our desires or needs to change, they would change. But there is nothing on which the moral law is based, save bare rationality itself. And there cannot be different kinds of bare rationality, or changes of rationality, as there can be different kinds of needs. In sum, all actions are governed either by necessary laws of rational nature, discovered a priori, or by contingent laws which depend on what we are, on our desirous nature, which we discover empirically, but none by both.

(2)[21] Hypothetical/Categorical. All actions can be represented either as fulfilling hypothetical imperatives or as fulfilling *the* categorical imperative, and none can be represented as fulfilling both. Hypothetical imperatives state only what is right for some purpose. The categorical imperative declares an action to be right without reference to any other purpose. If I issue a hypothetical imperative, you may ask of what it enjoins, what is it *good* for? This question is disallowed in the case of the categorical imperative. Following it is not *good for* anything. "What's the Good of following it?" does not apply.

Harking back to the first distinction, the goodness of what it commands does not depend on, is not contingent on, anything else. Now you cannot distinguish between the hypothetical and the categorical by a grammatical criterion alone, by asking whether or not the word "if" has an incidence in the imperative as formulated. The criterion is rather to be sought in how the imperative is backed if challenged, or, strictly, on whether the imperative is backed. Thus, "If something is divine, worship it" is hypothetical in form, whereas "Come here!" is categorical in form. But "If something is divine" gives you no incentive or further reason for worshipping what you should worship; if no backing is offered, then it is categorical, whereas the backing "Otherwise I'll strike you" can be offered for "Come here!" I say *can* be, because the imperative *may* not be backed, although Kant would say that such an imperative unless implicitly backed would never be obeyed. Unless, he believes, you can represent fulfillment of the imperative as satisfying some want of the person to whom it is issued, he will not follow it. The only imperative he will follow which is unbacked by a want is the imperative of duty, the moral law.

So now the criterion looks like being the possible incidence of the phrase "If you want . . . , then . . ." But even this is misleading. For consider the case, "Stand on the right."[22] In appearance this is categorical,

---

21 [The text at this point contains the remark: "[State what I want to do here—distinguish between them contentlessly, so that any imperative might be either.]"—Ed.]

22 Note that such signs commonly appear on escalators on the London underground, to allow those who want to travel more quickly to walk up or down on the left-hand side.

like "Come here." But we know that what it intends is, "If you want to stand, stand on the right." That is, you may walk instead of standing, but if you stand, it must be on the right. But standing on the right isn't something which fulfills my desire to stand or at any rate no better than standing on the left does. So the incidence of "If you want" fails as well.

The criterion which does the work is the following: an imperative is hypothetical if "If you want . . ." can have an incidence in it, not as a condition that makes the imperative applicable (as in the subway case) but as a ground for doing it: you do it *because* of something you want. The hypotheticity resides in the availability of a backing, and the "If you want to stand . . ." does not back in the way that "If you don't want to be struck" backs. The former only states when a categorical imperative is *in order*, when it applies, not *why* it applies.

Fusing 1 and 2, we get: an action is moral if and only if it exhibits a necessary law, and obeys a categorical imperative, and if and only if it does not exhibit a contingent law and does not obey a hypothetical imperative.

Hare: hypothetical imperatives are derivable from indicative minor premises alone. For example: "This acid burns: If you don't want to get burned, don't touch this acid." Hypothetical imperatives are thus reducible to indicatives: "If you touch this acid, you will get burned." This schema is inapplicable to the Tube stairway case. What indicative is "If you stand, stand, on the right," equivalent to? Not clearly, if you don't place yourself on the right, you won't stand. There is no indicative which can have the *force* of an imperative here. And this is what makes it categorical.

To be a nonnaturalist, to hold that you cannot move from "is" to "ought," is to hold that moral rules are imperatives irreducible to indicatives which have the same force.

(3) Desire/Will.[23] All action is either a result of desire or a result of will, of volition, and none is a result of both. This is OK *only* as a capsule formulation, though sometimes Kant will say it whole-hog. Actually will is present in the desire cases as well, but inefficacious will, will untrue to its own free nature, autonomous, in bondage to desire.

The distinction can be rephrased thus: in answer to the question "Why did he do x?" we will *ultimately* rest either at the answer because he desired x, or y, or because he willed x, or y. What you want you cannot will, though you can will a way to get it. You cannot will what you want, because when you want you are driven, unfree, and you only will when free. Conversely, what you will you cannot want, since you will freely, and you want in bondage. Skipping ahead to distinction 11, we see that

---

23   See Kant, *Groundwork of the Metaphysic of Morals* (448), p. 116, p. 109, for support.

Kant is a "wanting determinist," given distinction 6 as well. All action, phenomenally viewed, is caused by desire.[24]

This fusion is perhaps effected by a misconstruction of the propriety of always saying "Because I wanted to" at the end of the chain of explanations of what I did. For this often only means: no further reason, *not* I was spurred by desire. (In other words, we reach the want that is *entailed* by the action, and which therefore cannot explain it.) And that for which no further reason is given, no desire, for example, is freely willed, chosen: but many things are so willed, not merely moral behavior. So here we have one crucial breakdown in the series of equivalences. But continuing the evolution of the position, we now see that either what I do is contingent on a desire which pushes me to fulfill a hypothetical imperative, or will adopting a categorical imperative, in actions necessary in themselves, without further basis.

(4) Desire/Duty. All actions are undertaken either in order to fulfill a desire or in order to fulfill a duty and none for both. Note: this does not exclude the possibility of a dutiful action fulfilling a desire or a hedonic action fulfilling a duty: the exclusivity comes in at the level of "in order to," "for the sake of." This division is not difficult to appreciate, if you have followed what I have said so far. In the section "the exclusion of interest"[25] Kant explicitly says, "In the case of volition from duty all interest [i.e. desire—GAC] is renounced, which is the specific criterion of categorical as distinguished from hypothetical imperatives."[26] In the section "review of the whole argument"[27] he says that unless we are conceived as doing our duty, we must be conceived as subject to the physical law of our wants. So we either submit to desire, follow contingently grounded hypothetical imperatives, or will to do our duty, which is expressed in the categorical imperative, which needs no basis.

Tugendlehre: "A duty is a constraint to an end not gladly adopted."[28] Therefore duty cannot coincide with desire.[29]

(5)[30] Purpose/Principle. This seems a very odd distinction, not as readily assimilable as the rest. In fact it is crucial, as Kant's doctrine of the

---

24   Desire is by nature particular; will is by nature universal, not restricted by a particular passion: so 3 and 12 are connected: and cf. 5.

25   Kant, *Groundwork of the Metaphysic of Morals* (431). (Abbott, p. 59, Paton, pp. 99–100, pp. 93–95.)

26   [Here Cohen quotes the Abbott translation. The corresponding passage in Paton is p. 99, p. 94.—Ed.]

27   Kant, *Groundwork of the Metaphysic of Morals* (437–40), pp. 104–7, pp. 98–101.

28   Kant, *Metaphysical Principles of Virtue* (386), p. 43.

29   See also Kant, *Groundwork of the Metaphysic of Morals* (397–98), pp. 65–66, pp. 63–65.

30   See Sellars, "Thought and Action," pp. 136–39.

unique and original goodness of the good will, which I discuss after the distinctions, is connected with it. For he believes that the goodness of the good will is not contingent on the goodness of the purposes it pursues, but on the principle governing it.[31]

Now in the case of most of Kant's distinctions, their exclusivity seems to be in doubt: it often seems possible to present a counterexample, an action which is describable as *both*, e.g., sought out of desire and done for the sake of duty. But one can at least think of clear cases where one is present and the other absent, where dutiful action goes against desire and desire-driven action conflicts with duty. In the present instance, the prima facie difficulty is far more grave than this. Here it seems that not only are there counterexamples, but that there is not a single positive instance of an action done from principle but without purpose or vice versa. So far from it being an exclusive distinction, we may ask whether we have here any distinction at *all*. For there seems to be no difference between the questions "What was your purpose in Φ-ing?" and "What principle were you following in Φ-ing?" The same answers satisfy each. "My purpose in such situations is to save the women and children first."

But more careful scrutiny reveals that there is a difference here. First, consider what is meant by calling someone "unprincipled." The epithet clearly has condemnatory force. But we are not saying of the condemned that he has no purposes. Nor, even, are we saying that his purposes are bad. But we mean that he observes no limits, no forms, no *principles* in pursuing whatever purposes he has.

Again, when someone makes something "a matter of principle," quite typically he is sealing it off against all considerations of results or consequences: he is not willing to forbear, regardless of what purposes are frustrated in the adherence to his principle. The extreme of this principledness is the dictum "Fiat justitia, pereat mundus."

Now you may say that here he simply has one overriding purpose, and this he calls his principle. A principle is the name we give to a very big purpose. But this is not correct. For the difference between purposes and principles is that whereas the former may be fulfilled, attained, achieved, the latter *cannot* be, but the latter can be observed, adhered to, honored. This is not merely a verbal but a categorial distinction. It's not just if you call a purpose a principle then instead of fulfilling it you have to observe it. The point is that purposes are particular whereas principles are universal in character (to use distinction 12 to elucidate distinction 5). It can be my purpose, but not my principle, to fly to the moon or to eat a sour apple. We can date the times when these purposes are fulfilled. But if it

---

31   [The text at this point contains the remark: "(show how one might plausibly hold former view)."—Ed.]

is my principle *never* to treat a man unjustly, then the principle is always operative, does not mean to be so where it has been obeyed or adhered to: there can never be a time when it has been fulfilled: the principle, unlike the purpose, is universal in its reference. (Contrast "If anything is a man, I will not treat it unjustly" with "If anything is a moon, I will fly to it.")

Of course I can give up my principle, but this is not analogous to arriving on the moon, since I can give up that project before getting there. I've followed that principle all my life: if I say I've fulfilled that purpose all my life I may be asked—why did you repeat yourself so much? Well, I must mean, I've been in the process of fulfilling it all my life. But I am not in the process of following a principle all my life. Purposes aim at realizing *particular* states of affairs, even if these are of a general and temporally extended sort.[32] Principles do not aim at realizing particular states of affairs, because they do not aim at states of affairs, because they do not aim at all: rather they are observed when we are confronted by states of affairs.

Now connected with every principle there is a purpose or purposes and vice versa. If it is my purpose to amass wealth, I should make it a principle to cultivate wealthy friends. (Here we see connection between purposes and hypothetical imperatives.) If I am against drinking on principle, I adopt the purpose of furthering the aims of the temperance league. But *this* connection between principles and purposes doesn't damage Kant. He is distinguishing between actions which originate in principles, even though purposes are adopted in cleaving to the principles; and actions governed by purposes, even though principles are adopted to realize the purposes. In fact, Kant's principle is, "So act . . . ," and from this he distills the purpose of treating particular human beings on particular occasions as ends-in-se.

Why is Kant so committed against purposes and for principles? The reason is that he identifies having purposes with having desires, as is evident from "the formal principle of duty."[33] This is why he rejects all teleological ethics, and is the deontologist supreme. But the equivalence between purposes and desires is questionable. A temptation to equating them lies in the double use of "I want x," which can express either a purpose or a desire. But the way the statement would be verified would be different in each case. For in one sense "I can't want x" without trying to get it: this is the purpose sense. It isn't genuinely my purpose unless I pursue it. But it can be my desire even though I don't try to fulfill it. For I can suppress, restrain my desire: but I can't do this to my purpose—I can

32   [The next line in the text reads: "Principles are universal: doesn't follow *merely* such. (?)" Presumably more work on this thought is indicated here.—Ed.]

33   Kant, *Groundwork of the Metaphysic of Morals* (399–400), pp. 65–66, pp. 67–68.

only give up my purpose. My purpose is directly within my control; my desire is not. But to say the former is to sin against the whole teaching of Kant's ethics. But since he thought purposes were just desires, he had to build the ethics he did.

To summarize: actions either pursue purposes, fulfill desires, by obeying hypothetical imperatives, contingently rooted in our empirical natures: or observe the principle of duty, through an act of will, subscribing to the categorical imperative independent of our empirical natures.

As I suggested, Kant extracts the purpose of moral behavior, expressed in the two formulae of the end-in-itself and the kingdom of ends, from the principle of moral behavior expressed in the universalizability thesis. We are thus enjoined to act in a way which would foster the existence of a kingdom of ends. But it is important to realize just what is involved in "fostering" here. The moral action fosters the kingdom of ends because it is the sort of action which would be performed in it: the more people perform the action, the closer the kingdom of ends is to realization, in the sense that the resulting state of affairs approximates more to what a kingdom of ends is like. But Kant is not certifying actions which would bring about a kingdom of ends but are not themselves instances of the sort of actions undertaken in such a kingdom. By killing, lying, breaking promises, etc., I might help bring about the good society, but I am not permitted to do these things anyway, because they offend against the universalizability principle. There is nothing which falls under his kingdom of ends formula which does not fall under the universalizability formula. So the purpose pursued in moral behavior never takes leave of the principle which generates it.

In his essay "Politics as a Vocation," Max Weber distinguishes between an ethic of ultimate ends and an ethic of responsibility, and I think this division perfectly renders what Kant favors and what he is against.[34] What Weber calls an ethic of ultimate ends I call an ethic of principle. The ethic of ultimate ends is expressed in religious terms thus: "The Christian does rightly and leaves the results to the Lord." Kant explicitly does this, and brings in the Lord to make sure that, in the long haul, good results issue from moral behavior: this is why we *must* believe in God. By contrast the follower of an ethic of responsibility feels he must give an account of the foreseeable results of his actions. In an ethic of ultimate ends, "If an action of good intent leads to bad results, then, in the actor's eyes, not he but the world, or the stupidity of other men, or God's will who made them thus, is responsible for the evil."[35] The believer in an ethic of ultimate ends feels "responsible only for seeing to it that the flame of pure intentions is not quelched: for example the flame of protesting against the injustice of the

34 Weber, "Politics as a Vocation."
35 Ibid., p. 121.

social order [without, GAC, reckoning on the consequences, possibly negative, of such protest]. To rekindle the flame ever anew is the purpose of
his deeds, which are quite irrational when judged in view of their possible
success."[36] Precisely *this* attitude is the fruit of regarding the good will as
the only thing which is good without qualification.

(6) Caused/Free.[37] It is easy to see how this distinction connects with
those which precede it, at any rate on the left-hand side. Causes are contingent, I am caused, *by* desire to adopt a hypothetical imperative, and
purposes are equated with desires. It is less easy to see why caused and
free should be thought exclusive. For Kant *seems* here to be committing
the howler identified by Hume and Ayer: the equation of freedom and
causelessness, which turns freedom into chance and caprice.

Whether he *is* making *this* particular mistake depends on what we
think of the passage "The Concept of Freedom is the Key to explain
autonomy of the will." Here we are told that "the will is a kind of causality belonging to living beings in so far as they are rational, and *freedom*
would be this property of such causality that it can be efficient independent of foreign causes *determining* it."[38] That's to say, will is being
exercised, in truncated form, even when we obey hypothetical imperatives, the truncation stemming from the fact that the exercise of will is
determined by something else, a desire.

Kant goes on to argue that causality involves the notion of law. Thus
freedom, though uncaused, cannot be lawless, and therefore is not to
be identified with caprice. Free will is subject to law, but not to the law
of desire, of *particular* impulses, but to law as such, universal law. The
hatred of the particular, manifest in the Platonic tradition, is here given
prime metaphysical status. Not any particular causal connection, but the
notion of law as such, which is simply universality, is what guides the will
here. But this is only the will guiding itself, in independence of particular
desires. So freedom is connected with the will's autonomy, a formulation
of the categorical imperative. (So act "that the will can regard itself as at
the same time making a universal law by means of its maxim.")[39] Which
brings us to the next distinction.

(7) Heteronomous/Autonomous.[40] In order to explicate this distinction, we can profitably construct an analogy for it, in the realm of intellect.

36 Ibid.
37 [The text at this point contains the remark: "[Reformulate, bringing in will]."—Ed.]
38 [Cohen has quoted Abbott's translation, Kant, *Fundamental Principles of the
Metaphysics of Ethics*, p. 78.—Ed.] Kant, *Groundwork of the Metaphysic of Morals* (97),
p. 104, p. 107.
39 Ibid. (434) p. 101, p. 96.
40 [The text at this point adds a note: '[NB: THIS MATERIAL TO BE INTEGRATED
WITH SUPPLEMENT BELOW].' As no instructions are given about how the integration is
to be managed, the supplementary material is added in complete form below.—Ed.]

What would autonomy as opposed to heteronomy of the intellect be like? The philosopher who springs to mind as urging the autonomy of the intellect is Descartes. For his skeptical project consisted in disabusing himself of all deliverances which came from without his mind, and resting his thought on a truth which depended on his mind alone, namely the *Cogito*. The mind was incapable of denying this truth without denying itself, without denying its own existence. And the force of the proof of the *Cogito* depended on its clarity and distinctness. So this criterion, wrested out of the intellect itself, was made determinative of truth and falsity generally. Had Descartes passively accepted the opinions he subjected to scrutiny, he would have been deep in intellectual heteronomy.

Hume is the epistemological heteronomist par excellence. For with Hume there is no principle which the intellect, just because it is intellect, must accept, on pain of self-denial. All cognition is dependent, contingent, hypothetical, and even *putative categories* of cause and substance are only habits imposed on the mind by experience, not *order* imposed on experience by the mind.

This last remark makes us realize that Kant believed in the autonomy of the intellect as well, in its spontaneous generation of categories. If it fails to apply the categories native to it, it becomes a slave to custom and habit. Here is an interesting instantiation of this claim. If I write down a word or a number, and then perform an operation on it, following rules of grammar or arithmetic, my intellect is functioning actively, autonomously. If I write down a number or word and then put down "whatever comes into my head," if I don't direct my thinking, but simply let myself have thoughts, I will end up with a screed the subconscious origins of which can be traced. Just when I think I am freeing myself from rules, I am actually selling myself into cognitive bondage. So, to return to willing, if I do not opt for the law, which expresses the highest in me, I will not be free, but my behavior will be guided by desire. My will will be heteronomous, acted on from without, not fulfilling its true nature.

To be autonomous is to be subject to a law, but a law of our own making, since it expresses what is essential in us, our rationality. To act heteronomously is to act subject to laws not of our own making, laws which are contingent, laws which cannot be legislated or discovered a priori (see 9 and 10).

The doctrine of autonomy teaches that we are subject to the moral law because we are authors of the moral law. The theory is a metaphysicization of Rousseau's theory of the general will.[41] The idea in Rousseau is that my willing is directed both to particular objects and to objects valid

---

41   [The text at this point continues: "[as Burde's theory is a historicization and Hegel's a metahistoricization of that theory.]" "Burde" is presumably intended to be "Burke."—Ed.]

generally for all who have will. The former exercise is a derogation from the complete nature of will, assimilating it to desire. This is why when the state coerces me to follow laws embodying the general will, it is forcing me to be free. It is keeping me away from the path of heteronomy. This is why punishment is the right of the criminal in Kant: it expresses his true will in opposition to his heteronomous action.

Kant hovers over the distinction between autonomy and heteronomy.[42] But within heteronomy he distinguishes between empirical and rational principles, a distinction which jeopardizes the other sets of distinctions he relies upon. For unless rational principles of heteronomy can be reduced to empirical ones, the structure falls apart. Sometimes he seems to indicate such a reduction: we are attracted, because of our empirical natures, to certain conceptions of reason, not given in experience. But sometimes he insists on a threefold distinction, valid in itself, but out of accord with his other distinctions. For they depend on a rigorous adherence to a disjunction of desire and morality.[43]

Let us examine closely what he says. If the will passes beyond itself and seeks its law in the character of any of its objects, there always results heteronomy. The will does not give itself the law, but it is given by the object in its relation to the will. This relation, *whether* it rests on inclination or on conceptions of reason, admits only of hypothetical imperatives: I ought to do something because I wish for something else, whether by immediate inclination or by any satisfaction indirectly gained through reason (here the rational is assimilated to the empirical).

With empirical principles we are already familiar: they are given by desires. Rational principles, we are told, are built either on the rational conception of perfection as a possible effect, or on the will of God. By calling perfection a "rational conception" Kant means that no instance of it can be found in experience: unlike causation, it is a product of reason, not understanding.

Of empirical principles he says that the universality with which the moral law must hold for all rational beings is lost when its foundation is taken from the particular constitution or circumstances of human nature. The ontological conception of perfection is rejected because it is question-begging (does it include *moral* perfection? which of course we are urged to aim at—but then it is just another name for the moral law).

42   Kant, *Groundwork of the Metaphysic of Morals* (441–45) pp. 108–13, pp. 102–6.

43   [The text at this point continues: "(Perhaps criticism above can be averted: see my remark, p. 100)." This refers to a remark written in Cohen's personal copy of the 1947 edition of Paton's *The Moral Law*, which reads: "Note that heteronomous principles are those proposed by other moral philosophers, not ones actually acted on. This may solve the problem how there can be rational heteronomy (without desire)—there *can* be, in a false doctrine."—Ed.]

The will of God must either be judged to be good, which again is circular, or, if not, then this is a most heinous principle to follow, mere power-worship. I agree with both of these objections: but I cannot see how adopting either perfection or the divine will as a standard involves assent to a hypothetical imperative.

The important thing to remember is that *both* autonomy *and* freedom are connected with universality: Kant calls them reciprocal concepts.[44] So, in part 3, where he proves freedom, he takes himself to be proving the moral law.

(8) Selfish/Selfless

This distinction is the least important of the twelve. I throw it in, as it were, as a bonus. It simply adds to the series of conflations I listed when discussing distinction 6. By then it was clear that, as an empirically examinable being, all my behavior was subject to causation by desire, including my purposive behavior, given the assimilation of pursuing purposes and having desires. I am also a selfish being, since the desires which direct me are not yours but *mine*. Even if I seek to satisfy you, or more grandly, to realize the general welfare, it is only because *I* desire this end that I strive to bring it about:

> Out of love of humanity I am willing to allow that most of our actions may accord with duty; but if we look more closely at our scheming and striving, we everywhere come across the dear self, which is always turning up; and it is on this that the purpose of our actions is based—not on the strict command of duty which would often require self-denial.[45]

So not only is all my behavior governed by desire, but all my desires, viewed carefully, are selfish. This is a new claim, resting perhaps on a failure to distinguish between actions which afford me satisfaction and actions undertaken to afford me satisfaction. I may glow with content after sacrificing myself for you: but I don't necessarily do so in order to feel rosy. In fact, I may make the sacrifice even if I don't want to: but even if I do want to (and Kant would insist that I do) what I want is to help you, not to indirectly help myself.

There is another sense in which behavior is selfish. It is so because it follows from particular aspects of my nature, those aspects which make me specific, the specified, person that I am. This is contrasted with moral action, flowing as it does purely from what is universal, and in this sense selfless, about me, my rationality. My true self is that which transcends my self.

---

44   Kant, *Groundwork of the Metaphysic of Morals* (450), p. 118, p. 111.
45   Ibid. (407), p. 75, p. 72.

Thus there is no contradiction between supporting autonomy and rejecting springs of action which come from my *self*. It is not my empirical self which matters, but that which I have in common with any rational being, namely my reason, of which will is the practical exercise.

(9) and (10) Empirical/A Priori[46]

1. These two distinctions have to be treated together. The point is that Kant thinks he has made one distinction here, whereas actually there are two, however much the required equivalence relations may obtain between them.

2. The essential contention, embodied in the distinction, is that you cannot show the actuality of morality empirically, and so it is necessary to show it a priori (if it can be shown at all). But this vague phrase "actuality of morality" sometimes signifies "the objective validity of the moral law" and at other times "the existence of moral behavior." Clearly the moral law could be objectively valid without there being moral behavior. And conversely, moral behavior might exist, according to the prephilosophic as yet ungrounded but later shown to be sound conception of the moral law,[47] even if the latter were not shown to be sound. But let me show, textually, how two claims are being made, without being clearly differentiated.[48]

3. First let me draw your attention to the section "The need for pure ethics."[49] Here Kant asserts that it is universally admitted that for a law to have moral force it must carry with it absolute necessity: thus, e.g., "Thou shalt not lie" is not valid for men alone, but for all rational beings. From this it follows that the basis of obligation cannot be sought in man's nature and circumstances but a priori in the conceptions of pure reason. This is the nonempirical character of morality in the first sense. Before indicating the other sense (actuality of moral behavior), two objections are in order. First, what Kant takes to be obvious is hardly accepted by every plain man or even by every philosopher. Second, even if it is true that morality must be valid for *all* rational beings, it doesn't follow that its precepts are a *function* of their rationality, or that they can only be discovered a priori.

---

46 [At this point in the text contains the remark "N.B. THIS MATERIAL TO BE INTEGRATED WITH SUPPLEMENT. . . . BELOW'. Once again there are no instructions on how to integrate the material, and so the additional material is simply added as an appendix to this chapter.—Ed.]

47 [At this point the text contains the note: "Expand."—Ed.]

48 The ambiguity treated here is like that involved in "He had no motive for this action": (a) There was, in fact, no (good) reason to do it; (b) He did it for no reason. A skeptic about reasons could say these two things, just as Kant, as skeptic, supposes these two things about apparently moral reasons.

49 Kant, *Groundwork of the Metaphysic of Morals* (388), pp. 54–56, pp. 56–58.

4. At any rate, Kant is saying in the above that our *notion* of duty is not an empirical one. In the section entitled "The use of examples" he says this again, but attaches a totally different significance to it.[50] For here he says that we can never be certain in experience whether a given action flows from pure duty. (We shall not labor the point that we can, in experience, always be certain that it doesn't, since duty must be freely willed, and empirically viewed, action is determined.) To return, he says that we can never, even by the strictest examination, get completely behind the secret springs of action: since when the question is of moral worth, it is not with the actions which we see that we are concerned, but with those inward principles of them which we do not see. Now by "inward principles" Kant either means the phenomena of inner sense, in which case he here contradicts his avowed faith in the subsumability of these under discoverable laws; or he means noumenal activity, in which case, though we indeed discover a priori whether or not duty is being done, the answer is always in the affirmative. In fact I suggest Kant is cheating, confusing the two.

5. Anyhow, in the immediately following section ("Popular philosophy")[51] he says something in flagrant contradiction with the above. For he tells us that the pure conception of duty, the conception of a moral law, exercises on the human heart an influence so much more powerful than all other springs which may be derived from the field of experience, that in the consciousness of its worth, it despises the latter, and can by degrees become their master. How, one may ask, can such a phenomenological history be backed except by appeal to empirical data about human beings, an appeal which is supposed to be useless according to the previous section? How can you know how strong the sense of duty is in experience without looking at experience? In fact, the confusion stems from illegitimately looking at man as a compound of empirical and a priori *parts*, in tension, and saying that the latter element is destined to preponderate. But to transform standpoints, ways of looking at the same thing, into two parts of a single thing, is to commit a very juicy category howler indeed.

6. That Kant is assimilating two distinctions, a criticism separate from those I level at the way he treats each separately, *can best be seen*[52] by attending to the words of Paton, his chief English apologist. In *The Cat-*

---

50   Ibid. (406–9), pp. 73–75, pp. 71–73.

51   Ibid. (409–11), pp. 76–79, pp. 73–75.

52   [Here Cohen includes the following footnote: "No, look at Kant himself, p. 87." Assuming that Cohen is referring to his edition of Paton's *The Moral Law*, there are two marked passages on that page, but the one that corresponds most closely to Paton's remark reads: "[W]e must rather suspect that all imperatives which seem to be categorical may none the less be covertly hypothetical." Kant, *Groundwork of the Metaphysic of Morals* (419), p. 87, p. 82.—Ed.]

egorical Imperative the wily Scot has this to say: "Kant . . . insists that we can in no way establish the categorical imperative by an appeal to experience. He knows too well that seemingly categorical imperatives may conceal a motive of personal interest."[53] Now it is hard to see how a categorical imperative could do any such thing. How can a formula have a motive in it? What is easy to see is how action seemingly obeying a categorical imperative is actually motivated by a personal interest, is actually hypothetically inspired. But whether actions follow categorical imperatives is a question separate from whether there is a categorical imperative. And whereas one can at least plausibly maintain that the latter is not an empirical question, it is hard to see how the former can be anything but an empirical question.

Upshot: you can never be sure someone is moral. So the basis of morality must be *a priori*.

7. The fundamental assimilation at the basis of this confusion is Kant's conflation of psychological hedonism and philosophical hedonism.[54] He wants to reject both and thinks that the latter is implicated in the former: in his phenomenal account of human nature he commits the naturalistic fallacy. So he has to deny both that motivation can be established empirically and that value can be established empirically, but he never sees the difference between the two.[55]

APPENDIX

Kant is making several claims, all of which he subsumes under this distinction, and some of which contradict others.

(1) You cannot argue from an "is" (quite generally—the assertion need not be about somebody's behavior; it might be about human needs, or about conflictless societies) to an "ought."

(2) You cannot argue from a genuine example of moral behavior to the s.m.p.,[56] without a *petitio*.

(3) You can never be sure you are dealing with a genuine example.

(4) All empirical springs are desires—and these can't generate morality in a secure way (sometimes desire may lead to wrongdoing. But actually Kant has in mind a conceptual claim, not a probabilistic one).

53 Paton, *The Categorical Imperative*, p. 127.

54 [The text at this point contains the remark: "Expound each, show how he holds the former."—Ed.]

55 [The text continues here with a short appendix to this section. This is distinct from the supplementary material, referred to above, and included as appendixes below.—Ed.]

56 [Presumably this stands for "the supreme moral principle."—Ed.]

(11) Phenomenal/Noumenal[57]

There remains little further to say about this distinction, which I have referred to in explicating the previous two, and discussed at length in the opening lectures. Its function is to guarantee the remaining distinctions, by showing us a point of view from which the right-hand items are possible.[58] But it defeats itself, by showing that the left-hand items are illusory. In order for it not to be illusory, noumenon and phenomenon would have to be not standpoints, but parts, a way in which Kant sometimes illicitly treats them. He also sometimes (e.g., "the two standpoints")[59] treats them as a question of double membership: I belong to both worlds. But there are not two worlds but one world, conceived as it is in itself on the one hand and only as it appears on the other. In the section at hand he says: "So far as he belongs to the world of sense he finds himself subject to laws of nature (heteronomy); but as belonging to the intelligible world he finds himself under laws which being independent on nature have their foundation not in experience but in reason alone."[60] But he is not allowed to say this, for he makes it look as though I am to opt between sense and reason, whereas the option is not practical, actional, but epistemic.

Descartes, who made body and soul separate substances, found it difficult to account for their apparent interaction. Kant is more Spinozistic, seeing noumenon and phenomenon as modes of existence. It must be asked (1) How can two aspects of a thing interact? (2) Isn't their interaction necessary for there to be a will-inclination battle?[61] (3) Aren't the inclinations the phenomenal appearance of noumenal activity? (4) How can man *qua* noumenon will wrongly? Is he not *qua* noumenon a holy will? Isn't it illicit to say he *has* a moral will and *has* inclinations? (5) Oddly, Kant says (in second of "the two standpoints") that man is *really* a phenomenon in the world of sense as well:[62] this oddness is necessary to give the inclinations power. (Really, they're not on a par.)

But let us suppose that positing noumena behind phenomenal men is not a self-defeating move, and question whether the positing itself is legitimate anyway. Here I refer you to the *Critique of Pure Reason*:

---

57 [The text here adds a comment "To be integrated with Supplement." Once again there are no instructions for how the text is to be integrated, so it is included as an appendix.—Ed.]

58 [The text at this point contains the note: "(Remaining distinctions: analytical part; this: synthetical)."—Ed.]

59 Kant, *Groundwork of the Metaphysic of Morals* (450–453), pp. 118–21, pp. 111–13.

60 [Here Cohen quotes from the Abbott translation. The corresponding Paton translation is ibid. (108–9), p. 120, pp. 112–13.—Ed.]

61 But see ibid. (451–63), pp. 118–31, pp. 116–23: the doctrine is much more complex than is allowed here.

62 Ibid. (115–19), pp. 124–26, pp. 116–18.

If we entitle certain objects, as appearances, sensible entities (phenomena), then since we thus distinguish the mode in which we intuit them from the nature that belongs to them in themselves, it is implied in this distinction that we place the latter, considered in their own nature, although we do not so intuit them, or that we place other possible things, which are not objects of our senses but are thought as objects merely through the understanding [remember early lecture—we can *think* the noumenon, though we cannot think *about* it], in opposition to the former, and that in so doing we entitle them intelligible entities (noumena). The question then arises whether our pure concepts of the understanding have meaning in respect of these latter, and so can be a way of knowing them.[63]

First, note the reference to "other possible *things*," rather than other ways of looking at the same things, or conceiving them. This is the point I've been hammering at all too long, and which I now turn away from.

Now take the last sentence. We know that Kant's answer to this is in the negative, and that proving this answer is what the transcendental dialectic is all about. But since the answer is in the negative, it seems invalid for him to apply to the noumenon the category of plurality, which is the second category of quantity.[64] That is, he can have no ground for asserting a plurality of noumenal persons, but he must if I am to follow the dictates of *my real self*. But even *if* we could permit the use of this category, even if we could allow that the noumenon can be individuated into particulars, it seems unwarranted to make this individuation parasitic on the phenomenal individuation of particular people, which is what he implicitly does. Nor can he say of my noumenal being that it is a substance, as he must if I am to be held responsible for what I do. And finally, though this is an objection to the whole distinction, not just to the use he makes of it in morals, how can noumenal activity *cause* phenomenal appearances? He only evades this issue by saying, obscurely, that it *grounds* them. True, he says, we can't see *how* it causes. But he is sure *that* it causes; yet he can't make sense of this.

I am not suggesting that there is no value in his two standpoints notion. It is beautifully developed by Hampshire, and by D. M. MacKay. And stupidly by Strawson, in Pears.[65] I am only saying that it is impossible

---

63   Kant, *Critique of Pure Reason* B306, pp. 266–67.

64   Ibid. B106, p. 113.

65   [Cohen does not give further references. Strawson is clearly his contribution to a symposium with G. J. Warnock and J. F. Thomson, entitled "Determinism," which is a transcription of a BBC radio discussion. MacKay is most likely to be "On the Logical Indeterminacy of a Free Choice." The Hampshire is harder to pin down. Cohen is most likely to have in mind one or more of Hampshire's books *Thought and Action*, *Spinoza*, and *Freedom of the Individual*.—Ed.]

to see how it can lead to saying that I am obliged to act according to the moral law.

(12) Particular/Universal

This last distinction should by now be sufficiently familiar to warrant no further comment. But to understand it better, I refer you to the section "The categorical imperative."[66] Throughout we have stressed Kant's rejection of particular objects of particular desires. He takes the categorical imperative to be the sole alternative to the former. As the will has been deprived of all particular impulses, there remains nothing but the conformity of its actions to law in general, which alone is to serve the will as a principle, i.e. I am never to act otherwise than so that I could also will that my maxim should become a universal law.

Action is heteronomous when it is an instance of a particular empirical law of desire. The alternative to this is when it is an instance of law-abidingness in general. Distrustful as we are of Kant's assimilations, we might suppose that not all particular maxims are tied to desires, so that one could be moral, in the sense of not merely pursuing interest, without adopting the categorical imperative. In morality we obey a law just because it is a law, without any interest, but it doesn't follow from this that the law we obey is the categorical imperative; it may be quite particular, like: help the needy, which we may not feel called upon to *derive* from the notion of law-as-such. In sum, acting out of respect for law as such is not coterminous with acting out of respect for *the* law, with acting universalizably, and only universalizably.

SUMMARY

The burden of the distinctions can be put succinctly in this manner: the motivation of duty must be distinct from the motivation of desire; but for action to be motivated by desire (1) is for it to be caused (2), to be infected with particular (4) purpose (3), to be heteronomous (5), to be contingently (6) grounded, selfish (7), and an obeying of a hypothetical imperative (2); so duty must be inspired by universal principle, autonomous, categorical, selfless, and free; in *fact* men must treat themselves as free; so they must treat themselves as under the law; and they are entitled so to treat themselves because they are not aware of being otherwise, noumenally speaking. My account has focused on the genesis of the doctrine, not, as is more usual, on its applicability (of universalizability, etc.).

The latent pathology is the uncompromising association of freedom and the moral law. This association also poisons existentialism, in precisely

66   Kant, *Groundwork of the Metaphysic of Morals* (402–3), pp. 69–71, pp. 67–68.

the reverse manner. Here it's not that we're free because there is a law: we're free because there isn't. But "we are free to choose what we value" is ambiguous. It is the basis of the philosophy of total responsibility.

When discussing purpose/principle, I referred to Kant's doctrine that the only thing good simpliciter is the good will. And I said that this was unlike Mill. The point is: goodness is *not* derivable from purpose (purpose, being particular, is associated with desire). In sum, what he wills, not what he wants, decides a man's worth. And if he wills a particular purpose, not principle as such, then he wills heteronomously.[67]

APPENDIX: SUPPLEMENT[68]

DISTINCTION 7

We are concerned now with Kant's seventh distinction, according to which, in every action, the will is either autonomous or heteronomous. "Auto" means "self"; "hetero" means "other"; "nomous" comes from "nomos," which means law. So the difference between autonomy and heteronomy is one between action according to the will's own law or rule or principle and action according to some principle which is other than the principle governing the will, and is derived from some object external to the will.

I began to try to make sense of this difficult doctrine by recommending that we can understand Descartes's project in the *Meditations* as a search for the autonomy of the intellect. The intellect is concerned with discovering truth; the will is concerned with doing what is right. Kant is saying that a will wills rightly only when it wills according to the principle which defines its own nature—what this principle is and why it defines the will's nature I shall explain in a moment. So in the analogy the intellect would discover truth only when it thinks in accordance with its own principles, and does not accept any principles drawn from a source outside the intellect. Typical such sources for Descartes are sense-perception or traditional lore. These are banished, and then we try to see what the intellect can confidently assert without any recourse to them. And it turns out that the only thing which the intellect can assert without recourse to any external evidence is the *Cogito*. And what seems to guarantee the *Cogito* is its clarity and distinctness. So this principle, integral to the

67 [At this point the text continues with the following rough notes: "Connected view that evil man more praiseworthy. (The 'love' of the Gospels is practical, not pathological). A deep antinomy in our moral thinking (contrast with Nietzsche). Contrast rising above environment, above fiendish passion."—Ed.]

68 [It seems likely that this supplement was added when Cohen typed up his lectures in 1999.—Ed.]

functioning of the intellect itself, is the criterion of what can be asserted to be true in all cases: when and only when the intellect alone is functioning, we get clear and distinct ideas.

So to sustain the analogy, we must find a principle which defines the nature of the will in the way that clarity and distinctness define the nature of the intellect, and then, to will rightly, the will must follow this its own principle, just as, to think truly, the intellect must follow its own principle. And just as we determine in the Cartesian case *what* the principle is by asking what guides the intellect when it is acting without the influence of nonintellectual sources on it, we must ask what guides the will when no sources external to it are acting on it. And then we shall know what it is for the will to act according to its own nature.

Now from distinction 3 we know that an action is guided by and only by the will if and only if the will is not guided by any desire in the action it selects. Thus if the will is guided by desire, it is behaving heteronomously. And if it is not guided by desire, it is acting autonomously. But to be guided by desire, we know from distinctions 1 and 6, is for the subject's action to be subjected to some contingent law. But Kant thinks that all actions must take place in accordance with some law. So the will's action must be in accordance with some law but not in accordance with some contingent law, if the will is to be autonomous. But then all that is left is for the will to act in accordance with the notion of law in general; that is to say, the will is autonomous only when it causes an action which could always be willed, by any rational being, by any will, regardless of its desires, in the situation in which the will finds itself. In other words: whenever there is an action, there must be some law which it satisfies. Autonomous action cannot satisfy a particular law, so it must satisfy the law "Act so that . . . rational beings," since any other law is particular.

So to act according to the universalizability principle is to act according to a principle which is the only principle that can govern the will when nothing outside the will is moving it, and so to act according to the universalizability principle is to act autonomously. It is for the will to be subject to a law, but to a law of its own making (this has a pedagogically valuable ambiguity), unlike laws which are contingent on facts about the will's possessor which are independent of the fact that he has a will.

Now the will acts according to principles of heteronomy if its action is spurred not by its own principle but by some object external to it. Now that object may be of two kinds, and so there may be two kinds of principles of heteronomy. The object may be an empirical one, that is, one that we encounter in our experience, and the usual one provided by empirically heteronomous ethics is *happiness*. Or the object may not be found in experience but may be devised by reason, and here the usual one provided is the idea of perfection, whether as something to be achieved—so that I act in such a way that I shall become more perfect—or as something thought to be actual, namely a perfect being, namely God, to whose dictates I submit my will. But in all three cases, the will is bound to its object by desire, the desire to realize happiness, not necessarily my own, or the desire to become perfect, or the desire to follow God's will. In all three cases, so Kant claims, we can obey only a hypothetical imperative: if you will happiness, then you must will this; if you will to be perfect, then you must will this; if you will to follow God's dictates, then you must will this. But the if-clauses of hypothetical imperatives depend on contingent facts about the beings who obey them: thus, in these three heteronomous moralities, we are acting according to contingent, empirical laws, not valid for any rational beings, and hence not moral. The rational principles of heteronomy do not indeed direct us to seek items we have encountered empirically, but they are heteronomous principles because it is only a contingent fact about human beings that by their reason they devise the ideas of perfection and it is a contingent fact about them that they are attracted to these ideas.

Now in addition to rejecting the rational principles of heteronomy, on the grounds that they are heteronomous, Kant has special arguments against any ethic which recommends them. He claims that such ethics must be either circular or inadequate. And their rejection on this basis does not depend on their rejection on the ground that they are heteronomous. The rejection on the ground that they are heteronomous depends on Kant's complex argument that only an autonomous will can be a moral one. The argument that they are circular or inadequate does not depend on that thesis. They are circular if *moral* perfection is built into perfecting myself, or into the notion of God. For then I am not in receipt of a satisfactory answer when I ask what it is to be moral, for to say that it is to aim at perfection will involve saying that it is to aim at being moral, and to say that it is to follow the perfect will of God will involve saying that it is to follow a moral will, and each of these answers is inadequate. We asked the question to find out what morality is, and the answers presuppose that we know what it is. But if the answers are not circular, they must be inadequate, for why should I think myself duty-bound to perfect myself where my perfection does *not* involve moral perfection, but, say, the development of my strength and my talents alone? And why should I think myself duty-bound to obey a God who may not be moral, who may indeed be merely infinitely mighty?

So to build an ethic on seeking happiness, on perfecting oneself, or on obeying God is in each case to adopt heteronomous principles, since they are not derived simply and solely from the nature of the will itself: the will is acting according to a principle outside itself, and this is fatal to acting morally just as thinking according to what sense-experience and tradition suggest is fatal to thinking truly. And in the cases of rational principles, the doctrines are anyway either circular or uninviting when examined carefully.

So if there is such a thing as morality, it is realized when the will is subject to a law of its own making, since it is the only law defining the nature of the will itself, and it is the latter because it is the only law a will can follow when *not* guided from without. But, Kant will later argue, it is clear that to be autonomous, it is to be free. So in the final section of the book he tries to prove that we must believe ourselves to be free. Then he can say that we must take ourselves to be subject to the moral law.

DISTINCTIONS 9 AND 10

Here I want to claim that Kant is making two distinctions, while he thinks he is making one. He is putting forward two theses about what must be discovered *a priori*, or nonempirically, and the two things are different. I shall first explain what these two things are, and how they do differ; then I shall bring evidence to show that Kant in fact confuses them. Then I shall offer a comment on each thesis separately.

I shall begin with an ambiguous statement. Its two interpretations are the two theses which Kant is confusing. The statement: Morality cannot be discovered empirically, so if there is such a thing as morality, it must be discovered *a priori*. But this statement can mean one of two things, and Kant uses it to mean both: one thing it can mean is that "The moral law cannot be discovered empirically" and the other is that "Whether some-one is behaving morally cannot be discovered empirically." Alternatively, the first is, "Assembling observable facts will not enable you to prove the validity of the moral law"—you cannot move from an "is" to an "ought," and "assembling observable facts will not enable you to decide whether someone is behaving morally." Now the objective validity of the moral law might have to be shown a priori, but it would not follow that we would not tell empirically whether anyone is following it. Thus we show a priori that $2 + 2 = 4$, but we can tell empirically whether someone is respecting this truth. Conversely, we might be able to give some sort of utilitarian and hence empirical basis to morality but still be unable to tell whether someone is being moral.

To put this differently. There obviously could be a moral law without there being moral behavior. And there could be moral behavior in the prephilosophic sense without there being a moral law; that is, we might be able to show that *if* there is a moral law it is of such and such a char-acter, while failing to show that there *is* such a law, but succeeding in showing that there is behavior which would be moral if there were such a law.

Now let me point out where Kant asserts each thesis about the a priori character of morality, and then where he manifestly confuses the two theses. First look at the following:

> Every one must admit that a law has to carry with it absolute necessity if it is to be valid morally—valid, that is, as a ground of obligation; that the command "Thou shalt not lie" could not hold merely for men, other rational beings having no obligation to abide by it—and similarly with all other genuine moral laws; that here consequently the ground of obligation must be looked for, not in the nature of man . . . but solely a priori in the concepts of pure reason.[69]

Here he is claiming that we cannot know that there is a moral law or what it is by consulting experience or facts of observation. Now look at the following:

> In actual fact it is absolutely impossible for experience to establish with complete certainty a single case in which the maxim of an action in other respects right has rested solely on moral grounds and on the thought of one's duty. It is indeed at times the case that after the keenest self-examination we find nothing that without the moral motive of duty could have been strong enough to move us to this or that good action and to so great a sacrifice; but we cannot infer from this with certainty that it is not some secret impulse of self-love which has actually, under the mere show of the Idea of duty, been the cause genuinely determining our will. We are pleased to flatter ourselves with the false claim to a nobler motive, but in fact we can never, even by the most strenuous self-examination, get to the bottom of our secret impulses; for when moral value is in question, we are concerned, not with the actions which we see, but with their inner principles, which we cannot see.[70]

Here he is saying, not what he said before, that we cannot base the moral law on observable facts, but something quite different: that we cannot by the keenest observation be certain that a moral action has been performed.

Now why do I say that Kant confuses these separate things, both of which he thinks we cannot discover empirically? It is because in a number of places, for instance in the following, he passes from the premise that one can never be sure that someone is behaving morally to the conclusion that if there is a moral law it must be discovered or proved a priori:

69 Kant, *Groundwork of the Metaphysic of Morals* (389), p. 57, p. 55.
70 Ibid. (407), pp. 74–75, pp. 71–72.

Beyond all doubt, the question "How is the imperative of *morality* possible?" is the only one in need of a solution; for it is in no way hypothetical, and consequently we cannot base the objective necessity which it affirms on any presupposition, as we can with hypothetical imperatives. Only we must never forget here that it is impossible to settle *by an example*, and so empirically, whether there is any imperative of this kind at all: we must rather suspect that all imperatives which seem to be categorical may none the less be covertly hypothetical.[71]

Let me quote from Paton, *The Categorical Imperative*: "Kant . . . insists that we can in no way establish the categorical imperative by an appeal to experience. He knows too well that seemingly categorical imperatives may conceal a motive of personal interest."[72] But my point is that the only thing that can conceal a nonmoral motive is a case where *someone assents to or appears to obey* a categorical imperative. Someone who seems to be acting morally may be acting out of personal interest. But whether an *imperative* is categorical has nothing to do with whether a particular person is truly obeying a categorical imperative. The question whether or not there *is* a categorical imperative is quite independent of the question whether or not anyone ever genuinely obeys one.

Finally, I want to make a point about Kant's thesis that we cannot through experience establish that someone is behaving morally. He constantly speaks as though experience leaves us uncertain whether anyone ever behaves morally. But in fact his philosophical position commits him to saying something stronger than this. He is committed to saying that insofar as we restrict ourselves to what can be observed in experience, we must always conclude about a piece of putatively moral behavior that it is not in fact moral. For Kant thinks that every item in our experience must be represented by us as having a cause discernible in our experience. This is the teaching of *The Critique of Pure Reason*, and it is explicitly extended to cover human behavior, including its overt and covert manifestations.

Now as we shall see shortly, Kant thinks that we can adopt another perspective on the world from the observational one, and hence another perspective on human behavior, which is part of the world. From *that* perspective, he will urge that it is possible to say that we behave morally. (I shall show, however, that, from *that* perspective, we really always must behave morally, so that Kant proves too much.) But he is not entitled to say that he thereby answers in the affirmative a question which experience is unable to answer. He is rather answering in the affirmative a

71   Ibid. (419), pp. 86–87, p. 82.
72   Paton, *The Categorical Imperative*, p. 127.

question which, for Kant, experience must answer in the negative. And this is obviously a less tenable situation than the one he hopes he can be in. In fact, as we shall see, he illicitly transforms two ways of looking at human behavior into two forces operating in human behavior, and he makes the noumenal force occupy the place which he illicitly says we cannot know what occupies it from experience.

DISTINCTION 11[73]

This eleventh distinction is most important. The burden of it is that there is a nonempirical perspective which we can adopt on human beings, and from the view of that perspective the right-hand items, which exist if and only if morality exists, can be asserted to exist. For every action which we examine empirically must turn out to have all and only left-hand side features, and is hence, thus viewed not moral.

I divide my discussion of this important topic into six parts: (1) How Kant establishes the phenomenon/noumenon distinction; (2) Illegitimate ways in which he uses it; (3) Kant's practical proof of freedom; (4) Self-defeating character of appeal to noumenon; (5) How Kant avoids the problem that appeal is self-defeating by treating aspects as parts, and some other difficulties; and (6) Conclusion.

(1)[74]

> One observation is possible without any need for subtle reflexion and, we may assume, can be made by the most ordinary intelligence . . . the observation is this—that all ideas coming to us apart from our own volition (as do those of the senses) enable us to know objects only as they affect ourselves: what they may be in themselves remains unknown. Consequently, ideas of this kind, even with the greatest effort of attention and clarification brought to bear by understanding, serve only for knowledge of *appearances*, never of *things in themselves*. . . . it follows that behind appearances we must admit and assume something else which is not appearance—namely, things in themselves—although since we can never be acquainted with these, but only with the way in which they affect us, we must resign ourselves to the fact that we can never get any nearer to them and can never know what they are in themselves. This must yield us a distinction, however rough, between the sensible world and the intelligible world, the first of which can vary a great deal according to

---

73 [It is apparent from the manuscript that these final pages are more of a draft than the previous discussion, which underwent several revisions. It is included for completeness, as well as for the intrinsic interest of the material.—Ed.]

74 [Here the text contains the remark "Begin by reading pp. 118–9 sidelined. (And explain it.)" The passage is set out above, though no explanation is added.—Ed.]

differences of sensibility in sundry observers while the second, which is its ground, always remains the same.[75]

(2) Now in *The Critique of Pure Reason*, where this doctrine is expounded at much greater length,[76] Kant strenuously insists that we cannot apply what he calls the pure concepts of the understanding to what is noumenal. These are the concepts which are not gained through experience but are used by us when we organize experience. Three of these concepts are plurality, cause, and substance.[77] Thus we are not entitled to speak of a number of things in themselves, or to speak of causal transactions between things in themselves, or between things themselves and appearances, nor may we apply the concept substance to the noumenal, that is, we may not speak of enduring particular things within the noumenal. It's not merely that we can't answer questions like, how many noumenal things are there? Kant thinks he proves that the question cannot even be asked, that plurality cannot be a feature of the world as it is in itself. He thinks he shows that if you ask such a question you can prove contradictory answers to it (in the Transcendental Dialectic).

So an essential feature of the noumenal is that we cannot apply our categories to it. Yet this is precisely what Kant does in the *Grundlegung*. This is plain from the rest of the paragraph which I quoted earlier:

> Even as regards himself—so far as man is acquainted with himself by inner sensation—he cannot claim to know what he is in himself. For since he does not, so to say, make himself, and since he acquires his concept of self not a priori but empirically, it is natural that even about himself he should get information through sense—that is through inner sense—and consequently only through the mere appearance of his own nature and through the way in which his consciousness is affected. Yet beyond this character of himself as a subject made up, as it is, of mere appearances he must suppose there to be something else which is its ground—namely his Ego as this may be constituted in itself: and thus as regards mere perception and the capacity for receiving sensations he must count himself as belonging to the sensible world, but as regards whatever there may be in him of pure activity (whatever comes into consciousness, not through affection of the senses, but immediately) he must count himself as belonging to the intellectual world, of which, however, he knows nothing further.[78]

75   Kant, *Groundwork of the Metaphysic of Morals* (106), pp. 118–19, p. 111.
76   Kant, *Critique of Pure Reason* B306ff., pp. 266 ff.
77   Ibid. B106, p. 113, for the whole list.
78   Kant, *Groundwork of the Metaphysic of Morals* (106–7), pp. 118–19, 111–12.

Notice here that Kant has identified within the noumenal world a noumenal person to correspond to every phenomenal person. But to do this is to chop the noumenal world up into bits, and that is what we are forbidden to do. And even if we are not forbidden to chop the noumenal world into bits, to individuate particulars within it, what is the justification for making the individuation parasitic upon the individuation of particulars in experience? Of course we know *why* Kant does this. He must do it, for he's trying to prove that those beings who seem locked up by desire may in fact be free to behave morally. So they must, each of them separately, be members of the noumenal world. But his doctrine of the noumenal world forbids him even to entertain the idea of its having separate members. And even if that idea could be entertained, it is arbitrary to separate them on the basis of phenomenal divisions, and it is not only arbitrary but contrary to *everything* Kant says re noumenon, since we thereby know things about the noumenon, e.g. that it has so many human beings in it. Again, if those beings are to be capable of moral responsibility, which is precisely what Kant requires, then they must presumably be *substances* which endure through time so that past acts of theirs can be assigned to them in the present. But this talk is also quite illicit.

But in the rest of what I have to say, I ignore these criticisms. Let us pretend that Kant *can* say that each human agent is a noumenal being in reality, and only has desires, etc., in appearance. Let us see what he proposes to do with this conception which we have shown to be insupportable anyway.

(3) You will remember from discussion of autonomy that being moral turned out to be to will autonomously, and willing autonomously was the same as willing freely. Thus if Kant can prove that we are free, he can prove that we are subject to the moral law. Or so he thinks. It is plain that what freedom will prove is not only that we are subject to the moral law, but that we are always obeying it, because of the identities just asserted. This I show next. Then I show how Kant twists the phenomenal/noumenal distinction to avoid this unhappy conclusion. Right now let's see how he proves freedom. Here is the relevant text (with sentence numbers added for reference):

> (1) Now I assert that every being who cannot act except *under the Idea of freedom* is by this alone—from a practical point of view—really free; that is to say, for him all the laws inseparably bound up with freedom are valid just as much as if his will could be pronounced free in itself on grounds valid for theoretical philosophy. (2) And I maintain that to every rational being possessed of a will we must also lend the Idea of freedom as the only one under which he can act. (3) For in such a being we conceive a reason which is practical—that is, which exercises causality in regard to its objects. (4) But

we cannot possibly conceive of a reason as being consciously directed from outside in regard to its judgements; for in that case the subject would attribute the determination of his power of judgement, not to his reason, but to an impulsion. (5) Reason must look upon itself as the author of its own principles independently of alien influences. (6) Therefore as practical reason, or as the will of a rational being, it must be regarded by itself as free; that is, the will of a rational being can be a will of his own only under the Idea of freedom, and such a will must therefore—from a practical point of view—be attributed to all rational beings.[79]

Sentence 1: this is OK. If to be free is to be under the moral law, then if we must take ourselves to be free, we must take ourselves to have moral obligations.

Analogy: suppose you are a doctor treating a number of patients with a serum, but you can't know whether your current supplies of serum will be sufficient. If you assume they will be and they aren't, you have disaster. Then you are practically required to assume it won't. But then you must also assume all the consequences as much as if you knew them. (This is only partly analogous—for here it is *silly* to assume otherwise, whereas in Kant's example, it is inconceivable to assume otherwise.)

2: this is what he is trying to prove.

3: this is OK, this just means we have a will: a will is a causer of actions, even when it is moved by desire. (Notice that here will is practical reason: see early lecture.) So this doesn't beg the question, as it might seem to.

4 and 5: this I have discussed elsewhere.[80] I think it is true but with qualifications as I explain.

6. Contrary to what Paton says in his note, this is quite plainly an inference. Else why the "therefore"? And here I again refer you to the earliest part of these lectures on Kant, where I said that Kant wanted the will to be not separate from reason but a special exercise of it, because otherwise his proof of freedom of the will would not work. The proof is based on the freedom of the organ used in willing, and its freedom is established from its use in thinking. I leave you to assess the validity of the inference.

Let us suppose that this succeeds, that Kant has offered a practical proof of freedom. We have to take ourselves to be free. Now he immediately recognizes that this conflicts with what we know ourselves from experience. So he shows that we can consider ourselves from another point of view, and we have already traced how he does this. Now we *know* nothing about ourselves from that point of view, he says (though we have

---

79   Ibid. (448–49), pp. 115–16, pp. 108–9.
80   Cohen, "Beliefs and Roles," pp. 30–31.

seen that we must know something). But since we know nothing, we are entitled to make suppositions, if we have reason to. And we have a practical proof of freedom, which experience contradicts, and which therefore we are entitled to suppose fulfilled for what we really are.

(4) Now why do I say that making this distinction defeats Kant's purpose? His purpose is to show that though we appear to be able to act morally and hence not to be subject to the moral law, we are nevertheless subject to the moral law, we must nevertheless try to be moral, and we nevertheless, despite what experience tends to show, can succeed. And he says we realize we can be moral when we think of ourselves as members of a noumenal world, for as such members we are free. But this is the only world of which we are really members; therefore we must think of ourselves as really free without qualification—but being moral was, through the formula of autonomy, identified with being free; therefore we *are* moral, and we have nothing to worry about. No matter what we seem to be doing, we are behaving morally, since every phenomenal appearance is an appearance of noumenal activity, and all noumenal activity is free, and therefore moral.

(5) Kant escapes this disastrous consequence of his doctrine by grossest cheating, in two steps. For he gradually transforms these two standpoints we can take on ourselves, from one which is valid and another which is invalid, to two equally valid ones. And finally, he speaks as though we belong to two worlds and then as though we have a noumenal part and a phenomenal part which are in tension, and we behave morally when we favor the noumenal part of ourselves. What he is really doing is making what I appear to be into a part of what I am.

This is manifest from many passages.[81]

What he's trying to do is to produce a sophisticated philosophical doctrine which will carry the burden of a Christian spirit/flesh conflict. But there can be no conflict if the flesh is merely apparent and there can be no condemnation of what appears fleshly if what appears fleshly is really spiritual.[82]

(6) On the identification of freedom and morality. What Kant is saying. What Sartre says.

12TH DISTINCTION: WHAT KANT'S UNIVERSALIZABITY TEST IS NOT

(1) Not rule utilitarianism, for *its* test (if everybody behaved so, consequences would be bad) presupposes independent notion of what is

---

81   See Kant, *Groundwork of the Metaphysic of Morals* (452–53), pp. 120–21, pp. 112–13.

82   See Kant, *Metaphysical Principles of Virtue* (423), p. 84.

good. Kant is *not* saying the universalized state of affairs must not be unwillable.

(2) *Not* Hareianism, for his test is whether you think it right for others. Kant whether you can will others. Also first way of going wrong (logical one) absent in Hare.

(3) Not Golden Rule (a) The Golden Rule is positive—used to generate maxims, not test them. (b) The Golden Rule also eliminates first way of going wrong.

The two ways of going wrong: (a) Logical—associated with perfect duty—transgressions, datable and victims specifiable (promises, lies, breach of contract, severe injury (exception)). (b) Psychological—associated with imperfect duty—not datable—not specifiable. Latitude of choice is given. (Benevolence, due consideration (exception).)

Problems:

(1) What is the right description? The one under which the man acts: But then sincerity tests are required.

(2) Suppose a debt is onerous. Creditor wants to be paid, debtor to escape payment. If each universalizes, conflict remains. (Debtor proposes to pay, creditor to let him off.) Whose perspective rules? Utilitarian solution possible, but it is not a Kantian one.

(3) How can I will that anyone occupy this space? Maxim must be *general*.

(4) Billy Budd type case.[83]

---

83   [Presumably a reference to Peter Winch's famous discussion in "The Universalizability of Moral Judgements."—Ed.]

Chapter 6

HEGEL: MINDS, MASTERS, AND SLAVES

Hegel's writings offer *both* a general conception of reality and of history, to wit, Absolute Idealism, *and* specific, and sometimes brilliant, analyses of particular parts of reality and episodes and tracts of history. Now although the phrasing of his insightful examinations of particular problems about people, their communities, and their lives is usually informed by his general philosophy, we can often delete the heavy-duty philosophical terms that consequently appear within his discussion of particular problems, and concentrate on those claims which Hegel made about those problems that do not, or at least do not *appear* to, presuppose his general philosophy. We can, that is, examine those claims in disconnection from their place within Hegel's comprehensive philosophy, even though *he* might have regarded such a procedure as sheer butchery.[1]

One valuable analysis that we can, to some degree, isolate from the total structure of Hegel's thought is the discussion, in his *Phenomenology of the Spirit*, of Lordship and Bondage or, as it is more often called, the dialectic of the master and the slave. I shall summarize that dialectic below, after reviewing some tenets of Absolute Idealism that help us to see some of the more general philosophical questions with which *Hegel* was concerned in the course of his master/slave discussion. But I preconfess that the least satisfactory aspect of my presentation will be my treatment of the linkage between Hegel's *general* philosophy and this famous master/slave dialectic.

Hegel thought that everything the mind, any mind, experiences is in some sense a product of mind itself. One way of explaining how he arrived at this strange idea is by describing how he responded to the thought of Kant. Kantian philosophy features a set of dualities or oppositions, such as those between freedom and necessity, between the sensibility and the understanding, between the analytic and the synthetic, and between the infinite and the finite. Kant loved dichotomies. But Hegel, by contrast with Kant, abhorred ultimate dichotomies in the scheme of things. He objected to what he called, in his *Lesser Logic*, "the strict 'either-or': for

---

1 These lectures are based on Hegel's *Phenomenology of the Spirit*, trans. Miller, pp. 111–19. They were originally written October 1968, revised January 1998, tidied January 2004.

instance, the world is either finite or infinite; but one of these two it must be." He preferred to say such things as this:

> The soul is neither finite only, nor infinite only; it is really the one just as much as the other, and in that way neither one nor the other.[2]

So Hegel was a great reconciler, a mediator between ideas apparently hostile to one another, and *one way* of entering Hegel's thought is by recollecting a *fundamental* dichotomy in Kant's philosophy, and then exhibiting how Hegel rejected it.

Kant distinguished between the world as it is in itself and the world as it presents itself to us, or, as he put it, the world as it is *for* us, the world as far as our experience of it is concerned. We cannot know the character of the world as it is in itself: its *inherent* character is inaccessible to us. Our knowledge is rooted in and inseparable from our experience, and the content of our experience does not replicate the content of the world, because the features of our mental constitution, which we do not choose, cannot change, and cannot transcend, ensure that the world is presented to us only through the prism of our conception and perception of it. Because our minds contribute to the character of our experience, that experience fails to provide us with an unimpeded view of the experienced world. We are, in particular, capable of experiencing reality only by imposing on it the forms of space and time. Kant thought he proved that spatiotemporality is the mind's, not the world's, contribution to our experience of the world, and the fact that all our experience has

---

2 Hegel, *The Logic of Hegel* (*"The Lesser Logic"*), para. 32, p. 67. Terry Pinkard explains (*Hegel's Phenomenology*, p. 361, fn. 87):

> In his lectures on the history of philosophy, Hegel notes that the modern set of philosophical problems is dominated by a set of oppositions that philosophical theories seek to overcome or to reconcile. He mentions four such oppositions that play a central role in philosophical debate, which, he notes, do not play such a central role in ancient philosophy. They are (1) the *existence* of God and the *concept* of God; (2) the origin of evil, given God's supposed omniscience and omnipotence; (3) freedom and necessity (which itself is divided into problems of freedom versus God's omniscience, freedom versus natural necessity, and efficient versus formal causation); (4) the relation between mind and body. Hegel explains the domination of this kind of oppositional thought in modern philosophy as due to the influence of the Christian religion on the worldview of the moderns. It is with Christianity that these oppositions are either engendered or sharpened so that they become *the* philosophical problems of the culture. Likewise, the Christian promise of reconciliation (*Versöhnung*) is the basis for the philosophical community's belief that some kind of resolution of these problems is the major task of philosophical thought in the modern period. See *Vorlesungen über die Geschichte der Philosophie*, *Werke*, Vol. 20, pp. 66–69.

a spatiotemporal character means, for Kant, that none of it provides us with a portrayal of reality as it really is.

Most contemporary philosophers would argue that Kant's proposition that things as they are in themselves are beyond our grasp is incoherent. They would say that one cannot posit the existence of something one also says one knows absolutely nothing about.[3] They would agree with Kant that the mind shapes its experience, but they would say that it is through that very shaping that we acquire knowledge of *what* we experience. Our intellectual operations are *our way* of gaining purchase on the real world, and it is preposterous to represent the instruments we use to *gain* knowledge as barriers *to* our knowledge, as though the fact that in order to grasp an object I must grasp it in some particular way prevents me from truly grasping it. For most contemporary philosophers, there *is* a world independent of the mind, and the mind's activity is its way of coming to know that world.

Hegel *too* thought that Kant's unknowable thing-in-itself was an untenable notion, and for similar reasons. Hegel said that we cannot claim to know the existence of something we say we know nothing about. He also insisted that, far from being beyond the reach of our thought, the Kantian thing-in-itself is transparently a product of our thought, the product our thought produces by thinking away all the particular determinations of things. That resulting product is nothing but the empty idea of being.

I. 1.

When the Critical Philosophy understands the relation of these three Terms so as to make *Thoughts* intermediary between *Us* and *Things* in such a sense that this intermediary rather excludes us from things than connects us with them, this view may be met by the simple observation that these very things which are supposed to stand beyond ourselves, and beyond the thoughts referring to them, at the opposite extreme, are themselves things of thought, and, as being quite undetermined, are just one such thing (the so-called Thing-in-itself), the product of empty abstraction.[4]

Again:

The Thing-in-itself (and under "thing" is embraced even Mind and God) expresses the object when we leave out of sight all that consciousness makes of it, all

3   Cf. Jerry Fodor, "Cat's Whiskers," p. 17: "If you *really* can't say anything about the world except as it is represented, then one of the things that you can't say is that you can't say anything about the world except as it is represented."

4   Hegel, *Science of Logic*, 1, p. 44.

its emotional aspects, and all specific thoughts of it. It is easy to see what is left—utter abstraction, total emptiness, only described still as an "other-world"—the negative of every image, feeling, and definite thought. Nor does it require much penetration to see that this *caput mortuum* is still only a product of thought, such as accrues when thought is carried on to abstraction unalloyed . . . Hence one can only read with surprise the perpetual remark that we do not know the Thing-in-itself. On the contrary there is nothing we can know so easily.[5]

There is, so to speak, nothing to it.

But Hegel's inference from the supposed incoherence of Kant's position was not the inference which is favored today. As I have indicated in No. 2 in the chart below, both Hegel and our contemporaries agree that there is no unknowable thing-in-itself, where "thing-in-itself" means a thing that subsists utterly independently of consciousness (as opposed to where it means: how things really are, for Hegel certainly thought, as, of course, our contemporaries do, that there is a way that things really are). But our contemporaries conclude that there is a *knowable* thing-in-itself, and Hegel concludes instead that there is *no* thing-in-itself, where that means, once again, a thing that subsists utterly independently of consciousness. According to Hegel everything is, in Kant's terms, for us. In other words, everything exists only in relation to mentality.

Hegel arrived at this conclusion because, unlike our contemporaries, he accepted from Kant the following brief list of candidates for sources of our experience: 1. A world we cannot know. 2. The mind's own operations. He then, unlike Kant, dismissed the first item on the list, and was thereby forced to assert that the entirety of our experience is in some sense produced by mind, by, in fact, an infinite mind of which each of our finite minds is a part, or which manifests itself *as*, or at any rate, *in*, a series of finite minds, one of which each of us has.

I. 2. Philosophical positions of Kant, Hegel, and common sense philosophy (CSP):

		KANT	HEGEL	CSP
1.	There is a thing-in-itself, (that is, a reality independent of consciousness)	YES	NO	YES
2.	There is a thing-in-itself, and it is knowable	NO	NO	YES
3.	There is a thing-in-itself, and it is unknowable	YES	NO	NO
4.	Everything is only for us	NO	YES	NO
5.	We know only what is for us	YES	YES	NO
6.	We know how things really are	NO	YES	YES

5 Hegel, *The Logic of Hegel*, para. 44, p. 67.

REMARKS

1. The three positions set out above are the only (minimally) coherent sets of answers to the six questions. Proof: the answers to the first two questions determine the answers to the remaining four. Now, the second question may be answered yes or no. If its answer is no, then the first question may be answered yes or no. If its answer is yes, then the answer to the first must also be yes. Thus "NO, YES," respectively, is an inconsistent pair of answers to the first two questions. Accordingly, there are only three coherent pairs of answers to the first two questions, to wit, those exhibited above. And since, as already remarked, the answers to the first two determine the answers to the remaining four, the only (minimally) coherent sets of answers to the six questions are the three given above.

2. Hegel and CSP agree in rejecting Kant's answer to 3. It is Hegel's agreement with Kant on 2 which, given his agreement with CSP on 3, determines his differences with CSP on questions 4 and 5.

I. 3. A result of Hegel's response to Kant is that for Hegel all knowledge is self-knowledge. We all commonly distinguish between things we know about ourselves and things we know about external nature. But because he thinks mind constructs the world, Hegel must and does say that our knowledge of nature is really knowledge of ourselves, though it takes philosophizing to make us realize this. It is not immediately evident that all knowledge is self-knowledge, but the distinction between the subjective and the objective worlds disappears under rational scrutiny.

Perhaps we can understand the Hegelian thesis that everything a person experiences is in some sense a product of mentality by considering cases of experience where we might be prepared to say that this is so, that the object of a person's thought is also a product of his thought. Hallucination might be one such case. A writer's deliberations about a character he has invented might be another. A mathematician's work on a problem he has devised might be a third. But we would not say that when I see or think about that chair, I have to do with a creation of mind, whereas Hegel would say that I do. Hegel would not, of course, say that this chair was produced by Jerry Cohen's mind, but by a larger mind, an infinite mind, of which each of our finite minds is a part; or which manifests itself as a series of finite minds. Something transcending me creates the chair, but I am so intimately related to that creative me-transcending thing, to *Geist*, that, in knowing it, what I know is in some sense my own mind.

There is, then, finally no objective world which is not also subjective: all knowledge is knowledge by the subject of the subject, all knowledge is knowledge about the knower, and this is the deep metaphysical reason for the authority of mind over nature to which reference is made in the master/slave dialectic.

Hegel's book *The Phenomenology of Spirit* is, among other things, a narrative of the mind's progressive discovery of the essential unity between it and the objects of its experience. In the least sophisticated forms of our thinking the objects of our thought manifest themselves to us and have the value for us of things *other* than ourselves. This stage is not a misfortune. It is necessary at a certain point for the mind to misperceive as nonself what is actually self, because there are truths we can learn about ourselves only if throughout an initial period our investigations are governed by this error, this false distinction between what investigates and what is investigated. We learn about what appear to us to be independent objects and later discover that the information we acquire is really information about ourselves. Minds at first treat what they experience as something alien, yet it is, in fact, something from which they have confusedly alienated themselves. Eventually they recognize their confusion, reclaim the objects of their experience, and appropriate consciously what was always by right theirs. In the culmination of its journey, spirit "is at home with itself in its own otherness as such":[6] "the external reality which embodies us [that is, in which we are embodied] and on which we depend is fully expressive of us and contains nothing alien."[7]

II. 1. Hegel's dialectic of the master and the slave in the *Phenomenology of Spirit* expounds one stage in the mind's journey toward awareness of its oneness with the objective world, its journey toward complete self-knowledge and complete self-appropriation. The book opens with a consideration of the relation between subject and object in experience and knowledge of an object that is *apparently* independent of the subject, yet securely known by the subject. Hegel argues that the more we scrutinize that relation, the more plain it becomes that the object depends for its features on the subject related to it. The division between subject and object is therefore declared untenable, and we are required to examine modes of reality in which subject and object are fused.

The three modes of consciousness that precede those which fuse subject and object are entitled, successively, "sense-certainty," "perception," and "force and understanding: appearance and the supersensible world." By virtue of the obscurity of the relevant texts, and my own limited

---

6 [This is a quotation from the beginning of chapter 8 ("Absolute Knowledge") of Hegel's *Phenomenology of Spirit*. Cohen slightly altered J. L. Baillie's translation of the passage, by adding "own" before "otherness as such." The original is "in *seinem* Anderssein als solchem bei sich ist." Baillie's translation is published as Hegel *The Phemonenology of Mind*, and the passage occurs on p. 790.—Ed.]

7 Taylor, *Hegel*, p. 148.

telepathic powers, I cannot offer a limpid exposition of these sections of the book. But I can confidently say this much: in each case the pretension of consciousness that it knows a reality other than consciousness itself breaks down. We do not, it turns out, in the first stage, enjoy a secure and stable and incorrigible knowledge of *given* sense-data: Hegel rather modernly claims that we cannot so much as identify a sense-datum without presupposing truths about things that go beyond the content of our immediate consciousness. So we pass to perception, where what we think we know is not an object of sense but indeed an independent thing. But it then emerges that there is plenty of theoretical presupposition in our conception of thinghood: the thing is not, in truth, presented to us in all its independent glory, but manifests itself *as* a thing only under categories that we apply, categories that are refined by natural science, which is the third stage. The "supersensible world" in the name of that stage is the set of forces that scientific understanding posits beyond and in explanation of perceptual appearance.

Thus, if we consider the view of the supposedly external world which mature reflection on it develops, we find that natural science, which is such mature reflection, regards the world's appearances as derivative and misleading, and as produced by forces and laws, which are explanatory constructs of physical theory. But these constructs are not just the objects but also the products of the understanding mind. "Consciousness, in having these constructs as its object, actually has itself for an object. With the realization of this fact, consciousness becomes self-consciousness."[8]

Thus Hegel thinks that the physicist who speaks of discovering, e.g. forces, speaks misleadingly: he really invents them. And there is a certain plausibility in saying that he invents them. Newton did not stumble upon gravitational force as one might stumble upon a stone. But Hegel's conclusion, that the physicist's whole object of study is something invented by him, cannot be sustained. For either there is an *element* of discovery in the invention or there is not. If there is an element of discovery, then in some sense forces are in the world, even if it is also true that they are, in some sense, invented. But even if, to turn to the other possibility, the physicist's forces are truly and wholly invented, the reason *why* the physicist invents them is because they serve to *explain* or at least *order* information about sensory phenomena which cannot themselves be regarded as invented.

In any case, and as I said, such reasonings induce Hegel to embrace the conclusion that subject is not ultimately separate from object, and the associated thesis that all knowledge, all consciousness, is self-knowledge, self-consciousness. So he wants to examine the fusion of subject and object.

8 Soll, *Introduction to Hegel's Metaphysics*, p. 9.

II. 2. Hegel begins with the most primitive instance of that fusion: life, and the vital desires that accompany it, desires, that is, to incorporate seemingly external realities physically, in my being, thus achieving an elemental fusion of object and subject. Note that a living human being is both a natural being and a conscious being, and so, in the idea of life, and of life's impulses and metabolism with the world, the union of nature and spirit might seem to be achieved. As a liver I have as part of me the nature I located outside of me as a perceiver. My *vital* impulses and desires are equally mental and physical. The question: does my hunger belong to my body or to my mind? is not easy to answer. And though Hegel does not himself mention it, we can cite sexuality as a remarkable phenomenon in which the physical and the spiritual are inseparably united. To go in for sex, you need both a body and a mind: you lack specifically sexual desire unless you are both physical and mental.

II. 3. But the unity of subject and object provided by the fact that we are alive, desirous, and physically world-incorporating is inadequate, because the impulses embodying that unity are not finally, not in an ultimate sense, attributable to the subject who has them. According to Hegel, and, later, and following him, Sartre, a person can disengage herself from her drives and desires, repress or disown her impulses: she can deny the part of herself which is merely natural. Insofar, moreover, as I do act on a desire, it is only because I endorse it. It is not fully my desire; it presents itself as external to me save insofar as I take it up and give it the value of a project.

What I cannot disown are my thoughts. I can disaffiliate myself from my desires, and treat them as things. I can renounce a desire, and the desire may persist even though it is renounced. I can think of a desire I have as something alien which I shall fight against. But I cannot relate myself in this fashion to, I cannot disaffiliate myself from, for example, one of my beliefs. Either I am committed to my beliefs, and a whole range of propositional attitudes, or I do not have them. When, therefore, I reflect about what I think, I am reflecting about what I am. I am coming to know myself, and *what* I am coming to know is the same as the knower who is coming to know. Both are me.

II. 4. So now (though it's not so clear *why*) Hegel wants to focus on transactions not between the mind and external nature or between the mind and the physical nature to which it is attached but between the mind and itself. But Hegel announces that he will expound how consciousness seizes itself by telling a story about *two* consciousnesses, two people who are interested in self-knowledge, and what happens when they meet one another. Consciousness confronts itself, in the first instance, in another consciousness that confronts it. A person can be fully conscious of himself, can be in full and secure possession of himself, only by virtue of being recognized by another person: I become an object for myself through being an object for the other person. "Self-consciousness exists in and for itself when, and by the fact that, it so exists for another; that is, it exists only in being acknowledged."[9] If I am to know myself, another must know me, so that I can recognize myself in and through his recognition of me.

II. 5. But the transaction between me and him must be absolutely reciprocal. He cannot recognize me unless he is himself recognized. Therefore only if I give the other man my recognition can he recognize me and thus enable me to recognize myself. My recognition of him presupposes his recognition of me, and vice versa. What is required is an exchange of recognitions between us, in which our awarenesses of ourselves and of one another, all four awarenesses, grow together.

Why does Hegel demand this reciprocity, for true recognition (Anerkennung)? I think it becomes plain when we grasp that to recognize something, here, is not the merely epistemological matter of realizing that you have encountered it before: you don't, in the relevant sense, recognize a rock. It is, rather, a matter of acknowledging it as possessing a certain standing, or value, as when a state recognizes another state, or as when a person demands recognition from a contemning person who knows all too well that she exists, that she is there. To recognize here, is to acknowledge the value of, and four such acknowledgments are in question:

    a I acknowledge value in him
    b I perceive value in myself
    c He acknowledges value in me
    d He perceives value in himself.

We shall see that any one of a, b, c, or d entails the other three if we introduce two plausible principles: (1) I cannot attribute worth to another person unless I think I have some worth. For if I don't think I do, I can't think that I have the right to valorize him, or, indeed, though it's not immediately to the point here, to devalorize him, to depreciate him.[10] (2) I cannot feel worthy, perceive value in myself, unless I think another thinks me valuable, unless, that is to say, another confers value on me.

9 Hegel, *Phenomenology of Spirit*, para. 178, p. 520
10 Cf. Nietzsche: "Whoever despises himself still respects himself as one who despises." *Beyond Good and Evil*, p. 81. Cf. the rabbi: "Look who's talking."

Now if we take two people as forming a whole society for the purposes of recognition, then from these principles it readily follows that the
four "awarenesses" all presuppose one another, along the following endless and beginningless entailment-chain: a entails b (by (1)) which entails
c (by (2)) which entails d (by (1)) which entails a (by (2)). . . . [11]

This mutual dependence might be thought to necessitate that the per-
ceptions and conferrings grow gradually. For it might be thought that
there is otherwise a threat of circularity here. Maybe incomplete versions of a, b, c, and d are not as mutually dependent as the full-blown
versions are. [12]

II. 6. Now, instead of examining the relations between these four awarenesses Hegel imposes a second modification on the proceedings. (The
first modification was to present self-consciousness's possession of itself
as a matter of two self-consciousnesses recognizing each other.) He is
interested in an interchange which is completely mutual, but he decides
without any ado to present an interchange which is not mutual, in which
one person only recognizes and the other is only recognized. [13] I believe
he thinks it appropriate to begin with an unsatisfactory *one-sided* recognition because, at this stage of the development of consciousness, it is
unaware that true recognition must be fully mutual.

The one-sided exchange takes place between people who will come to
be called the Master and the Slave. We can divide what Hegel says about
them into three parts: (1) The struggle between the two people; (2) The
apparent outcome of the struggle; (3) The real outcome, which is not at
first apparent.

III. 1. (1) *The Struggle.* The persons confront one another as obstacles
in each other's paths, each with his own point of view, pursuing projects which include no recognition of the other's projects. Each implicitly

11   At the West Ham meeting in 1968 M. Rustin was exercised by the entailment relations about interpersonal valuation deployed here.

He said that if they are valid they provide a basis for a socialist commonwealth lacking
in other philosophies, such as utilitarianism, Kantianism, and existentialism. For none of
those three appreciates that men have an *essential* need for one another.

I answered that although the entailments indeed prove that men need a society they do
not prove that they need a socialist society. I said that as long as a man has achieved a sense
of personal value with some others he can then go on to exploit other others.

Rustin rightly complained that I had turned Hegel's interpersonal valuation into a once-
for-all socialization process, whereas it can in fact enter any dyad, so that in any exploiter-
exploitee, master-slave dyad, the absence of mutual recognition diminishes both.

12   On this whole matter see Schiller, *On the Aesthetic Education of Man*: "Ignorant
of his *own* human dignity, he is far removed from honouring it in others" (p. 114).

13   Hegel, *Phenomenology of Spirit*, para. 185, p. 112–13.

demands the recognition of the absolute validity of his own project by the other, and therefore resists acknowledgment of the validity of the other's projects. A struggle between them is therefore inevitable.

III. 2. In striving for the other's recognition, each agent in the encounter wishes to prove himself to be, and to be recognized by the other to be, more than a part of nature, more than just a brute obstacle in the other's path. To do so, he must transcend his biologicality; he must show "that [he] is not attached to any specific *existence*, not to the individuality common to existence as such . . . not attached to life."[14] And to show *that*, he must show that he is prepared to let his life be destroyed.[15] In other words, he must risk his life, for the sake of the recognition as naturetranscending to which he aspires, and he does so by entering battle with the other, by challenging the life of the other:

> It is only through staking one's life that freedom is won; only thus is it proved that for self-consciousness, its essential being is not [just] being, not the *immediate* form in which it appears, not its submergence in the expanse of life, but rather that there is nothing present in it which could not be regarded as a vanishing moment, that it is only pure *being-for-self*. The individual who has not risked his life may well be recognized as a *person*, but he has not attained to the truth of this recognition as an independent self-consciousness. Similarly, just as each stakes his own life, so each must seek the other's death, for it values the other no more than itself.[16]

So each risks his own life and thereby gives the other the opportunity of doing the same. (A convenient move, since the risk for either will obtain only if each challenges the other.) One must display a willingness to risk one's life in order to demonstrate that one is a free being, not a merely natural being: if one is unwilling to risk one's life, then one is tied down by it, one is not completely free, and that attachment to life, so we shall see, will lead one to be pure unacknowledged acknowledger, if the other is, by contrast, willing to persist with risking his life.

III. 3. Now if the antagonists struggle until one or both of them die, then they *do* stake and therefore *do* transcend their lives and they *do* prove their freedom. But, if they both die, then they do not prove their freedom

---

14 Ibid., para. 187, p. 113.

15 Cf. *Jenenser Realphilosophie*, as quoted by Wood, *Hegel's Ethical Thought*, p. 86: "To him as consciousness it appears that it is a question of the *death* of the other; but it is really a question of his own."

16 Hegel, *Phenomenology of Spirit*, para. 187, pp. 113–14.

to themselves, so neither has got what she wanted from the encounter. No one knows that she is free if they are both *simply* dead.[17] And even if *one* survives, he survives without the recognizer he needs to help him to perceive his own freedom. So a trial to the death will not deliver the goods. Life is a condition of the development of consciousness. What is needed is a negation of life which, unlike killing, does not destroy it. The person must develop beyond his absorption in his life without actually losing it.

III. 4. Hegel thinks this will be accomplished if in the course of the struggle one of the combatants gives up, putting life *before* his recognition by the other. So we suppose that one of them is willing to risk his life all the way, but that the other isn't. That other shows a greater attachment to life by surrendering, and he acknowledges the superiority of the first man, the man who persisted, the man who now becomes his master. The man who desisted becomes the slave.[18]

III. 5. Henceforth he exists for the sake of another person whose authority he recognizes. The loser's projects have validity only in the context of the victor's projects, which the loser's laboring activity serves.

IV. 1 (2) *The Apparent Outcome.* Hegel now describes the relation each man sustains to external nature, in the aftermath of their struggle. He associates external nature with the natural life which each had risked in different degrees, and the relation of each to external nature in the outcome reflects how he related himself to his natural life in the struggle.

By being willing to risk it completely, the master asserted himself completely against his natural life. He overcame it. Accordingly, he now relates himself to external nature without compromise or self-denial. For him nature consists of objects which the slave has so shaped that all the master does to nature is consume and enjoy it.

By contrast, because in the course of the struggle the slave allowed his desire for life to overcome him, because he remained tied to what was natural in him, he faces in the sequel to the struggle an external nature to which he is bound, one on which he must labor arduously. His labor on nature, like the master's consumption of it, is a kind of negation of it, but he cannot annihilate nature the way the master does by consuming it. Nature resists him, because his labor, like all labor, is directed at a material which he must fight, to make it assume the shape he has in mind.

17   Ibid., para. 188, pp. 114–15.
18   Cf. *The Encyclopedia*, para. 433: "One of those involved in the struggle prefers life, preserves himself as a single self-consciousness, but gives up being recognized, while the other holds [fast] to its reference to itself and is recognized by the first, who is his subject" (quoted by Wood, *Hegel's Ethical Thought*, pp. 86–87).

(3) *The Real Outcome*. But, so Hegel now proceeds to assure us, if we reconsider the outcome of the struggle, it shows itself to be different from what it first seemed to be. A more searching inquiry reveals that the real victor is the slave and the real loser is the master.

Let us reconsider the master's position, first vis-à-vis the slave, and then vis-à-vis external nature.

V. 1. The master is recognized by the slave, but the recognition he receives is defective. For in order to be a valuable recognizer *of* the master, the slave would have to be recognized *by* the master. But the master attributes no value to the slave: *he* does not recognize *him*. In dominating the slave the master has therefore failed to achieve what he wanted to achieve. He cannot perceive a dignity in himself because he perceives himself through a slave from whom he withholds recognition, to whom he assigns no dignity. So the master lacks the freedom that he seemed to have.[19]

V. 2. We now learn that, correspondingly, the slave has the freedom, or anyway *something* of the freedom, he was supposed to lack. He is the more independent of the two people, though he seemed utterly dependent, in thrall to the master and to external nature.

---

19 (1) For a brilliant elaboration of this theme, with relevant reference to the facts of American slavery, see Jon Elster, "Exploring Exploitation," p. 14. Elster aptly quotes John Donne's, "The Prohibition":

> Take heed of hating me,
> Or too much triumph in the victory.
> Not that I shall be mine own officer,
> And hate with hate again retaliate;
> But thou wilt lose the style of conqueror,
> If I, thy conquest, perish by thy hate.
> Then, lest my being nothing lessen thee,
>   If thou hate me, take heed of hating me.

Cf. Elster, *Logic and Society*, pp. 70–76.

(2) Compare the excellent remarks by Shklar at p. 78 of her "Hegel's *Phenomenology*: An Elegy for Hellas":

> By cutting himself off from creativity, action and experience, moreover, he distorts his vision. For as his own most basic experience is the contrast between his own passive superiority and the working creativity of his inferiors, he comes to see everything, from man to the cosmos, in terms of this radical dualism. . . . The possibility of a greater social awareness is cut off by the immediate consequences of battle. The victorious hero enslaves the vanquished and he becomes a user of human tools. That ensures the continued isolation of the hero, and it also arrests his development. His defined role is now that of a man who depends on others to do all work and creating for him. He is thus not as free as he believes, for his life is really in the hands of his servants. Despising creativity, he has also denied himself the possibility of new learning and development. . . . The lord in his contemplative independence cannot survive without his body-slave.

Why did he appear that way? Because we biased our examination of him by considering him only in relation to the master. In particular, we were interested in his labor only insofar as it was a service to the master, and we invidiously contrasted its rigors and pains with the master's unfettered enjoyment of nature. Now we retrace the slave's experience of the struggle and its aftermath, from his own point of view.

We know that in the struggle he experienced an extreme fear of death. That is what led him to surrender and what enabled the master to subject him. But now Hegel finds a supreme value in that supreme fear. The slave's fear brought him to the threshold of death, which is the disappearance of life. One could say that he experienced death as much as anyone who does not die can experience it. Hegel says that the consciousness of the slave

> does in fact contain within itself this truth of pure negativity [that is, of negation of all particular nature] and being-for-self, for it has experienced this its own essential nature. For this consciousness has been fearful, not of this or that particular thing or just at odd moments, but its whole being has been seized with dread; for it has experienced the fear of death, the absolute Lord. In that experience it has been quite unmanned, has trembled in every fibre of its being, and everything solid and stable has been shaken to its foundations. But this pure universal movement, the absolute melting-away[20] of everything stable, is the simple, essential nature of self-consciousness, absolute negativity, *pure being-for-self*, which consequently is *implicit* in this consciousness.[21]

I believe Hegel is saying that the slave's terror made him independent of his biological nature. He realized that he was nothing but a pure consciousness, independent of nature. In the moment of supreme terror, nothing was fixed, all that seemed solid and given melted away, and all that was left was pure freedom of thought, unharnessed to *anything*.[22]

Now if he became independent of his internal nature in the struggle, this fact must somehow be revealed in the struggle's outcome. And that means that the significance of the slave's labor on nature was not fully appreciated in the account of its deficiencies that we supplied above. We must reconsider the significance of the slave's labor. We must look for a new contrast between it and the master's consumption of nature.

20   *Flüssigwerden.* Marx's "all that is solid *melts*" is *verdampft.*
21   Hegel, *Phenomenology of Spirit*, para. 194, p. 117.
22   (1) Cf. Pinkard, *Hegel's Phenomenology*, p. 64: he thereby becomes "free in the sense that nothing can count as authoritative for [him]self unless [he] has freely elected it for [him]self." Hence the transition from the master/slave dialectic to Stoicism.

(2) Compare the significance of war in *The Philosophy of Right.* War liberates men from engulfment in everyday life and returns them to the universal idea embodied in the state.

V. 3. At this point Hegel reveals that the master's enjoyment of the objects with which he is supplied by the slave is an unsatisfactory mode of self-assertion over nature. It is too evanescent. The master from time to time consumes bits of nature, but he does not leave his mark on them; he does not impress himself on nature in a permanent way. The point is not to destroy nature but to develop it, to improve it, just as the point was not to destroy life but to enhance it. The one who was willing to kill or be killed can now *only* kill,[23] that is, destroy the bits of nature that the slave serves up to him.

V. 4. The slave, by contrast, imposes himself on nature in a permanent and stable way. His domination of nature is cumulative and perceptible in the forms he gives to objects. He externalizes the energies which constitute his being in what he makes, and he apprehends his powers, he recognizes himself, in the things he makes. He penetrates and subdues the alien natural reality before which he trembled in the struggle. As Terry Pinkard writes:

> [T]the natural objects of the world count as things of value only to the extent that *he*, the slave, integrates them into *a* scheme of satisfying desire (even if that scheme of desires is not his own).[24]

---

23   There would appear to be a connection between the stigma Hegel here attaches to the master and the words of Schiller at p. 116 of *On the Aesthetic Education of Man*, "An infinite perpetuation of being and well-being, merely for the sake of being and well-being, is merely an ideal of appetite and consequently a demand which can be put forward only by an animality that is striving after the absolute."

24   Pinkard, *Hegel's Phenomenology*, p. 62. See also Hegel, *Philosophy of Right*, para. 194, p. 79:

> The idea has been advanced that in respect of needs man lived in freedom in the so called 'state of nature' when his needs were supposed to be confined to what are known as the simple necessities of nature . . . This view takes no account of the moment of liberation intrinsic to work . . . Apart from this, it is false, because to be confined to mere physical needs as such and their direct satisfaction would simply be the condition in which the mental is plunged in the natural and so would be one of savagery and un-freedom, while freedom itself is to be found only in the reflection of mind into itself, in mind's distinction from nature, and in the reflex of mind in nature.

Compare Shklar, "Hegel's *Phenomenology*: An Elegy for Hellas," p. 79:

> The slave as a body-tool is not as immobilized by this situation as is the master. The slave learns. In his mortal fear he knows how to discipline himself. As he labours and produces for the benefit of the master, he imprints himself on the dead matter with which he works. In the process he not only creates things, but also himself. In his creative relation to objects he discovers his powers, and the really essential character of man. It is man as creator who is really self-aware and free, not the passive and dependent master. The slave achieves self-consciousness through his work.

V. 5. The master does not appreciate the dignity the slave achieves by his labor, and he therefore does not benefit from the acknowledgment of superiority he forces from the slave. He depends for his sense of self on the slave, and the sense he achieves is inadequate. But the slave creates selfhood for himself without mediation through the master, by translating his powers into the world through work, and by developing his powers against nature's resistance to his operations on it. To quote Schiller, who influenced Hegel greatly, "he turns outward everything internal, and gives form to everything external."[25] Note, however, that, as Taylor explains, the slave "owes his transformation to his subjection; only under the discipline of service would he have undertaken the work which has raised him above his original limits."[26] Compare Hegel's *Philosophy of Mind* (*Encyclopaedia*, para. 435), as quoted by Wood: "This subjection of the servant's selfishness forms the *beginning* of true human freedom, . . . a necessary moment in the formative education (*Bildung*) of every human being."[27]

VI. 1. There are many puzzles in Hegel's dialectic of the master and the slave, and I want to highlight just one of them. At the beginning of the story Hegel says that a *willingness* to sacrifice one's life is a prerequisite of achieving freedom, and his description of the *apparent* outcome of the struggle obeys that principle. But the description he gives of the *real* outcome of the struggle seems not to be motivated by that principle. It seems to be governed by another principle, to the effect that virtual loss of biological life is the prerequisite of freedom. The slave experiences that virtual loss of life. The master meets the condition announced at the beginning, that is, he is willing to risk his life, but in the end we learn that to fulfill that condition is to be merely destructive, abstractly negative. The ruling principle in the end is not "You must be willing to die in order to achieve your freedom" but "You must in a certain figurative sense die in order to be reborn free." If you're willing to die you either do and hence can't be reborn; or, if you don't die, it's because your opponent gives up and that means you never came close enough to death. You were willing to die but you never learned what death involves, and that lesson is the crucial lesson. The puzzle is: what justifies replacement of the first principle by the second? What are the respective authorities of these principles?

I am aware that I may not have convinced you of the power and interest of Hegel's dialectic of the master and the slave. You will have noticed

---

25 Schiller, *On the Aesthetic Education of Man*, p. 64.
26 Taylor, *Hegel*, p. 157.
27 Wood, *Hegel's Ethical Thought*, p. 88.

arbitrary steps in the deployment of the story, and I do not know whether the impression of arbitrariness is Hegel's fault or a defect in my understanding of him. What I do know is this: that it would be wrong to stigmatize as *a priori* illegitimate the kind of project Hegel is attempting, namely, the project of tracing what happens in a specially constructed situation where we suppose that two people meet and are interested in becoming self-conscious persons. For narratives based on such special constructions can be found even in British empirical philosophy, and if you think those narratives in principle valid you must think Hegel's project in principle legitimate. The difference between Hegel and the empiricist is that the empiricists Hobbes, Locke, Hume, and Adam Smith usually tell stories about what happens when people meet and seek to satisfy their *material* needs. Will they fight, or cooperatively labor, or exchange goods produced by separate labor, or establish over themselves an omnipotent state to assure that they do not slaughter each other? Hegel's story is intended to illuminate not our material needs but our needs for recognition and for a sense of our own personality. Such needs are ignored by empiricists. But we have them, and if we think Hegel's story curious, we can suggest other narratives in which the need for recognition is exhibited. Hegel's story might help us make up a better one.

VII. 1. It is a permissible conjecture, for which, however, there is, so far as I know, no direct evidence, that Karl Marx drew revolutionary inferences from this section of Hegel's *Phenomenology*. The master, or the capitalist, needs the slaving proletarian, but the latter does not need the former. This is true not only in the economic sense. It is not only that the bourgeois lives off the laboring man's labor, while the laboring man lives off his own labor. It is also that the capitalist's sense of personality depends on his exploitation of the worker, while the worker achieves that sense independent of the capitalist by laboring. The capitalist is irrelevant for his self-image, and this is one reason why he is going to get rid of him.[28]

---

28   If you sit next to a man on a plane in the United States and ask him what he does and he says, "I make plastics," you can confidently infer from his response, if he is being truthful, that he does not make plastics. He is identifying himself by reference to the activity of those whom he employs. He finds it most natural to offer a description of himself that is parasitic on the activity of others.

So we can give a Hegelio-Marxian explanation, in terms of parasitic identity, of that curious perversion in the meaning of the term "manufacturer" which has brought it about that a man is a manufacturer insofar as he does *not* work with his hands. To be sure, some (small) manufacturers make things with their hands, because they work side by side with their employees. But note. Suppose you ask a man, what do you do from 9 to 5, and he says, "I sew dresses." You might then say, "Ah, so you're not a manufacturer." He may then reply, "No. In fact I am a manufacturer, despite the fact that I work with my hands."

VII. 2. There is another element in Hegel's story which was important for Marx, and which I have not yet mentioned. Remember that the slave's labor was preceded by absolute fear. The value of his labor, its significance as an assertion of freedom against nature, derived from the fact that in the state of absolute fear the slave was freed of his own nature. Hegel adds that labor not preceded by absolute fear, labor not coerced on pain of death, cannot have the same value. It would, he says, be merely "a skill which is master over some things, but not over the universal power and the whole of objective being."[29] Marx similarly conceived the total subjection and degradation of the proletariat as a necessary prelude to its task of constructing a new world in which people would be completely free.

VII. 3. I want to instance a final conclusion that Marx might have drawn. Suppose we ask the question, what will happen if the master meets another master and if the slave meets another slave? Suppose a struggle like the one we described is duplicated elsewhere, and then the corresponding parties meet in new dyads: how will they relate to each other?

When one slave encounters another, two formed personalities, capable of creative relationship, meet. But when one master meets another, they can only act destructively toward one another. The real outcome of the struggle shows the masters to be restricted to a destructive attitude to persons and things.

(However, in corporate capitalism, there is to a certain extent an inversion of this inversion, insofar as the worker sometimes identifies himself as a limb of the fragment of capital that employs him. The status-seeking auto worker who says, "I am with GM." This is part of the syndrome of the soulful corporation, which ideology is a concerted effort to reverse the facts of capitalist reality. [For this last point, I am indebted to Pamela Zoline.])

29 Hegel, *Phenomenology of Spirit*, para. 196, p. 119.

Chapter 7

NIETZSCHE

LECTURE 1: LIFE

Friedrich Nietzsche was of mixed Prussian and Polish origin, and he stressed the Polish side whenever he was particularly disgusted by the Germans.[1] He was born on October 15, 1844, at Röcken, near Lützen, in the province of Saxony. For two generations back, all the males on both sides of his family had been Protestant pastors, robust men who lived long lives. An exception was Nietzsche's father, who died prematurely after falling down a flight of stairs, the blow to his head first driving him mad. Scholars used to debate whether or not Nietzsche's eventual insanity, which overtook him in 1889 and remained until he died, in 1900, was hereditary; and against the hereditary interpretation it was argued that Nietzsche's father's insanity must have resulted from the staircase accident. The whole question exercised the scholars because they thought that if Nietzsche's insanity was hereditary, then it must have been in some way operative throughout his life, and must therefore always have influenced his thinking. Nietzsche's thought was scary, and it would have been convenient if the scholars could treat it as a set of lunatic ravings. Today Nietzsche's thought is no longer so scary. This is either because his then revolutionary ideas and proposals have become more acceptable, or because the sting in his teaching has been interpreted away by many commentaries.

---

1 This essay was first written 1965, partially revised 1970. Sections 9 onwards remain in the 1965 version. [It is now widely believed that there is no basis to the claim that Nietzsche was of Polish descent, although he did claim as much toward the end of his life. On this issue see Hollingdale, *Nietzsche: The Man and His Philosophy*, p. 6. More generally, Cohen did not record what his sources were for his account of Nietzsche's life, although he explicitly cites, or quotes from, Lea, *The Tragic Philosopher*; Kaufman, *Nietzsche*; Danto, *Nietzsche as Philosopher*; and Morgan, *What Nietzsche Means*. Cohen's files include his reading notes on Kaufman and Lea. However, the general narrative and many, but not all, of the cited letters in their particular translations follow Halévy, *The Life of Friedrich Nietzsche*.—Ed.]

I know little about Nietzsche's very early years, but I can tell you that upon graduating secondary school, he achieved extremely good results, except in mathematics, at which he was judged "unsatisfactory." In 1864, at the age of twenty, he became a student in the University of Bonn, and pursued studies in theology and classics. Soon, however, to the consternation of his family, he abandoned theology,[2] and devoted himself to classics alone. He also rejected Christianity while still an undergraduate.[3]

He obtained a professorship at the University of Basle at the precocious age of twenty-four, and soon thereafter met the composer Richard Wagner. Both were passionate Graecophiles,[4] and their common cultural interests led to a brief but intense friendship, which was intensified further by Nietzsche's adoration for Wagner's wife, to whom he addressed ardent love letters after his mind had broken. Nietzsche and Wagner battled together against what they took to be the barrenness of contemporary German culture.

But Nietzsche began to perceive that Wagner was becoming attracted to Christianity, and was throwing in his lot with the nascent proto-Nazi movement. This led to an irrevocable schism between them, finalized by the inaugural operatic festival at Bayreuth in 1876,[5] where Wagner released his Christianizing works to an audience which was smug and bourgeois, whereas Nietzsche had anticipated a qualitatively fresh cultural explosion at Bayreuth, a sort of Woodstock Festival of Existence. After the estrangement, Nietzsche continued to express to his friends his admiration of Wagner's achievement, but he felt that Wagner had buckled under the strain of resisting the tide of mediocrity, that he had sold out.

Some sort of break with Wagner was inevitable, if Nietzsche was to live in practice his philosophical teaching, for in *Zarathustra* and elsewhere he enjoins disciples to reject their teachers: there are always new flames to kindle, new torches to carry. Once the teacher's creativity has infused you, it is time to abandon his doctrine and forge your own, to make of him an adversary, without forgetting your debt to him. One must not develop or criticize one's teacher's thought, but make a bold new beginning, for, Nietzsche says in a letter written in 1868: "One does

2   Lea, *The Tragic Philosopher*, pp. 333–50, laments this and claims that it blinded him to the essential Nietzscheanism of Jesus, and also of Paul!

3   [A handwritten note in the text says: "Ritschl said: only und[ergraduate] who could publish in his mag + first on whose success as a prof[essor] he'd stake his reputation." Friedrich Wilhelm Ritschl was Nietzsche's teacher of philology at Bonn. This is a paraphrase of part of Ritschl's recommendation for Nietzsche for his chair at Basle. See Kaufman, *The Portable Nietzsche*, p. 7.—Ed.]

4   Though see Morgan, *What Nietzsche Means*, p. 331.

5   [The typed manuscript has the date of the festival, incorrectly, as 1870. I thank Tom Stern for pointing out this error, which is almost certainly a typing mistake.—Ed.]

not write a critique of an outlook on the world; one just either accepts it or does not accept it. To me a third standpoint is unintelligible."[6] In an early work entitled *The Future of Our Educational Institutions*, he sketches, in the martial language which was to become his hallmark, the right relationship between teacher and student:

> [I]f the young man with a thirst for culture stands in need of a philosophical teacher, the teacher stands in no less need of sincere and devoted disciples. Without them he is in danger of succumbing to the hardships and temptations of isolation. [Hardships which, as we shall see, Nietzsche came to know well.] When, however, in spite of all this, leaders and followers, fighting and wounded, have found each other, there is an impassioned feeling of rapture, like the echo of an ever-sounding lyre.[7]

Nietzsche held his professorship at Basle for ten years, giving it up in 1879 partly because of failing health, and partly because he did not enjoy teaching and the academic atmosphere. He was, despite this, much loved by his students. When he refused a handsome offer to go teach elsewhere, they held a torchlight procession in his honor.

Having abandoned his chair, he now embarked on ten years of restless wandering throughout Europe. In this time he suffered long periods of depression, punctuated by spurts of remarkable creative work. The university decently provided him with a small pension, which he spent in northern Italy, the French Riviera, and in his favorite of spots, the Engadine range of lakes and mountains in Austria. He wrote *Beyond Good and Evil* in 1885–86, and *The Genealogy of Morals* in 1887. His breakdown occurred early in 1889. He spent the eleven years of his illness first with his mother at Naumburg, and then with his sister at Weimar, where he died on August 25, 1900. His body was taken to his birthplace, Röcken, where he lies buried in the churchyard.

Something must be said about Nietzsche's sister, before I tell you more about the circumstances in which he composed the two books I have asked you to read.[8] Elisabeth Nietzsche married a certain Herr Förster, who was an active right-wing nationalist and anti-Semite. She adopted her husband's poisonous views, and it was she who presided over the publication of Nietzsche's manuscripts and letters after he had been stricken ill. She pruned and distorted his thoughts, and made them

---

6 Quoted in Lea, *The Tragic Philosopher*, p. 57. (This is an early manifestation of Nietzsche's disbelief in truth, about which Professor Danto has written a stimulating study: *Nietzsche as Philosopher*.)

7 Quoted in Lea, *The Tragic Philosopher*, p. 58.

8 [Presumably *Beyond Good and Evil* and *The Genealogy of Morals*.—Ed.]

appear proto-Nazi in content. In fact Nietzsche had several times written that the anti-Semites of his day were the lowest grade of humanity, and he regarded the expansionist aspirations of Bismarck's new German state as a perversion of the drive for power which he constantly extolled. But a doctored Nietzschean corpus reached the public, and Hitler's scholars were able to claim him as a prophetic precursor, though even they prudently refrained from publishing all of Nietzsche's works. Many Western scholars, relying on the Försterised version of Nietzsche, and impressed by the amenability to fascist employment of his dicta, also saw him as an episode in the degeneration toward barbarism of Germany, and in recent years he has been regarded in some quarters as a principal cause of the Second World War.

How did *Beyond Good and Evil* and *The Genealogy of Morals* come into existence? In 1884 Nietzsche published *Thus Spoke Zarathustra*, but this long poem, subtitled *A Book for All and No One*, produced bewilderment and misunderstanding. No one knew what to make of it. At first Nietzsche proposed to rewrite it, for he had never completed it in the first place. But he changed his mind, and decided instead to expound the ideas contained in it in a nonpoetic form. He resolved to explain his philosophy more explicitly.

In June of 1885, after a revitalizing stay in Venice, where he recuperated from the disappointing reception accorded *Zarathustra*, Nietzsche returned to the Engadine, and set before himself the task of considering European moral values. He suspected that the valuations people made were connected with the type and amount of biological vitality they possessed. Some anticipation of this outlook may be found in the thought of Hobbes and Spinoza. Hobbes believed that "good" and "bad" were just names people gave for what they respectively desired or avoided. And he believed that objects were desired in the measure that they accelerated the motion of the blood, rejected in the measure that they impeded the heart's functioning. Nietzsche was after a more concrete typology of values, hoping to link particular value judgments with particular aspects of the physiological constitution. He also hoped to judge the value of the values, using as criterion the kind and degree of energy possessed by those who were attracted to them. (Hobbes had not undertaken this, since he merely accepted men's valuations as an irreducible fact about them which it would be confused to subject to ulterior assessment.) With these projects in mind, Nietzsche studied a book called *Biological Problems*, by a certain Rolph, in the expectation that he would find out about quanta of bodily energy and the sorts of attitudes they determined. But he found the work difficult, and fell victim to unrelenting insomnia. He never returned to precise physiological investigations. He continued to connect morality with questions of health, but we shall have to ask whether he meant this literally or metaphorically.

Having abandoned these researches, he left the Engadine for Germany, to bid farewell to his treacherous sister, who was departing for Paraguay with her skunk of a husband. After further wanderings, he arrived at Nice in November 1885, aiming to escape the harshness of winter by snuggling up in the Mediterranean climate. He wrote to a friend: "Here I am returned to Nice, that is to say, to reason."[9] But his initial feeling of hope and well-being gave way to disgust with the petty bourgeois surroundings of the little pension where he lived. And in late November, Nice became unusually cold, he couldn't pay for the fuel he needed to warm himself, and he longed for the stoves of Germany. But somehow, and in conformity with his Spartan teachings, he conquered the suffering his weak frame was undergoing. His depression was displaced by a period of tranquillity, and at the turn of the year he was able to write to his sister, "I have begun to sleep again, without narcotics."[10]

From January to March of 1886, his melancholy dispelled, he arranged his notes and papers, and decided to call his projected work *Beyond Good and Evil*, subtitling it *Prelude to a Philosophy of the Future*. But having completed the book, he sought in vain for a publisher. Houses in Leipzig and Berlin refused him, and he wrote to Elisabeth: "There is nothing else for me to do but to tie up my manuscript with a string and put it in a drawer."[11]

He went to Venice in the spring of 1886, but even here he continued to suffer. The bright sunshine stung the delicate nerves of his failing eyes. He shut himself up in his room, and could not enjoy the invigorating Italian weather. His thoughts moved to Germany, to the shades of its majestic forests. He began to wish to visit his mother, and to confront the Leipzig publishers who had refused his manuscript. So he left Venice for Leipzig, where he negotiated without success. Feeling it essential that his book should appear, he published it out of his own pocket, a step which entailed additional hardship.

He hurried from Leipzig to Naumburg, where he met his sad and lonely mother, who had lived by herself since her daughter's departure for Paraguay. His sister had deviously sent his writings to her, and she was distressed by their violent impieties. He gently advised her against reading his work, saying, "It is not for you that I write."[12] He spent a week at home, and was unable to restrain himself from giving utterance to his iconoclastic ideas, so by the time he took leave of his mother she was sadder still than when he had arrived.

9 Cited in Halévy, *The Life of Friedrich Nietzsche*, p. 304.
10 Ibid., p. 308.
11 Ibid., p. 309.
12 Ibid., p. 312.

Now he left Germany for the last time, never to return again of his own volition. He fled to the Engadine, whose mountain air had so often been salutary in the past. Here, in late July 1886, he experienced the first symptoms of the disorder which, two and a half years later, would precipitate a complete mental collapse. He stays in a mountain hotel, and the company is pleasant, but it is inadequate compensation for his lack of creativity. So in the autumn of 1886 he takes off again, this time for the Genoese coast.

In August 1886, having despaired of a hearing in Germany, he had sent copies of *Beyond Good and Evil* to two eminent foreign scholars. These were George Brandes, a Dane, and a follower of Kierkegaard, who responded, but only after a considerable time. The other was the French historian Hippolyte Taine. On October 17, 1886, Taine wrote him a gracious letter, praising the work, and this, a portent of the fame that was to come, gave him a much-needed respite, and filled him with joy. A friend visiting him near Genoa at this time, having not seen him for a year and half, reported that though he was physically emaciated, he was still wonderfully spontaneous and full of affection.

In the winter of 1887, he left Italy for Nice, but returned in the spring to Lake Maggiore. By now his health was in every respect impaired. He required a regime of baths, massages, and mineral waters. These he found at Coire in Switzerland, where he surrounded himself with doctors. In Switzerland he announced a new work. Herr Widman, a certain Swiss critic, had just published an attack on *Beyond Good and Evil*. Spurred by the welcome existence of an adversary, Nietzsche produced three remarkable essays in fifteen days, and these constitute what we know as *The Genealogy of Morals*. On the title page he explained that the book was intended to supplement and elucidate *Beyond Good and Evil*. On July 18, 1887, he wrote to a friend from Sils-Maria, in the Engadine:

> I have energetically employed these last days, which were better. I have drawn up a little piece of work, which, as I think, puts the problems of my last work in a clear light. Everyone has complained of not having understood me. And the hundred copies sold [of *Beyond Good and Evil*] do not permit me to doubt the truth of this. . . . Perhaps this little book which I am completing today will help to sell some copies of my last book . . . Perhaps my publishers will someday benefit from me. As for myself, I know only too well that when people begin to understand me, I shall not benefit from it.[13]

On July 20 he sent the manuscript to the publisher, but recalled it on July 24 to touch it up, and spent the rest of an arduous summer doing

13   Ibid., p. 329.

so. In September the corrected proofs were dispatched. The Engadine became cold. The wandering philosopher sought a new clime and new labor. Venice carried the day. But he meandered unproductively through lanes and piazzas. I shall not pursue him through the remainder of his travels, which consumed just over another year.

Franz Overbeck was an old friend of Nietzsche's, a scholar whom Nietzsche had known in the Basle days. On January 9, 1889, Overbeck was sitting with his wife at the window of his house in Basle. Suddenly he noticed that the old historian, Jacob Burkhardt, also a former confederate of Nietzsche's, was making his way to his, Overbeck's, front door. He wondered why, because Burkhardt was not a friend of his. Nietzsche was all that they had in common. In a flash Overbeck feared that Nietzsche was in some way the cause of the visit. For some weeks he had had disquieting letters from Nietzsche, who was now at Turin. In the event, Burckhardt showed him a long letter which all too poignantly confirmed Overbeck's suspicions. Nietzsche was raving mad. "I am Ferdinand de Lesseps," he wrote, "I am Prado, I am Chambige [two assassins then figuring in the French newspapers]; I have been buried twice this autumn."[14] He also said, "I would rather be a Professor at Basle than God but my ego is not so great that I can ignore the world crisis. I have summoned a meeting of all European chancelleries. Just now I am having all anti-Semites shot."[15]

Some few minutes later Overbeck received a similar communication, and all of Nietzsche's friends were informed of the tragedy. He had written to each of them. To Brandes, who had eventually responded to *Beyond Good and Evil*, he said, "Friend George, since you have discovered me, it is not wonderful to find me: what is now difficult is to lose me." This was signed "The Crucified."[16] To Peter Gast, a composer, who had taken an interest in musical compositions by Nietzsche: "A mon maestro Pietro. Sing me a new song. The world is clear and all the skies rejoice,"[17] and to Wagner's wife: "Ariane, I love you."[18]

Overbeck started for Italy immediately. He found Nietzsche banging on a piano with his elbow, wailing. Overbeck managed to bring him back to Basle and introduced him into a mental hospital, to which his mother came. She took him away with her.

---

14   Ibid., p. 360.

15   [Cohen's source for this quotation is unknown, although the last sentence is widely repeated, for example in Kaufman's *Nietzsche*, p. 50. The quotation is added in autograph to the 1970 typescript and so is presumably from a different source than the other material, which appears in the 1966 typescript as well as the 1970.—Ed.]

16   Cited in Halévy, *The Life of Friedrich Nietzsche*, p. 360.

17   Ibid., p. 361.

18   Ibid.

The first of his remaining ten years were agony, but he achieved a more tranquil state in time, without becoming less insane. He would from time to time recollect the past. "Have I not written fine books?"[19] he inquired pathetically. Upon seeing a portrait of Wagner he said, "Him I loved very much."[20]

One day his sister, sitting beside him, burst into tears. "Elisabeth," he started, "Why do you cry? Are we not happy?"[21]

His intellect was dead, but his disposition, toward the end, was sweet and charming. One day a young man who was publishing Nietzsche's work went with him on a promenade. Nietzsche noticed a little girl by the side of the road, and she captured his fancy. He walked up to her, stopped, and with his hand drew back the hair which lay low on her forehead. He contemplated her face and asked, in deep contentment, "Is it not the picture of innocence?"[22] Shortly after, on August 25, 1900, he died, at Weimar.

LECTURE 2

1. Nietzsche asks us to journey with him to a land beyond good and evil. Before joining him, let us perch on a tower on its borders in order to view the general lines of this foreign terrain.

Nietzsche proposes to do moral philosophy in an unorthodox way. Let us begin with a concise statement of the difference between him and most of the other moral philosophers it will be your privilege or burden to study. I say most, not all, because although Nietzsche differs, in ways I shall specify, very radically from Mill and Hume and Hobbes and Joseph Butler and possibly Kant and contemporary moral philosophers, he is much closer to the Greeks, and to Spinoza. What is the difference I have in mind? Whereas most moral philosophers ask what is the good *for* man, treating man as their fixed reference point, Nietzsche is asking something quite different: what is the good *of* man. In the way you might ask, not what's good for the flowers, but what's the good of them. The others ask what will satisfy mankind, or what actions, given man's needs and nature including the needs and nature of his fellows, ought men to undertake, Nietzsche is not taking man's nature as given, and he is asking, quite differently, what does a man have to be like in order *himself* to be of *value*. And he finds paradigms of valuable men in great

19   Ibid.
20   Ibid.
21   Ibid.
22   Ibid.

historical figures, who are great not because they benefit others, but because their constitutions are valuable in themselves. In the *Twilight of the Idols* (9.44) he says: "The great human being is a finale."[23] To exhibit his greatness, we display not what his presence led to or sponsored, but the majesty that his presence, in itself, *was*. So that Nietzsche writes in *The Will to Power*, "The value of a human being . . . does not lie in his usefulness: for it would continue to exist even if there were nobody to whom he could be useful."[24] The instructions generated by a utilitarian or Kantian moral code could not be followed by a marooned philanthropist or saint, because the instructions presuppose that he to whom they are directed is located amongst other men and called upon to relate himself righteously to them. But the Nietzschean saint or hero could continue to be that in virtue of which Nietzsche honors him in any kind of environment, without adjusting himself to it.

This shift in perspective, from what is good and right for man, to what is the good of man, the concern to make this shift, is prompted by Nietzsche's sincere and considerable anxiety that contemporary European man is losing his value, is ceasing to be valuable, is being diminished in substance, and precisely because of the supremacy of value systems constructed from the point of view which takes human nature for granted and ministers to it. In an early essay on "The Greek State," written before Nietzsche had addressed morals in any systematic way, the roots of this anxiety are discernible in his enunciation of an aristocratic political philosophy:

> In order that there may be a broad, deep and fruitful soil for the development of art, the enormous majority must, in the service of a minority, be slavishly subjected to life's struggle, to a *greater* degree than their own wants necessitate. At their cost, through the surplus of their labour, that privileged class is to be relieved from the struggle for existence, in order to create and to satisfy a new world of want. Accordingly we must accept this cruel-sounding truth, that *slavery is the essence of Culture*.[25]

So if we accept people's requirements, and minister to them, we serve men at the expense of man, at the expense of the development of the genius of the species. In fact the passage I have just recited is the secret teaching of Plato's *Republic*, a book which purports to design a community which will satisfy everybody, but in which—it is not difficult to prove—Plato is in fact aiming at a social pattern which will liberate the best human

---

23 Nietzsche, *Twilight of the Idols*, p. 548.
24 Quoted in Kaufman, *Nietzsche*, p. 314.
25 Quoted in Lea, *The Tragic Philosopher*, p. 63.

beings as much as possible, at whatever cost to the many. Now in a Europe resonating with ideas of democracy and equality, in a Europe in which the masses are making claims, in Nietzsche's Europe, the prospect for excellence in the species must, on this view, be limited. Hence the particular urgency of an inquiry into what man can be.

But that was a historical aside. Let me pick up the first theme I was expounding, the formal difference, not just the difference in attitude to society or to contemporary men, between Nietzsche and other moralists. Most moral philosophers take the nature of man as their point of departure, and relate their proposals to this datum. Nietzsche, instead, wants to scrutinize the credentials of the datum. He does not say, "Since men are of this character, this is what is good for them." He asks whether the way they are is a good way to be. It is perhaps ignoble and base, all-too-human? Must it not perhaps be rejected, replaced, by a different sort of human nature, a superhuman nature? Other philosophers take human interests for granted, and some contemporary philosophers, like Mrs. Foot, do so so extremely that they judge it a necessary truth that if X serves human interests then X is good.[26] But what if we find this creature and its interests revolting? Still other philosophers, like Professor Winch, do not believe in permanent historically invariant human interests which underlie the goals men pursue in particular societies: they see their goals as rooted in the life of their society, in what they call its form of life, and once a satisfactory connection with the form of life is made, the practice connected to it is justified, or at least not amenable to criticism.[27] Wittgenstein, Winch's master, said, "What has to be accepted, the given . . . forms of life."[28] But what if a certain form of life nauseates us when we contemplate it? In either case the Nietzschean response is that the phenomena which for the philosophers ground values require themselves to be grounded, or, if found worthless, then declared incapable of grounding values. So when the moral philosophy of utilitarianism argues from the alleged fact that men are so constituted as to desire happiness, Nietzsche disputed both the necessity and the value of that constitution. He rejects its necessity because he believes that men are concentrations of power which can turn in many direction, happiness being only one of them, and he indeed says, somewhere, that "Man does not desire happiness; only the Englishman does."[29] And he rejects its value because he believes that happiness is not a conspicuously elevated condition. The first riposte

---

26   [This view appears in Foot's "Moral Beliefs."—Ed.]

27   [This view appears in Winch's *Idea of a Social Science.*—Ed.]

28   Wittgenstein, *Philosophical Investigations*, p. 226.

29   [This is from *Twilight of the Idols*, Maxims and Arrows 12. For a slightly different translation, see Nietzsche, *Twilight of the Idols*, p. 468.—Ed.]

to such moralities as the utilitarian is: if the nature of man, as it is at present, can be shown to be worthless, then why strive to minister to its needs? Before developing moral rules adherence to which will satisfy human needs, one must ask whether the needs of this creature deserve to be satisfied.

2. Now that we have acquired a preliminary understanding of the project which occupies Nietzsche, we are entitled and obliged to raise three difficult questions: (A) How do we find out what sort of creatures men are? (B) How do we decide what sort of creature man ought to be? (C) Is it possible for man to transform himself into that sort of creature? These questions lead us beyond good and evil, because to frame them is to undermine the authority of the given structure of humanity, on which judgments of good and evil are based.

3. (A) How do we find out what sort of creatures men are? How do we diagnose the nature of man? In general, diagnoses are based on symptoms. What symptoms does Nietzsche think are relevant to the present inquiry? The symptoms are the moral precepts men affirm. And here is why the metaphor of "symptom" is apt: symptoms both *lead* the physician to the disease responsible for them, and they are what he seeks to remove in *treating* the disease. We seek to replace current values by better ones; we seek what Nietzsche calls a transvaluation of values. We must see what human type the values men currently espouse betoken, and we may hope for a salutary change in values as a result of an appropriate change in that type: indeed it is the type we care about, about the values only as its index and its expression.

In a sense, we traverse a route traveled by conventional philosophers, but in the opposite direction. Mill begins with inclinations and desires and ends with values; we begin with values and trace their genesis or genealogy in needs and desires in human strengths and weaknesses, only we feel differently about the strengths than we do about the weaknesses, while for Mill, they are on a par.

4. (B) We have now said something about the answer to the first question, how do we know what man is like? We turn to the second: How can we decide what sort of creature man ought to be or become?

Where do we obtain our new tablets, our fresh standards? On top of what mountain, and in the utterance of which God or lawgiver? Nietzsche does not answer this question directly, but a fairly definite answer is implied, or a set of answers, for he does not always seem to say the same thing. Sometimes the canons are aesthetic: the character and dispositions that would make a man worthwhile are those which it would be rewarding to contemplate, which would fill us with wonder and awe, induce in us the response we feel in the presence of great works of art. Few men give us aesthetic joy: there are the Leonardos, the Caesars, the Napoleons, and in paintings of such men what is painted is itself an aesthetic marvel; but most men offend against our sense of smell, make us turn away, unless we feel we have to stay. As Nietzsche says in *The Genealogy of Morals* (3.14):

> One who smells not only with his nose but also with his eyes and ears will notice everywhere these days an air as of a lunatic asylum or sanatorium. (I am thinking of all the current cultural enterprises of man, of every kind of Europe now existing.) It is the diseased who imperil mankind.[30]

So in this passage, and in many others, the aesthetic criterion is linked to a conception of health. It is the healthy specimen, and the bounteous overflowing strength of the truly great that provide joy to the onlooker: it is the diseased specimens who stimulate disgust. It needs no emphasizing that this is not health in the NHS sense. In what sense we shall have later to explore. But we can at least say that in some sense the Gods of beauty and health supersede the God of utility. We shall later question whether the marriage Nietzsche has arranged between his two Gods is really consummated in his thought.

5. (C) And now we take up our third question: Is it possible for man to transform himself into the kind of creature that earns Nietzsche's approval? If you tell men what they ought to be like, can there be any sense in your recommendation if you are unable to tell them how to become like that, if, indeed, it is impossible for them to become like that?

   To ask these questions is to raise the status of the time-honored philosophical maxim "Ought implies can," the principle that sentences of the form "You ought to Φ commit their utterers to sentences of the form "You can Φ." Now I do not think this principle is, as it stands valid. There may be no point in telling someone that he ought to do something which he is unable to do, but that may not diminish the validity of the ought-judgment. If you have no means of getting to the Costa Brava, it may be futile to tell you that you ought to visit it as a remedy for your illness, but it could still be true. The doctor might say, "Of course, you ought to go to the Costa Brava, but I know you can't." Or, in case you think this applies only to so-called nonmoral oughts, here is what would be considered a moral example: a man could say, "You ought to give him a hand, he's in trouble. Can you?" And if the answer is a truthful no, the

---

30   Nietzsche, *The Genealogy of Morals*, p. 258.

adviser's advice does not become false, just without practical use. To be sure, I cannot accuse you of being foolish or, in a moral case, blame you for what you failed to do, if you were unable to do it. If you fail to do the right thing but couldn't have helped it, then you are not culpable. But what you are not culpable for is precisely your failure to do what you ought to have done.

So value judgments do not imply the judgments of possibility that are obtained by putting "can" in the "ought"-space. And, significantly, this is abundantly true in the realm of art. The sculpture may be deficient in specifiable respects, we can see that it ought to have been other than it is, although the sculptor's talent may have been too limited to enable him to do it right. So we might decide, having accepted Nietzsche's teaching, that most men just are base and ignoble, even if we also decide that this is inevitably so. We might then shrug our shoulders and inefficaciously lament the matter. We might decide that we ought to be other than we are without seeing any way out of the way we are. It might then be pointless to try to realize new values, but we could still understand and affirm them.[31]

6. Happily, Nietzsche does tell us that we, or at least some of us, can change ourselves, though his explanation how we can do so reflects a pervasive incoherence in his philosophy of mind. Let me first indicate the answer, and then point to its difficulties. You will remember that I said Nietzsche rejects not only the worth of human nature as typically constituted, but also the *necessity* of that constitution. This suggests that he believes there is an answer to the question how a man can change himself. His answer depends on his notion of power. We are all vested with a fund of force or energy; indeed each of us is nothing more than a quantity of force or energy. This force is differentiated into different dispositions in different people. It is a repository of strength or power which may be harnessed by us to create *new* dispositions. We are once again confronting an aesthetic turn of thought, but this time we have to do not, as before, with the aesthetics of contemplation, but with the aesthetics of creation. We can regard ourselves as raw material out of

31   In the above I take "ought" implies "can" in its strongest version. Weaker claims are possible. For instance: you ought to Φ cannot be true unless it is possible for a human being to Φ. I mean, even if, if you ran at 200mph you'd save the damsel in distress, it doesn't follow that you ought to run at that rate, since nobody can. The act must be in some general sense, if not possible for you here and now, a possible act. And the emendations to the sculpture, if not possible for that sculptor, must be possible for the human activity of sculpting, for the powers of sculpting men define the sculptural form. It would be a work of great complexity to determine the strength of the challenge to Nietzsche of *this* version of ought-implies-can, if he thinks we in fact cannot. We shall bypass that work, because as we now report, he thinks the transformation that would be desirable *is* in some sense possible.

which we can fashion something noble. Most of us are infected with petty hatreds and resentments: rancor, or ressentiment, is, for Nietzsche, the mainspring of all-too-human values. But these passions are not stable elements with which our values must come to terms. For they are forms of power, power which can take other forms, and which can be made to take other forms by at least some of us.

His belief in this has made scholars judge Nietzsche as a forerunner of Sartre's existentialism, though Sartre's thought is also distinguishable from his. You will have heard of Sartre's slogan: Existence precedes essence. This announces that we make our own natures, that we are deposited featureless in the world, and that the features we come to have are created by us and last only as long as we sustain them: our creation of self is a continuous creation. Sartre's proclamation of this doctrine may indeed make it apt to call Nietzsche an existentialist, where we take Sartre as paradigmatic of that point of view. But notice two differences: whatever Nietzsche means by power, his attribution of it to the human substance means that we are not nothing, as Sartre thinks. I am not going to explain what Sartre means by saying that we are nothing, but one thing he means is that we lack the being, the determinacy of quality, possessed by all that is not conscious. This contrasts with Nietzsche, whose assertion that we are formations of power is an application of his somewhat Schopenhauerian doctrine that power is all there is in the universe; a tree, or a rock, or a rainbow is also power. In our case, organization of power is associated with consciousness, but consciousness lacks the central role it has in Sartre's philosophy. Nietzsche calls it our most fallible and weakest organ, whereas Sartre rests his whole view of man, including his dictum that existence precedes essence, on it.

Sartre's philosophy has mysteries which this is not the time to unravel. Nietzsche's philosophy is mysterious in other ways. And now let me justify my complaint that there is incoherence in Nietzsche's answer to the question, how we may change ourselves. If Nietzsche had really meant that *we* must redirect the power that we *have*, that would be all right. But he regards that formulation as a misleading figure, since his literal teaching is not that we have power, but that we are power. And this means that a distinction between the self and its energy cannot be drawn, and hence, so it seems to me, that the self cannot be called upon to rechannel its energy. In one place, and in consonance with what he literally believed, Nietzsche said that to appeal to a conqueror for mercy is like asking a river not to flow. Perhaps by sophisticated moves one could reconcile such teaching with the idea that man may survey and make his nature, but I have not discovered the method. As far as I can see, there *is* contradiction in Nietzsche's thought.

Now it is not as though something he says here or there conflicts with his main doctrine. It is not that kind of contradiction. It is a matter of thoroughgoing commitment to two conceptualizations which cannot both be sustained. Nietzsche wants what he says in figure to be literally true, even though taken literally, it contradicts the literal truth of which it is a figure. If we were exploring Nietzsche's metaphysics, we would concentrate on the pole of his thought at which men and their power are identified. Since we are exploring not metaphysics but morals, I shall, for the most part, ignore the identification doctrine, and allow Nietzsche his answer to our third question. It is sometimes profitable to let mercy season reason. If we insisted on the contradiction I have pointed to, we could lose interest in a lot in Nietzsche that is interesting. Now Nietzsche is not averse to men doing scandalous things. So I shall now commit the scandal, for such it is in a philosophy lecture, of commending to you the poet Walt Whitman's reply to the criticism that he contradicted himself: "Do I contradict myself? Very well then I contradict myself, (I am large, I contain multitudes.)"[32]

7. In answering the three questions I adverted to symptoms and diagnoses, and I exercised the concept of health. Let us look into this constellation of images. Nietzsche is, in a manner, setting himself up as a physician, a doctor to the human soul. But he is a special kind of physician. He aims not at providing medicine or therapy for his patients, but at showing them how they can cease being patients, how they can protect themselves against illness. In some ways he is like a physician who proposes exercise. Such a physician is asking the patient to remold his body, Nietzsche, to remold himself entire. The run of moralists tell us only how to deal with ourselves as we are. We are to organize a harmonious life by employing the categories and judgments of good and evil. Nietzsche would rather have us so transformed that we no longer need to reckon with good and evil, to make moral judgments, to reject and recommend. The image of the river about which it makes no sense to suggest an alternative course functions not only as an analogy to his philosophy of mind but also as an ideal of life to be attained.

Now in his attempts to assess human nature, Nietzsche is faced with a problem all psychiatry must face: namely, what is to count as health in the spiritual dimension, when is a soul diseased, what is *mens sana*? Standards of physical health are comparatively easy to establish. A healthy organism lives long and easily performs its characteristic functions. These criteria *can* conflict: there may be drugs and regimens which put brakes on performance but perpetuate the life span, and other procedures which bolster the metabolism but carry with their application premature death. But even though the criteria conflict, what they are is clear. And, moreover, conflict is rare. For evolutionary reasons, it must

32 Walt Whitman, "Song of Myself," in Whitman, *Complete Poems*, p. 123.

be rare. Creatures bent on using their bodies for life-diminishing purposes will tend to die off.

But where are the analogous criteria for the health of the soul? The first physical criterion was longevity. Unless we believe, as Nietzsche in no relevant sense did, in the possibility but not the guarantee of immortality, which could be won by directing our faculties to certain projects, there can be no psychic criterion comparable to the first physical one. If the soul perishes with the body, we must, as doctors to the soul, look to the other kind of criterion, and ask, what are the soul's proper functions? But here there is no agreement as there is in the case of what the legs or arms or stomach is for. The limits of the uses of our bodily organs, and the conditions of use under which they prosper, are fairly narrow, a matter, for the most part, of scientific observation. But the energy of intellect and will and feeling can run in many divergent channels, and associated with this fact is the fact that different projects have appeal to different men. It seems impossible to appeal to a notion of psychic health in order to assess human nature, since there is no agreed set of purposes for which our minds are to be used, or which should capture our hearts, from which we could derive what a healthy soul must be like, and even the most smug of psychiatrists are dogmatic only about what condition of mind is bad, unwilling to stipulate in any detail what condition is good.

So because the appeal to health is tenuous, Nietzsche's values always veer in the aesthetic direction, the two canons of wondrous to contemplate and creative. He continues to cloak his aesthetic norms in the language of hygienic regimen. But in substance the aesthetic orientation takes precedence. The soul is not seen as beautiful or graceful because it is healthy, but simply called healthy because it is experienced as radiating dignity and grace. Indeed, Nietzsche somewhere says that health is not the absence of suffering but the activity of overcoming it, and that activity is valued for its creative aspect. Remember that in my sketch of Nietzsche's life I reported that he gave up his research into correlations between physiology and moral precepts. There is no soul physiology whose proper alignment dictates valid values. Aesthetics defeats hygiene in the final reckoning. And the moving pronunciation which I shall now quote from Nietzsche's *Birth of Tragedy* presides over his entire oeuvre:

> For this one thing must above all be clear to us, to our humiliation *and* exaltation . . . that we have our highest dignity in our significance as works of art—for only as an *aesthetic* phenomenon is existence and the world eternally *justified*: — while of course our consciousness of this our significance hardly differs from the kind of consciousness which the soldiers painted on canvas have of the battle represented thereon.[33]

33   Nietzsche, *The Birth of Tragedy* (Haussmann translation), p. 50.

Before adding a comment on this passage let me protect you against a silly misunderstanding of it. I would not insult you by suggesting you may be suffering from it if I had not myself suffered from it for about seven years. By consciousness of soldiers Nietzsche means of the living soldiers who are represented in the painting, not of their painted representations. Having cleared that up, all I want to say is that in the passage there is both obviousness and paradox. Now: obviousness because if you demand a justification of the whole shebang, of the entire show, then since there is nothing outside it that it might serve, how but aesthetically, taken by itself in its uniqueness, could it pass muster? And paradox: because to whom is it supposed to afford aesthetic satisfaction, who can even recognize its value? Ex hypothesi not to us as individuals in it—see what is said about the soldiers. And there can be no God outside it not only because Nietzsche didn't believe in one but also for logical reasons: we are supposed to be justifying all existence here. Were there a God, he would be part of the universe to be justified. So if we pick at this passage there are problems. So let us leave it as it is. And anyway aesthetics functions not only in the mind-splittingly total way but also in the more modest dimension of our evaluation of single people, our theme to which we now return.

8. Men's judgments of good and evil, the nostra they cling to as medicines of the soul, must be judged according as they are healthy or unhealthy, or, more honestly, as they are beautiful or ugly. Of a judgment about good and evil we must ask from what human disposition does it flow, and what type is its acceptance likely to foster? The health or illness of disposition and type then determines the worth of the judgment. So in *The Antichrist* Nietzsche asserts that "what is bad . . . [is] . . . all that is born of weakness, or envy, or revenge"[34] because these are considered ugly and poisonous dispositions.

"All that is born of weakness." This standard provokes us, patient academics, to ask whether Nietzsche is not committing a famous mistake which pious moral philosophers have called, "the genetic fallacy." This supposed error involves estimating the worth of a product by reference to the worth of what produced it. It would be committed in declaring a work of music musically poor because it was written by a fascist, where this is the justification, not the explanation of the truth, of the musical judgment. Such a consideration, opponents of the genetic fallacy maintain, can never suffice. A thing must be judged on its own merits, not on the merits of what brought it into being. Now Nietzsche is charged with committing the genetic fallacy because he took as defective judgments which emerged from weak and petty creatures, simply because they emerged from them. I shall defend Nietzsche in two stages: (1) I shall question whether such

---

34 Nietzsche, *The Antichrist*, p. 647.

appeals to origin or genesis are universally fallacious. (2) I shall show that Nietzsche is concerned not only with the genesis but also with the function of value judgments which their genesis may reveal. One remark before beginning this defense: let no academic cretin *both* attack Nietzsche's thought because it was produced by a figure who lived on the border of insanity in the land of misery *and* accuse Nietzsche of committing the genetic fallacy. Plenty of Nietzsche-revilers would like to commit the inconsistency of doing both. The slyest way of doing so would be to say, Nietzsche judges ideas by their genesis, by the type of spirit that produced them; we shall judge his ideas by this standard. I impose on you as an exercise the question how such a devious critic may be rebutted.

Let us take a case where the genetic fallacy is unquestionably committed. I present you with what purports to be a proof of the Pythagorean theorem. I also tell you it was written at 7:00 p.m. yesterday by Wolfgang Bierquaffer. As it happens you were yesterday in the same pub as Bierquaffer, and you noticed that between five o'clock and five to seven he drank ten pints of Guinness. He doesn't have a prodigious capacity for alcohol, and by 7:00 p.m. he revealed all the signs of inebriation. So you say to me: that proof is faulty, it must have holes in it, because there were holes in the brain of the would-be geometrician who produced it. Obviously, this would be rash. For Wolfgang Bierquaffer may, despite his condition, have hit on a proper demonstration. Indeed a correct proof of the Pythagorean theorem may, through a bizarre ministration of Providence, appear on a piece of paper as a result of a certain coalescence and disaggregation of ink spots, after someone has spilled ink. No account of the origin of the demonstration can settle the question of its validity. That depends on examining the demonstration alone.[35]

---

35 So we concede that the fallacy may readily be committed in domains where there are objective standards. But even in such domains care is needed before accusations of genetic fallacy are lodged. Consider the following explication of the fallacy:

> [T]here is no reason why sociologists should not investigate the social background of physicists and compare it with that of biologists, nor why psychologists should not enquire whether there is a special type of personality that predisposes men to become scientists. Such enquiries, it will be seen, are quite irrelevant to the truth or falsity of the theories that the scientists put forward. . . . Whether a scientific theory is true or false is settled by scientific argument, not by reference to the nature of the propounder's motives. (Acton, *The Illusion of the Epoch*, 205)

It is possible that this passage evinces a naive conception of scientific argument, as an affair of disembodied unalloyed reason. What kinds of truth or falsehood scientists discover must depend on the nature of the scientific enterprise. This may well be at least partly a sociological question. So much must be pressed against those who would push the genetic fallacy idea too far, especially given the researches of Thomas Kuhn. Those researches would have to be shown to be misguided before we can certify Acton's remarks without demur. And it would be question-begging to stigmatize his researches as vitiated by the genetic fallacy.

Why was the genetic fallacy committed here? Because there was an independent means of considering the validity of the proof, by reference to the accepted geometry. Its availability guaranteed the ultimate irrelevance of Bierquaffer's state when he penned the proof. But now let us take another kind of case. Suppose it is discovered that they only believe in God who have had a certain sort of toilet training, or who, as children, were at the mercy of a tyrannical father. Now the content of their belief, to wit that God exists, may, as regards its truth, be independent of the origin of the belief. But here, unlike in the geometrical case, we lack a ready instrument for settling the truth of the claim. It is natural to abridge the significance of imputations of genetic fallacy in this domain. We might declare that even if a belief in God is not proved *false* by its origin, it is *discredited* by its origin. The assertor of the claim may, for all we know, have hit on a truth about the universe, but the explanation why he asserted it makes that most unlikely. (Karl Sternian replies to reductive moves against religion prove little.) Moreover, in a domain like the religious, the reasons for holding the belief seem essential to the nature of the belief itself, so that if the genetic story shows the official reasons to be spuriously such, it taints the belief as well. And the case of morals seems more readily assimilable to the case of religion than to matters of geometry. So there seems little trace of the genetic fallacy when a moral philosopher like Nietzsche discredits a moral conviction on the ground that only the weak and sickly tend to hold it. We may surely see sense in what he said in *Human, All Too Human* (1.10):

> Directly the origins of religion, art, and morals have been so described that one can explain them without having recourse to metaphysical concepts either at the beginning or along the way, the strongest interest in [metaphysical problems] ceases.[36]

One last point. There are many modes of the relation between the derived and the derivation. One mode is the expressive, where we can say of the product that it is an expression of what produced it. Now the relationship between an expression and what it is an expression of is particularly intimate—you cannot place one on one side and the other on the other. They interpenetrate and affect each other's correct description. Hence insofar as values may be seen as expressive of personality, it

---

In this connection, we must draw a distinction between what is relevant to the truth or falsity of theories and what is relevant to our decisions about the truth or falsity of theories. Even if background has no essential relevance to the former, we are in a position to treat only of the latter: we can get at truth only through procedures for deciding what is true, and these procedures may, as Kuhn has argued, embody a societal component.

36   Quoted from Danto, *Nietzsche as Philosopher*, p. 52.

is fair to draw conclusions about the values by studying the personality. Studying the personality is, to exaggerate a little, a way of studying the values.

The second point in my defense of Nietzsche is that he is not appealing to genesis alone but also to the function of judgments respecting good and evil. He not only asks, from what disposition do they arise? But also: to what disposition will their acceptance lead? Though, as I shall show in a moment, Nietzsche explicitly separated these questions, they are in fact closely allied. For it is a fair guess that if a man makes a judgment because he has a certain disposition, then following that judgment will reinforce and intensify the original disposition. Unable to cope with sexuality, I judge that it is evil: following my judgment is likely to incapacitate me further in the erotic field, to augment my aversion. So genesis may be a clue to function or effect, and no one says that there is, in addition to the genetic fallacy, a functional fallacy. For it is always appropriate to ask of something when considering its value, "To what use is it put? What does it lead to or result in?" This is a staple of evaluative reflection.

In the preface to *The Genealogy of Morals* questions about the genesis and the function of values receive separate mention: "Under what conditions did man construct the value judgments *good* and *evil*?" That is the genetic question. "And what is their intrinsic worth? Have they thus far benefited or retarded mankind?" [37] That is the functional question. And somewhere near the beginning of the book: "morals as effect, as symptom, as mask, as hypocrisy, as disease, as misunderstanding; but also morals as cause, as remedy, as stimulant, as hindrance, as poison." [38] Finally, Nietzsche asks (preface 3), "Do they betoken misery, curtailment, degeneracy, or, on the contrary, power, fullness of being, energy, courage in the face of life, and confidence in the future?" [39] The word "betoken" is conveniently ambiguous here. It means "mean." When we ask what value judgments mean, what is their import, we ask what constitution they spring from, and what constitution they produce, what constitution springs from them. We ask both the genetic and the functional question. Suppose I say, "Clouds mean rain" and also "People with umbrellas means rain." In the first case I point to function or result, in the second to genesis or origin. Nietzsche's questions point to both. As a historian he is mainly interested in genesis. As a moralist he is interested in both, and in function insofar as his ire is aroused by what he thinks clinging to the values we have will lead to.

37   Nietzsche, *The Genealogy of Morals*, p. 151.
38   [This is from the preface, section 6, p. 155. The quoted text is taken from the translation in Morgan, *What Nietzsche Means*, p. 144.—Ed.]
39   Nietzsche, *The Genealogy of Morals*, p. 151.

9. Talking of the function of value judgments seems identical with talking of their utility, and since we know that Nietzsche is opposed to utilitarianism, we must pause and sort things out, to forestall confusion. The difference is this: the utilitarian is interested in what is useful as productive of pleasure, of content, and Nietzsche is interested in what is useful as productive of men who have hygienically and aesthetically praiseworthy dispositions. And a man whose dispositions are bent to the search for pleasure is one whom Nietzsche would condemn as base and all-too-human. All-too-human, because all-too-animal.

It is true that Nietzsche says that values which are connected with miserly dispositions must be repudiated. He believes that they must be rejected in favor of values connected with healthy soul-stuff. But it is important to note that Nietzsche many times evinces a respect for *values-as-such*. That's to say, he prefers men who create tablets, even if these are forged out of ugly feelings, to men who fester in their disease and do not engage in the value enterprise at all. Thus he says in *The Genealogy of Morals* (1.8) first that the vengeance and hatred of the Jews was the deepest and sublimest hatred in human history since it gave birth to ideals and a new set of values. He pays them this tribute, though he rejects the values because they are rooted in hatred.[40]

Let us now raise once more the question, how can we arrive at standards of good and bad, healthy and diseased, and this time seek a new route for our answer. Let us adopt, for the moment, a linguistic approach to the problem. There are certain things of which we can say that they are good and bad, but not good and evil. An apple, for example, goes bad. We do not say that it goes evil. Now what is meant by calling an apple bad? Well, a bad apple is rotten. It is bad to eat. It is bad for a human being to eat. It is bad for a human being to eat if he wants nourishment and pleasant sensations of taste. These contextual qualifications are required to give sense to the judgment that an apple is bad: otherwise we could not speak of apples going bad, only of becoming more and more ripe. Now Nietzsche's ethic of good and bad is, in part, an attempt to assimilate people to apples. People are sound, healthy, good, or they are rotten. But what are the other terms in relation to which the health or rottenness of a human being is guaranteed? In the case of the apple, the guarantees were given by what kind of apple it is suitable to eat. What corresponds to edibility when we speak of the soundness or rottenness of a human being? Sometimes it seems that aesthetics gives the answer. A bad or rotten human being is one whose behavior it is disgusting to witness. So a slave, who is good by the standards of good and evil, because he is acquiescent, humble, respectful to his master, may not be good by

40 Ibid., p. 168.

the standards of good and bad, because his existence affords aesthetic displeasure. But to whom does his existence bring displeasure? We know he is displeasing to Nietzsche, and probably displeasing, aesthetically, to the masters. But he is probably not displeasing to people with equally servile temperaments. The analogy with rotten apples breaks down, since all people find the same apples sound and rotten. It emerges that Nietzsche is merely proposing a new set of values, not revealing a new value plane outside the accepted one from which he can assess the latter. In other words, it seems to emerge that his doctrine of good and bad is simply putting new content into the forms of good and evil. Except that he claims even slaves must reject themselves. And this means he values humanity highly—"he who despises. . . ."[41]

10. I shall begin by summarizing what I have said about Nietzsche up to this point. First, I pointed out the radical diversion of perspective his moral philosophy involves. Instead of asking what is valuable for man, he wants to know under what conditions man himself is valuable. He seeks not what is good for man, but asks what is the good *of* man? He denies that a man has value in the measure that he is useful to others: he rejects utilitarianism. He is loath to take human nature as his starting point. For this, he feels, may be ignoble and base, all-too-human. The human interests which philosophers like Mill take for granted—this is precisely what Nietzsche submits to criticism. He challenges the rights of the physical and emotional needs by reference to which more orthodox moralists justify their proposals.

Utilitarians argue that men by nature desire happiness. Nietzsche questions both the necessity and the value of such a constitution.

Given the intransigence, three difficulties face him: (1) How do we find out what sort of creatures men are? (2) How can we decide what sort of creature man ought to be, ought to transform himself into? (3) How is it possible to undertake this project of self-transformation?

(1) The symptoms which help us to diagnose human nature are the moral precepts men affirm. We find out what men are like by considering what they value. We do not, like Mill, build value on desires and propensities. We dig under the values to disclose these as their foundation. We show how pompous moral assertions originate in and minister to quite detestable traits in the ordinary run of folk.

(2) We answer this by applying fresh standards to men's needs and desires, instead of treating them as basic. But where do we get these new standards? Sometimes they are aesthetic canons: that man is worthwhile

---

41 [Possibly a reference to Proverbs 14:21: "He who despises his neighbor sins, but blessed is he who has pity on the poor."—Ed.]

whom it is edifying to contemplate. The appeal to aesthetic canons is connected with an elusive doctrine of soul hygiene. The healthy provide aesthetic satisfaction; the sickly stimulate disgust in the sensitive man. But we showed how the connection between health and beauty is a tenuous one, and how it falls apart on closer inspection.

(3) Having told men what they ought to be like, can we tell them how to become so? First I argued that we might not be able to do so, even though the judgment expressed in answer to the second question was valid. We might decide that we ought to be other than we are, without seeing any way out of being the way we are. It would then be pointless to stress man's inadequacy; but we could still understand what was intended in doing so.

But Nietzsche offers more hope than this. For he believes that we are all vested with a quantum of power or energy, which can be harnessed so as to develop new dispositions in us. This is an aesthetic idea, though it belongs not to the aesthetics of the spectator, but to the aesthetics of the creative artist. We are to regard ourselves, our selves, as raw material, out of which we can fashion something noble. Most of us are infected with petty hatreds and resentments. We must strive to eradicate these. We are able to do so, because we make our own natures. And because he believed this, Nietzsche was a forerunner of the existentialists, like Sartre. We can distance ourselves from our characters, our selves, assess, review, criticize, and change them.[42]

In answering the three questions I made use of certain notions of health and sickness. This was necessary because Nietzsche looks on the proper moral philosopher as a kind of spiritual physician. But he does not wish to administer palliative medicaments to relieve our maladies; he wants to show us how to avoid the malady in the first place, by shaping our souls properly; and also, if we have the maladies, how to use them rather than acquiesce and let them use us.

Then it had to be asked, of Nietzsche in particular and of psychiatry in general, what are the criteria of mental health? There seemed no notion of psychic hygiene parallel to that of physical hygiene, because we are not as clear on what we want to use our souls *for* as we are on what we want to use our bodies for. A healthy liver is one which secretes bile efficiently, etc., but the potentialities of the mental facilities of will, intellect, and feeling are too various to assign to them obvious functions success in the fulfillment of which settles whether or not they are healthy. Because the appeal to health is tenuous, Nietzsche often veers in the direction of aesthetic criteria as a substitute for it, the dual criteria of wondrous to

---

42 [At this point the text contains the note: "But 'punctuations' view subverts foregoing."—Ed.]

contemplate and creative. He continues to phrase his aesthetic norms in hygienic terms: but the two standpoints are no longer united in substance. The soul is not seen as beautiful because it is healthy, but simply called healthy because it is beautiful, or is experienced as such, and creates beauty. In the final reckoning, aesthetics defeats hygiene.

The judgments of good and evil made by men are themselves to be judged according to the criteria, good and bad. We have seen that the latter denote the healthy and the unhealthy, or, at other times, the beautiful and the ugly. It is asked of the judgment of good and evil, from what human disposition does it flow and what disposition will its acceptance tend to foster? The health or disease of the disposition, its nobility or baseness, will determine whether the value it inspires and/or feeds on is good or bad. Thus in *The Antichrist* Nietzsche asserts that "what is bad is all that is born of weakness, or envy, or revenge"[43] because these are considered ugly or poisonous dispositions.

Given that he believes this, we then considered whether the belief did not involve committing the genetic fallacy, the fallacy of supposing the worth of a product to be determined by the worth of what produced it. I then defended Nietzsche by arguing that the appeal to its genesis as a means of settling the worth of something was not always fallacious. In particular, the genetic fallacy is obviously involved where there is an independent method of assessing the production (as there is in geometry, but as there doesn't seem to be in religion). A moral conviction could be *discredited* by showing that only the weak and sickly would appeal to it. I also showed that Nietzsche asked not only the genetic question, but the functional one: what does this value lead to, and that there could be no functional fallacy parallel to the genetic one (although Kant thought there was).

Now talk about the function of value judgments smacks of an inquiry into their utility. And since we know that Nietzsche was antiutilitarian, it was necessary to point out that whereas the utilitarian fixes on what is useful as productive of pleasure, Nietzsche is concerned with what is useful as productive of hygienically and aesthetically valuable men. His is a *species* interest. A man whose dispositions were oriented to the search for pleasure would be condemned by Nietzsche as all-too-human, close to the animal and far from the übermensch.

Though Nietzsche repudiates values connected with miserly dispositions, he nevertheless often evinces a respect for values-as-such. He prefers men to create tablets, even if out of the stone of ugly feelings, to men who fester in their diseases and do not engage in the value enterprise at all. Thus he says (*Genealogy of Morals* 1.8) that the vengeance and

43 Nietzsche, *The Antichrist*, sec. 57, p. 647.

hatred of the Jews was the deepest and most sublime in human history since it gave birth to new values. His attitude here is governed by his appreciation of creative activity as such.

Finally, I reapproached the problem of establishing criteria of good and bad in a *linguistic* manner, by considering an object, namely an apple, which could be qualified as good or bad, but not as good or evil. I showed that a complicated context was required in order for an apple to count as bad. I wondered where this context was to be found when a man's soul is judged to be rotten. A rotten apple repels the eater. If a rotten soul repels the aesthetically oriented onlooker, who are we to choose as a qualified onlooker? All people agree on what makes apples sound or rotten. But what Nietzsche might call an ugly servile temperament would be represented as beautifully humble by others. In short Christians can adopt aesthetic metaphors to describe their value preferences: there where would Nietzsche be? He would simply be proposing a new set of values, a tiresome project which can be executed with but little imagination, whereas he had hoped to reveal a new value plane beyond the accepted one from which he could assess the latter.

Now we can, at least provisionally, rescue Nietzsche by construing the phrase "Beyond Good and Evil" in yet a new sense. To go beyond good and evil is no longer to look for new canons, but to probe more deeply into accepted moral precepts. It is to probe deeply into the people who assert the values, with the aim of exhibiting a discordance between their preachings and their practices, their feelings and the way they respond.[44] In other words, the transvaluation of values is not now interpreted— and I warn you that this is only a tentative suggestion, so I stress the "now"—as a new table of moral imperatives. Rather, it is an attack on the claims to authenticity and genuineness of those who subscribe to current values.

Thus the transvaluation of values is undertaken by Nietzsche in his role as dialectician. He sees it as his task to disclose as the hidden prong of an accepted value a tendency quite *opposite* to what the value itself enjoins. By saying he is dialectical I mean that wherever he sees A, he asserts not-A, not arbitrarily and fancifully, but with arresting psychological acumen. The current values are shown to be the opposite of what they purport to be. People disvalue arrogance: it is because they are afraid of boldness, and are unable to be bold; the wish to be bold is so strong, the incapacity so equally crippling, that boldness must be banished, declared worthless. When they counsel respect, we know it is only fear, which is close to hate, which is nearly the reverse of respect. They claim

44 For the view that all morality is immoral, see Morgan, *What Nietzsche Means,* pp. 170–75.

to be polite and considerate: they are in fact only obsequious.[45] They adopt maxims like "love thy neighbor" because they resent and hate their neighbor—these maxims do not flow from the core of their being. Nietzschean thought thrives on opposites such as these. He exploits the linguistic fact that any pattern of behavior which receives a laudatory characterization can equally be described in pejorative terms. How then, confronted by superficially similar modes of conduct, is he able to decide which is noble, which base? When is the positive account, when the negative, in place? When is apparent triumph defeat, when is love hate, when is chastity timidity? The answer is that the positive is in evidence when the conduct flows from and is informed by strength, power, exultation, fullness of being, and the negative is in evidence when the conduct is stimulated by and has the marks of cowardice and weakness. The notion of degrees of power, or, at times, what is quite different, degrees of the exercise of the power which constitutes every man, or the extent, in his later work, to which all human powers are governed by an integrating will-to-power (Nietzsche in his deterministic and libertarian moments—a tension in his thinking)[46] is the concept which emancipates us from the myopic concentration on good and evil. The powerful man is generous out of an urge to share his delight; he does not lose, he gains by giving: by giving he enlarges the scope of his influence; he embraces more of the universe. (Feuerbach, "Only the absolute, the perfect form, can delight without envy in the forms of other beings.")[47] The weak and sickly man is generous out of fear; for him giving involves self-laceration, resentment: he does not take the universe in; he lets himself be swallowed up in it, unable to stand alone. The powerful man is able to be savage and destructive: he is not therefore a ruthless beast, because he disciplines his passion. The weak man cannot be similarly self-assertive: the credit he arrogates to himself for his meekness is well beyond his due.[48] His laugh is nervous, cringing, self-abasing, while the powerful laugh confidently. The powerful man engages in the project of self-transformation: he joyously

---

45   [At around this point in the text a notecard is clipped to the manuscript, reading: "Feuerbach (*The Essence of Christianity* p. 314) is instructively Nietzschean in justifying approaching Christian wrongdoing and heathen wrongdoing differently: 'What then, speaking briefly, is the distinction between Christians and heathens in this matter [of sensuality GAC]. The heathens confirmed, the Christians contradicted their faith by their lives. [One might say, that it is part of *some* Christian faiths that the life *must* contradict the faith GAC]. The heathens do what they mean to do, the Christians do what they do *not* mean: the former, where they sin, sin with their conscience, the latter against their conscience; the former sin simply, the latter doubly; the former from hypertrophy, the latter from atrophy of the flesh'."—Ed.]

46   [At this point the text contains the remark "Expand."—Ed.]

47   Ludwig Feuerbach, *The Essence of Christianity*, p. 7n.

48   A passage in Morgan, *What Nietzsche Means*, p. 135, fully illuminates this.

shapes his soul into a form which *may* superficially resemble that of the weak man, but he lacks the rancor of the latter.

In thus explaining how Nietzsche manages to opt between competing characterizations of a single piece of behavior, whose worth is elusive, I have found it necessary to invoke three conceptions which are very important and should receive more extended examination. These are the conceptions of Nietzsche as a dialectician, the idea of power, which pervades his thought, and the notion of rancor, or resentment, or ressentiment, which is the capital Nietzschean sin.

11. Nietzsche's concern about man is a *species-concern*. He is not, to his discredit, greatly exercised by the lot of this or that man here or there in the universe. But he is anxious lest the health and worth of humanity-as-such suffers a decline. This worth is measured by the worth of its highest specimens. A single great man redeems the folly of a people, gives point to their existence. Thus he says in *Beyond Good and Evil* (126), "A people is a detour of nature to get to six or seven great men."[49] From this it would appear that the multitude is given a very subsidiary role to play in history.[50] But he says immediately thereafter, "Yes, and then to get around them." And I take this to mean that the ideal of the race must not fixate itself on today's heroes; it must constantly suffer transformation: so the people must persist, as a breeding place for new heroes, for new supermen, and as a recalcitrant leaven, inhospitable to total molding by its most exalted representatives. So the health of the bulk of men counts as well, and if mankind as a whole wanes, its exemplars will diminish in excellence. (An interesting account of the interplay between great men and the herd is given by Dostoyevsky, in *Crime and Punishment*.)[51] The great need enemies with whom to engage in battle: the better the enemy, the better the great man can become. Ideally, all men would be courageous warriors of the spirit, spurring one another on, like the pupils in a highly intelligent class.[52] The achievement of this ideal is, Nietzsche fears, endangered by the acceptance of Judeo-Christian values. In the preface (6) to *The Genealogy of Morals* he therefore says: "The intrinsic worth of these values was taken for granted as a fact of experience and put beyond question. Nobody, up to now, has doubted that the 'good' man represents a higher value than the 'evil,' in terms of promoting and benefiting mankind generally."[53] (Note: as opposed to ministering to the satisfactions of

49 Nietzsche, *Beyond Good and Evil*, p. 87. See also Morgan, *What Nietzsche Means*, pp. 78–81, 201, 205.
50 See Lea, *The Tragic Philosopher*, pp. 60–63.
51 Dostoyevsky, in *Crime and Punishment*, chap. 5, pp. 308–10.
52 Lea, *The Tragic Philosopher*, p. 58.
53 Nietzsche, *The Genealogy of Morals*, p. 155.

this and that man, here and there.) When we reflect on what Nietzsche has to say about suffering, we see this distinction clearly. By palliating the wounds of the sufferer, by giving him the pity he demands, you destroy his will-to-live, his will to discover, discover himself, uncover a new self; you destroy the possibilities of new manifestations, new flowerings of human creativity emerging from his suffering, from a *long* struggle with it. You help the man but you endanger his dignity, and especially the dignity of the race. But to return to the passage: "suppose the exact opposite were true. What if the 'good' man represents not merely a retrogression but even a danger, a temptation, a narcotic drug enabling the present to live at the expense of the future? More comfortable, less hazardous, perhaps, but also baser, more petty—so that morality itself would be responsible for man, as a species, failing to reach the peak of magnificence of which he is capable. What if morality should turn out to be the danger of dangers?"[54]

Let us now look more closely at Nietzsche's account of the origin or genealogy of the two competing value-orientations which we can roughly characterize as the ethics of health and the ethics of utility, of relief of suffering. We shall find that they differ not only in content, not only in their bases of power and weakness, respectively, but also in the sense that one is positive, affirmative, and derives a negative from itself; the other knows best how to negate, and only affirms itself indirectly. The one only negates because it posits or affirms; the other can only posit if it negates. The first treat themselves as good—if asked to justify this they would describe themselves. The second can only justify treating themselves as good by describing the evil whom they are unlike. The categories of good and bad can be construed as good and not good, or un-good. The categories of good and evil can be construed as evil and un-evil. If you probe the rejections of the morality of strength, you will find that they are in essence acceptances. Thus Nietzsche says somewhere, "I love the great despisers for they are also the great adorers."[55] The powerful exult in themselves and through experiencing the "pathos of distance" expel the weak from the court of worth. The weak have no strong support in themselves: they cringe before the strong, deny them rights, and only derivatively embrace as good their own fragility and pettiness.[56]

Let us see how Nietzsche gives historical content to these abstractions. He begins (*Genealogy of Morals*, 1.2) by rejecting an account of value

54   Ibid.
55   [This is from *Thus Spoke Zarathustra*, prologue, 4. Cohen has quoted the 1891 translation by Thomas Common. For a slightly different translation see Nietzsche, *Thus Spoke Zarathustra*, p. 127.—Ed.]
56   On good/bad good/evil see Danto, *Nietzsche as Philosopher*, pp. 158–59.

concepts which construes them as utilitarian in origin: speaking of those who hold this hypothesis he says:

"Originally," they decree, "altruistic actions were praised and approved by their recipients, that is, by those to whom they were useful. Later on, the origin of that praise, having been forgotten, such actions were felt to be good simply because it was the habit to commend them." We notice at once that this first derivation has all the earmarks of the English psychologists' work. Here are the key ideas of utility, forgetfulness, habit and, finally, error, seen as lying at the root of that value system which civilised man had hitherto regarded with pride as the prerogative of all men. This pride must now be humbled, these values devalued. Have the debunkers succeeded? [He feels that if utility is all, then value-as-such is devalued and even utility is a parasitic value-code.—GAC]

Now, it is obvious to me, first of all, that their theory looks for the genesis of the concept *good* in the wrong place: the judgement *good* does not originate with those to whom the good has been done. Rather it was the "good" themselves, that is to say, the noble, mighty, highly placed, and high-minded who decreed themselves and their actions to be good, i.e.: belonging to the highest rank, in contradistinction to all that was base, low-minded and plebeian.[57] It was only this *pathos of distance* that authorised them to create values and name them—what was utility to them? [The implication is that they required no utilitarian ethics since they were superbly self-reliant, needed to join in no lowly mutual aid society. Also what do they need contracts for? (See also 2.17.)—GAC] The notion of utility seems singularly inept to account for such quick jetting forth out of supreme value judgements. [The argument, roughly, is that utility is not something anybody can be expected to get very excited about.—GAC] Here we come face to face with the exact opposite of that lukewarmness which every scheming prudence, every utilitarian calculus presupposes, and not for a time only, for the rare, exceptional hour, but permanently. The origin of the opposites *good* and *bad* is to be found in the pathos of nobility and distance, representing the dominant temper of a higher ruling class, in relation to a lower, dependent one. . . . Such an origin would suggest that there is no *a priori* necessity for associating the word *good* with altruistic deeds, as those moral psychologists are fond of claiming.[58]

No *a priori necessity*. He claims that Judeo-Christian morality can have no monopoly as expressive of the human spirit. Response: the first time the human spirit gave itself shape in values, it did not take on such a mold. But whereas he denies that Judeo-Christian morals are the only morals, he does not say that they are not morals at all. He does not

57   See Lea, *The Tragic Philosopher*, p. 233.
58   Nietzsche, *The Genealogy of Morals*, pp. 159–60.

maintain that his genetic account makes such a morality impossible, but only unnecessary. That his contention is often no stronger than this, is proved by a passage in *Beyond Good and Evil* (212) where he insists only that Christian precepts have been overstressed: "The philosopher must include strength of will, hardness, and ability to make far-reaching decisions, in his ideal of human greatness. To this he has as much right as that with which the opposite teaching and the ideal of an abashed, renouncing, humble, selfless humanity was taught to an opposite era like the sixteenth century, for example, which suffered from a damned up energy of will and from the wildest torrents and flood waters of selfishness."[59] When the waters of selfishness flow over, the canons of good and evil, and the injunction to compassion, are needed to restrain them. Nietzsche only fears that exclusive stress on the latter will cause those waters, the liquid energy of the self, to dry up entirely.[60]

In *The Genealogy of Morals*, 1.7, it is the Jews who are debited with having inverted the aristocratic valuations, whose origins we encountered in *The Genealogy of Morals*, 1.2. Particularly through the wily intellects of their priests, they managed to wreak vengeance on their proud oppressors by inverting "the aristocratic value equations good/noble/powerful/happy/favored-of-the-gods and [maintaining], with the furious hatred of the underprivileged and impotent that 'only the poor, the powerless, are good; only the suffering, sick, and ugly, truly blessed' . . . It was the Jews who started the slave revolt in morals."[61]

12. It is in section 10 that Nietzsche reveals the contrast I sketched abstractly between the two sets of opposites, good and bad, good and evil. He also argues that if anyone displays the virtues demanded by slave ethics, the virtues of love and compassion, it is the noble who are despised by adherents of those very ethics. He does not maintain that all their energy is devoted to tending to others, but that more is *genuinely* so directed than is that of their slaves:

> All truly noble morality grows out of triumphant self-affirmation. Slave ethics, on the other hand, begins by saying *no* to an "*outside*," an "*other*" non-self, and that *no* is its creative act [which is to say that it is not capable of creativity at all—GAC]. This reversal of direction of the evaluating look, this invariable looking outward instead of inward, is a fundamental feature of rancor. Slave ethics requires for its inception a sphere different from and hostile to its own.

59   Nietzsche, *Beyond Good and Evil*, pp. 137–38. [Here Cohen has quoted the 1955 Marianne Cowan translation.—Ed.]

60   See further Morgan, *What Nietzsche Means*, p. 349.

61   Nietzsche, *The Genealogy of Morals*, pp. 167–68. [At this point the text includes the remark: "Here interpolate Christian and Nietzschean beatitudes."—Ed.]

[Thus the slaves depend on the masters, cannot get on without them; they can maintain no sense of self, no fixed identity. The masters, on the other hand, wrench their identity out of their *own* souls, don't need the souls of the underdogs to guide them to values and feelings.—GAC]. . . . The opposite is true of aristocratic valuations: such values grow and act spontaneously . . . in order to affirm themselves even more gratefully and delightedly.[62]

And here is what I indicated, that only the noble are capable of following even the slave ethics: "Such a man [the powerful man—GAC] simply shakes off vermin which would get beneath another's skin—and only here, if anywhere on earth, is it possible to speak of 'loving one's enemy.' The noble person will respect his enemy, and respect is already a bridge to love . . . Imagine, on the other hand, the 'enemy' as conceived by the rancorous man! For this is his true creative achievement: he conceived the 'evil enemy,' the Evil One, as a fundamental idea, and then as a pendant he has conceived a Good One—himself."[63] The noble man does not have to look at his enemy always as an enemy. He can suspend the antagonism, laugh together with him. He need not fear that by respecting his enemy he is losing his sense of self and his self-respect. But the slavish man cannot enjoy this confidence. For him to compromise his enmity, truly to love his antagonist, would be ethically suicidal: his values could not but crumble, premised as they are on denying all worth to those he resents.[64]

Connected with these opposed value postures are the contrasting uses the noble Greeks and the feeble Christians make of their gods or God.[65] The Greeks benefit from their gods, use them to still neurosis, not to create it. The Christian God is an instrument of punishment. Even when he is merciful, he punishes any claim to worth the fortunate sinners can hope for. For mercy, to differ from kindness, must presuppose a lack of desert. God's Grace is required because he is evil. This thought is developed by Nietzsche in *The Genealogy of Morals*, 2.23:

A single look at the Greek gods will convince us that a belief in gods need not result in morbid imaginations, that there are nobler ways of creating divine figments—ways that do not lead to the kind of self-crucifixion and self-punishment in which Europe, for millennia now, has excelled. The Hellenic gods reflected a race of noble and proud beings, in whom man's animal self had divine status and hence no need to lacerate and rage against itself. For a very long time the Greeks used their gods precisely to keep bad conscience [of

---

62 Nietzsche, *The Genealogy of Morals*, pp. 170–71.
63 Ibid., p. 173.
64 [At this point the text contains the remark "Is the temporal priority of good to bad in 'good and bad' and of 'good and bad' to 'good and evil' paralleled by a logical or conceptual priority?"—Ed.]
65 Nietzsche, *Human, All Too Human*, 1.114, p. 94.

guilt feelings—GAC] at a distance, in order to enjoy their inner freedom undisturbed; in other words they made the opposite use of them that Christianity has made of *its* God.[66]

And then he goes on to say that when a Greek has transgressed against a social principle his fellows would ask: "'How can such a thing happen to people like us, nobly bred, happy, virtuous, well-educated?' . . . 'Well, he must have been deluded by a God,' they would finally say, shaking their heads. This was a typically Greek solution. It was the office of the gods to justify, up to a certain point, the ill ways of man, to serve as 'sources' of evil. In those days they were not agents of punishment but, what is nobler, repositories of guilt."[67] By contrast, the Christian regards what is good as done by God.[68]

13. Part of our resistance to Nietzsche's attack flows, no doubt, from a well-grounded unwillingness to certify the lawless energies as much as he did. But part flows from another source: the fact that though we have a concept of morality, and of the moral man, we have almost completely lost a concept of virtue; we do not, in calling someone virtuous, mean anything different from what we mean when we call him moral. When we call someone moral, we usually make reference to the results, or, more sophisticatedly, the intended results of his behavior. If these benefit, he is moral; if they detriment, he is immoral. But the concept of virtue, as classically entertained, related less to the sorts of actions a man undertook and more to the sort of man he was, though the sort of man he was *might* be exhibited in his actions.[69] A libertarian might believe that a man's actions cannot be discovered by examining what sort of man he is: in consequence, the sort of man he is is not finally relevant to a moral evaluation of him. He may be jealous, cowardly, hot-tempered, but if he acts kindly in despite of the proddings of these dispositions, he is moral nonetheless, and some, like Kant, would say, far more conspicuously praiseworthy than the man who effortlessly does the right thing.

---

66 Nietzsche, *The Genealogy of Morals*, p. 227.

67 Ibid., p. 228.

68 [At around this point a typed card containing the following is attached: "Feuerbach (*Essence of Christianity*, p. 321) The standpoint of virtue is related to the standpoint of determinism, in a way well brought out in this passage: 'The poet *must* bring forth poetry, the philosopher *must* philosophise. They have their highest satisfaction in the activity of creation, apart from collateral or ulterior purpose. And it is just so with a truly noble moral action. To the man of noble feeling, the noble action is natural: he does not hesitate whether he should do it or not, he does not place it in the scales of choice; he *must* do it'."—Ed.]

69 See Morgan, *What Nietzsche Means*, pp. 155–56.

The standpoint of virtue is different from this.[70] Here the jealous man would be condemned, because of his rotten soul. And Nietzsche holds that his supposedly moral behavior must be a sham anyway, a cover-up, a dialectical distortion of his true nature. The nature underlying the action is what is assessed when we have virtue in mind. And this is a point of view inimical to a society whose orientation is mechanical, a society which places maximum value on getting things done, and confers only minimal import on the condition of the doers. The psychoanalytic orientation is a profound exception to this trend. It is in consequence no accident that Nietzsche is regarded as an anticipator of Freud.

I now want to justify further my frequent characterizations of Nietzsche as an aesthetic moralist. He first appears in this guise in the *Birth of Tragedy*, which he wrote in 1872. It was his first work, produced when he was a young professor (aged twenty-eight) at Basle. In section 5 he says: "Only as an aesthetic product can the world be justified to all eternity . . . Only as the genius in the act of creation merges with the primal architect of the cosmos can he truly know something of the eternal essence of art."[71] The phrase "to all eternity" warrants serious consideration. At the end of the lectures on Nietzsche, I may have time to say something about his doctrine of "eternal recurrence," a theory which is not to be found in either of the books I have asked you to read.[72] To put it roughly for the time being, Nietzsche believes that to approach the world in a healthy way is to approach it in a spirit of affirmation, of high optimism. Whether you are affirmative or not is tested by whether you can will that what you are now witnessing, experiencing, and doing be repeated endlessly, to all eternity, whether you can will that it recur forever. And the suggestion in the *Birth of Tragedy* is that you can only attain to this universe-embracing posture if you regard the universe from an aesthetic point of view. Furthermore it is the creative genius who can come closest to this viewpoint; he can see the universe as a wonderful creation when he himself engages in wonderful creation. Here we have an early seed of the notion of the superman, the man of surpassing strength, as the creative man. It will be recalled that the slavish people of "good and evil" are allowed as their single "creative" act the act of rejecting the powerful men, and this can now be seen as tantamount to rejecting creativity. This is why I suggested that resentment and rancor are Nietzsche's original sins. They offend against the aesthetic matrix. (An objection or elucidation: If we are only to justify the *entire* universe, we cannot do

---

70   See Nietzsche, *Human, All Too Human*, 1.60, p. 60.

71   Nietzsche, *The Birth of Tragedy* (Golffing translation), p. 42. [Above Cohen cites from the Haussmann translation, partially overlapping with this passage.—Ed.]

72   [Unfortunately there is no discussion of this topic in the manuscript.—Ed.]

this by showing how part of it is valuable for any other part of it, for this would leave the second part unjustified. To justify the entire universe cannot be to show how it is good for something other than itself, because by definition it is everything. So only the aesthetic way is open.)

That Nietzsche is an aesthetic moralist is further supported by the account of aesthetics I gave in the earlier portion of these lectures. I said there could be no rules for *judging* art, as for judging *actions*. One of the things I am also anxious to stress is that aesthetic creation, unlike righteous moral conduct, could not proceed according to rules. A man who follows moral precepts rigorously is a moral man, provided only he has fixed on the right moral precepts. But there can be no correct precepts in aesthetics, since, if there were, originality, which is essential to art, would be lost. There can be no rules for producing good paintings as there can be rules for producing good chairs.[73] This is just the difference between art and craft. For the expert craftsman is a master of the *rules*, and there are no expert artists, only brilliant ones. It does not follow that a chair cannot be a work of art: it only follows that such a chair was not produced by following rules. Of course, identical objects are possible, but one would not be an art object.

14. From the fact that no creative artist follows rules, it does not follow that what he creates lacks all order, that no structure can be discerned in or ascribed to it. I am not trying to give a conceptual justification for nonfigurative excesses. But the order or, one might say, rule, discoverable in the work, must not exist antecedent to the creation of the work. The norm does not make the work: the work makes the norm. And this is one reason why the powerful creative man cannot be attacked or criticized: there are no norms to appeal to other than the ones he establishes—he is a law unto himself.[74] Because a norm, though a self-imposed one, is thus involved in aesthetic creativity, Nietzsche's certification of power is not a certification of lawlessness, but of power formed and structured. And thus there emerges his aesthetic ideal of humanity, explicitly trumpeted in the following passage from *Joyful Wisdom/The Gay Science* (290):

One thing is needful. "Giving style" to one's character—a great and rare art! It is exercised by those who see all the strengths and weaknesses of their own natures and then comprehend them in an artistic plan until everything appears as art and reason and even weakness delights the eye. Here a large mass of

73 "Let us finally consider what a naivete it is in general to say 'Man *ought* to be thus and so!' Reality shows us a ravishing wealth of types, the luxury of an extravagant play and change of forms." Nietzsche, *Twilight of the Idols*, "Morality as Anti-Nature," 6, quoted in Morgan, *What Nietzsche Means*, p. 120.

74 See Nietzsche, *Human, All Too Human*, 1.170, p. 129.

second nature has been added: there a piece of original nature has been re-moved: both by long practice and daily labour. Here the ugly which could not be removed is hidden; there it has been reinterpreted and made sublime. . . . It will be the strong and domineering natures who enjoy their finest gaiety in such compulsion in such constraint and perfection under a law of their own . . . Conversely, it is the weak characters without power over themselves who *hate* the constraint of style . . . They become slaves as soon as they serve; they hate to serve. [This is so because the only service they know is service to an alien power—they have not the power to serve under, or lord over, themselves. They cannot, dialectically, be servant and master in one.—GAC] For one thing is needful: that a human being attain his satisfaction within himself—whether this be by this or that poetry or art; only then is a human being at all tolerable to behold. Whoever is dissatisfied with himself [to be dissatisfied *with* oneself is to be unable to find one's satisfaction *in* oneself—GAC] is always ready to re-venge himself therefore; we others will be his victims, if only by always having to stand his ugly sight. For the sight of the ugly makes men bad and gloomy.[75]

The final few sentences are important; they link the two moments in the aesthetic orientation which I have hitherto spoken of separately—the contemplative aesthetic and the creative aesthetic. For it now turns out that that which it is rewarding to contemplate is that which creates and has been created through aesthetic labor. Also, if you cannot create, you will be rancorous.

But let us now return to *The Genealogy of Morals*, which is the prin-cipal work we have to consider. In sections 11 and 12 of part 1 Nietzsche associates himself firmly with aesthetic in opposition to moral values. A moral community would be one in which no one menaced anyone else, in which each lent a helping hand to every other, in which all an-tagonism would be eradicated. Nietzsche questions the value of such a state of affairs, asking (11): "Who would not a thousand times prefer fear when it is accompanied [need it always be?—GAC] by admiration to security accompanied by the loathsome sight of perversion, dwarfish-ness, degeneracy?[76] And is not the latter our predicament today? What accounts for our repugnance to man—for there is no question that he makes us suffer? Certainly not our fear of him, rather the fact that there is no longer anything to be feared from him."[77]

75 Nietzsche, *The Gay Science*, p. 99.
76 [The following remark, which forms part of the typed text at this point, is marked "omit." However, it is not deleted. It is included here for reference. "Here Nietzsche reveals one of his important pre-suppositions—the assumption that it is impossible to curtail the forces in man which are socially disruptive without diminishing the strength and energy of the possible offenders against society. He is in favour of sublimation, but insists that it must operate on a personal level only, not on a social one."—Ed.]
77 Nietzsche, *The Genealogy of Morals*, p. 176.

In section 12 this claim is amplified. There is an insistence on the dialectical unity of fear and respect: value attaching only to an object which merits respect, it is impossible for a retiring, unaggressive humanity to be valuable: "The leveling and diminution of European man is our greatest danger; because the sight of him makes us despond . . . We no longer see anything these days which aspires to grow greater; instead, we have a suspicion that things will continue to go downhill, becoming ever thinner, more placid, smarter, cosier, more ordinary, more indifferent, more Chinese, more Christian—without doubt man is getting 'better' all the time . . . This is Europe's true predicament: together with the fear of man we have also lost the love of man, reverence for man, confidence in man, indeed the *will to man*. Now the sight of man makes us despond."[78]

One sort of man the sight of whom uplifts rather than depresses is described by Nietzsche in 2.17. They are conquering heroes, and their terrible advent is described, and thereby justified, in thoroughly aesthetic terms:

> Such beings are unaccountable; they come like destiny, without rhyme or reason, ruthlessly, bare of pretext. Suddenly they are here, like a stroke of lightning, too terrible, convincing, and "different" for hatred even. Their work is an instinctive imposing of forms. They are the most spontaneous, the most unconscious artists that exist. . . . They are actuated by the terrible egotism of the artist, which is justified by the work he must do, as the mother by the child she will bear.[79]

Notice that this is different from the characterization of the aesthetic hero we found in *The Gay Science*. There is an opaque mindlessness about these conquering men; they do not strenuously and subtly establish dominion over themselves—they recklessly establish their sway over others. These are very different uses to which one's power can be put, and Nietzsche seems to vacillate between them. In the next passage (2.18) he shows what happens when this power is directed against the self, and interpreting Nietzsche freely, we may say that in a more developed stage of humanity, its ideal can no longer reside in the savagery of conquest, but in the self-transformation of the creative artist, in a not very metaphorical sense of artists:

> Now the material upon which this great natural force was employed was man himself, his old animal self—and not, as in that grander and more spectacular phenomenon—his fellow man. This secret violation of the self, this artist's

78   Ibid., pp. 177–78.
79   Ibid., p. 220.

cruelty, this urge to impose upon recalcitrant matter a form, a will, a distinction, a feeling of contradiction and contempt . . . has it not given birth to a wealth of strange beauty and affirmation? Has it not given birth to beauty itself? Would beauty exist if ugliness had not first taken cognisance of itself, not said to itself, "I am ugly"?[80]

Thus we see that grandeur can be shaped out of pettiness, if only that pettiness is not certified by, e.g. the Christian religion. And this, again, is a deeply dialectical proposition, followed up by what he says in 3.4: "An artist must resist the temptation to 'analogy by contiguity' which would persuade him that he, himself, *is* what he imagines and expresses. The truth of the matter is that if he *were* that thing he would be unable to express it: Homer would not have created Achilles, nor Goethe Faust, if Homer had been an Achilles or Goethe a Faust."[81] Nor could Nietzsche be Zarathustra. Thus Wagner succumbs to the typical velleity of the artist,[82] failing to be content with portraying Christianity and becoming Christian.

Here Nietzsche is reversing the genealogical approach: for the latter involved assessing the product by examining what produced it; here he is certifying the producer because of the beauty of the product, though in himself, if he had not created something *out of himself* (a phrase with many meanings), he would be worthless. These issues put on the agenda the question of Nietzsche as dialectician, to which I shall now turn.

More than once I have said that Nietzsche thinks dialectically. Less than once have I explained what the word "dialectical" means. We can elucidate its developed philosophical meaning by considering its crude, primitive meaning. The latter is connected with the word "dialogue" which in turn means two words, or a double flow of words. But dialectic, as we find it in Plato, is not just any dialogue; it is not mere chat, but dialogue with a certain structure. The structure, or rather rhythm, is a series of negations and counternegations. Thus I say, "Political society is best organized in a democratic manner. Thereby everybody has a say." And you reply, "No, because too many people will be disposed to say the same thing, and so minorities lose their say in thorough democracies. What is wanted is enlightened aristocracy, which permits liberty to everyone." "Yes, ideally perhaps. But in fact aristocracy will lead to abuse, and curtail the liberty it is supposed to secure against the dangers of democracy. So democracy, while imperfect, is the best we can have." Now such a discussion has a superiority over solitary contemplation since it is all too

80   Ibid., p. 221.
81   Ibid., p. 235. But cf. Nietzsche, *Human, All Too Human*, 1.200.
82   [A reference to *The Genealogy of Morals*, 3.4, p. 236. I thank David Owen for pointing this out.—Ed.]

easy to jump to a conclusion to which an antagonistically inclined interlocutor may have an insuperable objection. Dialectical thinking consists
in internalizing this rhythm, in cultivating the disposition to entertain
the opposite of everything you are inclined to say, and then arbitrate
somehow between the contending assertions. The dialectician's faith is
that truth will lie in some subtle synthesis of the opposed moments. I
say subtle, because the synthesis is not always a case of each being true
to some extent but each being totally true but in different ways. A fully
dialectical proposition is one which can only be true if its negation is true,
exhibitable as P if and only if not P. There can be pleasure if and only if
there is pain. There can be liberty if and only if there is authority. There
can be surface if and only if there is an interior. And so on.

So far I have shown how dialectic is a method of thinking. Nor can
I fully characterize this method by giving its rules. For this itself would
be undialectical. The rules of the dialectic must themselves harbor their
opposites, and so only training and practice, not appreciation of precept,
can teach you to think dialectically. But some philosophers have construed dialectic not as a principle of thought, or not only as that, but as
a principle of reality. Not as a kind of quasi-logical sequence of propositions, but as a temporal sequence of events and stages of reality as well.
Most clearly associated with dialectic in this more ambitious sense is
Hegel. Hegel believed that the essence of reality is mind, which matter, a
creation or construct of mind, imperfectly reflects. And since the principle
of mind, of the individual thinking mind, is the movement of opposites,
this is the principle of the world as well. All action provokes a reaction
in physics, all political suppression gives way to political freedom, health
stimulates disease, poverty leads to wealth, tranquillity produces explosion. It is not just the concept of each which must be connected with the
concept of the other, but the reality of each must generate the reality of
the other.[83] Later German thinkers who did not accept Hegel's idealism,
his reduction of matter to mind, still accepted the dialectical character
of reality. In Marxism, this leads to what is called dialectical materialism. And in Nietzsche it takes a less easily summarized form. But I have

83   [Around this point in the manuscript a typed card is attached, stating: "Feuerbach,
(*Essence of Christianity*, p 250) is relevant to the question of Nietzsche's dialecticality. What
he said is worth quoting: ' . . . the characteristic principle of religion [is] that it changes that
which is naturally active into the passive [and thus corrodes man's power, man's will GAC].
The heathen elevates himself, the Christian feels himself elevated. The Christian converts
into a matter or feeling, of receptivity, what to the heathen is a matter of spontaneity. The
humility of the believer is an inverted arrogance,—an arrogance nonetheless because it has
not the appearance, the external characteristics of arrogance. He feels himself pre-eminent:
this pre-eminence however, is not a result of his activity, but a matter of grace; he has been
made pre-eminent; he can do nothing toward it himself. He does not make himself the end
of his own activity, but the end, the object of God.' It is, of course, arrogant, to regard yourself as important to such a being as God."—Ed.]

referred to instances of dialectic in his work. There is his reversal of values into their opposites, his demonstration that Judeo-Christian morality is fundamentally immoral, by its own lights, at its roots. There is his insistence on the need for both tables of values, on the danger of adhering exclusively to one pole of the value antithesis (here dialectic becomes not descriptive, analytical, but normative). And there is his account of the master and slave ethics as sets of opposites, the former containing an affirmation and a negation, the latter a negation and a negation of the negation (the flower's development as negation of the negation). And there is the insight that in order for there to be a Faust, there must be a not-Faust, namely Goethe. I want now to give other cases of dialectic in Nietzsche.

In part 1, section 14 of *The Genealogy of Morals* he gives a picturesque account of how the slaves transform certain of their characteristics into their opposites:

> Impotence, which cannot retaliate, into kindness; pusillanimity into humility; submission before those one hates into obedience to One of whom they say that he has commanded this submission—they call him God. The inoffensiveness of the weak, his cowardice, his ineluctable standing and waiting at doors, are being given honorific titles such as patience; to be *unable* to avenge oneself is called to be *unwilling* to avenge oneself—even forgiveness . . . They call the thing they seek not retribution but the triumph of justice; the thing they hate is not their enemy, by no means—they hate injustice, ungodliness; the thing they hope for and believe is not vengeance, the sweet exultation of vengeance . . . but the "triumph of God who is just, over the godless."[84]

15. In part 3, section 2 there is the suggestion that chastity and sinful lust are connected, as are chastity and healthy sensual pleasure. We know who move in the first division, who in the second. And because opposites define one another, because *omnis determinatio est negatio*, the chastity of the slaves differs from the chastity of the masters. Thus Nietzsche says, "There is no inherent contradiction between chastity and sensual pleasure: every good marriage, every real love affair, transcends these opposites."[85] It transcends the opposites, or their opposition, by honoring each, and neither can be honored without honoring the other. The slaves are unable to appreciate the flesh, they can't manage it, so they have no true understanding of the value of abstention *as* abstention either: "On the other hand . . . once those pigs who have failed as pigs (and there are such) come round to the worship of chastity, they will view it simply as their own opposite and will worship it with the most tragic grunting

---

84 Nietzsche, *The Genealogy of Morals*, pp. 180–82.
85 Ibid., p. 232.

zeal."[86] This can be compared with Hegel's account in the *Philosophy of Right* of the abstinence of monasteries, which he rightly saw conferred on the flesh a tremendous importance.[87]

The phenomenon of masochism is inexplicable to the undialectical mind. For it involves a coalescence of the pleasant and the painful. But if you are Nietzsche you can see no unacceptable paradox in the fact that the slaves, and their leaders, the ascetic priests, enjoy their suffering. The self-torture they inflict must, he believes, be a kind of joy to them. The apparently antibiological asceticism of the priest *must* have some function in the history of the species. So we now see that, in the third section, Nietzsche's dialectic leads him to reject his own unqualified rejection of slave ethics, though he accepts it not on its own terms, but as partially ministering to health (see 3.11).[88] The point is put most forcibly in 3.13, which I urge you to read carefully. It ends by saying, "When this master of destruction, of self-destruction, wounds himself, it is that very wound that forces him to live."[89] We now see that Nietzsche's idea of health is as subtly dialectical as all of his other ideas. For health is no bland burping solid stability; it is conquest of disease, not absence of disease. Health thrives on illness. But illness is always only the necessary condition of health: it must be battled against. Goethe cannot remain only Goethe: he must create Faust as well.

It remains to consider and try to tie together topics we have already mentioned: suffering, pity, friendship, enmity, and power. We know that Nietzsche measures value by degree of power, and we also know that he deplored the utilitarian rejection of suffering. We have just seen how these two views are connected: health, or power, requires illness, or suffering. Health is not a fortunate lack of infection, but the active capacity to overcome disease. The self which the powerful man overcomes is the self as passive, as prone, as susceptible. Even the creation of beauty is the response of the potentially healthy individual to the challenge of illness. Thus Nietzsche says in the *Twilight of the Idols*: "Whatever does not destroy me makes me stronger"[90] and "One must need to be strong—otherwise one will never become strong."[91] And in *Ecce Homo*: "For the healthy type, just sickness may be an energetic *stimulant* to life, to more life."[92]

---

86   Ibid., p. 233.

87   [It is not clear what Cohen had in mind with this comment.—Ed.]

88   Nietzsche, *The Genealogy of Morals*, pp. 252–54.

89   Ibid., p. 257.

90   Nietzsche, *Twilight of the Idols*, Maxims and Arrows 8, p. 467.

91   Nietzsche, *Twilight of the Idols*, Skirmishes of an Untimely Man 38, p. 542.

92   Nietzsche, *Ecce Homo*, "Why I Am So Wise" 2, p. 224. [Here Cohen uses a translation I have not been able to trace.—Ed.]

Because of this valuation of suffering, as necessary for the development of power, *compassion is devalued*; as I showed, pity, commiseration, speedy aid, palliating medicines, are construed as fundamentally more destructive than helpful to the suffering.[93] Pity is rejected for deeper reasons as well, not only because of what it leads *to*, but also because of what the demand for pity and the willingness to offer it flow *from*. The sufferer crying out for aid is deviously trying to dominate. The project of arousing pity comes from a wish to hurt, to implicate others in my suffering. The sick, he says in *Human, All Too Human* (1.50): "still have one power in spite of all their weakness, the power to hurt."[94] Pity is also a sign of misallocated power: I commiserate in order to remind myself how well-off I am, comparatively speaking. Pity, he believes, always includes condescension and contempt, and the judgment that the sufferer cannot help himself. The true friend is one who asks and gives no pity, so that he and his friend may both achieve self-mastery.

In point of dialectical fact, your truest friend is your truest enemy, if friends are those who help you to flourish and enemies those who offer you resistance. This is clear from Nietzsche's account, in *The Genealogy of Morals* 3.7, of the basis of the philosopher Schopenhauer's genius: "Schopenhauer absolutely required enemies to keep him in good spirits; . . . he loved atrabilious words, he fulminated for the sake of fulminating, out of passion; he would have sickened . . . had he been deprived of his enemies, of Hegel, of woman, of sensuality, of the human will to survival . . . It was his enemies who kept him alive . . . His rage was his balm, his recreation, his compensation, his specific against tedium, in short, his happiness."[95]

So we are told not to pity the weak. But we are not told to step on them either. We are told either to ignore them and let them struggle or to challenge them, but to carefully weigh challenge to capacity to respond.[96] The powerful man is not to express his power in oppressing others: only the weak man "*wishes* to hurt and to see signs of suffering."[97] ("*Wish*" is important here, since wishes express what you are more reliably than doings.) True power is self-mastery, and often the urge to conquer is only a token of inadequate power: others may be subdued when I am unable to subdue myself. Nietzsche's developed and thoroughly humane view can be gathered from a late fragment:

---

93 See Morgan, *What Nietzsche Means*, pp. 177–79.
94 Nietzsche, *Human, All Too Human* 1.50. p. 54. [Cohen here too uses a translation I have not been able to trace.—Ed.]
95 Nietzsche, *The Genealogy of Morals*, p. 241.
96 See Lea, *The Tragic Philosopher*, pp. 234–35.
97 Nietzsche, *The Dawn*. Quoted in Kaufman, *Nietzsche*, p. 194.

I have found strength where one does not look for it: in simple, mild, and pleasant people, without the least desire to rule—and, conversely, the desire to rule has often appeared to me as a sign of inward weakness: they fear their own slave soul and shroud it in a royal cloak; (in the end, they still become the slaves of their followers, their fame, etc.). The powerful natures *dominate*, it is a necessity, they need not lift one finger.[98]

In the last sentence that aspect of Nietzsche which I have occasionally mentioned, is manifest: Nietzsche as determinist, whereas we know that so many of the things he says depend on a libertarian view. I have not been able to find any resolution of this contradiction which does not smack of sophistry.

A necessary condition for the validity of Nietzsche's teaching is a threefold distinction which is often invoked, by him and many others, but never carefully hoovered conceptually. I mean the distinction between indulging one's passions, extirpating or suppressing one's passions, and channeling or organizing one's passions.[99] This problem is independent of the free will/necessitation contradiction, because we can put the issue either as three different things you can do to your passions, or three different things that happen to them. Clearly Nietzsche wants us to channel our passions, or, put in the determinist way, regards those passions as best which have been channeled. Though the trichotomy seems intelligible, it becomes cloudy when we try to apply it. Let us take the sexual drive as a paradigm instance of a passion. What would count as indulging it? Clearly it cannot be indulged unless some steps are taken, unless a sex object is sought, and is this not a form of rudimentary channeling? What about suppressing it? Well, this is often known as sublimation: when we suppress our sex drive, it is diverted; it stimulates us to write poetry and undertake chivalrous deeds. Isn't *this* a channeling? The problem here is to get the criteria of identity for a passion: are we to say that the sex drive has been directed to an artistic object, or are we to say that the sex drive has been extirpated and an artistic one has replaced it? If we differentiate passions by their objects, then we say the latter, for writing poetry is not an essential, intrinsic object of the sex drive, which could be used to individuate it. But if we do so individuate passions, then are we not already dealing with channeled passions, with drives to which a direction, an end-point, has been given? But if we do not use objects as criteria of individuation, and rely on some vague apprehension of what's pushing us, then what we vaguely apprehend will itself be vague in its boundaries and it will be impossible to say when it has been suppressed and when

---

98   Nietzsche, *Will to Power*. Quoted in Kaufman, *Nietzsche*, p. 252.
99   See Morgan, *What Nietzsche Means*, pp. 99–100, on sublimation.

it has been given a direction or goal. Are monks to be condemned for suppressing their desires, or applauded for vesting the energy in them in ritual observance? We know that Nietzsche vacillates on this, telling us that the slave cannot realize his energies on the one hand, and on the other congratulating the ascetic priest for bottling up his instincts. (Perhaps the trichotomy is unsustainable *without* the use of the free will/determinism dichotomy in the form of the distinction "within my control.")

I commend this problem to your own reflection. One instrument I invite you to use in thinking about it is the Platonic device of illuminating a problem about the individual soul by projecting it on a social canvas. Thus we can think of drives as restless elements in a population, and conceive rulers as faced with the choices of hanging them, giving them what they demand, and encouraging them to seek other goals. Will the latter be partial suppression and partial indulgence, or true channeling? This Platonic technique has many applications. It can, for example, be used in considering part 2, section 10 of *The Genealogy of Morals* where Nietzsche says:

> Whenever a community gains power and pride, its penal code becomes lenient, while the moment it is weakened or endangered the harsher methods of the past are revived. The humanity of creditors has always increased with their wealth. . . . It is possible to imagine a society flushed with such a sense of power that it could afford to let its offenders go unpunished. What greater luxury is there for a society to indulge in? "Why should I bother about these parasites of mine?" such a society might ask. "Let them take all they want. I have plenty."[100]

This can be read, though I am not arguing that Nietzsche intended it so, as an analogue of what is true of individuals, their power, and their unruly desires. Whenever a person gains in power and pride, the degree to which he has to suppress his evil instincts is diminished. The slave cannot afford to give his passions any free rein, for then they would dominate him, not he them. The powerful master mentality can permit himself excess: his reserves of strength allow him to.

And thus ends the account of the moral philosophy of Friedrich Nietzsche, the 121st anniversary of whose birth we celebrate this year.

---

100 Nietzsche, *The Genealogy of Morals*, p. 205.

PART TWO

Papers

Chapter 8

BOURGEOIS AND PROLETARIANS

I. BOURGEOIS AND PROLETARIANS

In *The Holy Family* Marx draws an important distinction between the alienation endured by the worker and the alienation endured by the capitalist in bourgeois society:

> The possessing classes and the class of the proletariat present pictures of the same human self-estrangement. But the former class feels at home in and confirmed by this self-estrangement, recognizes its estrangement as its special power, and enjoys in it the semblance of a human existence; the latter feels annihilated in its estrangement, and glimpses in it its impotence and the reality of an inhuman existence.[1]

My first task is to explain what Marx means in this difficult passage, and why he thinks it is true. It is impossible to fulfill this task without drawing upon material from works other than *The Holy Family*. This is because the passage is embedded in a section which throws little light on it, since it uses the distinction to argue that the proletariat is revolutionary and the bourgeoisie conservative, without elaborating the distinction itself. Furthermore, almost the entire text of *The Holy Family* is given over to polemic of an unusually minute, clownish, and altogether dated kind. Serious theoretical discussion occurs only in fragments. I shall therefore explore the meaning of the *Holy Family* passage by paying attention to

---

1 "Die besitzende Klasse und die Klasse des Proletariats stellen dieselbe menschliche Selbstentfremdung dar. Aber die erste Klasse fühlt sich in dieser Selbstentfremdung wohl und bestätigt, weiss die Entfremdung als ihre eigene Macht, und besitzt in ihr den Schein einer menschlichen Existenz; die Zweite fühlt sich in der Entfremdung vernichtet, erblickt in ihr ihre Ohnmacht und die Wirklichkeit einer Unmenschlichen Existenz." Karl Marx: *Die Frühschriften*, p. 317. Translations alternative to the one offered above are given by Bottomore, in Marx, *Selected Writings in Sociology and Social Philosophy*, p. 231; and by Dixon in *The Holy Family*, p. 51. They translate the text less literally, though without, I think, any gain in intelligibility.

a characterization of the human essence which is offered in *The German Ideology* and to the doctrine of alienation as it unfolds in the *Paris Manuscripts*. These materials do solve the puzzles in the text I have quoted.[2] I begin with *The German Ideology*:

> Men can be distinguished from animals by consciousness, by religion, or anything else you like. They themselves begin to distinguish themselves from animals as soon as they begin to *produce* their means of subsistence.[3]

I shall treat this as a declaration about man's essence, because one way of fixing the essence of something is by allocating it to its genus

---

2   To illuminate one work by means of passages drawn from another is often, exegetically speaking, problematical. In the present case the problems are multiplied, for a number of reasons:

(1)   There is the alleged division of Marx's writings into those which belong to his "young" period and those which belong to his "mature" period. And if there is such a transition in Marx, it may reasonably be located within the time during which the three texts mentioned here were written. The *Manuscripts* were composed between April and August 1844; *The Holy Family* from September to November 1844; and *The German Ideology* in 1845–46. Their composition thus occupies a small number of months, but these were months of great ferment in Marx's thinking.

(2)   Many of Marx's works were not published: the *Manuscripts* remained manuscripts, and *The German Ideology* was "left to the gnawing criticism of the mice." This fact reduced the pressure on Marx to signal shifts in his use of concepts or changes in his general orientation. Two other facts had the same consequence:

(3)   The works which were published were often intended for a largely nonacademic audience.

(4)   Marx did not see his own writings, both published and unpublished, as the work of someone undergoing an exclusively intellectual development. He often wrote in response to (what he conceived to be) the changing demands of the social struggle.

Notwithstanding these reasons for caution, I regard my exegetical procedure as legitimate, since I use the other writings not to embellish a passage which already has a clear meaning, but to establish a meaning where Marx's intentions are somewhat dark. When a passage is very difficult the interpreter must be liberal in his choice of instruments; the main test of their validity will be their success in rendering the passage less puzzling. But it is also important that Marx wrote *The Holy Family* immediately after writing the *Manuscripts* so that they constitute, in a sense, a continuous *oeuvre*. And although *The German Ideology* (the other work which flanks *The Holy Family*) is very different in theme from the *Manuscripts*, it echoes the latter's stress on man as an essentially productive being. Finally, I concede that there is a measure of artificiality in distributing so much additional material around the *Holy Family* passage. My main object is to depict a worker/capitalist contrast which runs inexplicitly through the *Manuscripts*, and I begin with *The Holy Family* because in that work the same contrast is explicitly, though obscurely, drawn.

3   Marx and Engels, *The German Ideology* (Moscow edition), p. 31 (emphasis in original).

and species, its species being determined by the differentia between it and other species of its genus; and it is man's differentia which Marx is providing. Men belong to the genus animal, or at any rate to a genus of which animals are the other species. To ask which species man is is to ask what distinguishes men from (other) animals. Marx's answer is that man himself does the distinguishing. Man makes that part of his essence in virtue of which he is not an animal. This means that it is man's nature to make his nature,[4] that he is by nature a maker, or producer, in the most general sense: he produces what he is.

But Marx is also proposing that man is a producer in a more specific sense. For he performs the act of distinguishing himself from animals— the act which is productive in a general sense—by engaging in particular acts of production, in the making of things. Those acts are the concrete content of man's universal act of self-creation.

For Marx, a man is self-estranged if his existence is not in conformity with his essence. Since man is really a productive being, he should behave like one in his empirical life,[5] and his empirical life conditions should support the possibility of such behavior. Productive activity must be each individual's purpose, his fundamental interest and aim, since essence is the proper end of existence. To be nonalienated, therefore, is to engage in productive activity as an end-in-itself, to use one's powers in order to exercise them, and to exult in manifesting them. The fact that neither capitalist nor worker does this explains the first sentence of the *Holy Family* passage, which asserts that they are both alienated. The capitalist does not produce at all: he is not a producer, but an owner. And the proletarian produces, not in order to realize his powers, but for an alien reason: to stay alive.

But why is the bourgeoisie content in its self-estrangement, and the proletariat not? The answer falls into two parts: (a) the bourgeoisie, unlike the proletariat, cannot *hope* to escape its alienation; and (b) the bourgeoisie, unlike the proletariat, has no *desire* to escape its alienation.

(a) Capitalists and workers are, respectively, owners and producers. It is possible to be a nonalienated producer, but it is not possible to be a nonalienated owner. It follows that a worker can *hope* to become disalienated: the transformation is no threat to his identity. He is identified as a producer, even though he produces for alien reasons, and, as

4 Marx's view should not be overassimilated to Sartrean existentialism. It is not an originally featureless being, or Nothingness, which makes its nature, but a certain kind of animal. Animalhood rather than mere existence precedes essence for Marx.

5 If he fails to behave in this way, he sometimes comes to resemble an animal; he slips back into animalhood, from which he is essentially distinguished. There are suggestions of this kind in the *Manuscripts*. See Marx, *Early Writings*, p. 125. [The references to Marx, *Early Writings*, in this chapter are to the Bottomore edition—Ed.]

we shall see, in an alien way.[6] But a capitalist can hope for no salvation from alienation, for "nonalienated owner" is a *contradictio in adjecto*. An owner cannot cease to be alienated without ceasing to be. The capitalist must cling to his alienated life, since there can be no nonalienated life for him.

It might be objected that though the capitalist, insofar as he is a capitalist, cannot wish to be disalienated, this need not be true of the man who is a capitalist; it appears true of the man only when we focus on one of his aspects: his ownership of capital. But (at least for some purpose) Marx did treat the capitalist abstractly. He developed a phenomenology of the abstract man who is purely an owner, and nothing besides. The lines of this phenomenology will be traced later in the paper. The justification of the abstract perspective will be provided elsewhere. (A brief version of it is given in IV-3, below.)

(b) The contrasting *desires* of capitalist and worker are explicable if the following maxim, to which Marx was committed, is accepted: If a person is aware that the conditions of his life are antagonistic to the realization of his essence, he will be dissatisfied with his life situation. To this must be added the general principle that a man can demand or desire only those states of affairs of which he has some conception. The conjunction of these propositions entails that a man will desire to be disalienated if and only if he is in some way aware that he is alienated. It remains to show that the worker is conscious of his alienation, while the capitalist is not. This will explain their discrepant desires.

I shall introduce the explanation by means of an analogy. Let us say that to be nonalienated is analogous to possessing a fine human body. To be alienated is to lack a fine human body. When the capitalist confronts himself in the mirror, he sees a finely clad body. He does not realize that he lacks a fine body, because he does not even see his body—it does not exist for him: he sees only his clothes. When the worker gazes in his mirror he sees a naked but bruised and misshapen human body. He sees his body, and he sees that it is not fine. And so he desires a fine body, while the capitalist does not.

To interpret the analogy. The worker is forced to labor, and in laboring he confronts his specifically human powers, but is frustrated through being unable to exercise them properly. The capitalist never engages with his powers, even in an alienated way. *His* powers are utterly dormant, because his money exerts power *for* him: it hides his powers from him

---

6   The worker's activity is a paradigm of the activity of mankind throughout history, which is also conceived as alienated production. Mankind has revealed its essence through the "history of industry" which is "an open book of the human faculties," though it shows us the essential human faculties in an alienated form. (Marx, *Early Writings*, pp. 162–63.)

as his clothes hide his body in the analogy. He experiences no frustrating exercise of his faculties, for he does not exercise them at all.

We are now close to what Marx meant when he said that the bourgeoisie had a semblance of a human existence. He did not mean that they are nearer to being really human than are the workers. He meant that their capital, their money, the machines they own, *are* human for them: their possessions take on human powers, in a manner which will be elaborated later. They feel no need to be truly human, for they have the full gamut of human powers in their capital.[7] They have a substitute or *ersatz* humanity. The proletariat lives a truly inhuman life, while the bourgeoisie lives a falsely human life. And this is why the proletariat desires to be truly human and the bourgeoisie does not.

It is because the capitalist has lost all perception of and contact with his essence that he tolerates his alienation. But the worker daily glimpses his essence at a distance from him and experiences his humanity in a distorted form,[8] so that he hopes and desires to live in a nonalienated world. The idea that the worker possesses his humanity in a warped form while the capitalist has lost it completely can be defended by reference to the well-known characterization of alienation as the circumstance in which man becomes a thing. For the thing which the worker is said to become is a thing very like man—namely, a machine, a thing conceived and described in the vocabulary of human powers. But the thing which the capitalist becomes, as we shall see, is much more grotesque, and quite lacking in human qualities, since it lacks all qualities. The capitalist, it will emerge, is a bearer of properties which he does not have.

I have been trying to illuminate the *Holy Family* passage by means of the notion that the worker is a productive, active being, while the capitalist is not. Additional light is cast in the same direction by Marx's suggestion that whereas the workers really suffer, the capitalists do not. While not systematizing his views on suffering, Marx does reveal an attitude to

---

7   They therefore feel themselves to be active and productive: see Lukács, *Geschichte und Klassenbewußtsein*, p. 182: "[F]ür den Kapitalisten ist diese Verdoppelung der Persönlichkeit, dieses Zerreissen des Menschen in ein Element der Warenbewegung und in einen (objektiv-ohnmächtigen) Zuschauer dieser Bewegung vorhanden. Sie nimmt aber für sein Bewusstsein notwendig die Form einer—freilich objektiv scheinbaren—Tätigkeit, einer Auswirkung seines Subjekts auf." "For the capitalist also there is the same doubling of personality, the same splitting up of man into an element of the movement of commodities and an (objective and impotent) observer of that movement. But for his consciousness it necessarily appears as an activity (albeit this activity is objectively an illusion), in which effects emanate from himself." Lukács, *History and Class Consciousness*, p. 166.

8   That the worker has his essence in a warped form is suggested in the *Manuscripts* (Marx, *Early Writings*, p. 126), where we read that his activity manifests itself as passivity, his strength as powerlessness, his creation as emasculation. (The capitalist lacks activity, strength, and creation in any form.)

it in the *Manuscripts*. The topic enters the first paragraph of the work, where Marx, following Adam Smith, speaks of the separation of capital, landed property, and labor, which bourgeois society has wrought. It has sundered factors of production which were more integrated at an earlier period of economic history. (The capitalist division of labor is a fragmentation of what is already a fragment.) And Marx points out that this loss of unity (which for him betokens alienation, since he thinks any incidence of discrete spheres in society does) is *harmful* only for the workers.[9]

Two pages later, he gives an ontological formulation of this thesis:

> [I]t should be noted that where both worker and capitalist suffer, the worker suffers in his existence while the capitalist suffers in the profit on his dead Mammon.[10]

Earlier we found that the capitalist does not act on the world. Marx is now contending that he is, equally, not acted on by the world; it cannot make *him* suffer. His money insulates him against the impact of things in the world. It is only when his dead Mammon suffers, when his capital is depleted, that he has any relation to suffering, and that relation is completely external. To return to the mirror analogy: his clothes can be violated, but his body cannot be harmed. Sometimes, when he looks in the mirror, he notices that his garments are torn.

This is obviously meant to be true not of particular capitalists, but of an abstract being who is nothing but an owner of money. Yet empirical exemplification of the point is available. For three-dimensional capitalists worry when their fortunes decline, even when there is no chance that the decline will be great enough to disturb their mode of life in any way. In the Marxian contention, they are upset because they identify themselves with their capital, and they do so because, not being producers, they lack a human identity without it. They can possess human powers only derivatively, through their capital. The worker, by contrast, suffers directly. He suffers inhumanly, but he does suffer, just as he produces inhumanly, but does produce.

Marx's understanding of the significance of suffering confirms what was urged above: that the workers know that they are alienated, while

---

9   Marx, *Early Writings*, p. 69. For the original integration and its dissolution, see Marx, *Pre-Capitalist Economic Formations*, pp. 67, 86–87, 97–99. On how capitalism prepares a future integration, see Marx, *Capital*, vol. 1 (Chicago edition), p. 554 (Penguin edition, p. 637). For the most relevant passages in Smith, see *The Wealth of Nations*, 1:41–48, 57–60.

10   Marx, *Early Writings*, p. 71. What might be called the *empirical manifestation* of this is given on p. 76: "In the declining state of society, the worker suffers most. The particular severity of his hardship is due to his situation as a worker, but the hardship in general is due to the condition of society."

the capitalists do not. For in Marx's early thought suffering is a mode of knowledge. In certain later writings he asserts that the workers' misery prevents them from entertaining illusions about their position and sharpens their insight into social processes in general. He appears to think that he who knows the Woe must know the Vale. But in the *Manuscripts* the relation between suffering and knowledge is more intimate and less situational: suffering is itself a way of knowing.[11] This result is attained through a series of conceptual assimilations. Suffering *from* something is associated with suffering or undergoing that thing, that is to say, *experiencing* it, which is in turn related to *perceiving* it, that is, gaining knowledge of it. It seems that the English word "suffer" has nuances which stimulate a development of this kind. We have only to think of the interchangeability of locutions like "I suffered many years of torment" and "I knew many years of torment."[12] And the German word *leiden*, which is the one Marx used in the present connection, has similar shadings. So it appears that Marx's idea of suffering helps to explain the vision of reality of which he speaks in the *Holy Family* passage. But I am committed to elucidating that passage by means of his account of the essence of man, and suffering, it seems, failed to enter into that account.

It does not enter explicitly, but it is a corollary of the stress on production. Man cannot produce without using his body, without bringing it to bear on things in the world, and in that contact the world acts on man, and must be borne by him. On the Marxian view, activity and passivity entail one another, since each entails and is entailed by commerce with the world: "As soon as I have an object, this object has me for its object."[13] Thus productivity has a passive dimension, and since Marx is prepared to treat any passive relation to the world as a form of suffering, we are able to conclude that suffering is part of man's natural estate.

In sum: the man who works for a living encounters the world both as agent and as patient, though in an alienated way; while the man who owns for a living is separated by what he owns from both active and

11   Marx, *Die Frühschriften*, p. 275: "Sinnlich sein ist *leidend* sein. Der Mensch als ein gegenständliches sinnliches Wesen ist daher ein *leidendes* und weil sein Leiden empfindendes Wesen ein *leidenschaftliches* Wesen. Die Leidenschaft, die Passion ist die nach seinem Gegenstand energisch strebende Wesenskraft des Menschen." "Man as an objective sensuous being is therefore a suffering being, and because he feels his suffering, he is a passionate being. Passion is man's essential power vigorously striving to attain its object." Marx, *Early Writings* (Penguin edition), p. 390. For similar remarks, see Feuerbach, *Principles of the Philosophy of the Future*, especially sec. 33. The latter work appeared in 1843.

12   We also say, "I knew many years of happiness," which is replaceable not by "I suffered . . ." but by "I enjoyed many years of happiness." So knowledge has no special association with suffering, but only with passivity in general. The link with suffering is more obvious to Marx, since he is speaking of suffering and passivity as equivalent.

13   Marx, *Early Writings*, p. 208.

passive contact with things outside him. In the rest of the paper I shall explore proletarian and bourgeois alienation in greater detail.

II. THE WORKER'S RELATION TO HIS MACHINE

Capital is the link between the worker and the capitalist, since the former works at a machine, which is a physical form of capital, and the latter owns money, which is convertible into capital. I shall discuss the worker's alienation in his relation to the machine, and the capitalist's in his relation to money, since I wish to compare their situations, and capital provides a convenient meeting-point for the comparison.[14] This means that I shall neglect certain aspects of alienation, such as man's distance from his fellow man, and his incapacity for sensuous enjoyment of nature. In treating the capitalist, I shall try simply to expound Marx, since exposition of his views on this subject is rarely offered. By contrast, many discussions of the worker's alienation are available. Indeed, often what is presented as an account of man's alienation is restricted to a consideration of the worker. I hope the present paper shows such a procedure to be mistaken. As to the worker, I shall confine myself to three possible criticisms of the relatively familiar Marxian description of his position. They concern (1) product-alienation and process-alienation; (2) aspects of process-alienation; and (3) the dictum that "Man becomes a machine."

(1) Product-alienation resides in the fact that what the worker makes is taken from him. The result of his labor does not benefit him: the more he produces, the more impoverished he becomes. In addition, there is alienation "in the process of *production*, within *productive activity* itself."[15] Marx thinks that these two modes of alienation are intimately connected:

> How could the worker stand in an alien relationship to the product of his activity if he did not alienate himself in the act of production itself? The product is indeed only the *résumé* of activity, of production. Consequently, if the product of labour is alienation, production itself must be alienation—the alienation of activity and the activity of alienation. The alienation of the object of labour merely summarizes the alienation in the work activity itself.[16]

This seems unacceptable. "Active alienation" consists in the soul-destroying effects laboring at the machine has on the worker. It seems

14   See Marx, *Pre-Capitalist Economic Formations*, p. 108, where Marx asserts that money becomes convertible into capital just when labor becomes powerless, when workers cease to own their means of production. Hence the machine achieves its power over the worker just when capitalists become possible.
15   Marx, *Early Writings*, p. 124 (emphasis in original).
16   Ibid., p. 124.

that these cannot entail product-alienation, since we can consistently suppose that a man controls the product he makes by inhuman toil. If the division of labor removes this possibility, because under its sway there can be no product on which any man has a special claim, the community of workers could still own the goods they slavishly produce: at the very least those goods need not be used, as product-alienation demands, to enslave them further. Isn't Marx just wrong in thinking that from what happens to the worker within the factory one can infer what happens to the product after it leaves the factory?

Marx is also committed to the converse implication, that product-alienation entails process-alienation. (A close reading of the text reveals that he thinks the entailment is mutual. His metaphor of summation alone suggests this, since in one sense series and sum entail one another.) And this proposition seems equally dubious. For we can imagine men who have some dignity in the labor-process, although their products are taken away. Indeed many Marxists concede this, when responding to liberal claims that work has been or can be made enjoyable and fulfilling, by arguing that this only conceals alienation, since the product is still taken from the worker. These defenders abandon Marx when they give this answer, for they are separating what he connected.

Notwithstanding these objections, I think the two modes of alienation can be seen to associate naturally with each other. This begins to be clear once we recognize how bizarre it is to suggest that the workers might control the products of the factory in which they slave. For they would have the power to do so only if they owned the factory, and if they owned it, they would not submit themselves to a debasing regimen. If they controlled the product, they would not let the process alienate them. But the man who in fact controls the product is willing to rob the worker of the fruits of his toil. Such a man will naturally make working conditions as exploitative as possible. He shows himself oblivious to the worker's needs in the way he treats his product. Consistency will lead him to shape the man to the needs of the machine in the process of production. One cannot reply that the capitalist would provide salubrious conditions for the worker if he thought it profitable to do so. For the capitalist with whom we are concerned is only the agent of the machine. *It is the machine that exploits the worker.* The capitalist exploits him only because he owns the machine. He does not exploit him by means of the machine. (These asseverations are defended in III-3.)

Finally, the worker brings to the factory a consciousness that he is not working for himself, and this affects him negatively in the throes of the labor-process.

It might be thought that the filiation between product- and process-alienation traced here could be short-circuited in the following way. Product-alienation means that the product is used to enslave the worker, and that means that the product is (or is used to build) a new machine, which facilitates further process-alienation. On this interpretation, the product stays within the factory, or within the factory-system, to increase the agony of industrial life. But this solution to the problem eliminates much of what Marx comprehended in the notion of product-alienation.[17]

(2) We have seen that Marx wishes to fuse product-alienation and process-alienation. He also thinks that a number of seemingly separable elements of process-alienation are inextricable from one another. These are listed in the *Manuscripts*:[18] (i) the worker denies himself instead of fulfilling himself, (ii) he feels miserable, (iii) he does not develop his energies, (iv) he is exhausted, (v) he is debased, (vi) he works involuntarily, (vii) his work is not the satisfaction of a need but the means to the satisfaction of his needs, (viii) he works for another.

These indexes of alienation do take on a certain coherence if we begin with (vii) and use the definition of and principles about human nature which were advanced earlier in the paper. (vii) is outlawed by the definition of man. It therefore entails (v), since "debased" means "dehumanized"; and it entails (iii), since the negation of (iii) is activity in accord with man's essence. Again, we have seen that the worker knows that he is alienated in his work, and that a man will resent what he knows alienates him. This allows us to infer (ii) and (vi). (viii) is licensed by the insistence that no one would impose alienating work conditions on himself. This leaves (i) and (iv). (i) is simply a way of summarizing aspects already dealt with, and (iv) need not be true if physical exhaustion is intended, but it is certainly warranted by the picture I have tried to compose, if emotional exhaustion is allowed to count.

(3) In the *Manuscripts* Marx approvingly quotes Wilhelm Schulz, who, one year prior to the time at which Marx was writing, maintained that "the important distinction between how far men work *with* machines or *as* machines has not received attention."[19] Marx addresses himself to this question, and selects the second alternative: hence his dictum that *man becomes a machine*. It is perhaps worth registering that he does not mean

17   In this section alienation has been rooted in the fact that the worker does not receive the product he makes. Earlier, alienated labor was identified as work not performed for its own sake. These formulations seem at best independent, at worst, inconsistent. But they can be reconciled. Producing is not the worker's freely chosen end, because he is bound by contract to work, and he enters this contract to satisfy needs other than the need to exercise his powers. That the product is not his is a sign that his activity is alienated, though it does not and need not follow that if the product were his, he would not be alienated. If he does not receive the product, there can be no joy in his work, yet true joy in work is not to be had from the prospect of receiving the product.

18   Marx, *Early Writings*, p. 125.

19   Ibid., p. 80. The quotation is from *Die Bewegung der Produktion. Eine geschichtlich-statistische Abhandlung* (Zurich, 1843), p. 69.

this literally. He does not think that what is left of the human being is a robot. What he holds is that man is forcibly adapted to fit the machine, rebuilt to accommodate its demands on him.[20] He is accorded the treatment proper to a machine, and in the factory his behavior resembles that of a machine.

I do not think this famous dictum should be retained by Marxists. I think it should be replaced by a formulation which is critically different. It is better to say that man is transformed into a *tool*, or, in the words of Marx elsewhere, into an appendage of the machine.[21] Here is why the latter terminology is preferable. The craftsman wields a tool. The industrial worker cannot be said to wield a machine, for the machines of modern industry cannot be wielded. Marx wishes to say that the machine wields the worker, since he conceives him as placed at its disposal, to be pushed and pulled. A machine in operation is a system in motion and the man is what is moved. But this makes it impossible to characterize the worker as a machine (as opposed to a machine-part). The same conceptual barrier which prevents us from thinking of the worker as wielding the machine blocks the thought that the worker has become a machine once it is asserted that the machine wields *him*. The machine relates to the worker as the craftsman relates to his tool, and not as the worker ought to relate to the machine, since machines cannot be wielded. If we turn from wielding to the more general concept of controlling, under which it falls, we can then say that the worker ought to control the machine although the machine controls the worker. But if we comprehend this control concretely, then we must allow that what the machine does to the worker is not something the worker can do to the machine.

My rejection of the machine dictum as a succinct label for alienation in the factory is supported by Alan White's enlightening remarks on the meaning of the word "mechanical":

> "Mechanical" describes the manner in which we carry out some continuous train of action, such as knitting or playing the piano. It is typically used of routine or *skilled* performances which from practice we can go through without

---

20 For the empirical content of this idea in contemporary factory work, see Blauner, *Alienation and Freedom*, pp. 19–22.

21 Marx and Engels, *Manifesto of the Communist Party*, 1:40. "Appendage" is predicated of the worker in many places throughout Marx's writings. See, for example, *Capital*, vol. 1 (Chicago edition), pp. 421, 462, 530, 708. But note that in ibid., p. 436, "machine" rather than "appendage" is used. [Note that some of the above page numbers have been corrected from the previously published versions of this essay. The corresponding page numbers in the Penguin edition (Fowkes translation) are, respectively: 508 (note the term "appendage" is not used here), 548, 614, 799, and 523.—Ed.]

attention to the details and, hence, without showing or needing originality or liveliness; in short, like a smoothly functioning machine.[22]

Now this is perhaps not the noblest kind of work given to man. But it is difficult to see how it is possible or why it should be thought desirable to abolish it, for to do so would be to abridge our repertoire of skilled performances. So the machine dictum not only fails to sum up alienation in the factory; it fails to point at an unambiguously depressing idea. Anyone who insists that all mechanical activity is alienated or objectionable is being overdemanding and even silly. But if supreme value lies in realizing men's productive powers, then it is necessary to reject activities in which man resembles not a machine, but a tool.

Marx may have overlooked productive work of the kind White mentions because of his wavering perception of the difference between human productivity and what appears to be productivity in animals. He commonly cites advance planning as a distinguishing factor.[23] But certain *bona fide* skills are acquired just because they eliminate the need to apply a plan in the course of the work they enable.

Earlier in this paper I treated the idea that the worker becomes a machine as a mark of his superiority over the capitalist. That idea must be abandoned, but the point can still be made, in a different way. For the worker, though a tool, remains intimately involved in the productive process;[24] and he is a living tool, never utterly inert. He is still closer to the essence of man than the capitalist is.

III. THE CAPITALIST'S RELATION TO HIS CAPITAL

(1) At least four images of the capitalist can be found in Marx's writings: (i) He who owns things instead of producing them, or the capitalist as *Owner*; (ii) He who accumulates and hoards things instead of enjoying them, or the capitalist as *Miser*;[25] (iii) He who consumes things instead of producing them, or the capitalist as *Consumer*; (iv) He who is a most stupendously productive individual, as a member of a class under whose dominion man has changed the shape of nature.

---

22   White, *Attention*, p. 123 (emphasis added).

23   He offers other differentiae as well. See Marx, *Early Writings*, pp. 126–28; *Capital*, vol. 1 (Chicago edition), pp. 197–205, esp. pp. 199–200 (Penguin edition, pp. 283–291, esp. pp. 285–66); Marx, *Pre-Capitalist Economic Formations*, p. 91.

24   This becomes less true in those modern industrial settings in which workers do not engage with machines but merely "tend" them. See Bell, *The End of Ideology*, p. 270.

25   Marx, *Early Writings*, p. 171.

The first of these conceptions must be treated as dominant and must be carefully explored if the quotation from *The Holy Family* is to be understood. It appears irreconcilable with the fourth conception, so boldly sketched in *The Communist Manifesto*,[26] of the capitalist as dynamic director of man's conquest of nature. In *The Holy Family* Marx is suppressing this aspect of the capitalist, and in the *Manuscripts* we see the result of making this abstraction: the capitalist becomes a mere appendage of his capital,[27] though he is not appended in the same way as the worker. The legitimacy of the abstraction cannot be considered here. It must suffice to point out that although capitalists are energetic and entrepreneurial in the first phases of capitalism, Marx thought that they would tend to become pure owners, divorced from the productive process, as capitalism developed its distinctive character, so that the first image is more revealing than the fourth.

While (i) appears to exclude (iv), it is plainly compatible with (ii), though it does not entail it. As I expound (i) in detail it may come to seem incompatible with (iii), and (ii) and (iii) are apparently incompatible as they stand. Yet I believe it is possible to entertain an idea of the capitalist which embraces all three elements, in which the profligate life of the self-indulgent bourgeois (iii) is represented as a mode of existence of the capitalist who is a Scrooge (i and ii). This synthesis is articulated in the *Manuscripts*:

> Of course, the industrial capitalist also has his pleasures, . . . but his enjoyment is only a secondary matter . . . it is . . . a *calculated, economic* enjoyment, for he charges his pleasures as an expense of capital and what he squanders must not be more than can be replaced with profit by the reproduction of capital. Thus enjoyment is subordinated to capital and the pleasure-loving individual is subordinated to the capital-accumulating individual.[28]

The enjoyment of the capitalist as consumer is "calculated" and "economic" because he does not surrender himself to it. He cannot give

26 Marx and Engels, *The Communist Manifesto*, p. 35. For the values latent in capitalist production, see Marx, *Pre-Capitalist Economic Formations*, pp. 84–85.

27 See also *Capital*, vol. 1 (Chicago edition), p. 365 (quoted in fn. 34 below) and pp. 648–69 (Penguin edition, p. 450, pp. 738–39).

28 Karl Marx, *Early Writings*, p. 179 (emphases in original). Cf. *Capital*, vol. 1 (Chicago edition), p. 650–51 (Penguin edition, pp. 740–41). It may also be possible to bind (ii) and (iv), and hence all the four images, thereby rendering unnecessary the concession that (i) excludes (iv). The relevant text is *A Contribution to the Critique of Political Economy*, pp. 178–80, where Marx asserts that "the hoarding of money for the sake of money is the barbaric form of production for production's sake" (Cf. ibid., p. 217). This permits us to call capitalist production (iv) a sophisticated form of hoarding or miserliness (ii). Capitalist (ii) and capitalist (iv) both seek to collect as much exchange-value as possible, but the latter realizes that exchange-value can be acquired more effectively by producing than by hoarding.

himself up to it, because he remains tied to his money. We must now examine the nature of this tie, the nature of capitalist ownership. We must try to answer the question: What is it to be fundamentally an owner?

(2) For Marx, capital cannot exist without a capitalist who owns it. "The concept of capital implies the capitalist."[29] Property must have a human embodiment if it is to be allowed entry into economic equations. But although capital must be possessed by a capitalist, the relation of possession which unites them is most peculiar. For, as I shall try to show, it follows from the fact that the capitalist owns property that he himself lacks proper*ties*.[30] Only someone who is in a certain sense qualityless can qualify for the role of Owner. In the terms of the mirror analogy, there is no body under the capitalist's clothes, but only empty space.

Now for Marx all truly human properties are powers, or propensities to have effects on the world. He forbids us to predicate a feature of a human being unless the standard effects of possessing that feature are realized. A capitalist may appear ugly, but if his money buys beautiful women for him, then, Marx says, he is not ugly, since the effect of ugliness, its power to repel, is annulled by money.[31] This restriction on what is to count as a human feature derives from Marx's view of man as an essentially productive being, through a generalization in which productivity covers *all* powers. It is in this sense of properties that the capitalist has none: his self is not manifested in the world. And the explanation of this is the fact that he owns property, which keeps the world at a distance from him. The workers do operate on the world, in an alienated way, so that they have a dehumanized humanity, but the capitalist's humanity is a void.

Let us turn to the *Manuscripts*:

> The less you are, the less you express your life, the more you *have* . . . Everything which the economist takes from you in the way of life and *humanity*, he restores to you in the form of money and wealth. And everything which you are unable to do your money can do for you; it can eat, drink, go to the ball and to the theatre. It can acquire art, learning, historical treasures, political power; and it can travel.[32]

29   Marx, *Pre-Capitalist Economic Formations*, p. 118. See Schumpeter, *Capitalism, Socialism and Democracy*, p. 45.

30   Marx plays in a similar way with the two senses of "property" in *The German Ideology*, pp. 248–49.

31   Marx, *Early Writings*, p. 191. Cf. Feuerbach, *Principles of the Philosophy of the Future*, sec. 16: "The more qualities I have . . . the greater is the circumference of my effects and influence."

32   (a) Marx, *Early Writings*, p. 171 (emphases in original). It should be noted that Marx is speaking of anyone's money, not just the capitalist's. I take the liberty of applying what he says to the capitalist in particular, since while the worker's money latently possesses

We shall shortly consider how money performs for the capitalist, so that he does nothing himself, and therefore lacks a nature, just because he owns capital, which has such a rich nature ("it is the true opulence").[33] But first I want to indicate how Marx contrasts this form of ownership with the relation the feudal lord enjoys to his property:

[I]n feudal landownership . . . there is an appearance of a more intimate connexion between the owner and the land than is the case in the possession of mere *wealth*. Landed property assumes an individual character with its lord, is knightly or baronial with him, has his privileges, his jurisdiction, his political rights, etc. It appears as the inorganic body of its lord.[34]

It is crucial that the landowner does not see his property as something he can sell. Instead, he has entered into an "honorable marriage with his land."[35] If he comes to treat his property as alienable, he possesses it only contingently, since the very same thing could be possessed by another, and he is on the way to being a capitalist, whose ownership can be so abstract that in some instances neither he nor anyone else can say *what* he owns, but only how *much*. Manors maketh men, but factories maketh owners, and the capitalist merely owns his wealth. He engages in no intimate interaction with what he owns; he never really *has* it, where to have it is to hold it. (I intend that sense of "have" in which it is incorrect to say of an object that I have it when it is neither within my grasp nor under my control. In this sense, I do not *have* the spectacles I have left at home.) With the advent of bourgeois society "all personal relationships between

---

similar powers, there is never enough of it for these powers to spring into action. (b) The next sentence but one after this excerpt reads: "But although it can do all this, it only *desires* to create itself, and to buy itself, for everything else is subordinated to it." This confirms and extends what was argued above, that the Scrooge notion of the capitalist subjugates and limits the Consumer idea. (c) For one sense in which money can travel see *Capital*, vol. 2 (Chicago edition), pp. 169, 184 (Penguin edition, pp. 225, 242).

33 Marx, *Early Writings*, p. 171.

34 Ibid., p. 114 (emphasis in original; I have corrected the translation). Note that here property assumes the features of its owner, rather than vice versa, as is the case in capitalism. The bond between a person and his property counts as personal if it depends on the person's characteristics. See Marx and Engels, *The German Ideology*, p. 93.

At one point in *Capital* Marx refuses to offer special compliments to the feudal lord: "It is not because he is a leader of industry that a man is a capitalist; on the contrary he is a leader of industry because he is a capitalist. The leadership of industry is an attribute of capital, just as in feudal times the functions of general and judge were attributes of landed property" (Chicago edition, 1:365; Penguin edition, p. 450). Contrast ibid., vol. 3 (Chicago edition), p. 1027 (Penguin edition, p. 1021). For further nuances see Avineri, *The Social and Political Thought of Karl Marx*, p. 30.

35 Marx, *Early Writings*, p. 115. Cf. *Capital*, vol. 1 (Chicago edition), p. 101 (Penguin edition, p. 183).

the property owner and his property . . . cease."[36] No one is firmly connected with the particular property he owns and the result is that

> the medieval adage, *nulle terre sans seigneur*, is replaced with a new adage, *l'argent n'a pas de maître*, which expresses the complete domination of living men by dead matter.[37]

Let us examine the character of this domination.

(3) I have already cited a number of capacities which Marx ascribes to prodigious capital, in its money form. But what is it for my wealth to eat and drink and go to the ball or the theater *for* me? Well, the ball and the theater are essentially social occasions, where men and women get together. Marx means, I think, that money defines who comes, that I come *qua* money-owner, and that I am interested in going only *qua* money-owner. Money attracts me and brings me to these places. It is money which actually pays them a visit, and it drags me along. If eating and drinking are also understood in their social aspects, similar interpretations could be offered.

Chief among the features of capital is its "*power of command* over labor and its products." And Marx tells us that "the capitalist possesses this power, not on account of his personal or human qualities, but as the *owner* of capital," and that "capital itself rules the capitalist."[38] It would thus be a mistake to conceive the capitalist as a human being who forms the intention of controlling the worker and uses his capital to do so. On the contrary, it is capital, the machine, which controls the worker, and the capitalist does so only derivatively and abstractly, as an extension of capital, not because of any personal aspirations or through any individual virtues, such as were needed by feudal lords, who exacted respect through their own breeding and bearing.

The way in which capital wreaks an alchemical transformation on its owner is most strikingly expressed in the following passage:

> What I *am* and *can* do is . . . not at all determined by my individuality. . . . As an individual I am lame, but money provides me with twenty-four legs. Therefore I, am not lame.[39] I am a detestable, dishonorable, and stupid man,

---

36 Marx, *Early Writings*, p. 105.

37 Ibid. Cf. *Capital*, vol. 1 (Chicago edition), note, p. 163 (Penguin edition, p. 247); vol. 3 (Chicago edition) p. 724 (Penguin edition, p. 755). Similar to Marx's discussion is Hannah Arendt's distinction between property and wealth. See *The Human Condition*, p. 56. The distinction between feudal lord and capitalist takes a radical turn in and is essential to the work of Schumpeter. See *Capitalism, Socialism and Democracy*, pp. 137ff.

38 Marx, *Early Writings*, 85 (emphases in original).

39 Therefore I cannot even suffer. See above.

but money is honored and so also is its possessor. Money is the highest good, and so its possessor is good. Besides, money saves me the trouble of being dishonest; therefore I am presumed honest. I am *stupid*, but since money is *the real mind* of all things, how should its possessor be stupid?[40] . . . I who can have, through the power of money, everything for which the human heart longs, do I not possess all human abilities? Does not my money, therefore, transform all my incapacities into their opposites?[41]

As Bottomore translates the passage, the capitalist has these faculties *through* rather than *by means* of money. (The German preposition is *"durch,"* which can be translated either way.) I believe Bottomore's decision accords with Marx's intentions, for I do not think Marx meant that capital is an *instrument* I use to get what I want. Rather, my capital gets it and has it *for* me, and I have it only *through* my capital. Money shines on my life and makes it bright, but the light in my life is always a reflection. Marx is not saying that a woman falls in love with me because I am rich, or that I entice her by means of my money. Rather, she is attracted *to* my money, she is seduced *by* my money, not by means of it, and it is even money which satisfies her. Again, when I am honored because of my money, it is my money which is honored, and I only as its keeper. I have neither love nor honor, but complete semblances of both, since my money has both, and my ownership of my money is only a semblance of real possession.[42]

These theses can be called philosophical: it is not easy to establish precise verification-conditions for them. Yet they correspond to some observable tendencies in capitalist society. Some capitalists do have abilities which decay because they have no need or occasion to use them. When a society tends to make a healthy body and a healthy mind mere means to survival or enrichment, the powers of mind and body tend not to be used when money can secure whatever they enable a man to get. Thus the ontological topsy-turvy is accompanied by psychobiological corruption.

IV. CONCLUDING REMARKS

(1) The contrast between bourgeois and proletarian may now be restated. For Marx, human characteristics are powers, and powers are interpreted as capacities to produce. In bourgeois society property is what

---

40   "Stupid" and "mind" are translations of *geistlos* and *Geist*.

41   Marx, *Early Writings*, p. 191 (emphases in original). On the ignorant capitalist's ownership of knowledge, see *Capital*, vol. 1 (Chicago edition), pp. 397, 422n, 462 (Penguin edition, pp. 483, 508n, 548).

42   For the meaning of real possession, see Marx, *Early Writings*, pp. 193–94.

is produced, so that to have properties is to create property. The worker does create property, in an alienated way; therefore he has properties, of a deformed sort. The capitalist, as mere Owner of property, has no properties. He does not even *have* the property he *owns*, for to have a thing is to be in intimate active contact with it. The capitalist is more distant from being truly human than the worker is. He is not a creator and he is therefore not even a real possessor: he is a sham possessor. The worker is a degenerate creator, and this is thought to be better.

Each is a man who is dominated by a thing, namely capital, whose most immediate form for one is the machine, for the other, money. In the body of the paper I have tried to show the objective differences between the two relations of domination. Now I wish to bring into relief certain more psychological aspects. To this end I propose the following schedule of possibilities.

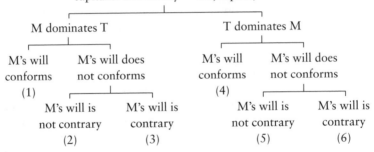

CHART OF PSYCHOLOGICAL POSSIBILITIES
Relation between Man and Thing
(worker and machine — i.e., capital;
capitalist and money — i.e., capital)

M dominates T   T dominates M

M's will   M's will does   M's will   M's will does
conforms   not conforms   conforms   not conforms
(1)   (4)

M's will is   M's will is   M's will is   M's will is
not contrary   contrary   not contrary   contrary
(2)   (3)   (5)   (6)

The chart distinguishes six states of mind. I am using "will" in a very general sense, comprehending any mode of desire or volition. My will conforms to my situation (1, 4) if I enjoy what I am doing, if I feel fulfilled in it. If my will fails to conform (2, 3, 5, 6), this may be because I am opposed to what I am doing and I find it oppressive (3, 6) or because I merely acquiesce in my position, without investing my self in it (2, 5).

The images of capitalist and worker which we have examined both belong on the right-hand side of the schedule, for they are both alienated. Marx usually locates the worker under (6), portraying him as disposed to resent and react against his position. The worker never falls under (4): he never enjoys his alienated life. Some things Marx says about the worker warrant the application of (5). But (6) must be standard for the worker: he can satisfy (5) only temporarily, since otherwise his revolutionism would disappear.

In the *Holy Family* passage, the capitalist is allocated to category (4): he enjoys his alienated life. I have found confirmation and explanation of this in the *Manuscripts*, although some of the texts I have used might be construed so as to deposit the capitalist in category (5), making him a dull and passive agent of his capital. But no interpretation could make him satisfy (6).

What would satisfy the descriptions on the left-hand side of the schedule? It seems that (1) applies to the energetic capitalist presiding in the early phases of bourgeois society. Such a capitalist is as close as any can be to being nonalienated. I hesitate to say that he would be regarded as fully nonalienated, since Marx would perhaps consider him too removed from concrete productive processes to deserve this title. Items (2) and (3) could represent resourceful industrialists who, in different ways, get no satisfaction out of their activity. Such types do not occur in Marx's writings, at any rate not as central characters for the purpose of theory.

A worker who fell under (1) would be a genuinely nonalienated man. There cannot be workers of types (2) and (3), for this would violate the principle that it is satisfying to live in accordance with the definition of one's essence. Nevertheless many contemporary alienation-hunters would be prepared to find cases of (2) and (3), and would declare that they instantiate alienation, since psychological indexes are now often treated as sufficient for that designation. Again, much of what is now identified as alienation falls under (4), another category containing no workers for Marx. This is the worker as described by semi-Marxist radicals who make concessions, like those I referred to in II-1. C. Wright Mills's "cheerful robot"[43] probably belongs in this category.

(2) The present paper can be read as a reply to a recent article by D. C. Hodges, who claims that the only party to alienation in the *Manuscripts* is the worker, and that the capitalist is free in the measure that the worker is alienated. I do not know what Hodges would say about the *Holy Family* passage, for he does not mention it. That his case with respect to the *Manuscripts* is weak has, I think, been demonstrated here.

Hodges[44] deals with the power of money by saying that "to the enlightened bourgeois it is a means and not an end."[45] But we find no such enlightened bourgeois in the *Manuscripts*. Hodges exploits Marx's assertion that "if the worker's activity is a torment to him, to another it must be *delight* and his life's joy."[46] But the *Holy Family* passage shows that

---

43 Wright Mills, *White Collar*, p. 233. Wright Mills, *The Sociological Imagination*, p. 171.

44 Hodges, "The Young Marx—A Reappraisal."

45 Ibid., 228.

46 Ibid., 227. Quoted from Martin Milligan's translation: *Economic and Philosophic Manuscripts of 1844*, p. 79.

Marx took this kind of delight to be compatible with the deepest alienation. I am in qualified agreement with one of Hodges's theses: Marx's doctrine of alienation does not refer to "the human situation as such."[47] He is concerned with the alienation of particular kinds of men. But I deny that the worker is the only kind of man who is alienated.

I do not agree with Hodges that to embrace the capitalist within the alienated fold is to reduce emphasis on the proletariat as the agency of revolutionary social change. I am against drawing this inference, for I have sought to explain (in I) why the capitalist cannot be expected to revolt against his situation.

(3) I would like to suggest that, in proposing his concept of the capitalist who merely owns, Marx adumbrates the idea of the separation of ownership and management, which has been so popular since Berle and Means.[48] It might be thought that in making this attribution I am trying to vault an impassable gulf between metaphysics and economics, but it is significant that Marx refers to an ownership/management cleavage in the third volume of *Capital*,[49] and assigns a crucial importance to it.

But why, it may be asked, do I suppose that there can be a connection between the phenomenological study of the abstract capitalist, considered in this paper, and the remarks Marx made on a more empirical basis about the tendencies in capitalist development which lead to the atrophy of the capitalist, as far as the production process is concerned? To generalize the objection: why is it supposed that from the sort of analysis provided in this paper one can reach an understanding of real capitalists in the real world?

I believe I can answer these questions, but here I shall only outline the steps I would take: (1) It can be shown that the worker whose alienation Marx describes is also a product of abstraction, and was known to be such by Marx. (2) The justification of treating both worker and capitalist abstractly is that bourgeois political economy implicitly does so. (3) The justification of beginning with the abstractions of political economy in an inquiry which purports to be relevant to three-dimensional people is that, for Marx, that science sums up, anticipates, and even prepares the future development of capitalism, for the movement of modern history

---

47   Hodges, "The Young Marx—A Reappraisal," 224. The first sentence of the *Holy Family* passage (". . . the *same* human self-estrangement") shows that the argument must be qualified.

48   Berle and Means, *The Modern Corporation and Private Property*.

49   Marx *Capital*, vol. 3 (Chicago edition), pp. 449–59, 516–18, (Penguin edition, pp. 535–45, 601–3). Avineri, *The Social and Political Thought of Karl Marx*, pp. 174ff., provides an original and illuminating discussion of the passages.

is a movement toward abstraction, and political economy is the ideal expression of that movement.[50]

Complete abstraction can never be achieved because men cannot become completely dehumanized. What halts the increasing alienation is the socialist revolution,[51] to which bourgeois economists are blind. But Marx thought and said that their vision was acute when they described the condition of man under capitalism.

---

50 The *Manuscripts* passages most relevant for establishing these interpretations are in Marx, *Early Writings*, pp. 76–77, 82, 137–39, 181.

51 In which the proletariat brings human existence into harmony with the human essence: Marx and Engels, *The German Ideology*, pp. 54–55.

Chapter 9

THE WORKERS AND THE WORD: WHY MARX
HAD THE RIGHT TO THINK HE WAS RIGHT

[W]hile Marx was so much alive to the ideological character
of systems of ideas with which he was not in sympathy, he was
completely blind to the ideological elements present in his own. But
the principle of interpretation involved in his concept of ideology
is perfectly general. Obviously we cannot say: everywhere else is
ideology; we alone stand on the rock of absolute truth. Laborist
ideologies are neither better nor worse than any others.

—JOSEPH A. SCHUMPETER, *A History of Economic Analysis*, p. 33–34

Ein allbekanntes und in den Augen der bürgerlichen
Wissenschaft entscheidendes Argument gegen die Wahrheit des
historischen Materialismus besteht darin, daß er auf sich selbst
angewendet werden muß.

—GEORG LUKÁCS, *Geschichte und Klassenbewußtsein*, p. 234[1]

In this paper I want to defend Karl Marx against the kind of argument
typified by the remarks of Schumpeter quoted above. The argument I
propose to refute belongs to a class of arguments, the members of which
are bound together by a shared formal structure. The arguments are
pressed against many theorists, Marx being only one of them. What these
theorists have in common is that they try to account for the workings of
human thought by means of explanations which may be called *reductive*,
since they end by assigning to human thinking a status lower than the
one it receives from those who hold no such theory. They demote human
thinking to a lower grade, because they entail that human thought is not
primarily an effort to arrive at *truth*, in the normal acceptation of that
word. The objection takes the form of a *tu quoque*, a complaint that the
theorist cannot claim validity for his own views, since he has chosen to

---

1 "A common argument against the validity of historical materialism and one regarded by bourgeois thought as decisive, is that the methods of historical materialism must
be applied to itself." Lukács, *History and Class Consciousness*, p. 228.

268

doubt that it is profitable or right to assess views for their validity. The objector's argument might run as follows:

(1) According to you, human thought-processes have a status lower than what they are usually conceived to have. In particular, you maintain that it is inappropriate and/or impossible to assess them for their truth or falsity.
(2) But your theory is itself a series of human thoughts.
(3) Therefore it must have the properties you ascribe to human thinking in general.
(4) Therefore you cannot advance it in the spirit in which you advance it, as a candidate for truth.
(5) In short, the character of your theory makes it illicit for you to put it forward.

An example of a theory often dealt with in this fashion is relativism, the doctrine that what is true for one person may be false for another, that truth and falsehood are not properties of propositions, but of propositions as held by this or that person, where that p is true for X does not entail that p is true for Y, and where that p appears true to X entails that p is true for X. The objector will point out that he need not regard this theory about truth as true for anyone other than its propounders. It may be true for you, he says, but it does not appear true to me. And you cannot, on your own principles, prevent me from dismissing your theory in this way.

Another victim of the *tu quoque* argument is that version of pragmatism which declares that a proposition is true if and only if it is useful to believe it, or that there really is no property truth which attaches to propositions but only the property utility. The natural objection is that pragmatism shall be accepted only if *its* utility is demonstrated, that its utility can be demonstrated only by showing that it is useful to believe that pragmatism is useful, and the latter proposition can be supported only by showing that it is useful to believe that it is useful to believe that pragmatism is useful, and so on endlessly; so that pragmatism, while not immediately self-stultifying, like relativism, is nevertheless prevented by its own principles from being a theory which anyone can claim he knows he has a right to hold. One can advance the theory, but one cannot hope to argue successfully for it.

Relativism and pragmatism, as just sketched, are thin and uninteresting theories, and I know of no noteworthy philosopher who has put either forward in quite so spare a form. It is therefore perhaps unsurprising that they seem so open to the charges put by *tu quoque* argument. But this form of argument has also been used against elaborate theories of distinguished pedigree. One such theory can perhaps be constructed out of a certain trend in Freud. It cannot be characterized as Freud's settled and consistent view, but it is in the Freudian corpus, and it is certainly sponsored by some followers of Freud. It is the theory that people who purport to be seeking the truth are really only sublimating unfulfilled needs, or gratifying a voyeuristic disposition, or driven by some neurosis which has no interest in truth at all. The reply will be that the Freudian cannot regard himself as dispassionately researching into the psychology of knowledge or as revealing truth when reporting his results.

Some physiological psychologists might be indicted in this way, and also some radical behaviorists, such as B. F. Skinner. The first treat thoughts as processes in the brain, the second as behavioral responses to stimuli, and within each camp are those who claim to dispose of the notion of truth when characterizing the nature of thought. The response to them will be: Why should *I* take an interest in *your* brain-processes? And: Why should I be guided by what you have been reinforced to say? Indeed in the second case, the case of Skinner, one might reply: Why should I allow you to condition me to think as you do?

I shall point to no fallacy in the *tu quoque* argument. My quarrel is not with the argument but with those who use it with such undiscriminating eagerness that they often misapply it. For what frequently prompts its employment is a desire not to consider the detail of the theory being attacked. And what just as frequently makes the attack irrelevant is that the theorist is willing to claim an exceptional status for his theory. Once he does this the crucial premise used by the critic has vanished, for that premise is "*All* human thought-processes have the character indicated by the theory." The theorist can evade the critic's argument simply by asserting that his theory is not among the ideas to be treated in the manner in which his theory treats ideas. The critic can then justly demand from the theorist a defense of his assertion that his theory enjoys a special immunity. The *tu quoque refutation* is thereby transformed into a *challenge*, and instead of closing discussion of the theory, the critic succeeds in opening it, in a potentially fruitful way. Instead of giving the wrong sort of argument he puts the right sort of question. We shall now see how this question arises for a theory held by Karl Marx, and how we may imagine him answering it.

The *tu quoque* charge against Marx depends on the way he sought to explain the social theories of thinkers who preceded him. When Marx considered such theories, when he asked why Plato said what he did in the *Republic*, why Thomas Aquinas thought as he did about society and government, why Hobbes held the views he held, and why they differed as they did from Locke's, he began his answer to such questions by identifying each thinker as the intellectual representative of a certain class, and he called his theory the *ideology* of that class. For a thinker to be

the intellectual representative of a class two conditions are necessary:
(1) His theory must serve the interests of the class, in the sense that if it
is generally accepted, the class will flourish, will be able to seize power,
or to protect the power it has. (2) The members of the class must feel
drawn to the theory; they must find it natural to believe in it. Not that
they must recognize it for what it really is, a weapon fashioned for their
use. On the contrary, it is demanded by Marx's theory that they do not
deem their ideology particularly appropriate to their needs and aspirations. They must find their representative's ideas plausible whenever they
are disposed to reflect on man and society, even when their class interests
are far from their minds. For Marx all interesting and significant social
theories have this secret class character. They are not therefore what they
purport to be, for they are not the result of unbiased efforts to arrive at
the truth. They are rather to be understood as expressing and supporting
the interests of classes, and for this reason Marx calls them "ideologies,"
a term he uses to suggest error and illusion.

The critic now claims to have found an incoherence in Marx's view.
We may imagine him addressing Marx as follows: your theory, the very
theory with which you explain social theory, is itself a social theory.
Therefore it represents the interests of a certain class, in fact those of the
working class. It follows that your theory has the properties you have assigned to all class-bound theories. It is the ideological reflex of the working class. It embodies the particular kind of false consciousness to which
laboring men are prone. It is your role to articulate this consciousness.
You are therefore forbidden to regard your work as genuinely scientific.

There is no doubt that Marx would feel moved to resist this indict-
ment. He would begin by granting that his doctrine was expressive of
proletarian interests. But he would argue that the situation of the proletariat has unique features which ensure that its intellectual representative
is developing a theory which is not an ideology, that he is possessed of
a correct rather than an illuded consciousness of reality. The position of
the workers is such that they have a privileged access to the facts about
reality in general and society in particular. The circumstances of their life
and struggle bring them into contact with the Word, with truth itself. This
licenses their intellectual representative's scientific posture. The workers
and the Word are destined for each other, and the scientific status of
Marxism is a result of that destiny.[2]

---

2 In his essay "Der Funktionswechsel des historischen Materialismus" ("The Changing Function of Historical Materialism") Georg Lukács replies to the critic in a manner
which differs importantly from the one sketched here, and he too thinks he is speaking for
Marx. He believes that Marx would be prepared to judge his own doctrine in the way he
judged the best work of political economy, which he regarded as true for its time, but false
insofar as it extended its claims to all human history instead of restricting them to men as

I want to explain and defend the response I have attributed to Marx. But let me make clear what I shall be defending. The critic's argument does not purport to show that Marx's theory is false. It aims at showing only that he lacks the right to regard it as true. I believe that Marx's theory is to an important degree true, but in this paper I shall sponsor only his right to think it true.

It is important to separate the position of Marx on the issue which concerns us from an attitude to which it might loosely be assimilated, and which once can associate, at least loosely, with the name of Stalin. For Stalinists also thought that theories devised and presented on behalf of the proletariat were true. Why? Because the proletariat is fated to be the dominant class, and the final victor in the battle of history. And that is the beginning and the end of the Stalinist argument for this thesis. For them truth is *identified* with whatever theories help the workers to prevail. They really revise the concept of truth, since for them there is no *objective* standpoint from which the claims of Marxism might be judged true.

This is not the way in which Marx thought that theories which expressed the interests of the proletariat were true. He does not deny that there can be an objective standpoint. On the contrary he asserts that the proletariat occupies that standpoint. Marx is not departing from the standard idea of truth, according to which true statements correspond

---

they behaved on nascent capitalism (see *Geschichte und Klassenbewußtsein*, pp. 234–35). Lukács's essay opposes vulgar Marxism, which in his view extends historical materialism in an analogously illegitimate way. Lukács counterclaims that the principles of historical materialism are very difficult to apply to precapitalist epochs (*Geschichte*, p. 238).

I do not think Lukács's position is supported by Marx's writings. I believe that in a curious way Lukács himself commits what Marx took to be the error of bourgeois economists. For he takes the notion of "economics" in a narrow, capitalist sense, and only by this means succeeds in restricting its explanatory scope. He himself seems to recognize this (see *Geschichte*, p. 247), but he does not appreciate the consequence of his usage: it separates him from historical materialism, within which terms like "economics" and "production" are applied not, of course, loosely, but liberally, the generality of the notions enabling Marx to theorize about all past history and not merely about capitalism, as Lukács would have it.

Lukács (*Geschichte*, p. 239) cites as evidence for his contention certain statements in Engels's *Origin of the Family*. But the use he makes of these was refuted in advance by Plekhanov, in the course of his polemic against N. I. Kareyev and others (see *The Development of the Monist View of History*, pp. 167–70). Finally I must mention a passage in the first volume of *Capital* (Chicago edition, p. 93; fn. 2, Penguin edition, pp. 175–76), which explicitly and decisively rejects the sort of interpretation Lukács favors.

Lukács also attacks the vulgar Marxists for being aprioristic and unsubtle in their deployment of the base/superstructure category. Here, I believe, he writes in complete conformity with Marx, but he fails to distinguish this problem from the question of the *scope* of Marx's theory.

In these footnotes I refer frequently to the Lukács of *Geschichte und Klassenbewußtsein*, since he was much exercised by the issues considered in the present paper, but treated them in a very different and much more exciting and interesting way. While I cannot adopt his approach, I find his work too impressive to ignore.

to what is the case in the world, independent of any person's interests, or any class's interests. For him the situation of the proletariat *brings it about* that its worldview, unlike that of any other class, is correct. But this is not the beginning and the end of the argument, as it seems to have been for Stalin. The workers do not automatically have the Word just because they are workers. But because they are workers they have certain features which make it immensely likely that they will have it. It is a matter of fact that only the proletarians have such features: it is therefore a matter of fact that they possess the truth. It is not a matter of definition as it is for Stalin.

This means that between the premise that the workers will prove triumphant in the class struggle, and the conclusion that their views, and therefore Marx's theories, are correct—between this premise and this conclusion there are in Marx's thought a number of links which warrant the inference from the one to the other. It is my object to explore these links. I shall do this by presenting a series of arguments, all taken from Marx, though not all designed by him for the purpose to which I shall put them. The arguments offer the missing steps which Stalinism dogmatically neglects to provide. Their aim is to demonstrate *both* that the way the proletariat perceives the world is specially immune from illusion, that information reaches them without passing through a distorting medium, *and* that where information is not something which presents itself but something which has to be sought, the proletariat is specially well equipped to find out what is true.

The critic's challenge is that one important part of Marx's social theory, namely his account of the nature of social thought, subverts his own doctrine. The only way to meet the challenge is to refer the critic to statements in the doctrine that should silence him. But the critic may say that since such statements are part of the doctrine, they are part of what he is putting into question. Now if he insists on this, he is demanding too easy a victory for himself. We have already seen, when discussing the *tu quoque* argument more generally, that he is not entitled to say that there *couldn't* be anything in Marx's theory which makes it exempt. And that there are legitimate exempting clauses is what I shall be concerned to show.

For the inquiry to be fruitful, one Marxian thesis must be accepted: the claim that the workers will make a successful revolution. Now it scarcely follows immediately from this that the workers have the Word. What I want to display is the complex route through which Marx would hope to reach this conclusion, once a fair-minded critic has granted that premise.[3]

---

3 In some of the argumentation which follows, the claim that the workers will make a successful revolution functions not as a premise but on the contrary as a difficulty which Marx must surmount. The claim can sometimes be used by the critic and sometimes by Marx himself, and for this reason I impose it on the discussion: it serves to situate the debate.

The missing-link arguments are four in number. The first is the most powerful of them. In fact, it will emerge that the other three are either highly inconclusive or dependent for what strength they have on the first argument.

After giving the four arguments, I shall describe and examine a view held by the American theologian Reinhold Niebuhr. For he believes that if the workers are to make a successful revolution they must suffer illusions. I have said on this hypothesis one can show that the workers possess the truth. Niebuhr claims that on the same premise one can show they are blind to it. I shall end my defense of Marx by disposing of Niebuhr's thesis.

I now pass to the first argument:

(1) For Marx every class which makes a revolution does so in order to advance its own material interests. But its revolution cannot be successful unless it is certified and supported by allies in other classes, who will not benefit from it. For this reason a class will not achieve victory unless its intellectual exponents manage to propagate the idea that the aims of revolution have comprehensive validity, that they promote the interests not only of the class initiating the revolution, but of most men in the society. And so, to take an example which strongly conditioned Marx's thinking, the bourgeoisie made the French Revolution in order to liberate itself as a class, to emancipate capitalism from feudal restrictions. But it had to adopt the slogan "Liberty, Equality, and Fraternity for *all men*" in order to obtain—what it needed to succeed in its undertaking—the support of other classes. The French bourgeoisie succeeded because, to quote Marx,

> [there was] . . . a moment of enthusiasm in which it associated and mingled with society at large, identified itself with it, and was felt and recognized as the *general representative* of . . . society . . . [For] . . . it is only in the name of general interests that a particular class can claim general supremacy.[4]

Yet it is not the case that a French bourgeoisie—or even its intellectual representatives—played a cunning trick on the rest of society. They were not being devious when they disseminated false doctrine about what their revolution was intended to achieve. To convince others of the cogency of their ideas they had to propound them with passion and vigor, and they could do this only because they themselves believed that they were aiming at general prosperity. A gap exists between the interests of the

---

4 *Contribution to the Critique of Hegel's Philosophy of Right. Introduction*, pp. 55–56 (in *Early Writings*, ed. Bottomore). I have made an innocent change in the tense of the first sentence, to suit the present context. This doctrine of revolution can also be found in the *Eighteenth Brumaire*, as is shown by the next passage quoted in the paper. See also Marx and Engels, *The German Ideology*, pp. 62–62, 313. See Lukács (*Geschichte*, pp. 209–10) for a variation of this conception.

revolutionary class and those of society as a whole, but the class must deny even to itself the existence of the gap, for only then can it prosecute its aims with enough resolve to succeed. And so, to fulfill its revolutionary project a class must fall into illusion.

We encounter here Marx's belief that human beings will be stirred to action of world-historical importance only if they are inspired by the proclamation of universal ideals.[5] Thus sectional interests must believe themselves to be sponsors of humanity as such in order to act in a revolutionary way. But this pretense is not hypocrisy. Hypocrisy on so grand a scale is beyond the capacity of men, but self-deception of equal measure is not. And so, to quote again, the men of the bourgeoisie

> found . . . the self-deceptions that they needed in order to conceal from themselves the bourgeois limitations of the content of their struggles and to keep their enthusiasm on the high plane of the great historical tragedy.[6]

Marx used these essentially psychological principles to explain not only why the French bourgeoisie succeeded in making a revolution, but also why the German bourgeoisie failed to make one. The Germans, he thought, were too petty in spirit, too engrossed in very private and limited concerns to extricate themselves from them except in fantasy. They were grand in their theories, but they were too modestly self-centered, and too easily satisfied to make ambitious claims about their own historical roles. They lacked romantic ardor. And so they were unable to live their illusions.[7] And so they were unable to act on the sort of doctrine which obscures from view the gaps between the interests of different classes.

---

5   This suggests a contrast with Hegel. For Hegel "nothing great has been achieved . . . without passion" (*Introduction to the Philosophy of History*, p. 23) and reason must cunningly employ passion in order to manifest itself. For Marx passion (interest) is historically impotent if unaided by reason, and unharnessed by some ideal. But even in Marx the economic interests which use ideals ultimately also serve to realize them.

6   Marx, *The Eighteenth Brumaire of Louis Bonaparte*, p. 248. Lukács also believes that the bourgeoisie requires self-deception: "Aber die Verschleierung des Wesens der bürgerlichen Gesellschaft ist auch für die Bourgeoisie selbst eine Lebensnotwendigkeit" (*Geschichte*, p. 78). ("But the veil drawn over the nature of bourgeois society is indispensable to the bourgeoisie itself" [*History and Class Consciousness*, p. 66].) But for him it is necessary not so much while the bourgeoisie is acquiring its hold over society but rather when its dominion is crumbling. The bourgeoisie must convince itself that capitalism is vigorous when manifestly it is not, for capitalism will be overthrown when and only when the bourgeoisie no longer believes in it. This correlation between class position and class consciousness is stronger, I think, than any Marx would wish to posit. See also fn. 17 below.

7   This suggests that for Marx some nonproletariat classes may not have ideologies in the full sense. See fn. 23 for an elaboration of this point.

And unless those gaps are through appropriate action made to seem to disappear, a successful revolution is impossible.[8]

In short, for all classes except, as we shall see, the working class, the fact that a gap exists between them and other classes means that they must lose contact with the truth if they are to develop a theory which will further their interests.

Now why is the proletariat an exception to this rule? Marx thinks they are exempt because there is no serious difference between their interests and those of mankind.[9] And he gives two sorts of justification for this claim. The first sort occurs in his earlier writings, where the proletariat is pictured as a reflection of the essence of man: all other classes represent man in a warped shape. This is because what distinguishes men from other animals is their capacity to produce, and it is the workers who play the role of producers in society. This makes them essentially human,[10] and therefore their interests cannot contradict those of man as such. Furthermore, their insurgency is only superficially the mutiny of a *class*, for they have no class interests to defend, no status or acquisitions to protect or increase. They act in response to needs which any human being, regardless of his social situation, must want fulfilled. And their intense suffering is so comprehensive that it is a summation of the suffering of all men throughout history: in revolting against it they are therefore revolting on behalf of all mankind.

---

8   For Marx's remarks on the Germans, see *Contribution to the Critique of Hegel's Philosophy of Right*, pp. 56–57. In his assessment of the German character, Marx follows Hegel, who charged the Germans with political idealism and a fixation on forms in his essay *The German Constitution* esp. pp. 147, 180, 190, 206, 238. Both saw the roots of this tendency in petty selfishness, world historical cowardice, and an inability to focus on anything except narrow privilege. German thought embodied universal principles: German practice endorsed a chaos of particular interests. But the Marxian echo is in fact a rejoinder. For although Hegel was aware of the futility of constitutional ritual, of the "philosophical illusion," he shared with the French as Marx described them (*The German Ideology*, p. 51) the "political illusion." He thought that a well-ordered state would bring salvation; a new polity, not a new society. He wanted a Theseus to bring this to Germany. Marx called for a proletarian class, with radical chains, enjoining it to unite and socialize Germany in a revolution to be heralded by the crowing of the cock of Gaul. But the bird was laryngitic, and Bismark usurped Theseus's role.

9   But Lukács argues (*Geschichte*, pp. 83–85) that because there is a gap between the immediate interests and final goals of the workers, they too can suffer illusions. I shall not enter this important and essentially Leninist problematic, though some of my remarks on Niebuhr, below, are relevant to it.

10   This claim can be substantiated despite the fact that the workers produce in an inhuman way. See my "Bourgeois and Proletarians," chapter 8 in this volume, especially section 1. For what follows in the text, see Marx, *Contribution to the Critique of Hegel's Philosophy of Right*, p. 58.

I shall not assess this argument, not because I think it is below scholarly consideration, but because I am proposing to deal with Marx as a social theorist, rather than as a philosopher. That is, I am in this paper concerned with those among his claims which are empirically testable, and his characterization of the proletariat as the universal class raises *philosophical* questions which I do not wish to deal with here. I therefore pass to the second sort of justification Marx gives for denying a significant difference between the workers' interests and those of others, a justification which is less grandiose, and which emerges in his later writings. The second justification is very simple. It is that the workers form the overwhelming majority of the members of society, and that for this reason there is no gulf which they must bridge by making and believing false theories.

But is there in fact no gulf? Certainly it can be argued that since the society to be introduced by the proletarian revolution will be classless, there will be no groups with discrepant interests in it. But this contention is inadmissible here, since we are concerned with the proletariat while it is making its revolution, not with the state of affairs it hopes to realize. We have allowed Marx to presuppose that the workers' revolution will be successful, but only in the sense that they will defeat their opponents. We did not include in this success the realization of their conception of the future society. Had we done so we should have begged entirely the question whether their thoughts about themselves and society are true, since the belief that their efforts will bring about a socialist society is central to those thoughts.

The question, is there a gap between proletariat interests and those of other classes? therefore reasserts itself, and the obvious answer is that there is a gap, since the proletarian ascendancy frustrates the interests of the bourgeoisie, on any plain interpretation of "interests."[11] But this does not mean that Marx was wrong, for he said that there was no gulf which had to be *bridged*, and there is indeed no gulf of this sort. Because of its numerical strength, the proletariat is not constrained to summon other classes to its aid. So the gap exists, but it is quite consistent to argue that in the case of the workers, and only in their case, the gap does not matter. I would therefore claim for the first argument considerable power. It is a good argument for the thesis that the workers are in a position which makes it unnecessary for them to embrace false theories.

Thus the intellectual representative of the proletariat need not advocate any ideology. This does not, of course, entail that he will not. But I

---

11 It could be argued that the human interests of capitalists, taken severally, are also served by the proletarian revolution. But it is class interest which is relevant here, and a class can have no interest in its own extinction.

think Marx would accept a principle which would enjoin the entailment, the principle that it is not only the office but also the natural aim of intellectuals to discover truth, so that social theorists will arrive at it if nothing impedes them.

(2) The second argument is that the suffering of the proletariat in capitalist society is so great that their true situation cannot but be painfully evident to them, and they are consequently unable to entertain illusions about it.[12] The workers' suffering is total: they undergo everything that happens in capitalist society, they are the raw material in the process of that society, they are what it uses, so that whatever happens in it has such a strong impact on them that they cannot divert their minds from it. Every rhythm in the dynamic of capitalism comes home to them as a keenly felt deprivation.[13]

There are several ideas clustering here. One is the notion that when something hurts you, you come to know it very well. Another is the supposition that men who are made miserable by a state of affairs cannot accept theories which would distort the character of that state of affairs. And finally there is a metaphysical thought, arrived at by a kind of conceptual compression, which argues that suffering does not merely give rise to knowledge but is itself a mode of knowing. This is achieved by relating suffering from something to suffering or undergoing that thing, that is to say, experiencing it, which in turn is related to perceiving it, and indeed to perceiving it veridically, that is, gaining knowledge about it. It seems that the English word "suffer" has nuances which stimulate an elaboration of this kind, and the German word *leiden*, which is the one Marx uses in this connection, is similarly shaded.[14]

I do not think we can draw much from this second argument, in any of its forms. For reasons already stated, I shall decline to consider its most philosophical version. And the idea that what hurts you presents itself to you clearly is obviously exposed to a rich array of counterexamples, which only the most sophisticated could hope to surmount. The other idea, that one does not develop illusions about a situation in which one

12   Note that here suffering is being put to a use different from the one it had in the philosophical part of argument (1). There it was considered a reason for saying that the workers are typical of human kind; here it is a reason for saying that they have knowledge.

13   Hence Lukacs says: "[F]ür diese Klasse ihre Selbsterkenntnis zugleich eine richtige Erkenntnis der ganzen Gesellschaft bedeutet" (*Geschichte*, pp. 14–15) and "Der historische Materialismus . . . bedeutet *die Selbsterkenntnis der kapitalistischen Gesellschaft*" (ibid., p. 235, emphasis in original. P. 182 is also very interesting in the present connection). "[T]he fact that a class [sc. the proletariat] understands itself means that it understands society as a whole" (*History and Class Consciousness*, p. 2) and "Historical materialism . . . means the *self-knowledge of capitalist society*" (ibid., p. 229).

14   See Marx, *Early Writings*, p. 208. The original is available in Marx, *Die Früh-schriften*, p. 275.

is mishandled, that he who knows the Woe knows the Vale—this might, at a pinch, show that the workers know the nature of capitalism. But the same suffering makes them prone to enormous illusions about what conditions they may hope to enjoy in the future. The Marxian analysis of capitalism might therefore be defended by these anyhow dubious means, but the very same considerations jeopardize the Marxian projection of a communal future for all.

(3) The third argument is this: in the course of and because of their revolutionary struggle, the workers develop their critical powers, their ability to discern the nature of the society they are attempting to change, and their insight into the future which is gestating in the womb of the present. Marx says:

> [P]roletarian revolutions . . . criticize themselves constantly, interrupt themselves continually in their own course, come back to the apparently accomplished in order to begin it afresh, deride with unmerciful thoroughness the inadequacies, weaknesses and paltrinesses of their first attempts.[15]

To make a socialist revolution, Marx seems to think, it is vital to have a clear view of things. Truth is so necessary that the proletariat is forced to discover it.[16]

This argument is of questionable value. For plainly a commitment to revolution does not automatically sharpen anyone's wits. In fact participants in socialist movements have always been plagued by fantasies of power or of impotence. But there is a more decisive objection. The workers are not the first to make a revolution. The bourgeoisie made one too. Why, then, were *its* eyes not opened in the process? To answer this Marx would have to appeal to the first argument, about the bourgeoisie's need to close a gap the workers need not close, and therefore what strength the third argument has depends upon the cogency of the first argument.

(4) The final argument involves a trend in Marx's thought which cannot, perhaps, be considered dominant, and for this reason the argument has limited value even if it is valid. The premise is that when a class is secure in its position it needs no illusions. It needs them only when it is weak and firmly subjected, or when, although it is in power, its rule is threatened. Thus Marx declares that the economic theories of the

---

15   Marx, *The Eighteenth Brumaire*, p. 250. See also Marx and Engels, *The German Ideology*, pp. 86, 229–30.

16   Cf. Lukács, *Geschichte*, p. 34: "[E]s für das Proletariat ein Lebensbedürfnis, eine Existenzfrage ist, die vollste Klarheit über seine Klassenlage zu erlangen." See also pp. 80, 181. "[F]for the proletariat the total knowledge of its class-situation was a vital necessity, a matter of life and death" (*History and Class Consciousness*, p. 20).

bourgeoisie remain genuinely scientific as long as working-class opposition to capitalism is very feeble. But after 1830, when the capitalist order begins to be seriously challenged, "the death-knell of scientific bourgeois economy is sounded," and economists become the "hired prize-fighters" of the ruling class.[17]

The opposite holds for the place of truth and falsehood in the career of the proletariat. This emerges in Marx's assessment of the historical role of the Utopian Socialists who preceded him. He says that these men theorized when the proletariat was weak, and that they were for the most part visionaries who improvised fantastic schemes which an immature working class was willing to accept. But once the proletariat begins to feel and show its strength, it becomes possible for it to enlist a genuine social science as its ally.[18]

I have said that this trend is not dominant. Indeed, to speak strictly and candidly, it contradicts the Marxian thesis we have been investigating: that the doctrines of and for the workers are true. For on the view just expounded, the social thought of the bourgeoisie begins by being true and ends by being false, while the social thought of the proletariat undergoes the reverse development. But why, anyway, should the workers' doctrine *remain* true? Presumably because there will be no section of society capable of challenging them once they begin to exercise hegemony. Therefore, as we probe the fourth argument, it reveals itself as yet another dependent of the first argument.

This ends the exposition of four arguments intended to show that if Marx's theory serves and represents the working class, then it is reasonable to think it is correct. I now turn to Niebuhr's accusation, which occurs in the introduction to his book *Moral Man and Immoral Society*:

> No class of industrial workers will ever win freedom from the dominant classes [unless] . . . they . . . believe rather more firmly in the justice and in the probable triumph of their cause than any impartial science would give them the right to believe . . . [Only if they have these unwarranted beliefs] . . . will they have enough energy to contest the power of the strong.[19]

---

17   *Capital*, vol. 1 (Chicago edition), pp. 17–19 (Penguin edition, pp. 96–98). See also Marx, *The German Ideology*, pp. 316–17. Lukacs (*Geschichte*, pp. 231ff.) tells a somewhat different story. For him early bourgeois ideology is robust and confident, and in that measure illuded about the ultimate promise of capitalist society. When capitalism begins to fail, disillusion and a more correct consciousness emerge. This does not really conflict with Marx, since the latter is thinking within the polarities science/apologetic, while Lukács is concerned with the polarities utopian confidence/despair. Obviously despair can lead to self-deceptive apologetic, while confidence can stimulate a scientific approach to at least some questions.

18   See *The Poverty of Philosophy* (Progress Press edition), pp. 112–13.

19   Niebuhr, *Moral Men and Immoral Society*, p. xv.

Niebuhr thinks that, in order to effect its revolution, the proletariat must be under two illusions. They must think their cause more just than the evidence suggests it is, and they must think themselves more likely to succeed than any objective observer would.

The second allegation is very strange. It says that in order to be victorious they must be more confident of victory than they have a right to be. But what is the proper verdict on their belief if it turns out that they *are* victorious? It must then be clear that their confidence was not excessively great. The criticism is paradoxical, for it says that the proletariat will prevail only if it has an unwarranted belief that it will prevail. The belief may be partly self-warranting, but this does not make it unwarranted: even a person who issues a self-fulfilling prophecy cannot be reproached with confusion about what is going to happen.

In advancing this objection, Niebuhr was missing an important fact about the relation of human thought to human action, a fact which Marx sought to accommodate in his idea of the unity of theory and practice. One aspect of this idea has been stressed in our time by Stuart Hampshire:[20] that men can find a basis for their beliefs about the future not only by reviewing the evidence external to their intentions, but also in their own resolutions and decisions about what they are going to do. Marx would agree that part of what makes it certain that the workers will win is the fact that they intend to and therefore believe that they will. But if the belief that they will win helps them to win, in fact, it is difficult to stigmatize it as unwarranted.[21]

Still, Niebuhr was speaking about "impartial science." And the question may be raised whether a belief that grows out of a resolution is based on impartial science. Answer: it is not based on impartial science, but it cannot be forbidden by impartial science either, and it is the latter consideration which is relevant, since Niebuhr spoke of what impartial science gives one the right to believe, that is, what it allows one to believe. And if Hampshire's claims about thought and action are correct, no science can subvert them, however much it fails to confirm them. But Niebuhr's submission is open to a more telling refutation still. For the impartial

20   Especially in *Thought and Action*.

21   Lukács touches on the idea of knowledge gained through the resolution to engage in certain praxis. He poses the question how one can be certain that the workers' revolution will succeed, and answers thus: "Für diese Gewißheit kann es keine 'materielle' Gewähr geben. Sie ist uns nur methodisch—durch die dialektische Methode—garantiert. Und auch diese Garantie kann nur durch die Tat, durch die Revolution selbst, durch das Leben and Sterben für die Revolution erprobt und erworben warden" (*Geschichte*, p. 55). "There can be no 'material' guarantee of this certitude. It can be guaranteed methodologically—by the dialectical method. And even this must be tested and proved by action, by the revolution itself, by living and dying for the revolution" (*History and Class Consciousness*, p. 43).

scientist observing social movement when the proletariat is making its revolutionary bid would himself have to treat as a datum its belief that it will succeed, and we have seen that Niebuhr grants critical efficacy to this belief, although he wrongly thinks it unreasonable. So the impartial scientist who takes account of the proletariat's convictions will, on Niebuhr's own authority, be able to predict reasonably that workers will succeed.

Niebuhr's other claim is in no way paradoxical. In fact I think it is correct, but that it does not weaken the case which I have presented in this paper. The workers believe excessively in the justice of their own cause, if, for example, they imagine themselves utterly pure and the capitalists utterly wicked, but it is difficult to conceive how men engaged in a revolution against them can always avoid believing that they are. They can hardly shout across the barricades, "We have nothing against you personally." Or feel great compassion for them while confiscating their property. The nature of revolution demands that those who make one experience strong feelings against those who resist them, and such feelings are bound to embody irrational beliefs about the villainy of their opponents.

So I grant Niebuhr his claim. But I think it fails to affect the thesis for which I have argued, because of a distinction which I now wish to draw. We have to separate the doctrine of a class, the theory which its advocates put forward, and with which its members associate themselves when they are disposed to theorize—we have to separate this from the passions and observations of the members of the class, which weigh with them in their nontheoretical moments. Even if the doctrine is to be regarded as expressive of the passions, it need not reproduce the errors embedded in them: it is one of the functions of expression to refine what it expresses.[22]

The distinction is not constructed simply to save the workers and Marx from Niebuhr's criticism, since it holds for the thinking and feeling of all classes. Thus the ideology of the English bourgeoisie of the seventeenth century is contained in writings like those of Hobbes and Locke and Calvin, because the ideas of these men gave shape to the political behavior of that class. But the English bourgeoisie of the seventeenth century also had its narrowly emotional attachments and resentments,

---

22 Note that the concession that the workers may have many false notions does not violate the argument on which this paper has relied: that the proletariat needs no false *theory* to play its world-historical role and that therefore its intellectual representative is free to devise a true one. I appeal principally to argument (1) because it is concerned with the way a class speaks to other classes, with the message it projects into the wide social world. This is where Marxian doctrine is to be located, and in this sphere self-involved passions are transcended.

which would not normally be regarded as part of its ideology.[23] Like the proletarians', their emotions involved illusions, such as an ungrounded pride in their own spiritual worth. But in addition to such *personal* illusions of the *heart*, they had *theoretical* illusions, illusions of the *head*, and such, it has been argued, the proletariat lacks.

Now one might accept this distinction but complain that I have attributed too little significance to what I wish to call the personal factor. After all, does it not play a larger role in the worker's daily life than his articulate theoretical consciousness does? Niebuhr is entitled to press this point, and indeed to maintain that the proletarian's theoretical life is not only less vital than his personal life, but so marginal as to deserve no attention at all. But the same line of attack is not open to Marx's *tu quoque* critic, since he must accept, for the purposes of his argument and his challenge, the Marxian view that classes have substantial theoretical lives, and that Marxism is the substance of the proletariat's theoretical existence: only thus can he hope by his simple means to show that Marx's theories are unscientific. We can acknowledge the force of Niebuhr's point and still use the argument of this paper in support of the hypothetical proposition that if the workers have a theoretical life, there is reason to think it is a lucid one, And this is enough to silence the *tu quoque* critic.[24]

23   The way in which Marx speaks about the Germans (see above) is evidence that he would agree with this restriction on what is to count as ideology. The Germans lacked an ideology because they remained at the subjective level. But what about *The German Ideology* itself? To what does the title of the book refer? To a set of doctrines developed in Germany, but not for the benefit of any German class. For the Germans were "the *philosophical* contemporaries of the present day without being its historical contemporaries" (Marx, *Contribution to the Critique of Hegel's Philosophy of Right*, p. 49 [emphases in original]). The German ideology did have a class association, but only on the other side of the Rhine. The Germans developed not their own ideology, but that of others. Hence Hegel, *The German Constitution*, p. 206: "The principle which Germany has given to the world it has not developed for itself, nor has it known how to find in it a support for itself."

24   I am indebted to Isaiah Berlin, Steven Lukes, Alan Madian, John McMurty, and Richard Wollheim, all of whom commented helpfully on an earlier version of this paper.

Chapter 10

REPLY TO ELSTER ON "MARXISM, FUNCTIONALISM, AND GAME THEORY"

Jon Elster and I each worked sympathetically on Marxism for a long time, and each of us independently came to see that Marxism in its traditional form is associated with explanations of a special type, ones in which, to put it roughly, consequences are used to explain causes. In keeping with normal practice Elster calls such explanations *functional* explanations, and I shall follow suit here.[1] He deplores the association between Marxism and functional explanation, because he thinks there is no scope for functional explanation in social science. It is, he believes, quite proper in biology, because unlike social phenomena, biological ones satisfy the presuppositions that justify its use. Elster therefore concludes that the Marxist theory of society and history should abandon functional explanation. He also thinks it should, instead, draw for its explanations on the resources of game theory.

I do not think that course is open to historical materialism. I believe that historical materialism's central explanations are unrevisably functional in nature so that if functional explanation is unacceptable in social theory then historical materialism cannot be reformed and must be rejected. But I do not think functional explanation is unacceptable in social theory. My judgment that historical materialism is indissolubly wedded to functional explanation reflects my conception of the content of historical materialist theory. To display, then, the grounds of that judgment, I shall expound what I think historical materialism says. I shall provide a résumé of the theory that I attribute, on a textual basis, to Marx, and that I explicate and defend in my book *Karl Marx's Theory of History*.[2]

---

1   For reasons given in my "Functional Explanation, Consequence Explanation, and Marxism" I am not certain that explanations of causes by consequences should be considered functional explanations, but that issue is irrelevant to Elster's article ("Marxism, Functionalism, and Game Theory: The Case for Methodological Individualism"), so I shall here fall in with the standard practice of regarding what I would call consequence explanations as functional explanations. Much of this reply has already appeared in the article mentioned above, published in *Inquiry*, and I am grateful to the editor of that journal for allowing it to be reproduced here.

2   Cohen, *Karl Marx's Theory of History*, henceforth referred to as *KMTH*.

In my book I say, and Marx says, that history is, fundamentally, the growth of human productive power, and that forms of society rise and fall according as they enable and promote, or prevent and discourage, that growth. The canonical text for this interpretation is the famous 1859 "Preface" to *A Contribution to the Critique of Political Economy*, some sentences of which we shall look at shortly. I argue (in section 3 of chapter 6) that the "Preface" makes explicit the standpoint on society and history to be found throughout Marx's mature writings, on any reasonable view of the date at which he attained theoretical maturity. In attending to the "Preface," we are not looking at just one text among many, but at that text which gives the clearest statement of the theory of historical materialism. The presentation of the theory in the "Preface" begins as follows:

> In the social production of their life men enter into definite relations that are indispensable and independent of their will, relations of production which *correspond* to a definite stage of development of their material productive forces. The sum total of these relations constitutes the economic structure of society, the real *basis, on which arises* a legal and political superstructure.[3] (emphasis added)

These sentences mention three ensembles, the productive forces, the relations of production, and the superstructure, among which certain explanatory connections are asserted. Here I say what I think the ensembles are, and then I describe the explanatory connections among them. (All of what follows is argued for in *KMTH*, but not all of the argument is given in what follows, which may therefore wrongly impress the reader as dogmatic.) The productive forces are those facilities and devices used in the process of production: means of production on the one hand, and labor power on the other. Means of production are physical productive resources; e.g., tools, machinery, raw materials, and premises. Labor power includes not only the strength of producers, but also their skills, and the technical knowledge (which they need not understand) they apply when laboring. Marx says, and I agree, that this subjective dimension of the productive forces is more important than the objective or means of production dimension; and within the more important dimension the part most capable of development is knowledge. In its higher stages, then, the development of the productive forces merges with the development of productively useful science.

Note that Marx takes for granted in the "Preface," what elsewhere he asserts outright, that "there is a continual movement of growth in

---

3 Quoted in *KMTH*, p. vii.

productive forces."[4] I argue (in section 6 of chapter 2 of *KMTH*) that the relevant standard for measuring that growth in power is how much (or, rather, how little) labor must be spent with given forces to produce what is required to satisfy the inescapable physical needs of the immediate producers.[5] This criterion of social productivity is less equivocal than others that may come to mind, but the decisive reason for choosing it is not any such "operational" advantage, but its theoretical appropriateness: if kinds of economic structure correspond, as the theory says they do, to levels of productive power, then this way of measuring productive power makes the theory's correspondence thesis more plausible.[6] (I do not say that the only explanatory feature of productive power is how much there is of it: qualitative features of productive forces also help to explain the character of economic structures. My claim is that insofar as quantity of productive power is what matters, the key quantity is how much time it takes to reproduce the producers.)

We turn to relations of production. They are relations of economic power, of the economic power[7] people enjoy or lack over labor power and means of production. In a capitalist society relations of production include the economic power capitalists have over means of production, the limited but substantial economic power workers (unlike slaves) have over their own labor power, and the lack of economic power workers have over means of production. The sum total of production relations in a given society is said to constitute the economic structure of that society, which is also called—in relation to the superstructure—the basis, or base, or foundation. The economic structure or base therefore consists of relations of production only: it does not include the productive forces. The "Preface" describes the superstructure as legal and political. So it at any rate *includes* the legal and state institutions of society. It is customary to locate other institutions within it too, and it is controversial what its correct demarcation is: my own view is that there are strong textual and systematic reasons for supposing that the superstructure is a lot smaller than many commentators think it is.[8] It is certainly false that every non-economic social phenomenon is superstructural: artistic creation, for example, is demonstrably not, as such, superstructural, for Marx. In these

4   Marx, *The Poverty of Philosophy* (Lawrence and Wishart edition), p. 166.

5   As opposed, for example, to their socially developed needs, reference to which would be inappropriate here (though not, of course, everywhere).

6   For a set of correspondences of relations to forces of production, see *KMTH*, p. 198.

7   I call such power "economic" in virtue of what it is power over, and irrespective of the means of gaining, sustaining, or exercising the power, which need not be economic. See *KMTH*, pp. 223–24.

8   The common practice of overpopulating the superstructure is criticized in my review of Melvin Rader's *Marx's Interpretation of History*.

remarks I shall discuss the legal order only, which is uncontroversially a part of the superstructure.

So much for the identity of the three ensembles mentioned in the "Preface." Now relations of production are said to *correspond to* the level of development of the productive forces, and in turn to be a *foundation* on which a superstructure rises. I think these are ways of saying that the level of development of the productive forces explains the nature of the production relations, and that they in turn explain the character of the superstructure copresent with them. But what kind of explanation is ventured here? I argue that in each case what we have is a species of functional explanation.

What sort of explanation is that? It is, very roughly, an explanation in which an event, or whatever else, if there is anything else that can have an effect, is explained in terms of its effect. But now let us be less rough. Suppose we have a cause, e, and its effect, f. Then the form of the explanation is not: e occurred because f occurred—that would make functional explanation the mirror image of ordinary causal explanation, and then functional explanation would have the fatal defect that it represented a later occurrence as explaining an earlier one. Nor should we say that the form of the explanation is "e occurred because it caused f." Similar constraints on explanation and time order rule that candidate out: by the time e has caused f, e has occurred, so the fact that it caused f could not explain its occurrence. The only remaining candidate, which I therefore elect, is: e occurred because it would cause f, or, less tersely but more properly, e occurred because the situation was such that an event of type E would cause an event of type F.[9] So in my view a functional explanation is an explanation in which a dispositional fact explains the occurrence of the event-type mentioned in the antecedent of the hypothetical specifying the disposition. I called the laws justifying functional explanations *consequence laws*. They are of roughly this form:$(E > F) > E$ (a more precise specification of their form is given in section 4 of chapter 9 of *KMTH*). If this account of what functional explanations are is correct, then the main explanatory theses of historical materialism are functional explanations. For superstructures hold foundations together, and production relations control the development of productive forces: these are undeniable facts, of which Marx was aware. Yet he asserts that the character of the superstructure is explained by the nature of the base, and that the base is explained by the nature of the productive forces. If the intended explanations are functional ones, we have consistency between

---

9 Small letters represent phrases denoting particular events, and capital letters represent phrases denoting types of event. Where the letters are the same, the particular event belongs to the type in virtue of the meanings of the phrases denoting them.

the effect of *A* on *B* and the explanation of *A* by *B*, *and I do not know any other way of rendering historical materialism consistent.*

I now expound in greater detail one of the two functional explanatory theses, that which concerns base and superstructure. The base, it will be recalled, is the sum total of production relations, these being relations of economic power over labor power and means of production. The capitalist's control of means of production is an illustration. And the superstructure, we saw, has more than one part; exactly what its parts are is somewhat uncertain, but certainly one *bona fide* part of it is the legal system, which will occupy us here. In a capitalist society capitalists have effective power over means of production. What confers that power on a given capitalist, say an owner of a factory? On what can he rely if others attempt to take control of the factory away from him? An important part of the answer is this: he can rely on the law of the land, which is enforced by the might of the state. It is his legal right that causes him to have his economic power. What he is effectively able to do depends on what he is legally entitled to do. And this is in general true in law-abiding society with respect to all economic powers and all economic agents. We can therefore say: in law-abiding society people have the economic powers they do because they have the legal rights they do.

That seems to refute the doctrine of base and superstructure, because here superstructural conditions—what legal rights people have—determine basic ones—what their economic powers are. But although it seems to refute the doctrine of base and superstructure, it cannot be denied. And it would not only seem to refute it, but actually would refute it, were it not possible, *and therefore mandatory* (for historical materialists), to present the doctrine of base and superstructure as an instance of functional explanation. For we can add, to the undeniable truth emphasized above, the thesis that the given capitalist enjoys the stated right because it belongs to a structure of rights, a structure that obtains because it sustains an analogous structure of economic power. The content of the legal system is explained by its function, which is to help sustain an economy of a particular kind. People do usually get their powers from their rights, but in a manner that is not only allowed but demanded by the way historical materialism explains superstructural rights by reference to basic powers. Hence the effect of the law of property on the economy is not, as is often supposed, an embarrassment to historical materialism. It is something that historical materialism is committed to emphasizing, because of the particular way it explains law in terms of economic conditions. Legal structures rise and fall according as they sustain or frustrate forms of economy that, I now add, are favored by the productive forces. The addition implies an explanation why whatever economic structure obtains at a given time does obtain at that time. Once more the explanation is a functional one: the prevailing production relations prevail because they are relations that advance the development of the productive forces. The existing level of productive power determines what relations of production would raise its level, and relations of that type consequently obtain. In other words: if production relations of type R obtain at time t, then that is because R-type relations are suitable to the development of the forces at t, given the level of their development at t.[10]

Now to say that A explains B is not necessarily to indicate *how* A explains B. The child who knows that the match burst into flame because it was struck may not know how the latter event explains the former (because he is ignorant of the relationship between friction and heat, the contribution of oxygen to combustion, and so on).[11] In this sense of "how," we can ask: how does the fact that the economic structure promotes the development of the productive forces (or that the superstructure protects the base) explain the character of the economic structure (or the superstructure)? Consider an analogy: to say, correctly, that the species giraffe developed a long neck because of the utility of that feature in relation to the diet of giraffes (acacia tree leaves) is not to say how the utility of that feature accounted for its emergence or persistence. To that question Lamarck gave an unacceptable answer and Darwin an excellent one. To the corresponding questions within historical materialism no one has given excellent answers. I make some unexcellent attempts in chapter 10 of my book. This seems to me an important area of future research for proponents of historical materialism, because the functional construal of the doctrine cannot be avoided.

Let me now summarize my argument for the thesis that the chief explanatory claims of historical materialism are functional in form. Historical materialism's central claims are that:

(1) The level of development of the productive forces in a society explains the nature of its economic structure, and

(2) its economic structure explains the nature of its superstructure.

I take (1) and (2) to be functional explanations, because I cannot otherwise reconcile them with two further Marxian theses, namely that

(3) the economic structure of a society promotes the development of its productive forces, and

(4) the superstructure of a society stabilizes its economic structure.

---

10   For a detailed account of the nature of the primacy of the forces, see section 5 of chapter 6 of *KMTH*, which also discusses the transitional case.

11   In a widely favored idiom, he may not know the mechanism linking cause and effect, or, as I prefer to say, he may be unable to elaborate the explanation. I use both forms of expression in the sequel.

(3) and (4) entail that the economic structure is functional for the development of the productive forces, and that the superstructure is functional for the stability of the economic structure. These claims do not by themselves entail that economic structures and superstructures are *explained* by the stated functions: A may be functional for B even when it is false that A exists, or has the character it does, *because* its existence or character is functional for B. But (3) and (4), *in conjunction with (1) and (2)*, do force us to treat historical materialist explanation as functional. No other treatment preserves consistency between the explanatory primacy of the productive forces over the economic structure and the massive control of the latter over the former, or between the explanatory primacy of the economic structure over the superstructure and the latter's regulation of the former. I did not come to associate historical materialism with functional explanation because I thought functional explanation a good thing and I therefore wanted Marxism to have it. I began with a commitment to Marxism, and my attachment to functional explanation arose out of a conceptual analysis of historical materialism. I do not see how historical materialism can avoid it, for better or for worse. Contrast Jon Elster's attitude to Marxism and game theory. He wants Marxism to liaise with game theory because he admires game theory and thinks Marxism can gain much from the match. He wants to put Marxism and game theory together. I would not say that I want to put together Marxism and functional explanation, because I think functional explanation is inherent in Marxism.

At the beginning of his article Elster complains that Marxist social analysis has been contaminated by the principles of functionalist sociology. I am sure that claim is both historically and conceptually incorrect. Marxists do not indulge in functional explanation because they are influenced by the bad bourgeois science of functionalist sociology, and it is not open to them to use the better bourgeois science of game theory instead. They indulge in functional explanation because they are committed to historical materialism. Because functional explanation cannot be removed from the center of historical materialism, game theory cannot be installed there in its stead. But it might be thought that game theory could also figure at the center of historical materialism, not as a replacement but as an addition. Yet that, too, I argue, is false. Game theory may be, as Elster says, "tailor-made for Marxist analysis,"[12] but it is irrelevant to historical materialism's central theses, which are propositions (1) and (2). Its relevance, as I now explain, is to theses immediately peripheral to (1) and (2).

---

12   Elster, *Ulysses and the Sirens*, p. 34.

Elster makes deft use of game theory in a discussion of the dialectics of class struggle that I greatly admire. And it is not surprising that game theory illuminates class behavior. But Marxism is *fundamentally* concerned not with behavior, but with the forces and relations constraining and directing it. When we turn from the immediacy of class conflict to its long-term outcome, game theory provides no assistance, because that outcome, for historical materialism, is governed by a dialectic of forces and relations of production that is background to class behavior, and not explicable in terms of it. Game theory helps to explain the vicissitudes of the struggle, and the strategies pursued in it, but it cannot give a Marxist answer to the question why class wars (as opposed to battles) are settled one way rather than another. The Marxist answer is that the class that rules through a period, or emerges triumphant from epochal conflict, does so because it is the class best suited, most able and disposed, to preside over the development of the productive forces at the given time.[13] That answer may be untenable, but I cannot envisage a game-theoretical alternative to it that would qualify as historical materialist.

Elster says that "game theory is invaluable to any analysis of the historical process that centers on exploitation, struggle, alliances, and revolution."[14] But for Marxian analysis those phenomena are not primary but, as it were, immediately secondary, on the periphery of the center: they are, in the words of the 1859 "Preface," the "forms in which men become conscious of the conflict [between forces and relations of production] and fight it out."[15] To put the point differently, we may say that the items on Elster's list are the actions at the center of the historical process, but for Marxism there are also items more basic than actions at its center.[16] By "revolution" Elster must mean the political phenomenon of transfer of state power, as opposed to the transformation of economic structure political revolution initiates or reflects. Many facts about political revolutions are accessible to game theoretical explanation, but not the world-historical facts that there was a bourgeois revolution and that there will be a proletarian one. Elster urges that game theory bears on strategic questions of great importance to Marxists. I accept that contention, which is amply supported by the excellent illustrations in his article. When faced with a strategic problem, such as how to transform society, we need strategic, not functionalist, thinking. But when Marx called on the workers to revolutionize society, he was not asking them

---

13 See *KMTH*, pp. 148–49.

14 Elster, "Marxism, Functionalism, and Game Theory," p. 453.

15 Cited in *KMTH*, p. vii.

16 Hence to say, as some Marxists do, that "class struggle is the motor of history" is to abandon historical materialism.

to bring about what would explain their doing so: the exhaustion of the progressive capacity of the capitalist order, and the availability of enough productive power to install a socialist one.

The concepts exercised in the previous sentence take us away from game theory to the fundamental context of historical materialism, that of forces and relations of production. There exists a splendid unpublished essay by Jon Elster entitled "Forces and Relations of Production." The essay makes no use of game theory. That is striking confirmation of my view that it is irrelevant to the foundational claims of Marxism: it shows that Elster himself agrees, in practice, with that view. Having constructed a rigorous theory of contradiction between forces and relations of production, Elster says that "the great weakness of the theory is that it is very difficult to link it to action." Now despite my insistence on the centrality in historical materialism of things that are not actions, I do appreciate that actions are prominent proximate causes of social effects. If links with action cannot be forged, if the question how the functional explanations of historical materialism explain cannot even in principle be answered, then that would have lethal significance for historical materialism. And this brings me to Elster's critique of functional explanation.

I remarked earlier that even when A is functional for B, A's existence or character need not be *explained* by that fact. Thus to confer credibility on the claim that B functionally explains A, one must supply evidence in excess of that needed to show that A is functional for B. Elster and I disagree about what sort of further evidence is necessary. He demands that the claim that B functionally explains A be supported by a plausible story that reveals how B functionally explains A. I think that is sufficient, but not necessary. For I think one can support the claim that B functionally explains A even when one cannot suggest what the mechanism is, if instead one can point to an appropriately varied range of instances in which, whenever A would be functional for B, A appears.[17] This is an application to functional explanatory claims of a general truth about explanatory claims. There are always two ways of backing them up. Suppose, for example, that Elster and I notice a dead body in the library of the country house the morning after the dinner party, and that we hypothesize that its owner died because of something he ate the night before. Further research can take either of two forms. We might open him up to see whether there are any poisons in him, which would be analogous to what Elster thinks we must do to back up functional explanations, or we might find out what he ate, what other guests ate, and which other guests took ill or died, and that would be analogous to the

---

17   That is the simplest way of confirming a functional explanation without establishing a mechanism. For more complicated ways, see *KMTH*, chap. 9, secs. 5 and 7.

way I say we can proceed with functional explanations. In my procedure we look for appropriately consonant and discrepant parallel instances. In Elster's we rely on preexisting knowledge about parallel instances at a more basic causal level and we look for a mechanism in the given case that is consonant with that knowledge.

I can illustrate what is at stake by reference to the case of Lamarck and Darwin. Darwin showed how functional facts about the equipment of organisms contribute to explaining why they have it: the answer lies in the mechanism of chance variation and natural selection. Now I claim, and Elster denies, that, before Darwin thereby advanced the science of natural history, the belief that the useful characters of organisms are there because they are useful was already justified, by the sheer volume of evidence of adaptation. The belief was certainly widely held, by people who had no idea how to elaborate it and by others, such as Lamarck, who had what proved to be an unsatisfactory idea of how to elaborate it. And I contend, and Elster denies, that it was a justified belief. This debate is pursued elsewhere, and I shall not take it further here.[18]

Now because I concede that Marxists have not yet produced good elaborations of their functional explanatory theses, I concede that historical materialism is *at best* in a position like that occupied by natural history before Darwin transformed the subject. But I am not convinced that it has got even that far. For whereas Elster and I disagree strongly about what would confirm functional explanations, we disagree less about whether Marxists have actually produced well-confirmed functional explanations. The essays in Marxist functional explanation which he discusses are sadly representative, and I have no desire to defend them against his criticisms. Here we can make common cause. Many Marxist exercises in functional explanation fail to satisfy even the preliminary requirement of showing that A is functional for B (whether or not it is also explained by its function(s)).[19] Take, for example, the claim that the contemporary capitalist state functions to protect and sustain the capitalist system. Legislation and policy in the direct interest of the capitalist class

18 See the exchange between Elster and myself in *Political Studies*: Elster, "Cohen on Marx's Theory of History"; Cohen, "Functional Explanation: Reply to Elster." See especially Elster p. 126, and Cohen, p. 133–34, and "Functional Explanation, Consequence Explanation, and Marxism." One result reached in the latter article bears mention here. I show that if Elster is right about what functional explanation is (he says what it is in *Ulysses and the Sirens*), then he is wrong that natural selection is necessary to sustain functional explanations in biology. It follows that he is also wrong in the corresponding claims about sociological functional explanation at p. 455 and p. 463 of "Marxism, Functionalism, and Game Theory: The Case for Methodological Individualism."

19 Elster does not always distinguish this criticism from the one I make in the next paragraph; see, for example, his comments (p. 458) on the passage from *The Eighteenth Brumaire*. If he is right, both criticisms apply, but he does not properly separate them.

can reasonably be regarded as confirming it. But what about putative counterexamples, such as social welfare provision and legal immunities enjoyed by trade unions? These too might be functional for capitalism in an indirect way, but that is something which needs to be argued with care, not just asserted. But those who propound the general claim about the state rarely trouble to say what sort of evidence would falsify or weaken it, and therefore every action of the state is treated as confirmatory, because there is always some way, legitimate or spurious, in which the action can be made to look functional. Methodological indiscipline is then compounded when, having established to his own satisfaction that state policy is functional, the theorist treats it, without further argument, as also functionally explained. He proceeds from "*A* is functional for *B*" to "*B* functionally explains *A*" without experiencing any need to justify the step, if, indeed, he notices that he has taken a step from one position to a distinct and stronger one.[20]

Most Marxists are methodologically unself-conscious. If they were more sophisticated, they might provide a better defense of the functional explanations they offer. And then, again, they might not. I do not know how to be confident about this, one way or the other. But I maintain my insistence, first, that historical materialism cannot shed its commitment to functional explanation, and, second, that there is nothing inherently suspect in it. Elster's philosophical criticisms of historical materialist functional explanation still strike me as without force, by contrast with his polemic against particular essays in functional explanation. Our

---

20   And sometimes it is unclear that a step has been taken from a statement of functionality to a functional explanation, and, therefore, it is correspondingly unclear that a fallacy has been committed. Thus, for example, I do not share Elster's confidence that Marx's use of the word "means" in the quotation from vol. 3 of *Capital* on p. 457 proves that Marx is offering a functional explanation, and I am sure that he is wrong when he claims (p. 456) that Marx subscribed to "the main functional paradigm."
[This is the passage from Marx:

The circumstance that a man without fortune but possessing energy, solidity, ability and business acumen may become a capitalist in this manner [i.e., by receiving credit]—and the commercial value of each individual is pretty accurately estimated under the capitalist mode of production—is greatly admired by the apologists of the capitalist system. Although this circumstance continually brings an unwelcome number of new soldiers of fortune into the field and into competition with the already existing individual capitalists, it also reinforces the supremacy of capital itself, expands its base and enables it to recruit ever new forces for itself out of the substratum of society. In a similar way, the circumstance that the Catholic Church in the Middle Ages formed its hierarchy out of the best brains in the land, regardless of their estate, birth or fortune, was one of the principal means of consolidating ecclesiastical rule and suppressing the laity. The more a ruling class is able to assimilate the foremost minds of a ruled class, the more stable and dangerous becomes its rule. (Marx, *Capital*, vol. 3 [International Publishers], p. 600–601 [Penguin Edition, pp. 735–36].)—Ed.]

philosophical disagreement is pursued in *Political Studies* and *Inquiry*. In fn. 8 of his present contribution Elster offers two new objections to my own theory of functional explanation, both of which are misguided. His first objection is that even when it is true that whenever *A* would have favorable consequences for *B*, *A* appears, *A* might not be explained by its possession of such consequences, because a third factor, *C*, might both cause *A* to have favorable consequences for *B*, and cause *A* to appear, without causing the latter as a result of causing the former. That is so, but it is not an objection to my theory.[21] The form of an ordinary causal law is: whenever *A* occurs, *B* occurs. Once again, this might be caused by a third factor, *C*, so related to *A* and *B* *A* does not qualify as causing *B*. But there are tests which, when appropriate results are forthcoming, render the hypothesis that there exists such a *C* implausible, and suitably analogous tests may be conducted in the case of consequence laws.[22] Elster's second fresh objection rests on the premise that I do not mention time in my characterization of consequence laws. It is true that I do not mention particular amounts of time when describing the form of such laws in general terms, just as one does not when one describes the form of ordinary causal laws as "whenever *A* occurs, *B* occurs." But causal laws are not therefore "vacuously confirmable," because particular causal laws include appropriate temporal specifications. All that need be said in general terms about consequence laws and time will be found on pp. 260–61 of *KMTH*.

I now take up two issues in the part of Elster's article in which he successfully conjoins Marxism and game theory. In a highly original account of the ideology and practice of social democratic capitalism, Elster sets the stage by describing the dissolution of the marginalist illusion, and the action unfolds along lines scripted by Zeuthen and Nash on the one hand and Lancaster on the other. I have two criticisms of this treatment. The first is that Elster misidentifies the illusion that survives after the marginalist one has been dissolved. He calls it "the presentist illusion,"[23] and attributes it to "diachronic alienation."[24] Workers are alienated "from their own history, i.e., from past generations of workers who produced the means of production currently used," and they overcome that alienation "by taking possession of their history."[25] Elster would agree that unrevolutionary workers believe that the capitalist is entitled to a return because he is the morally legitimate owner of the means of production. He thinks

---

21 It is, indeed, a point I made myself: see *KMTH*, pp. 267ff.
22 See, further, my "Functional Explanation."
23 Elster, "Marxism, Functionalism, and Game Theory: The Case for Methodological Individualism," p. 472.
24 Ibid., p. 474.
25 Ibid., p. 472.

the presentist illusion explains why they think the capitalist's ownership is legitimate. But in what does the illusion consist? In a false belief that the means of production were not produced by workers in the past? But workers know better than that. They know, if they reflect on the matter, that means of production were produced by earlier workers, but just as they believe that their own employer is entitled to a return, so, in parallel, they think the employer of earlier workers was; whence, in particular, employers of workers producing means of production came to possess them legitimately and passed them on, directly or indirectly, through market exchange and gift (especially inheritance), to the employers of today. If there exists any kind of presentist illusion, why should workers not project it backwards when they think about their predecessors?

My second criticism of the game theoretical part of Elster's article concerns his remarks on the locus of exploitation. He writes

> that the exploitation of the working class . . . does not consist *only* in the capitalists' appropriation of surplus-value but also in the workers' exclusion from decisive investment choices that shape the future.[26]

Much the same sentence occurs in an earlier version of Elster's article, except that the word "mainly" occurs where the word "only" appears in this final version. This reply was originally composed in response to that earlier version. Having read my response, Elster changed "mainly" to "only," thereby partly spoiling some criticisms I had made of the original version. I shall nevertheless enter the following paragraph of criticism of his original formulation (the one with "mainly") here, not only out of vanity but also because it still applies, if with reduced force, against his revised formulation, and most importantly because I think it is useful to try to identify rather precisely what exploitation consists in.

I do not doubt that workers are excluded from investment decisions, but I deny that they are thereby *exploited*. If someone robs me of the power to control my own life, he does not *ipso facto* use me unfairly to his own advantage, which is what, very roughly, exploitation is. Authoritarian parents do not, by virtue of being authoritarian, qualify as exploiters of their children, and authoritarian parenthood is a good analogue to the relationship Elster highlights here, which is one of subordination, not exploitation. That subordination is, moreover, a consequence of exploitation in the traditional sense, which is therefore not displaced by (what is anyway wrongly considered) a further form of exploitation. It is because capitalists appropriate surplus value that they are able to decide what to do with it, to consume and invest in whatever proportions

26   Ibid., p. 476 (emphasis added).

they choose. And the exploitation of the worker lies in the appropriation, not in the subsequent disposal over what has been appropriated. Part of what moved Elster to make his (original) statement was the fact, which he emphasizes elsewhere, that only a small proportion of total social product remains for capitalist consumption after workers' income and capitalist investment have absorbed their shares.[27] But because there are relatively few capitalists, that small proportion enables them to enjoy a life of comfort and freedom inaccessible to workers. The difference in *per capita* personal income remains massive, and it matters a great deal to the self-perception and sense of dignity of working people. Working-class existence, even in America, is full of strain unknown to wealthy people. Elster's (original) formulation overlooks that sheer difference in standard of living between the classes remains a major part of the injustice of capitalism.

My present view about the matters in contention between Elster and myself is as follows: (1) Functional explanation lies at the heart of historical materialism. (2) Game theory therefore cannot replace functional explanation within Marxist social analysis. (3) Nor is there a place for game theory at the heart of historical materialism, alongside functional explanation. (4) But game theory is very helpful in relation to claims near, but not quite at, historical materialism's heart. (5) There is no methodological error in historical materialism's functional explanatory theses. (6) But Marxists have not done much to establish that they are true. If Marxian functional explanation remains as wanting in practice (as opposed to high theory) as it has been, the foundational claims of historical materialism might need to be severely modified. Positions of great traditional authority might have to be abandoned. One of Elster's achievements is that he has shown how fruitfully what would remain of the doctrine we have inherited can be enriched and extended.

---

27 See "Exploring Exploitation," p. 12, where he concludes that "in modern capitalist economies the notion of exploitation should be linked to the lack of power over investment decisions rather than to the fact (or to the possibility) of capitalists having a high level of consumption at the expense of workers."

Chapter 11

REVIEW OF *KARL MARX*, BY ALLEN W. WOOD

This addition to Ted Honderich's imposing "Arguments of the Philosophers" series is, at the time of writing, the best philosophical introduction to Marx in English. It is a well-organized, well-written, and, with one big exception—to which most of this review will be devoted—supremely balanced work. Wood is properly and acidly skeptical about many of the claims about Marx and about the world which Marxists have made, but he is also largely persuasive in his enthusiastic recommendation of what he thinks is abidingly valuable in Marxism.

The book is divided into five parts. The first part, on Alienation, begins with the liberating observation[1] that one should not expect to identify a *theory* of Alienation in Marx, since the fragments carrying his ideas on that topic present phenomena too disparate for theoretical unification. Wood nevertheless succeeds in unifying his own discussion by providing a judicious account of the much-unanalyzed idea of self-realization: various failures to achieve self-realization generate correspondingly various alienations.

In part 2, on Historical Materialism, Wood joins those who seek to reinstate a toughly materialist reading of Marx's theory of history, in the face of sixty years of Hegelian and other idealist interpretation of it. He devises many good distinctions, such as those which enable him to present historical agents' lack of self-knowledge as a social rather than a psychological matter,[2] and others which support his nuanced denial that historical materialism is a determinist doctrine.[3] He also lodges many particular claims with which I disagree, too many, indeed, to discuss here, where I shall comment on one very general issue only.

That issue is the relationship between two branches of Marxism, its philosophical anthropology (or conception of human nature), and its theory of history, which correspond to parts 1 and 2 of Wood's book. I think Wood associates the two too closely. It is easy to do that, since the concept of production is at the center of each, but it plays contrasting

---

1 Wood, *Karl Marx*, p. 4.
2 Ibid., pp. 88, 93, 112.
3 Ibid., pp. 111–17.

roles. In the philosophical anthropology people are by nature creative beings. They flourish only in the cultivation and exercise of their manifold powers, and they are especially productive—which is to say, *here*, creative—in the condition of freedom conferred by material plenty. But in the theory of history people produce not freely but because they have to, because nature does not otherwise supply their wants; and the development in history of the productive power of *man* (as such, as a species) occurs at the expense of the creative capacity of the *men* who are the agents and victims of that development. They are forced to perform repugnant labor which is a denial, not an expression, of their natures: it is not "the free play of [their] own physical and mental powers."[4]

Wood writes: "Historical progress consists fundamentally in the growth of people's abilities to shape and control the world about them. This is the most basic way in which they develop and express their human essence. It is the definite means by which they may in time gain a measure of freedom, of mastery over their social creations."[5] The first sentence is ambiguous, because of "people's abilities," which may denote either abilities inherent in individuals or the Ability of Man, and only under the latter interpretation is the sentence true. And the second sentence is, consequently, false: people do not develop and express their human essence in activity which thwarts that essence. The third sentence, taken out of context, might still be true, since an essence-frustrating cause could have essence-congenial effects, but if we take it to mean that humanity engages in self-denying labor *in order* "in time" to achieve self-fulfillment, then what it says is too extravagantly teleological. Teleological or (as I prefer to consider them) functional explanations are, I am sure, fundamental in historical materialism, but it does not follow that history as a whole has an overall purpose which humanity pursues.

After Historical Materialism comes the book's most original part, on Marxism and Morality. Here Wood departs from sobriety and defends, with considerable skill, the unlikely thesis which he launched in his seminal article on "The Marxian Critique of Justice" that Marx did not think capitalism was an unjust society. He argues that the common and natural supposition that Marx did think it unjust reflects misunderstanding of his social philosophy, according to which principles of justice are never to be taken as they present themselves but are always to be understood

---

4 *Capital*, vol. 1 (Chicago edition), p. 291 (Penguin edition, p. 375). [In the original text Cohen cites the Moscow 1961 edition, which also uses the Moore and Aveling translation. In the Chicago edition the text reads: "the free-play of [their] bodily and mental activity."—Ed.]

5 Wood, *Karl Marx*, p. 75.

reductively, as the ideological sublimates of effective power relations which it is their function to endorse and thereby reinforce.

For Wood's Marx that is just, in a given society, which conforms to the ground plan of that society, and there are no criteria of justice by reference to which its ground plan might be criticized. Wood infers that, for Marx, the contract between capitalists and worker is not only not unjust, but just, at least in the standard case where the worker gets the market value of the labor power he sells. There are no noncapitalist criteria of justice which impugn a properly formed labor contract, just as there are no criteria of justice which impugn slave ownership in a slave society, where it is not only not unjust, but just.[6]

Marx condemns capitalism because it displays, not injustice, or any other moral evil, but what Wood considers to be nonmoral evils: it cripples human creativity and it fosters inhumane social relations. "Although capitalist exploitation alienates, dehumanizes and degrades wage labourers, it does not violate any of their rights, and there is nothing about it which is wrongful or unjust,"[7] since in capitalist society there exist no rights beyond those which capitalist exploitation honors.

This is a patently interesting interpretation of Marx, and Wood makes a strong textual case for it. But the case is not invulnerable, and a number of authors have plausibly reinterpreted many of the texts he uses and adduced other ones which embarrass his position. Ziyad Husami's "Marx on Distributive Justice" and Gary Young's "Justice and Capitalist Production" are especially effective contributions, and I also recommend Young's "Doing Marx Justice."[8]

I cannot review the many relevant texts here, but there is a well-known passage in volume 1 of *Capital* which is particularly germane, and I shall turn to it after I have expounded a pertinent bit of Marx's economic theory.

A main object of *Capital* is to explain how capitalists are able to turn given sums of money, or value, into bigger ones. Marx thinks the explanation cannot in general be that the capitalist exchanges what he has for something more valuable, for then the other party loses whatever the capitalist gets, and there is no net gain: what needs to be explained is the (for Marx) manifest fact that fresh value comes into being, and none comes into being when one person gets value which another loses. Marx concludes that the only way, in general, in which a capitalist can increase his stock of value is by purchasing, at its value, a commodity which can

---

6   Ibid., p. 131.

7   Ibid, p. 43.

8   This is published in the bumper Supplementary Volume 7 (1981) of the *Canadian Journal of Philosophy*, entitled *Marx and Morality*, which contains an excellent bibliography.

be used to create more value than it, that commodity, has. He then identifies the worker's labor power as the requisite commodity. It is sold in daily or weekly packets to the capitalist, who pays for it a sum corresponding to the number of hours required to produce it (to produce, that is, the commodities the worker must consume to remain alive and able to work). Since, according to the labor theory of value, the value of a commodity depends precisely on how many hours are required to produce it, the worker gets the value of his labor power, but the capitalist nevertheless gains (newly created) value, because the value of the worker's labor power is less than the value of what it produces: a worker can work more hours per day than are required to produce what he must consume to work that many hours in a day.

In this operation "equivalent is exchanged for equivalent," since the worker gets the full value of his labor power, but "the transaction is for all that only the old dodge of every conqueror who buys commodities from the conquered with the money he has robbed them of (*mit ihrem eigenen, geraubten Geld*)," since capitalists pay wages with money they get by selling what workers produce. Thus the worker, though paid the full value of his labor power, does not get the extra, or surplus, value he produces, and capitalist profit, and therefore capitalism, are "based on theft (*Diebstahl*) of another's labour time."[9]

Now when Marx speaks here (and elsewhere: this is not an isolated text) of "robbery" (or "theft"), he cannot mean "robbery according to the rules of capitalism," since the transaction he considers robbery obeys those rules: what is wrong with capitalism is that the appropriation of surplus labor is not, by its rules, robbery, that when and because the worker gets the full value of his labor power, he is robbed. When, therefore, Wood stresses against his critic Husami that the *Capital* passage speaks of an exchange of equivalents,[10] he exhibits a singular and uncharacteristic obtuseness, since Marx's point is that equal exchange enables the capitalist to rob the worker. Wood treats the assertion of equivalence as though Marx intended it to show that moral condemnation of capitalism is out of place, when its purpose, for Marx, is to emphasize that the transaction he goes on to condemn does not violate the rules of market exchange.

Now since, as Wood will agree, Marx did not think that by capitalist criteria the capitalist steals, and since he did think he steals, he must have meant that he steals in some appropriately nonrelativist sense. And since to steal is, in general, wrongly to take what rightly belongs to another, to

---

9   Marx, *Grundrisse*, p. 705.
10   Wood, *Karl Marx*, p. 256.

steal is to commit an injustice, and a system which is "based on theft" is based on injustice.

Did Marx, nevertheless, lack the belief that capitalism was unjust, because he failed to notice that robbery constitutes an injustice? I think the relationship between robbery and injustice is so close that anyone who thinks capitalism is robbery must be treated as someone who thinks capitalism is unjust, even if he does not realize that he thinks it is.

And perhaps Marx did not always realize that he thought capitalism was unjust. For there exist texts, ably exploited by Wood, which suggest that, at least when writing them, Marx thought all nonrelativist notions of justice and injustice were moonshine. *If* the texts really show that he thought so, then I would conclude that, at least sometimes, *Marx mistakenly thought that Marx did not believe that capitalism was unjust*, because he was confused about justice.[11]

At one point Wood approaches a thesis about Marx on capitalism and justice which resembles the one just stated, but he retreats from it on the ground that "there is no sign that Marx sees anything morally wrong or unjust about . . . capitalism."[12] I think calling it "robbery" is such a sign, and that saying, "Capitalist justice is truly to be wondered at!,"[13] with the sense the remark carries in its context, is another one.

So I uphold the conventional idea that Marx thought capitalist exploitation is unjust, and I shall now argue that Wood's denial (see above) that exploitation is unjust leads him into a false account of what exploitation is, in fact and in Marx. He says that exploiters get something from those they exploit without giving anything in return, but that not all unreciprocated transfers are exploitative. I more or less agree with that, although there are problems, touched on below, about what is to count as absence of reciprocity. But Wood and I disagree about what the other features of exploitation are. I would claim, conventionally enough, that nonreciprocity is exploitative only when it is unfair, but Wood cannot acknowledge that exploitation is unfair, and he proposes this different account of the concept: Marx's idea is that A exploits B whenever A lives off the fruits of B's labor and is able to do so not because A makes any reciprocal contribution to social production but because the social relations in which A stands to B put A in a position to coerce B to work for A's benefit.[14] But coercion, I shall argue, is neither a necessary condition, nor, when added to nonreciprocity, a sufficient condition, of exploitation.

11   The italicized thesis is misreported, in two different ways, at pp. 9 and 42 of the *Canadian Journal of Philosophy*, Supplementary Volume, *Marx and Morality*, because of bad (copy?) editing.

12   Wood, *Karl Marx*, p. 151.

13   Marx, *Capital*, vol. 1 (Penguin edition), p. 815.

14   Wood, *Karl Marx*, p. 232.

To see that it is not a necessary condition, consider a rich capitalist, A, who, for whatever reason, voluntarily works for another capitalist, B, at a wage which is such that, were A a worker, he would count as exploited. On my view, and also Marx's, A, though not forced to work for B, or for anyone else, is exploited by B. We might ask A why he lets B exploit him and he might give any of various answers: "I don't think B is exploiting me," "I don't mind being exploited," "I bet C that I would get B to hire me," "I want to see what it is like to be a worker," and so on. Being a rich capitalist, he could not reply: "I have no choice." Yet on Wood's view it is truistic to say of an exploited person that he is forced to work for his exploiter.

So I do not agree with Wood that the reason why "people who live on welfare do not exploit taxpayers" is that "the taxpayers are coerced by the state and not by the welfare recipients":[15] exploiters do not necessarily coerce those they exploit. In my different view, one reason why welfare recipients are not exploiters is that the relevant transfer payments are not unjust. For the same reason, they are also not beneficiaries of exploitation. (A nonexploiter may be a beneficiary of exploitation, as Wood would no doubt agree that capitalists' children are, and as he might agree that he and I are.) Is Wood willing to say that people on welfare are beneficiaries of exploitation, since others—the state—force taxpayers, who receive nothing in return, to sustain them? He seems committed to that unfortunate claim.

I would also deny that coercive nonreciprocity is a sufficient condition of exploitation. Wood purports to illustrate the sufficiency thesis by urging that "welfare recipients would exploit taxpayers if—as some right-wing fanatics claim—the state were in the hands of good-for-nothings who used its taxing powers to plunder hardworking citizens,"[16] but by describing the hypothetically coercing welfare receivers as good-for-nothings he obscures the issue whether it is their coerciveness or their undeservingness which makes them exploiters. For a better test of the sufficiency claim, imagine not good-for-nothings but involuntarily unemployed adults with plenty of children to feed who force earners to make modest payments to them, by threatening violence in the streets, or, more fancifully, under a constitution which confers legislative power in welfare matters on unemployed people. "Right-wing fanatics" would call those people exploiters. How could Wood disagree?

Right-wing fanatics—and even nonfanatics—would say that on Wood's definition of exploitation capitalists are not exploiters, since they provide workers with means of production and thereby make a "reciprocal contribution to social production." I would reply that the said

15   Ibid., p. 267.
16   Ibid., p. 268.

"contribution" does not establish absence of exploitation, since capitalist property in means of production is theft, and the capitalist is therefore "providing" only what morally ought not to be his to provide. But how could Wood, steering scrupulously clear of moral judgment, resist the claim that there is a reciprocity in the capital/labor relationship which disproves the charge of exploitation?

The last and least interesting parts of *Karl Marx* are devoted to Philosophical Materialism and The Dialectical Method. Wood's discussion of these matters is far superior to most, but that is not high praise since, as many will agree, Marxist research has been particularly infertile in these areas. The part on Philosophical Materialism is a refreshing treatment of a dry subject, but I was less impressed by Wood on dialectic. He relies too much on an unexplicated notion of "organic wholeness," and I cannot agree with him that "inherent tendencies to development" (with which he associates dialectic) and "causal laws"[17] represent fundamentally contrasting sources of explanation of phenomena, since the first notion seems to depend on the second. I also think that, in his chapter on "Dialectic in *Capital*," Wood is too kind to the labor theory of value, but there is no space to substantiate that here.

I disagree with *Karl Marx* on a number of important counts, but I would reiterate that it is a splendidly well-constructed book, and quite the best general philosophical treatment of Marx in English.[18]

---

17   Ibid., p. 211.
18   I thank Arnold Zuboff for his brilliant criticisms of a draft of this review.

Chapter 12

REASON, HUMANITY, AND THE MORAL LAW

1. You might think that, if you make a law, then that law binds you, *because* you made it. For, if you will the law, then how can you deny that it binds you, without contradicting your own will? But you might also think the opposite. You might think that, if you are the author of the law, then it *cannot* bind you. For how can it have authority over you when you have authority over it? How can it *bind* you when you, the law*maker*, can change it, at will, whenever you like?

Now, in that pair of arguments mutually contradictory conclusions are drawn from the self-same premise, the premise that you make the law. So at least one of the arguments is invalid. But, even if they are *both* invalid, they might still be unignorable, because they might have elements of truth in them. They might be healthy argument-embryos out of which sound arguments could develop. And, whatever else is true, each of the arguments is sufficiently persuasive that, mutually contradictory though they are, each was affirmed in Hobbes's *Leviathan*, in much the form in which I just stated them.

There are, by my count, four arguments in Hobbes for the conclusion that the citizen is obliged to obey the law. Three of the arguments don't matter here.[1] The one that matters here has two premises, the first of which is that every act of the sovereign is an act of each citizen, since "every man gives their common represener authority from himself in particular; and owning all the actions the represener doth, in case they give him authority without stint," and there is, of course, no stint in the authority Hobbesian people give their sovereign. Accordingly, "the subject is the author of every act the Sovereign doth."[2]

Having thus possessed himself of the premise that I am the author of what the sovereign does, hence of each law he enacts, Hobbes now enters his second premise, which is that it is absurd for me to object to what

---

1 They are (i) the consequentialist argument that the state of nature is intolerable, (ii) the argument of hypothetical consent: any rational person would agree to submit to government, and (iii) the argument of actual consent: all citizens in fact agree to submit to government.

2 Hobbes, *Leviathan*, pp. 221, 265, and cf. ibid., p. 276.

I myself do. Accordingly, it is absurd for me to object to any law that I pass, and I must therefore, on pain of absurdity, obey the sovereign's law.[3] I must obey it because I made it.

Now you might think that, if I am subject to the law *because* I make it, not, albeit, directly, but through my representative, then that representative himself, the sovereign, is equally or even *a fortiori* subject to the law, because *he* makes it, and, indeed, makes it more directly than I do. But that is not Hobbes's inference. Not only does Hobbes not infer, using the same reasoning that he used in the case of the citizen, which should, it seems, also apply to the sovereign, that the latter *is* subject to the law he makes; but Hobbes concludes, oppositely, that the sovereign is *not* subject to the law. And the reason that Hobbes gives for that conclusion is the very same one as the reason that he gives for concluding that the citizen *is* subject to the law, to wit that he, the sovereign, *makes* the law. Here is what Hobbes says:

> [T]o those laws which the Soveraign himselfe, that is, which the Commonwealth maketh, he is not subject. For to be subject to Lawes, is to be subject to the Common-wealth, that is to the Sovereign Representative, that is to himself; which is not subjection, but freedom from the Lawes.

> The Sovereaign of a Common-wealth, be it an assembly, or one man, is not subject to the civil laws. For having power to make, and repeal laws, he may when he pleaseth, free himself from that subjection, by repealing those laws that trouble him, and making of new; and consequently he was free before. For he is free, that can be free when he will: Nor is it possible for any person to be bound to himself; because he that can bind, can release; and therefore he that is bound to himself only, is not bound.[4]

3   Stepwise, the argument runs as follows:

	What the sovereign does, I do.
But	The sovereign makes the law.
So	I make the law.
Now,	It is absurd to object to what I myself do.
So	I cannot object to the law.
So	I must obey the law.

In a different version of the argument, which Hobbes also gives, the further premise is not that I cannot object to what I myself do but that I cannot "injure" (that is, do an injustice to) myself. The argument then runs as follows:

	What the sovereign does, I do.
But,	A man cannot injure himself.
So	The sovereign does not injure me.
So	I cannot object to what the sovereign requires of me.
So	I must obey the sovereign.

4   Hobbes, *Leviathan*, pp. 367, 313, and see Hobbes, *De Cive*, 12.4, 11.14.

This argument says (in the fuller version of it to be found in the second quoted passage, and very slightly reconstructed):

> The sovereign makes the law.
> So   The sovereign can unmake the law.
> So   The sovereign is not bound by the law that he makes.

Hobbes claims that, when the citizen violates the law, he contradicts his own will: he, in the person of the sovereign, made the law, and therefore cannot without absurdity violate it. Yet it is precisely because the sovereign makes the law that he is *not* bound by it: according to Hobbes, it is conceptually impossible for him to violate it.

There is no inconsistency in the idea that two make the one law, for one makes as author what the other makes as representative of that author. But it cannot follow from "X makes the law" both that X is subject to it and that X is not subject to it. You cannot say both: because you make the law, you must obey it; and: because you make the law, it has no authority over you, so you need not obey it. The inference of the argument about the citizen requires the principle that, if I make the law, then I am bound by it. The inference of the argument about the sovereign requires the principle that, if I make the law, then I am not bound by it. At least one of those principles must be wrong.

Now, the truth of this whole matter is complicated, but the parts of it that concern us here seem to me to be this. I pass a law. Either the law says that everyone must act thus and so, or its scope is restricted to, say, everyone except me. If the latter is true, then I am clearly not obliged to obey the law: so the first point to make about the first argument is that the terms of the law need to be specified before the inference in that argument can be examined.

Suppose, then, that the law is indeed universal, or that it includes me within its scope by virtue of some other semantic or pragmatic feature of it. Then, if I had the authority to legislate it, it indeed binds me, as long as I do not repeal it. (It remains unclear, even then, that it binds me *because*, if I violate it, I contradict my will: so the kernel of truth in the first argument may be quite a small one.) The necessity to add that rider reflects the important element of truth in the argument about the sovereign, which is also incorrect in its unmodified form. The big mistake in that argument is the supposition that if I *can* repeal the law, then it fails to bind me even when I have not *yet* repealed it. Hobbes is wrong that, if you can free yourself at will, then you are already free, that "he is free, that can be free when he will." But other important things do follow from my being able to free myself at will, for example, that I cannot complain about my unfreedom. And, more pertinently to our theme, although you may be bound by a law that you can change, the fact that you can change it diminishes the significance of the fact that you are bound by it. There's not much "must" in a "must" that you can readily get rid of.

2. In Christine Korsgaard's ethics, the subject of the law is also its author: and that is the ground of the subject's obligation—that *it* is the author of the law that obliges it. That sounds like Hobbes's first argument. So we should ask a question inspired by Hobbes's second argument, the one about the sovereign: how can the subject be responsible to a law that it makes and can therefore unmake? As we know, Korsgaard's answer relates to the circumstance that the subject has a practical identity.

Now Korsgaard's ethics descends from Kant, but it contrasts in important ways with Kant's ethics. Korsgaard's subject is unequivocally the author of the law that binds it, for its law is the law of *its* practical identity, and the subject itself "*constructs*" that identity. But in Kant the position is more equivocal. We can say that the Kantian subject both is and is not the author of the law that binds it. There is an important duality with respect to the source of the law in the following characteristic text from the *Grundlegung*. In previous moral philosophy, Kant says,

> Man was seen to be bound to laws by his duty, but it was not seen that he is subject to his own, *but still universal*, legislation, and that he is bound to act only in accordance with his own will, which is, however, *designed by nature to be a will giving universal law*. For if one thought of him as *only* subject to a law . . . this necessarily implied some interest as a stimulus or compulsion to obedience because the law did not arise from his own will. Rather his will had to be constrained by something else to act in a certain way. This might be his own interest or that of another, but in either case the imperative always had to be conditional, and could not at all serve as a moral command. The moral principle I will call the principle of *autonomy* of the will in contrast to all other principles which I accordingly count under *heteronomy*.[5]

Kant thought that if the moral law came *just* from my own will, then it would have no claim on me, rather as the law of the sovereign has none over the sovereign in Hobbes. If, on the other hand, the law was *just* externally imposed, and did *not* come from my own will, then it would be heteronomous slavery for me to obey it, and the challenging argument that Hobbes uses about the citizen, that he must obey the law because it is his *own* law, he must obey it on pain of inconsistency, would not be available. So the passage I've exhibited, while stating that man is subject to his *own* law, and bound to act only in accordance with his *own* will, is quick to add that man's legislation, though his own, is still universal, emanating

---

5 Kant, *Foundations of the Metaphysics of Morals*, pp. 49–50 (emphases added, except on "autonomy" and "heteronomy").

from a will "designed by nature to be a will giving universal law." And that makes Kant's person different from Hobbes's sovereign. Kant's person indeed makes the law, but he cannot unmake it, for he is designed by nature to make it as he does, and what he is designed to make has the inherent authority of reason as such. So Hobbes's sovereignty argument does not apply, and Kant can stay with the citizen argument. He can give the citizen argument for obedience and rebut the sovereignty argument for freedom from law by pointing out that *this* law is *not* one that the agent can unmake. In the moral realm, we are, Kant says, "subjects . . . not sovereigns."[6]

So the Hobbesian reflection about the sovereign and the law sheds light on Kant's insistence that the imperative of morals must not come from *human* nature, nor even from human *reason*, should there be any respect in which human reason differs from reason as such. For it is reason as such that is sovereign over us, and that gives determinacy, stability, and authority to a law that would otherwise lack all that: "the ground of obligation must not be sought in the nature of man . . . but a priori solely in the concepts of pure reason."[7] "For with what right could we bring into unlimited respect something that might be valid only under contingent human conditions?"[8] And

> whatever is derived from the particular natural situation of man as such, or from certain feelings and propensities, or even from a particular tendency of human reason which might not hold necessarily for the will of every rational being (if such a tendency is possible), can give a maxim valid for us but not a law . . . This is so far the case that the sublimity and intrinsic worth of the command is the better shown in a duty the fewer subjective causes there are for it and the more there are against it.[9]

Since Kant was certain that to root the moral law exclusively in human nature was to derogate from its authority, Korsgaard is not entirely right when she says that

> Kant, like Hume and Williams, thinks that morality is grounded in human nature, and that moral properties are projections of human dispositions.[10]

---

6   Kant, *Critique of Practical Reason*, p. 85: "We are indeed legislative members of a moral realm which is possible through freedom and which is presented to us as an object of respect by practical reason; yet we are at the same time subjects in it, not sovereigns, and to mistake our inferior positions as creatures and to deny, from self-conceit, respect to the holy law is, in spirit, a defection from it even if its letter be fulfilled."

7   Kant, *Foundations of the Metaphysics of Morals*, p. 5.

8   Ibid., p. 24.

9   Ibid., p. 42. cf. pp. 28, 65, and Kant, *Critique of Practical Reason*, p. 19.

10   Korsgaard, *The Sources of Normativity*, p. 91.

For Korsgaard, morality *is* grounded in human nature,[11] and that difference between her and Kant is consequential here, for Kant has a ready answer to Hobbes's argument about the sovereign, whereas Korsgaard may have no answer to it, because she has abandoned the element of Kant that transcends merely human nature. She appears to agree with the insistence she attributes to Pufendorf and Hobbes, that the only possible source of obligation, not of its being good or sensible or beneficial or desirable that you do something, but of your *having* to do it, is that you are ordered to do it by a lawgiver. No "ought" without law and no law without a lawgiver. Korsgaard affirms all that,[12] but she adds that the only person "in a position" to give that law is the self-commanding self. Accordingly, to secure the binding force of law, Korsgaard has to have a way of answering Hobbes's second argument, and she does not have Kant's way.

If Hobbes's position can be rendered consistent, if he can bind the citizen to obey while nevertheless freeing the sovereign from all duty of obedience, then legislating *qua* sovereign must for some reason *not* be self-binding whereas legislating through a sovereign representative *is*. But Korsgaard's persons are autonomous self-legislators: no delegation or representation occurs here. Accordingly, it is hard to see how anything becomes a law for them that they *must* obey. So Korsgaard can maintain the authority of the law over its subject legislator neither in Kant's way nor in the just hypothesized revisionist Hobbesian way.

Suppose I ask: *why* should I obey myself? Who am *I*, anyway, to issue a command to *me*?[13] Kant can answer that question. He can say that, although you *legislate* the law, the content of the law comes from reason, not from anything special about you, or *your* reason, or even *human* reason, but from reason as such. And, when that is so, then, perhaps, reflective endorsement of the law is inescapable. But if the content of the law

---

11   See, ibid., e.g., pp. 131–32.

12   See her conclusion, ibid., pp. 164–65. Korsgaard's claim that the solution to the problem of normativity must be imperativist puzzles me. She brings out, brilliantly, the difference between doing logic because of its merits as a subject and doing it because it is a required course (pp. 25–27, pp. 105–7), but why isn't it good enough if our reason for being moral is as good as the one a person has for doing logic where that isn't a required course? This question relates to the point that morality is a choice within rationality, not a requirement of it: see Section 5 below.

13   Korsgaard rejects Pufendorfian voluntarism, remarking that "the very notion of a legitimate authority is already a normative one and cannot be used to answer the normative question" (p. 29). In her own answer to that question, *I* am the legislating will, so *I* must possess legitimate authority for my legislation to be valid. Does it follow, in a defeating way, that I cannot cite *my own* legitimate authority any more than Pufendorf can cite God's, by way of answer to the normative question? I *think* that Korsgaard's answer would be that I *must* have authority for me, in virtue of some or all of the argumentation that I discuss in Section 7 below.

reflects *my* nature, my engagements and commitments, then could I not *change* its content? Trafficking at the human level as she does, Korsgaard must say that my practical identity, with which the law is bound up, is inescapable, but one may doubt both that there is a special connection between morality and practical identity and that practical identity is inescapable. One may therefore doubt that Korsgaard can achieve her goal, which, so I read it, is to keep the "must" that Kant put into morality while humanizing morality's source.[14]

I have said that, for Korsgaard, morality is rooted in human nature. But at one place Korsgaard says the somewhat different thing, that "value is grounded in rational nature—in particular in the structure of reflective consciousness—and it is projected onto the world."[15] But rational nature, if it means the nature of reason, is different from human nature, at least for Kant, and Korsgaard returns us to the fully human when she adds the gloss referring to the structure of reflective consciousness, for, as she will surely not deny, all manner of all-too-human peculiarities can gain strength in reflective consciousness. Kant can say that you must be moral on pain of irrationality. Korsgaard cannot say that.

3. What Korsgaard says, instead, is that you must be moral on pain of sacrificing your practical identity, which is to say, who you are from a practical point of view. You act morally because you could not live with yourself, "it could be. . . . worse than death," if you did not.[16]

But I find it very difficult to put together the motif of practical identity with the emphasis on law that Korsgaard takes from Hobbes and Pufendorf and, especially, Kant. *If* morality is to do with law, then the liaison between morality and practical identity is questionable, since the commitments that form my practical identity need not be to things that have the *universality* characteristic of law. Practical identity is a matter of loyalty and identification, and whereas there is indeed such a thing as loyalty to general principles, there also exists loyalty to family, to group, to another individual; and no credible characterization of what practical identity is, in general terms, would yield a general priority for principled over particularistic identifications. Being Jewish plays a role in my practical identity, and so does being a Fellow of All Souls. But neither of those features signifies an attachment for me *because* I believe some principle that says: cleave to the ethnic group to which you belong, or to the College that was sufficiently gracious to receive you. As Bernard Williams

14   For further comment on Korsgaard's project, so conceived, see the final paragraph of the present reply.

15   Korsgaard, *The Sources of Normativity*, p. 116.

16   Ibid., p. 18.

famously said, if I save my wife not *just* because she is my wife, but because I believe that husbands in general have special obligations to their wives, then I act on "one thought too many."[17]

My sacrifice for a person need not come from a general belief about right and wrong, but from solidarity with that person, and not because of characteristics which she and I have and which are such that, where characteristics of that kind obtain, solidarity is always required. I might find it hard to live with myself if I gave nothing to Oxfam, which is for me a matter of principle, but I would find it harder still to live with myself if I gave to Oxfam instead of paying for the operation that my mother needs. It does not distinguish my moral from my other commitments[18] that if I resile on my principled ones I prejudice my practical identity.[19]

Korsgaard writes:

> The reflective structure of human consciousness requires that you identify yourself with some law or principle which will govern your choices. It requires you to be a law to yourself. And that is the source of normativity. So the argument shows just what Kant said that it did: that our autonomy is the source of obligation.[20]

The reflective structure of human consciousness may require, as Korsgaard says, following Harry Frankfurt, that, on pain of reducing myself to the condition of a wanton, I endorse the first-order impulses on which I act, that, as we say, I *identify* myself with them. But it does not follow, and it is not true, that the structure of my consciousness requires that I identify myself with some law or principle. I do not do that when I identify myself with the impulse to save my own drowning child. What the reflective structure requires, if anything, is not that I be a law to myself, but that I be in command of myself. And sometimes the commands that I issue will be singular, not universal. If, as Korsgaard says, "the necessity of acting in the light of reflection makes us authorities over ourselves," then we exercise that authority not only in making laws but also in issuing singular edicts that mean as much to us as general principles do.[21]

---

17 Williams, "Persons, Character, and Morality," p. 18.

18 And—see below—it is not even true of all of my moral ones, any more than it is true of all of my nonmoral ones.

19 For a sensitive defense of the claim that one can act unselfishly for the sake of a collective to which one belongs, and other than for reasons of principle, see Oldenquist, "Loyalties." For an illuminating application of the point to Marx on proletarian solidarity, see the section on "Morality" in Miller, *Analyzing Marx*, especially pp. 63–76, and see too, in the same connection, Whelan, "Marx and Revolutionary Virtue," pp. 64–65.

20 Korsgaard, *The Sources of Normativity*, p. 174.

21 The text continues: "And in so far as we have authority over ourselves, we can make laws for ourselves and those laws will be normative" (p. 165). Yes, we *can* make laws

Using Richard Hare's terms, we can say that Korsgaard's solution is imperativist or prescriptive, but not universally prescriptive. And whether or not the moral *must* be law-like *if* it is prescriptive, Korsgaard says that it is law-like, yet it is just not true that every claim on me that survives reflection is, or, presupposes, a law.

Korsgaard remarks that, if she calls out my name, and I do not stop, then I am rebelling against her.[22] She then asks, "But why should you *have* to rebel against me?" Why should my failure to stop *count* as rebellion? Her answer is that "[i]t is because I am a law to you. By calling out your name, I have obligated you. I have given you a reason to stop." Well, suppose we accept that, just by calling out my name, you've given me a reason to stop. I think that could be regarded as extravagant (maybe you've [also] given me a reason to speed up), but suppose we accept it. Then, even so, what you have given me is no law but just an order, a singular order lacking the universality of law.

Now whether or not morality is, as Korsgaard thinks, a matter of law, it is false that whatever I do for fear of compromising my practical identity counts as moral, and also false that whatever counts as moral is done for fear of compromising identity. It is a huge exaggeration to say, as Korsgaard does, that "an obligation always takes the form of a reaction against a threat of a loss of identity."[23] I could remain me both in the evident banal sense and in every pertinent nonbanal sense if I gave nothing to help the distant dying who oppress my conscience. I just wouldn't *feel* very good about myself. And I might even say, in morose reflection, "How typical of me, to be so bloody selfish." And I might lose my grip on myself if I suddenly found myself being very philanthropic. So this is not Korsgaard's point that my identity is solid enough to withstand a measure of wrongdoing that contradicts it.[24] This is the different point that plenty of what I do that I regard as wrong does not challenge my identity at all.

4. Korsgaard provides two (entirely compatible) characterizations of the problem of normativity, one general and unexceptionable, and the other more specific and of a sort which makes the problem so difficult that it seems impossible to solve. With the hard version of the problem in hand, she finds it easy to dismiss rival solutions to it. I shall argue that, if we press the problem in its harder form against her own solution, then it too fails. But I shall also hypothesize that the resources of Korsgaard's

---

in exercise of our authority, if, indeed, we have it. But, as I've just protested, we can do other relevant things too, in exercise of that (supposed) authority.

22   Ibid., p. 140.
23   Ibid., p. 102.
24   Ibid., pp. 103, 158–60.

solution might be used to produce an interesting candidate for solving the normative problem if we characterize that problem differently, but not altogether differently, from the way she does.

Introducing the problem, Korsgaard says that what "we want to understand" is "the normative dimension," which is that "ethical standards . . . make *claims* on us: they command, oblige, recommend, or guide. Or at least, when we invoke them, we make claims on one another."[25] The question is "Why should I be moral?" "We are asking what *justifies* the claims that morality makes on us. This is what I am calling 'the normative question.'"[26]

Korsgaard lists three conditions which the answer to the normative question must meet. It must "succeed in *addressing*" someone who is in "the first-person position of the agent who demands a justification of the claims which morality makes upon him." Consequently, and this is the second condition, a successful normative theory must meet the condition of "transparency": when I know what justifies my acting as required, I must "believe that [my] actions are justified and make sense." Third, "the answer must appeal, in a deep way, to our sense of who we are, to our sense of our identity . . . [Moral claims] . . . must issue in a deep way from our sense of who we are."[27]

I shall concentrate, in Section 5, on the first condition, that the answer to the normative question must address the agent who asks it, for, as I shall argue, Korsgaard presents that agent as asking that question in so intransigent a spirit that I doubt that such an agent could be satisfied by any theory, Korsgaard's included. Here I remark that Korsgaard's third condition of adequacy on an answer is inappropriate in its assigned role. It is question-begging to say in *advance* that the answer must appeal to the agent's sense of her own identity, even if that should indeed turn out to be a feature of the right answer.

5. Korsgaard's answer to the normative question is that the reason why ethical standards make claims on me is that they represent commands that I give to myself, either *in virtue* of my practical identity or *in exercise* of my practical identity: I am not sure which of those is the right way to put her claim. On the first interpretation, the cost of violating ethical

25   Ibid., p. 8.
26   Ibid., pp. 9–10.
27   Ibid., p. 16–18. I cannot here forbear from the comment which restates, in a different way, points made in Section 3, that who we are is not what we are. Who I am is a matter of my specified situation. And that takes us miles away not only from Kant, for whom only *what* we are enters the moral, but from the *specifically* moral, on *any* account of morality.

standards is loss of the practical identity that I would otherwise still have had; on the second, the cost is failure to have a practical identity, where I might never have had one anyway. I shall suppose that the first interpretation is correct—it fits more of what Korsgaard says.

Now, as I said, the further specification that Korsgaard attaches to the normative problem, the specification that fells the candidate solutions to it which are rival to her own, makes the problem so hard that, so I believe, her own solution too is seen to fall if, as she did not, we forthrightly confront it with her tough specification of the problem.

Return to the general characterization of the problem. The problem is to answer the question "Why should I be moral?" But consider two very different discursive contexts in which that question can occur. The first is the context of protest. "Why should I be moral? If I behave morally here, I wreck my career, I lose friends, I become poor . . ." The second is the context of self-justification. "Why should I be moral? Why should I act morally, like a decent human being? I'll tell you why I should act morally. Because I could not live with myself if I did not." Now, Korsgaard has to fashion an answer which meets the question in its first, protestant, guise. But I doubt whether anything can be *guaranteed* to persuade *that* questioner, and I am certain that Korsgaard can do no better at persuading him than the rivals she criticizes do. Yet her answer does fit what the person figured above says when he addresses the question in its second, and milder, guise.

At various points in lecture 1 Korsgaard taxes moral realism in particular with incapacity to answer the normative question in its protestant form. We are told, first, that

> when the normative question is raised, these are the exact points that are in contention—whether there is really *anything* I must do, and if so whether it is *this*. So it is a little hard to see how realism can help,[28]

since all that realism can say is: well, it's in the nature of things that this is what you must do. But, we have to ask, when so radical a stance of doubt is struck, how Korsgaard's own answer can be expected to help. Again:

> If someone finds that the bare fact that something is his duty does not move him to action, and asks what possible motive he has for doing it, it does not help to tell him that the fact that it is his duty just is the motive. That fact isn't motivating him just now, and therein lies his problem. In a similar way, if someone falls into doubt about whether obligations really exist, it doesn't

---

28 Ibid., p. 34.

help to say "ah, but indeed they do, they are *real*." Just now he doesn't see it, and therein lies his problem.[29]

But when he is in such a state, a state in which he does not feel the force of reason or obligation, that can be because in such a state, and, indeed, if Korsgaard is right, that *must* be because in such a state he does not feel the force of, does not see what is involved in, his practical identity; and, echoing Korsgaard, we can say: therein lies his problem. He asks: why should I continue to dedicate myself like this? And then there is no point saying to him: because that is what you are committed to. Korsgaard says that "the normative question arises when our confidence ['that we really do have obligations'] has been shaken whether by philosophy or by the exigencies of life,"[30] and that someone's confident affirmation of the reality of obligation will then do nothing for us. But one thing which life's exigencies can shake is a person's practical identity, and, when that happens, then Korsgaard's answer will not help. Something shatters my sense of being and obligation in the world, consequently my confidence that obligation is real. It is then useless to tell me that it lies in my practical identity to be thus obliged. When I doubt that "obligations really exist," or do not recognize that moral "actions" are "worth undertaking,"[31] I am setting aside any relevant practical identity that the philosopher might have invoked.

In expressing skepticism about whether Korsgaard's—or anyone else's—theory could address and convert the radically disaffected, I am not committing myself to skepticism about moral obligation. What I am skeptical of is the requirement that an answer to the normative question, in its general specification, has to sound good when addressed to the radically disaffected. If we scale down the difficulty of the question, we can, I think, find illumination in Korsgaard's answer to it.

"The normative question," says Korsgaard, "is a first person question that arises for the moral agent who must actually do what morality says . . . You . . . ask the philosopher: Must I really do this? Why must I do it? And his answer is his answer to the normative question."[32] But, to repeat my objection, if his answer is that it belongs to my practical identity to do it, then why am I asking the question in the alienated style on which Korsgaard insists?

If, on the other hand, we turn the thing around, we get something better. Suppose, again, that I am the moral agent, but this time not an

29   Ibid., p. 38.

30   Ibid., p. 40.

31   Ibid., p. 38 (quoted more fully in text to note 29 above) and p. 102 (quoted more fully in text to note 36 below).

32   Ibid., p. 16, and see pp. 85–86.

alienated one, and *I* am faced by the skeptic who knows it will cost me to go on the march and who asks me why I bother. Then I can say a great deal that is persuasive about my practical identity. If I say, in radical disaffection: "I do not know why I should march," then it is fatuous for you to reply: "Because your conscience compels you to." But if *you* ask why *I* am going to do it, at substantial sacrifice of self-interest, it is not at all fatuous for me to reply, "because my conscience compels me to." "Hier steh ich, ich kann nicht anders" makes sense. "Dort stehst du, du kannst nicht anders" is manifestly false for the case of extreme disaffection which Korsgaard insists a moral theory must address.

If Korsgaard's defense of morality does not meet her own standard, which is that it should be capable of convincing the disaffected, then that could be because hers is the wrong standard, or hers is the wrong defense, or both. For my part, I am more clear that the standard is wrong than that the defense is. I do not think that we can show the intransigent why they should be moral. But I think that I can show the sincere inquirer why *I* must be moral. I have to be moral because, indeed, I could not otherwise live with myself, because I would find my life shabby if I were not moral. I can show that morality is *a* rational way, without being able to show that it is *the* (only) rational way.[33]

That morality is an option within rationality rather than a requirement of rationality necessitates the indicated first-person approach, in which the defender of morality is the moral agent herself. In the defense I sketch, the defender speaks in the first person, in Korsgaard's in the second person, to *me* as a sincere but disaffected inquirer. So I am not against the proposal that the issue be framed in I-thou terms, but I think that the roles of speaker and audience need to be reversed.

Korsgaard calls her solution "the appeal to autonomy," and in one place she describes it as follows:

> [T]he source of the normativity of moral claims must be found in the agent's own will, in particular in the fact that the laws of morality are the laws of the agent's own will and that its claims are ones she is prepared to make on herself. The capacity for self-conscious reflection about our actions confers on us a kind of authority over ourselves, and it is this authority which gives normativity to moral claims.[34]

---

33   I said earlier that not all instances of failure to be moral compromise my practical identity. But to not be moral at all *would* wreck my practical identity, and that of all my fellow nonsociopaths. (I am conscious that this qualified rehabilitation of Korsgaard may achieve nothing more than a return to the Williams position that she wanted her own to supersede.)

34   Korsgaard, *The Sources of Normativity*, pp. 19–20.

I have asked some questions about our supposed authority over ourselves in Section 2 above.[35] Right now I want to register that the rhetoric of the foregoing passage is more suited to how I would explain why I bother to be moral than to what someone else could say if *I* intransigently insist on being told why I *must* be moral.

Your practical identity is given by the

[d]escription[s] under which you value yourself . . . description[s] under which you find your life to be worth living and your actions to be worth undertaking . . . these identities give rise to reasons and obligations. Your reasons express your identity, your nature: your obligations spring from what that identity forbids.[36]

I think all that is powerful stuff for me, the moral agent, to say to my interrogator, but it is entirely impotent when addressed to someone who, being disaffected, *ex hypothesi* finds no actions to be worth undertaking, or, more pertinently and more plausibly, no *moral* ones. It is powerful to say, "I couldn't live with myself if I did that,"[37] but off the mark to say, "You couldn't live with yourself if you did that," to someone who is evidently managing to do so.[38] The intransigent person who insists on a justification for being moral is close to saying: "As far as my deep identity goes, I feel no force in morality's claims." To that little can be said, so that, if we set Korsgaard's answer to the normative question against her own too demanding description of that question, then her answer to it does not work.

6. I have objected to Korsgaard's claim that "[a]n obligation always takes the form of a reaction against a threat of loss of identity." It is an overstatement, whatever may be the truth that it overstates.[39] Not all obligations are like that. But, even if they were, it would remain true that, as I have

---

35   Recall the Hobbesian conundrum with which I began, the problem of whether I have the authority to legislate over myself. If you say to me: but look, it is your law, your practical identity, then I might say: yes, but who am I to impose such a law on me? But when I say, "Hier steh ich," then it is odd for you to say: but who are you to issue such a command to yourself?

36   Korsgaard, *The Sources of Normativity*, pp. 101.

37   Ibid.

38   "A human being is an animal whose nature it is to construct a practical identity which is normative for her. She is a law to herself. When some way of acting is a threat to her practical identity and reflection reveals that fact, the person finds that she must reject that way of acting, and act in another way. In that case she is obligated" (ibid., p. 150).

But you can't *get* me to construct a practical identity that will matter to *me*. And, if I do have one, then there is *my* answer to *you*.

39   See above for the protest against it and note 33 for the element of truth in it.

also complained, not everything that *is* like that is an obligation of the sort for which, we can suppose, Korsgaard wants to supply foundations.

Consider an idealized Mafioso: I call him "idealized" because an expert has told me that real Mafiosi don't have the heroic attitude that my Mafioso displays. This Mafioso does not believe in doing unto others as you would have them do unto you: in relieving suffering just because it is suffering, in keeping promises because they are promises, in telling the truth because it is the truth, and so on. Instead, he lives by a code of strength and honor that matters as much to him as some of the principles I said he disbelieves in matter to most of us. And when he has to do some hideous thing that goes against his inclinations, and he is tempted to fly, he steels himself and we can say of him as much as of us, with the same exaggeration or lack of it, that he steels himself on pain of risking a loss of identity.

What the Mafioso takes to be his obligations can be made to fit Korsgaardian formulae about loss of identity as much as what most of us would regard as genuine obligations can be made to fit those formulae. So it looks as though what she has investigated is the experience or phenomenology of obligation, not its ground or authenticating source. Autonomy, she says, "is the source of obligation, and in particular of our ability to obligate ourselves,"[40] but the Mafia man has that as much as anyone does, this capacity to transcend impulses through reflection and endorse or reject them.

Korsgaard realizes that she might be interpreted as I interpret her when I press the Mafioso example. Accordingly, she emphasizes that "the bare *fact* of reflective endorsement . . . is [not] enough to make an action right."[41] It cannot be enough, she says, because, while there always is at least a minimal reflective endorsement of action, not all action is right. The argument has merit as far as it goes, but it is unreassuring, since it is consistent with the view that *more* than minimal reflective endorsement *does* always make an action right. It is unreassuring that the reason given for denying that reflective endorsement always makes an action right does not confront the reason we have for fearing that it might, reasons like this one: that the Mafioso is entirely capable of (more than minimal) reflective endorsement.

At 3.4.4 Korsgaard seems to grant the present insistence, that the apparatus of reflective endorsement and practical identity is content-neutral: she thinks that it gains its different contents from the different social worlds that self-identifying subjects inhabit. But then we do not have what was demanded in the original characterization of the problem

40   Korsgaard, *The Sources of Normativity*, p. 91.
41   Ibid., p. 161.

of normativity, which was an answer to the question why I must do the specifically *moral* thing. Unless, again, we turn the question around, and *you* are asking *me* why *I* undertake the labor of morality, as such. If I do undertake it, I can explain why. If I don't, Korsgaard supplies nothing sure to work that *you* can say to *me*, for morality might not be part of the practical identity that *my* social world has nourished. Or, worse, my social world might indeed be a morally constituted one, but the nourishment might have failed to take in my case.

7. An attempt to derive *specifically* moral obligation is prosecuted in Korsgaard's lecture 3: see, in particular, sections 3.4.7–3.4.10 and the important summary at 3.6.1. I shall here articulate the argument which I believe to be embodied in the cited sections, and which I find multiply questionable. I shall then pose some of the questions that I have in mind.

Here, then, is what I take to be Korsgaard's argument:

1.	Since we are reflective beings, we must act for reasons.
But	2. If we did not have a normative conception of our identities, we could have no reasons for actions.
So	3. We must have a normative conception of our identities (and our factual need for a normative identity is part of our normative identity).[42]
So	4. We must endorse ourselves as valuable.
So	5. We must treat (all) human beings as valuable.
So	6. We find human beings to be valuable.
So	7. Human beings *are* valuable.
So	8. Moral obligation is established: it is founded in the nature of human agency.

The above argument can be decomposed into four subarguments, on each of which I now invite focus: (1) from 1 to 3, (2) from 3 to 5, (3) from 5 to 7, and (4) from 7 to 8.

(1) The passage from 1 (which I shall not question) to 3 rests on 2, but I do not see that 2 is true, except in the trivial sense that, if I treat something as a reason, then it follows that I regard myself as, identify myself as, the sort of person who is treating that item, here and now, as a reason. I do not see that I must consult an independent conception of my identity to determine whether a possible spring of action is to be endorsed or not, nor even that such endorsement must issue in such a conception, other than in the indicated trivial sense. When I am thirsty, and, at a reflective level, I do not reject my desire to drink, I have, or I think that I have, a reason for taking water, but not one that reflects, or commits me to, a

42   See, in particular, ibid., pp. 125–26.

(relevantly) normative conception of my identity. Merely acting on reasons carries no such commitment.

(2) The inference from 3 to 5 depends on the idea that, being, as we are, inescapably reflective, we must employ the normative conception of our identities (that we therefore necessarily have) to "endorse or reject"[43] the impulses which present themselves to us as possible springs of action. But the very fact (supposing that it is one) that I must endorse *and* reject shows that I do not endorse a human impulse just *because* it is a human impulse. Human impulses are not, therefore, of value just because they are human. So, consistently with the structure of reflective consciousness, I can pass harsh judgment on my own, or on another's panoply of desires and bents, the more so if that other *is* disposed to endorse them. And if my endorsement of a given impulse means that I regard my humanity as *pro tanto* of positive value, then, by the same token, my rejection of another impulse must mean that I regard my humanity as *pro tanto* of negative value. No reason emerges for the conclusion that I must treat human beings, as such, as valuable, or for the requirement, which some might think a Kantian morality embodies, that I must treat them as equal in their value.

(3) The inference from 5 to 7 might be thought to illustrate the fallacy of equivocation, for it seems to depend on an ambiguity in the expression "to find,"[44] which is sometimes a success-verb, where what is found to be thus and so must be so, and sometimes not. There is a sense of "find" in which 6 follows from 5, and another one in which 7 follows from 6: but Korsgaard needs one sense, on pain of equivocation. Yet this comment of mine may reflect boneheadedness on my part about the character of transcendental arguments, for this is supposed to be one: maybe, in a transcendental argument, "find" in its (normally) weaker sense is good enough to derive such a conclusion as 7. Accordingly, being uncertain whether there is any objection worth raising here, I pass on.

(4) My final comment concerns the passage from 7 to 8. My difficulty with it is that it appears to me that the Mafioso can accept 7, in any sense in which what precedes it shows that it is true (I rely here on points made in comment (2) above), yet reject 8. For the Mafioso can honor human beings the springs of whose actions are congruent with his *own* practical identity. So whatever endorsement of humanity as such comes out of this argument, it seems to me not to distinguish the Mafioso ethic from morality, and therefore not to move us beyond the mere phenomenology of obligation to providing a foundation for specifically *moral* obligation.

The problem lies in our freedom at the level of endorsement, the old problem with which these remarks began: that the sovereign can change

---

43   Ibid., 120.
44   See ibid, pp. 123–25.

the law. To hammer that home a bit more, I want to look at Harry Frankfurt's concept of free personhood.

8. The debt that Korsgaard acknowledges to Frankfurt[45] is instructive in connection with my related claims that she has offered an option for the first person rather than a constraint that the second person must accept, and that what she has enabled the first person to provide is a defense of any set of commitments and not of specifically moral ones.

For Frankfurt, I am free when my will conforms to a higher-order volition, when, that is, I act on a first-order volition that I wish to act on, when the spring of my action is one that I want to be moved by.

We should pause to modify this formula. We should add a restriction, a further condition for such conformity to betoken freedom, which has to do with the *direction* of the conformity. That is, the direction of conformity must be that my lower will conforms to my higher one, for, if it goes the other way, if my higher adjusts to my lower, then we have not freedom but second-order adaptive preference formation.[46] That category covers the addict who has come to endorse his own pursuit of drugs: he now likes desiring drugs, and he likes acting on that desire. (I do not say that a willing addict's second-order volition could not be determinative: I am just using as an example the more plausible case in which it is not.)

But there is no restriction either in Frankfurt's presentation or in fact on what the content of second-order volition can be, or, better, for this weaker claim will suffice here, no restriction sufficiently restrictive to yield moral obligation.[47] Thus, to return to my example, the ideal Mafioso is entirely capable of Frankfurt freedom: he can prescribe the Mafia ethic to himself. Yet, to repeat my qualified defense of Korsgaard, *I* can defend *my* ethic even to him. I can explain why I strive not to succumb to some of my first-order desires, including some that move him.

---

45   Ibid., p. 99n.

46   *Second-order* adaptive preference formation because you adapt, here, not your first-order desire to the course of action that's available, but your second-order desire to the first-order desire that's available, or even unshakable.

47   Frankfurt himself supports the stronger claim:

> In speaking of the evaluation of his own desires and motives as being characteristic of a person, I do not mean to suggest that a person's second-order volitions necessarily manifest a *moral* stance on his part toward his first-order desires. It may not be from the point of view of morality that the person evaluates his first-order desires. Moreover, a person may be capricious and irresponsible in forming his second-order volitions and give no serious consideration to what is at stake. Second-order volitions express evaluations only in the sense that they are preferences. There is no essential restriction on the kind of basis, if any, upon which they are formed. (Frankfurt, "Freedom of the Will and the Concept of a Person," p. 19, fn. 6)

Reference to Frankfurt also reinforces the point made earlier, that Korsgaard's legislator is too like the Hobbesian sovereign, as opposed to the Hobbesian citizen, to serve as the sort of model she requires. The Kantian reflective endorsement is inescapable, but Frankfurt's person, like Hobbes's sovereign, is at liberty to reassess his commitments.

So, I return to the thought that something transcending human will must figure in morality if it is to have an apodictic character. Kant was right that, if morality is merely human, then it is optional, as far as rationality is concerned. But it does not follow that morality cannot be merely human, since Kant may have been wrong to think that morality could not be optional. What does follow is that Korsgaard's goal is unachievable, because she wants to keep the "must" that Kant put into morality while nevertheless humanizing morality's source.

PART THREE

Memoir

Chapter 13

G. A. COHEN: A MEMOIR

Jonathan Wolff

G. A. Cohen, universally known as Jerry, died unexpectedly on August 5, 2009. Born on April 14, 1941, he had recently retired as Chichele Professor of Social and Political Thought at Oxford University, and had taken up a part-time post as Quain Professor of Jurisprudence at University College London. UCL was where he had begun his lecturing career in 1963, before his election, in 1984 at a youthful forty-three, to his Oxford Chair, which had previously been held by G.D.H. Cole, Isaiah Berlin, John Plamenatz, and Charles Taylor. He took up the Chair in 1985, the same year in which he was also elected to the British Academy.

The question of who would be appointed to the Chichele Chair was, somewhat surprisingly, a matter of discussion in the national press. Cohen was relatively unknown and an unlikely candidate, at that time the author of just one book, *Karl Marx's Theory of History: A Defence*, and a handful of papers. On his appointment the satirical magazine *Private Eye* speculated that the committee may have been influenced by Cohen's reputation as a wit and raconteur, and the need to enliven the quality of dinner-table conversation at All Souls. Certainly Cohen had a unique and memorable gift for entertaining those around him—his conversation crackled with jokes, snatches of show tunes, and impressions of great philosophers, real and imagined—but in truth, the committee understood that he also had a rare, perhaps unique, philosophical talent, and their confidence in him was amply rewarded.

Cohen was born into a Jewish Marxist family, and his life and character were woven into his philosophical work in an unusual way, to the point where some of these writings contain extended descriptions of his upbringing and family. For example, chapter 2 of his 1996 Gifford Lectures *If You're an Egalitarian, How Come You're So Rich?* is entitled "Politics and Religion in a Montreal Communist Jewish Childhood" and paints a moving picture of his childhood, his parents, their convictions, and their social milieu as factory workers and, in the case of his mother,

Communist Party member and activist.[1] To read it is to be transported into another world: the world of a Cold War Canadian child, from an immigrant family, first convinced of the truth of Marxism and the moral superiority of Soviet Communism, but later trying to come to terms with the behavior of the Soviet Union in the 1950s. Cohen's upbringing, his family, his Jewishness (as distinct from Judaism), and his need to position his own beliefs in relation to Marx and to Soviet Communism were central to his life and work, in terms of both its content and, often, its presentation.

Equally important to his work was his training in philosophy, especially at Oxford, where he moved from undergraduate study at McGill, in 1961. There he came under the influence—the "benign guidance"[2]—of Gilbert Ryle and received a thorough grounding in the techniques of analytical philosophy, with its emphasis on rigor and fine distinctions. It was armed with such techniques that Cohen began his earliest project, resulting in his Isaac Deutcher Memorial Prize–winning book *Karl Marx's Theory of History: A Defence. (KMTH).*[3] Later he said it was a type of "repayment for what I had received. It reflected gratitude to my parents, to the school which had taught me, to the political community in which I was raised."[4] It was an attempt to state and defend Marx's theory of history in a fashion that met the standards of rigor and clarity of contemporary analytic philosophy, in the face of criticisms from Plamenatz and others that this could not be done. The project proceeded relatively slowly. Cohen first published a handful of papers on Marx-related themes. These include two papers on what might be thought of as social epistemology. One, his first published paper, considers the question of whether one's social role can determine what one can think and believe; Cohen argues that human freedom requires one to believe as a human being, rather than attributing one's beliefs to a social role that one plays.[5] A second paper asks how a Marxist understanding of the materialist production of ideas affects the question of whether any such ideas can be regarded as true.[6] This is clearly a matter of huge importance for a Marxist philosopher, and, no doubt, a question Cohen felt he had to settle before taking any further steps. His response is that while other classes need, falsely, to represent their ideas as universal, in the sense of being in the interest of the great majority, the proletariat have no such

---

1   Cohen, *If You're an Egalitarian, How Come You're So Rich?*, pp. 20–41.

2   Cohen, *History, Labour, and Freedom*, p. xi.

3   Cohen, *Karl Marx's Theory of History: A Defence.*

4   *History, Labour, and Freedom*, p. xi.

5   Cohen, "Beliefs and Roles."

6   Cohen, "The Workers and the Word: Why Marx Had the Right to Think He Was Right." [Chapter 9 in the present volume—Ed.]

need of pretense or deception. For their ideas really are in the interest of the majority.

Both these papers are, in a way, prefatory to his project of defending Marx's theory of history, in that they are questions he needed to answer in order to carry out the project with confidence. A third paper from the period, however, is much more closely aligned to the book-length project. Published in 1970, it is called "On Some Criticisms of Historical Materialism" and was presented to the Joint Session of the Aristotelian Society and Mind Association at its annual meeting.[7] Here Cohen responds to some earlier criticisms of historical materialism by H. B. Acton and John Plamenatz, and Acton then replies to Cohen's paper.

Although this paper was published some years before KMTH, several of the innovative themes of that work are foreshadowed here. First, Cohen praises Acton for applying the standards of rigor of analytical philosophy to Marxism, and suggests that in his own work he will apply even higher standards. For this reason, arguably, this 1970 paper may well be the first appearance of what was later to be called "Analytic Marxism," using the techniques of analytical philosophy and formal economics and social science to defend Marxism, rather than to criticize it. Second, Cohen takes Marx's 1859 "Preface" to A Contribution to the Critique of Political Economy as the central source for his reading of Marx's theory of history. Finally, he presents a sketch of how the device of functional explanation can be used to overcome some difficulties in the formulation of the theory, which was to become one of the central aspects of his later reconstruction. The main topic of the symposium is the question of the relation between the economic base and the legal and political superstructure in historical materialism. The economic base is understood to be the set of relations of production, such as the relations between capitalists and workers, or masters and slaves, within the economy. Thus the base is, broadly speaking, the economic system. Plamenatz had argued that it was impossible to characterize economic relations of production except in terms of legal powers. For example, a proletarian is someone who has the right to sell his or her labor, unlike the serf or slave who has no such right. Yet to use the language of rights is to use a set of concepts belonging to the superstructure, and hence, so it is argued, it is impossible to define the economic structure except in superstuctural terms. If this is so, then, it is argued, it cannot be the case that the economic structure has explanatory priority over the superstructure, as orthodox Marxism dictates.

Cohen does not question Plamenatz's claim that it is necessary to provide an independent account of the economic structure for it to play the role Marx requires of it. Rather he takes on the challenge of providing

---

7 Cohen, "On Some Criticisms of Historical Materialism."

such an account—what he calls a "rechtsfrei" interpretation. He argues that the economic base should be understood, strictly speaking, as constituted by powers, rather than rights. The superstructure, as a set of legal rights, exists in order to consolidate the powers belonging to the economic base. This is a direct and explicit appeal to functional explanation. The superstructure exists because it has a function: the function of protecting economic power. The solution is elegant. The base and superstructure can be characterized independently of each other, and while the superstructure has a causal effect on the base, it exists in order to have that effect. Therefore the economic base has explanatory priority even though causal influence goes in the opposite direction.

Although many of the elements were in place by 1970, and other important papers on Marx were published in 1972 and 1974,[8] it was not until 1978 that Cohen published *KMTH*. Part of the reason for delay was his perfectionism in trying to get the details as precisely right as he could. But another explanation was that he was faced with a much more urgent project. In 1973 Robert Nozick published a long article in *Philosophy and Public Affairs*, which was to become the heart of the libertarian political philosophy elaborated in *Anarchy, State, and Utopia*.[9]

Cohen reports that Nozick's ideas were first drawn to his attention by Gerald Dworkin in 1972, and, in an important episode in his life, in 1975 he visited Princeton for a semester, lecturing on Nozick and making important connections with Tom Nagel and Tim Scanlon.[10] On encountering Nozick's arguments Cohen felt a need to divert his focus from his work on Marx, for the time being, to answer Nozick. Nozick, of course, sets out a natural rights–based form of libertarianism, defending a minimal state, and condemning any form of redistributive transfer as coercive and unjust. For many left-liberals, Nozick's was a dazzling defense of an obviously false and heartless view: a view that required attention because of the intellectual strength, wit, and elegance of many of the arguments of the book, but not because the overall doctrine presented gave them any cause to doubt their own heartfelt convictions. For Cohen, however, the situation was quite different. As he later put it, in a paper revealingly entitled "Marxism and Contemporary Political Philosophy, or: Why Nozick Exercises Some Marxists More Than He Does Any Egalitarian Liberals,"[11] Cohen's Marxist-inspired critique of capitalism was based on the idea that the relation between capitalist and worker is exploitative,

---

8   Cohen, "Karl Marx and the Withering Away of Social Science"; Cohen, "Marx's Dialectic of Labor"; and Cohen, "Being, Consciousness and Roles."

9   Nozick, *Anarchy, State, and Utopia*.

10   Cohen, *Self-Ownership, Freedom, and Equality*, p. 4.

11   Reprinted as chap. 6 of ibid.

because it involves "the theft of another person's labour time." Yet in *Anarchy, State, and Utopia* Nozick argues that redistributive taxation has exactly that character. According to Cohen, Marxists such as himself at that time believe in the principle of self-ownership, that people are the rightful owners of their own powers, but exactly this principle is argued, by Nozick, to yield not communism, but a stark form of capitalist individualism. Refuting this view, then, became another essential "ground-clearing" task in the defense of Marxism, but also very important for its own sake.[12]

Cohen's classic paper on Nozick, "Robert Nozick and Wilt Chamberlain: How Patterns Preserve Liberty," was published in 1977.[13] (A slightly revised version was published in 1995 in *Self-Ownership, Freedom, and Equality*. Like many of his reprinted papers the later version contains a number of small corrections and amendments.) Nozick vividly argued that any attempt to introduce a "pattern" of distributive justice, such as equality, will require the state to prevent individuals from making voluntary transactions that might disrupt the pattern. Yet if the state were to do this, it would restrict individual liberty, needing to coerce individuals into conformity to the designated distribution, and so those who value liberty should resist any attempt to implement a pattern. Cohen makes many points in criticism of Nozick's argument, but his main response is that Nozick has overlooked the fact that a distribution of property is already a distribution of liberty. One person's ownership of an item of property entails that other people are not at liberty to use it without the owner's permission. Therefore it can be the case that a pattern is needed to preserve the liberty of those who would otherwise suffer in an unpatterned distribution. Hence, Cohen argues, patterns preserve liberty. He notes that Nozick attempts to avoid this, by redefining liberty as, essentially, the freedom to do what one has a right to do, and so a nonowner's inability to use the property of its owner is no longer a detriment to liberty. But if this move is made, it then becomes question-begging to try to defend a view of private property in terms of liberty, for any account of liberty already assumes a view of justified property. This critique is arguably the most powerful and influential of those that attempted to engage with Nozick's argument.

Cohen finally published *KMTH* in 1978, and shortly afterward a brilliant, critical examination of Marx's labor theory of value and its relation to the theory of exploitation.[14] On the publication of *KMTH* Cohen established his position as among the world leading interpreters of Marx's

---

12 Ibid., pp. 144–64.
13 Cohen, "Robert Nozick and Wilt Chamberlain: How Patterns Preserve Liberty."
14 Cohen, "The Labour Theory of Value and the Concept of Exploitation."

thought. The book is a considerable extension of the earlier paper "On Some Criticisms of Historical Materialism" and sets out a clear account of the core of Marx's theory of history. According to Cohen the two central theses of historical materialism are the "development thesis" and the "primacy thesis." The development thesis states that society's productive forces tend to develop throughout history, in the sense that human productivity tends to become more powerful over time. The primacy thesis is a combination of two claims: that the nature of the productive forces explains the economic structure, and that the nature of the economic structure explains the superstructure (the claim we saw explicated and defended in the earlier paper). Put together, this is a form of technological determinism: the ultimate explanatory factor for all other significant facts about society is the nature of technology available. As Marx himself puts it, in *The Poverty of Philosophy*, "the hand-mill gives you society with the feudal lord, the steam mill society with the industrial capitalist."[15]

This theory is distinctively Marxist in that it divides history into epochs—preclass society, slavery, feudalism, capitalism, and communism—and understands the transition from epoch to epoch as the result of class struggle and revolutionary change. The claim is that an economic structure, such as capitalism, will persist for as long as it is optimal for the development of the productive forces (an application of functional explanation), but eventually it cannot contain all the growth it has stimulated. At that point the economic structure "fetters" the development of the productive forces, and must give way, to be replaced by a new economic structure that will continue the development of the productive forces.

Although the basic theory can be stated simply, *KMTH* is a complex book. First, it enters into many disputes regarding the detailed understanding of Marx, attempting to settle contested points of textual interpretation. Second, Cohen builds detailed and ingenious arguments for many of the positions taken. The book, after all, is an interpretation of Marx and a defense of Marx's position. Accordingly the discussion encompasses questions not raised by Marx, such as how to formulate and deploy the central device of functional explanation, or how to argue for the claim that the forces of production tend to develop throughout history.

On publication the book received wide acclaim. At the same time, naturally enough, it received various forms of criticism. Some of this criticism was aimed at the interpretation of Marx. One oft-leveled charge was that Marx's theory of history was not, at bottom, one of technological determinism. Some of these critics pointed out that Cohen had downplayed Hegel's influence on Marx, and, accordingly, had not taken seriously dialectical forms of reasoning. However, Cohen's project of incorporating

15   Marx, *The Poverty of Philosophy* (Progress Press edition), p. 95.

analytic philosophy into Marxism was designed precisely to overcome what he saw as the damaging obscurantism of Hegelian Marxism, especially that transmitted via the work of Althusser.[16] A related, and less doctrinaire, criticism was that Cohen allowed only a relatively minor role for class struggle. In Cohen's reading, class struggle is the agent of change from epoch to epoch, rather than the engine of history at all times, as appears to be indicated by Marx's remark that "history is the history of class struggle." Yet Cohen was convinced that his interpretation of Marx was correct on this point, accepting that class struggle is the "immediate driving power of history" but not its "underlying" driving force.[17]

Other lines of criticism concerned the theory itself, rather than whether it was a true depiction of Marx's thought. Jon Elster, for example, strongly criticized the use of functional explanation, arguing that it retained an unacceptable teleology. As Elster observes, suggesting that economic structures rise and fall as they further or impede human productive power seems to assume that history is goal directed, or even that there is some sort of external agency ensuring that progress continues to be made.[18] Andrew Levine and Erik Wright take issue with Cohen's argument that the development of the productive forces can be explained in terms of what they call "rational adaptive preferences." They suggest that Cohen does not take sufficiently into account problems of collective action.[19] Joshua Cohen made similar criticisms and adduced evidence that there have been long stretches of history in which the productive forces declined in strength (most notably on the fall of the Roman Empire).[20] Richard Miller pointed out that the account of fettering was unclear.[21] Did the productive forces have to stop developing, or was it enough that they developed more slowly than they would under some other economic structure? Furthermore, the use of the productive forces and their development are quite different. One could argue that capitalism greatly develops the productive forces but uses them poorly. Is this fettering or not?

Each of these criticisms brought forward important responses and further clarifications of the theory. In response to Elster, Cohen pursued the analogy with the Darwinian use of functional explanation in evolutionary biology, which does not presuppose teleology or "nature's purposes."[22] In response to Joshua Cohen, and Levine and Wright, Cohen, together

16   Cohen, *Karl Marx's Theory of History* (expanded edition), p. xxi.
17   Cohen, *History, Labour, and Freedom*, p. 16.
18   Elster, "Cohen on Marx's Theory of History"; and Elster, *Making Sense of Marx*.
19   A. Levine and E. Wright, "Rationality and Class Struggle."
20   J. Cohen, review of *Karl Marx's Theory of History*.
21   Miller, "Productive Forces and the Forces of Change," review of *Karl Marx's Theory of History*.
22   Cohen, "Functional Explanation: Reply to Elster."

with Will Kymlicka, wrote a detailed rebuttal of their argument,[23] and in response to Richard Miller, Cohen broadly accepted the criticism that the theory of fettering was unclear, and wrote a detailed clarification, which was first published in *History, Labour, and Freedom* and was ultimately incorporated as an additional chapter in the expanded edition of *KMTH*.

Yet in the face of these criticisms and reformulations Cohen began to see that the theory was not as clear-cut as he had thought. He also had begun to develop reservations of his own, especially about historical materialism's apparent neglect of people's apparent need for self-definition: that is, the need to identify with groups in society that are less than the whole. This in turn leads Marxism to a dismissive and reductionist approach to religion and nationalism. These anxieties are recorded in two other papers that also appeared first in *History, Labour, and Freedom* and then in the expanded edition of *KMTH*: "Reconsidering Historical Materialism," and "Restricted and Inclusive Historical Materialism." Others might, at this point, have seen the enterprise as a "degenerating research program." Instead of using the theory to illuminate and explain ever more aspects of empirical reality, it appeared to require increasingly intricate internal development, specification, and qualification, to defend it against criticism, thereby reducing its explanatory power. Indeed, Cohen explains that his attitude to historical materialism had changed upon his completion of the book. While writing it he was sure that Marx's theory of history was correct. After, he said, it was not so much that he believed it to be false, but that he did not know how to tell whether or not it was true.[24]

During this time Cohen was a founder and very active member of the Non-Bullshit Marxism Group (later called the September Group), which was a remarkable, interdisciplinary group of scholars who first met in 1979 and again in 1980, to discuss exploitation. They then met annually, and then biennially, to discuss wider themes. The core membership of the original group, aside from Cohen, were Jon Elster, John Roemer, Hillel Steiner, Philippe van Parijs, Robert van der Veen, Adam Przeworski, Erik Olin Wright, Pranab Bardhan, and Robert Brenner, although the membership changed considerably over the years.

The September Group was founded to discuss themes within Marxism, but their allegiance to the themes lasted longer, typically, than their allegiance to Marx. This development was foreshadowed, to some degree, by Cohen's earlier paper "The Labour Theory of Value and the Concept of Exploitation," in which he had argued that the concept of exploitation

---

23   Cohen and Kymlicka, "Human Nature and Social Change in the Marxist Conception of History."

24   *History, Labour, and Freedom*, p. 132; *Karl Marx's Theory of History* (expanded edition), p. 341.

does not rest on the labor theory of value. As Cohen continued to work in the 1980s and beyond, one might characterize his writings as working out how to formulate his opposition to capitalism and allegiance to socialism without the underpinnings of Marx's theory of history. As he put it, "In the past, there seemed to be no need to *argue* for the desirability of an egalitarian socialist society. Now I do little else."[25]

This next phase in his career takes up themes that emerged in his criticism of Nozick: the relations between capitalism, socialism, and freedom, and the nature and consequences of the thesis of self-ownership. These are the topics of the last few papers reprinted in *History, Labour, and Freedom*, and all of his next collection, *Self-Ownership, Freedom, and Equality*.

In the 1980s, Cohen was especially exercised by the Marx-inspired question of how to understand the unfreedom of workers under capitalism, given that they exist in a structure that places freedom of choice at its center, and no worker is forced, so it appears, to work for any particular capitalist. Yet at the same time there seems to be a vital sense in which workers in the capitalist system remain unfree. One important part of the analysis is to provide a definition of being forced to do something in which saying that a person is forced to do something does not mean that it is the only option available to him or her, but that any other options he or she has are not acceptable or reasonable.[26]

One obvious response to the claim that workers are forced to sell their labor-power to the capitalists, on this definition, is that workers do have an acceptable alternative; they can become petty bourgeois shop owners or self-employed in some way. Here Cohen accepts that this escape route is available to some workers, yet, he argues, although any individual worker is free to leave the proletariat, the proletariat is collectively unfree, for there are nothing like as many escape routes as there are members of the proletariat.[27]

The notion of the worker's right to freedom and the thesis of self-ownership are linked through the idea of a person's right to control his or her actions and labor. Cohen characterizes self-ownership as the thesis that "each person enjoys over herself and her powers, full and exclusive rights of control and use, and therefore owes no service or product to anyone else that she has not contracted to supply."[28] This is, of course, qualified by the condition that rights of self-ownership do not permit one to interfere coercively in the lives of others. In a series of papers Cohen

25 *Self-Ownership, Freedom, and Equality*, p. 7.
26 *History, Labour, and Freedom*, p. 247.
27 Ibid., pp. 239–304.
28 *Self-Ownership, Freedom, and Equality*, p. 12.

considered the relation between self-ownership and what he refers to as "world-ownership": rights over those parts of the world that are not persons. Essentially Cohen set out to rebut the Nozickian argument that rights to self-ownership entail rights to world-ownership (i.e., individual property rights) that are in principle unrestricted. Nozick had argued that any attempt to redistribute worldly resources in effect conscripts one person, willingly or not, to work for another.

Cohen notes that those who are in favor of redistribution have the option merely to deny self-ownership, and assume that we have noncontractual duties of noninterference. Yet he argues that a stronger defense is to accept, for the purposes of argument, the thesis of self-ownership, and show that the Nozickian conclusion does not follow. In a now-classic discussion of Nozick's account of justice in initial acquisition, Cohen points out that it is essential to Nozick's argument that the external world is, initially, unowned, and therefore available for initial acquisition. However, Nozick does not show that the world is not jointly owned by all human beings. If that were the case, the conditions for appropriation would be much more strict, and would not yield the type of property rights favored by libertarians. Hence, at the least, Nozick has not shown that radically unequal distribution can follow from self-ownership. Furthermore, even if the world is not jointly owned, Cohen argues that Nozick's defense of initial appropriation— roughly, an appropriation is acceptable as long as it makes no one worse-off—contains a strong element of paternalism that Nozick would reject in other circumstances.[29]

As his work on this topic developed, Cohen seemed close to endorsing the thesis of self-ownership, especially, as we noted above, because he saw it as very similar to the views that underlie the Marxist opposition to exploitation. Yet he came to believe that self-ownership and an attractive form of egalitarianism were in conflict. In "Are Freedom and Equality Compatible?" he argues that assuming that egalitarianism should be characterized by the thesis that the world is jointly owned by everyone is far too restrictive. It would require everyone else's consent before anyone could use anything at all. This, Cohen argues, thereby renders self-ownership "merely formal" (a criticism that also applies to libertarianism, for the self-ownership of those without property is also merely formal, and they would rely entirely on the cooperation of others for survival). He continues with the argument that the egalitarian alternative of parceling the world into equal individual shares fares no better, at least from an egalitarian point of view, as it will allow outcomes to be strongly determined by the exercise of differential talent, and fails to guarantee support for those who cannot produce for themselves.[30]

29   Ibid., pp. 67–91.
30   Ibid., pp. 92–115.

Eventually, therefore, he found the principle of self-ownership unhelp-ful, and in a pair of papers published for the first time in *Self-Ownership, Freedom, and Equality* he came to accept the position that many of his liberal egalitarian friends and colleagues had urged upon him for years: the rejection of the principle. While he defends the coherence of the idea of self-ownership, he argues against its adoption. His position is not so much to find a direct argument against the thesis, but rather to demon-strate that the motivations that lead in the direction of self-ownership do not take one all the way. That is to say, one can oppose slavery, advance autonomy, and object to treating a person as a means without adopting self-ownership.[31]

Self-Ownership, Freedom, and Equality largely pursues a single theme: the thesis of self-ownership, and it is something of an anticlimax that the work ends on a largely negative note. Yet this should not detract from the point that the essays together add up to the most powerful and influential detailed rebuttal of Nozick's libertarianism that has been produced, one that is unlikely to be surpassed. The essays, executed with supreme rigor, are full of insight and interest even when their point is to warn against a wrong turning, rather than build a new construction.

Modestly Cohen characterized himself as essentially a reactive phi-losopher. This, as a more general conception of philosophy, comes out clearly in a remarkable paper, "How to Do Political Philosophy," written for use in teaching a graduate class at Oxford, where it is clear that Cohen conceives of philosophy as an activity that takes place against an oppo-nent.[32] In the first phase of his career Marx was the clear inspiration, and the opponents were analytic critics of Marx, such as Plamenatz, and ob-scurantist defenders, such as Althusser. The second phase was dominated by the need to answer Nozick's libertarianism. In the third phase Ronald Dworkin was the focus of his reflections, and in particular Dworkin's two seminal articles on equality of welfare and equality of resources.[33] Cohen found himself very sympathetic to what later came to be called "luck egalitarianism." Dworkin's achievement, said Cohen, in a much-quoted passage, was to perform "for egalitarianism the considerable service of incorporating within it the most powerful idea in the arsenal of the anti-egalitarian right: the idea of choice and responsibility."[34] Indeed, there is a strong residue of Cohen's earlier reflections on Nozick in this comment.

The leading idea of luck egalitarianism is to make a distinction between those aspects of one's fate for which one is responsible, and those aspects

31   Ibid., pp. 209–44.
32   Cohen, "How to Do Political Philosophy."
33   Dworkin, "What Is Equality? Part 1, Equality of Welfare" and "What Is Equality? Part 2, Equality of Resources."
34   Cohen, "On the Currency of Egalitarian Justice."

for which one is not. Dworkin makes a distinction between "brute luck" and "option luck," and on this view the project is to set out principles that allow people to reap the benefits, but also suffer the burdens, of good and bad option luck, but at the same time to insulate people from the effects of good and bad brute luck. There are, at least, two central questions that must be answered in order to settle how this doctrine is to be formulated. One is the question of how exactly to define the "cut" between those factors for which a person is to be held responsible, and those for which he or she is not. A second is the "currency" of justice: should equality be defined in terms of welfare, resources, capabilities, or something else again? Dworkin is very clear on the second question: equality of resources is the right currency. His response to the first question—how exactly to draw the cut—was less easy to discern from his writings.

Cohen's contribution to this debate was initially set out in two papers, "On the Currency of Egalitarian Justice," mentioned above, and "Equality of What? On Welfare, Goods and Capabilities."[35] Cohen broadly accepts Arneson's characterization of Dworkin's theory as one of equality of opportunity for resources.[36] However, in opposition to Dworkin and Arneson, Cohen's preferred position is one of "equality of access to advantage," of which the more important modification is "advantage" instead of "resources" or "welfare." Cohen's point is that an egalitarian must be sensitive to certain types of resource deficiency, however they impact on welfare, as well as certain types of welfare deficiency, however they impact on resources. Accordingly he defines a new notion—advantage—which straddles resources and welfare (although he does not attempt to specify how the two elements are to be combined).

One primary issue between Cohen and Dworkin comes down to the question of whether low welfare should engage egalitarian concerns. Dworkin admits the immediate appeal of such a view but marshals a range of considerations to put it into doubt. Perhaps surprisingly, the focal example for deciding between different cases is that of "expensive tastes." If a person cannot enjoy those things others typically take pleasure in—beer and hen's eggs, say—but to achieve comparable levels of enjoyment, she must consume expensive champagne and plover's eggs, should she receive a social subsidy so that she can achieve the same level of enjoyment as the rest of the population?

Dworkin's position is that one should not receive a subsidy for expensive tastes, unless they are a form of compulsion or craving, akin to mental illness. Cohen, by contrast, argues that there is a difference between those people who find themselves with expensive tastes, by bad

---

35   Cohen, "Equality of What? On Welfare, Goods and Capabilities."
36   Arneson, "Equality and Equal Opportunity for Welfare."

brute luck, who should be subsidized, and those who deliberately cultivated them, who, in the spirit of luck egalitarianism, should be required
to bear the consequences of their freely made choice. Dworkin argues
that the key factor for deciding whether or not subsidy is due is whether
the person identifies with his or her tastes. It would be "alienating" to
offer people subsidy for aspects of what they regard as their personality.
In reply Cohen makes the important distinction between identifying with
the taste and identifying with its cost. One can fully identify with the taste
yet regret that it is expensive. If one has not deliberately cultivated it,
then, in Cohen's view, subsidy is due. The debate between Dworkin and
Cohen went through several exchanges, both making strong and plausible arguments and neither side prepared to concede ground.[37]

When luck egalitarianism—in all its versions—came under attack from
Elizabeth Anderson[38] and others for its apparent inhumanity, such as its
"abandonment of the irresponsible" (those who have freely chosen paths
with disastrous consequences and would therefore have no claim for
help), Cohen took pains to point out that his project was only to define
and argue for a theory of equality as an account of distributive justice,
and not to argue that any society should adopt an unmodified principle
of equality. Rather, he reminded his readers of a point that he had made
explicit in his earlier paper. He accepts that concerns other than those of
egalitarian justice could turn out to be more important in practice.[39] In
making this point he develops an early version of a distinction that, as we
will see, became important in the last period of his work: the distinction
between theories of justice and what he was to call "rules of regulation."

The next phase in Cohen's work began with three papers that stand
with *Karl Marx's Theory of History*, and the critique of Nozick, as the
high points of his career. These are the Tanner Lectures of 1992, "Incentives, Inequality, and Community,"[40] "The Pareto Argument for Inequality" (1995),[41] and "Where the Action Is: On the Site of Distributive
Justice" (1997).[42] The last of these papers was also included in Cohen's
superbly readable and engrossing book *If You're an Egalitarian, How
Come You're So Rich?* and together they also constitute the first three
chapters of his final major book, *Rescuing Justice and Equality*. The
essential question is, how, as a believer in equality, should one behave
in one's personal economic life? In particular Cohen is concerned to

37 Cohen, "Expensive Tastes and Multiculturalism"; Dworkin, *Sovereign Virtue*;
Cohen, "Expensive Tastes Rides Again"; Dworkin, "Replies."
38 Anderson, "What Is the Point of Equality?"
39 Cohen, *Rescuing Justice and Equality*, p. 271.
40 Cohen, "Incentives, Inequality, and Community."
41 Cohen, "The Pareto Argument for Inequality."
42 Cohen, "Where the Action Is: On the Site of Distributive Justice."

question how it could be consistent both to pursue a high income and to espouse egalitarianism. Much of this work is aimed at the criticism of one particular attempt to defend such a combination to be found in the work of John Rawls, who, in effect, became Cohen's last philosophical opponent. Rawls's famous "Difference Principle" states that inequalities in income and wealth are justified when they are to the greatest possible benefit of the worst-off.[43] An apparently naive reply to Rawls is to question how inequalities could ever be to the benefit of the worst-off. Inequalities can be removed if money is transferred from the richer to the poorer; this achieves equality by making the worst-off better-off. The Rawlsian reply is that such a transfer would, of course, be better if it were possible. But the Difference Principle also anticipates situations where such a beneficial transfer is not possible; that is, where equalizing would make everyone worse-off, at least in the longer term. Broadly this doctrine is thought to be sensitive to the economic argument that everyone can be better-off if the highly productive are provided with material incentives to work harder. This, in turn, leads to inequalities that are to the advantage of all.

Cohen, however, pushes the argument to another stage. How can there be circumstances where equality is impossible at a higher level for all? Presumably, only because those who are well-off will not contribute as much effort at a lower level of income. This may be an understandable response, if not admirable, for those who do not believe in equality. Yet one of the conditions of Rawls's account of a "well-ordered society" is that everyone should believe in the Rawlsian principles of justice, and in particular endorse the principle that the worst-off should be made as well-off as possible. Therefore people in a Rawlsian society should not seek higher wages than others, unless there is some special reason why they cannot (as distinct from will not) be more productive on the same income as others. Therefore, Cohen argues, the Difference Principle justifies much less inequality than it is often thought to do, and Rawlsian principles of justice must be supplemented by an "egalitarian ethos" to guide choices in everyday life.

There are several resources in Rawls to try to combat this line of argument, although Rawls himself never confronted it in detail. One important response is that the Difference Principle is intended to regulate the "basic structure" of society, rather than personal behavior. This, and several other strategies, are discussed, and rebutted in detail, in the first half of *Rescuing Justice and Equality*. The second part of the book, while still engaged with Rawlsian theory, changes tack, extending an argument first

43   Rawls, *A Theory of Justice*.

presented in a paper entitled "Facts and Principles."[44] Here the project is to attempt to show that basic principles of justice must be "fact free" in the sense of not depending on any empirical facts. This contrasts with a Rawlsian "constructivist" approach in which facts about human nature and society are taken into account at the most basic level in formulating principles of justice. Here Cohen accuses Rawls and his followers of failing to respect the distinction mentioned above between rules of regulation and (pure) principles of justice.

While this work has attracted respectful and detailed attention, many readers have been surprised by this turn in Cohen's work. Although it is the fruit of several years of sustained endeavor, in contrast to most of his other work it is much less clear what the payoff is, as his opponents are not convicted of any substantive error regarding what is to be done, as distinct from conceptual confusion regarding the nature of justice. However, for Cohen conceptual clarity for its own sake was of supreme importance.

Nevertheless, certainly for the chapters in part 1, the book is already a classic in political philosophy, and it may well be that in time the significance of part 2 will come to be better understood. Furthermore, in presenting his ideas in book-length form, Cohen came to reflect on a number of items that are foreshadowed in earlier work but explicitly clarified here. For example, there is a short discussion of Cohen's attitude to moral realism,[45] and a more explicit endorsement of pluralism than is found elsewhere.[46]

Cohen's final book, *Why Not Socialism?*, was completed before he died but published posthumously.[47] The book is very short, and published in small format. It begins with an account of a camping trip and persuasively argues that under such circumstances the trip would be much more enjoyable for all participants, and more efficient, if the campers adopted certain anti-individualist principles of community and equality that could fairly be described as socialist, rather than capitalist market principles, to govern their interactions. The book continues with the question of why it should be that such socialist principles are not adopted in broader social and economic life. Here Cohen refuses to accept the pessimism about human nature that suggests that natural human selfishness makes socialism impossible. Rather, he points out, we have not (yet?) been able to devise social mechanisms that allow us to organize large-scale economic interaction on the basis of human generosity, in contrast to the

44 Cohen, "Facts and Principles."
45 *Rescuing Justice and Equality*, pp. 230, 257
46 Ibid., pp. 3–6.
47 Cohen, *Why Not Socialism?*

capitalist free market, which can turn individual greed and fear to general advantage, although, if course, it has many disadvantages too.

At his death Cohen left a number of works in progress as well as a series of lectures on moral and political philosophy that he had intended to prepare for publication. Much of this work will be published in the next few years.[48] One of the most intriguing previously unpublished papers is called "One Kind of Spirituality." The importance of Cohen's Jewish background has already been remarked upon, but many assumed that he had no interest in any issues of religion or spirituality, especially given what he has described as his "anti-religious upbringing." However, two of his three children, Gideon and Sarah, took a different direction, Gideon adopting Rastafarianism and moving to Ethiopia, and Sarah spending much of her time in an ashram in the southern Indian state of Kerala. Cohen's love and respect for his children no doubt encouraged him to take their views seriously. In his Gifford Lectures for 1996—normally given on a theme in Philosophy of Religion—Cohen stated that he was agnostic, not an atheist. But more surprisingly for many readers, he revealed himself as a long-standing and regular Bible reader of both Testaments. In the lectures he showed a respectful and tolerant attitude to religion, and especially Christianity.

It should be clear from the foregoing how important family was to Cohen. His first major philosophical project was seen as a type of repayment to his parents, to whom his first book was dedicated. He married Margaret Pearce in 1965, and they had three children, Gideon, Miriam (who now teaches philosophy in London), and Sarah. The marriage was dissolved but Cohen remained on very good terms with Maggie, and both remarried, Cohen to Michèle Jacottet in 1999. His second marriage was a very happy one, spent in the company of what was now a complex and growing extended family.

Cohen's contribution to political philosophy has been extensive, defending what many would regard as the most thoroughgoing and radical egalitarianism to be found among analytical philosophers. However, his own positive view was not developed in the detail that characterizes the work of other leading figures, such as John Rawls, Ronald Dworkin, or John Roemer. Rather, as noted, Cohen considered himself more a reactive than an individually creative philosopher. In this his skill was unrivaled. His style is often that of an expert demolition worker: finding what might look like a rather banal difficulty, but probing and probing until the edifice collapses. Cohen knew exactly where to locate his criticism, and how to develop it to greatest effect. At first sight the criticisms

---

48 Footnote added in 2013: This volume is, in fact, the last of the three posthumous volumes referred to above.

can look pedantic or fussy, but as the arguments develop, something of great power emerges. Those who have the instinct to defend the views he attacks find themselves with a much more difficult task than they first assumed.

Cohen will be remembered for his work, but just as much for his wit and his support for other people. Even in prestigious public lectures he would crack jokes, burst into song, or imitate other philosophers. He would do the same thing in restaurants, drawing waiting staff or diners at other tables into the fun and good-natured mischief. His valedictory lecture at Oxford in 2008 included a series of imitations or parodies of many well-known philosophers, and was said by many members of the audience to be the funniest and most entertaining lecture they had witnessed. Fortunately some video and audio recordings of Cohen survive, most notably a TV program, *No Habitat for a Shmoo*, made in 1986, some videos of lectures and impersonations delivered in Madison, Wisconsin, in 1998, and an imperfect audio recording of the valedictory lecture.[49]

In 2009, about half a year before his death, a conference at Oxford was held in celebration of his work and career. In remarks at the end of the conference Cohen observed how odd it is that in this country we honor people by attempting to rip their work to pieces. But in these remarks he also made clear how extremely proud he was of his former students—of how confident they had become, and of how much they had become their own people. Cohen was extraordinarily generous with his time, and not only for his own students, and not only on his own topics. His native intelligence—honed by tutorials with Gilbert Ryle—enabled him to grapple with any topic put to him, and fifteen minutes with Cohen would leave anyone understanding both more and less about his or her own view or argument. All of those who met him, or read his work, will realize what a gap his unexpected death has left. He gave so much, yet he still had so much more. Any attempt to express how much he will be missed by his family, friends, colleagues, and even those who never met him, will seem trite or formulaic.[50]

---

49 The text of this lecture appears in *Finding Oneself in the Other*, a collection of Cohen's work, edited by Michael Otsuka. The recording is posted to http://press.princeton.edu/titles/9886.html.

50 My thanks to Miriam Cohen Christofidis, Veronique Munoz Dardé, Michael Otsuka, Michael Rosen, Hillel Steiner, and Arnold Zuboff, for very valuable comments on an earlier version. A few paragraphs of this piece appeared previously in an obituary I published in the *Philosophers' Magazine*. I thank the editors for permission to reuse the material.

Works Cited

Acton, H. B. *The Illusion of the Epoch*. London: Cohen and West, 1955.

Adkins, Arthur W. H. *Merit and Responsibility*. Chicago: University of Chicago Press, 1960.

Aeschylus. *The Persians*. P. Vellacott, trans. London: Penguin, 1962.

Altham, J.E.J. "Reflections on the State of Nature." In Ross Harrison, ed. *Rational Action*. Cambridge: Cambridge University Press, 1979.

Anderson, Elizabeth. "What Is the Point of Equality?" *Ethics* 109 (1999): 287–337.

Annas, Julia. *An Introduction to Plato's Republic*. Oxford: Clarendon Press, 1981.

Arendt, Hannah. *The Human Condition*. New York: Doubleday Anchor, 1959.

Aristotle, *Politics*. 350 BCE. Ernest Barker, trans. Oxford: Clarendon Press, 1946.

———. *Politics: Books III and IV*. 350 BCE. Richard Robinson, trans. Oxford: Oxford University Press, 1962. Reprinted 1995.

Arneson, Richard. "Equality and Equal Opportunity for Welfare." *Philosophical Studies* 55 (1989): 77–93.

Avineri, Shlomo. *The Social and Political Thought of Karl Marx*. Cambridge: Cambridge University Press, 1968.

Barnes, Jonathan. *The Presocratic Philosophers*. London: Routledge, 1982.

———. "New Light on Antiphon." *Polis* 7 (1987): 2–5.

Berle, A. A., and G. C. Means. *The Modern Corporation and Private Property*. New York: Macmillan, 1932.

Bell, Daniel. *The End of Ideology*. New York: Free Press, 1962.

Bennet, John. "A Note on Locke's Theory of Tacit Consent." *Philosophical Review* 88 (1979): 224–34.

Bierce, Ambrose. *The Devil's Dictionary*. D. E. Schultz and S. J. Joshi, eds. Athens: University of Georgia Press, 2000.

Blauner, Robert. *Alienation and Freedom*. Chicago: University of Chicago Press, 1964.

Bradley, F. H. "My Station and Its Duties." In his *Ethical Studies*, 2nd ed. Oxford: Oxford University Press, 1927.

Burns, Robert. *Selected Poems*. London: Penguin, 1993.

Burnyeat, Myles. "The Impiety of Socrates." *Ancient Philosophy* 17 (1997): 1–12.

Castiglione, Dario. "History, Reason, and Experience: Hume's Arguments against Contract Theories." In D. Boucher and P. Kelly, eds. *The Social Contract from Hobbes to Rawls*. London: Routledge, 1994.

Cavell, Stanley. *Must We Mean What We Say?* New York: Scribner, 1969.

Cohen, G. A. "Beliefs and Roles." *Proceedings of the Aristotelian Society* 67 (1966–67): 17–34.

———. "On Some Criticisms of Historical Materialism." *Proceedings of the Aristotelian Society: Supplementary Volume* 44 (1970): 121–41.

———. "Karl Marx and the Withering Away of Social Science." *Philosophy and Public Affairs* 1 (1972): 182–203.

———. "Being, Consciousness and Roles." In C. Abramsky, ed. *Essays in Honour of E. H. Carr*. London: Macmillan, 1974.

———. "Marx's Dialectic of Labor." *Philosophy and Public Affairs* 3 (1974): 235–61.

———. "Robert Nozick and Wilt Chamberlain: How Patterns Preserve Liberty." *Erkenntnis* 11 (1977): 5–23.

———. *Karl Marx's Theory of History: A Defence*. Princeton: Princeton University Press, 1978. Expanded ed., 2000.

———. "The Labour Theory of Value and the Concept of Exploitation." *Philosophy and Public Affairs* 8 (1979): 338–60.

———. "Functional Explanation: Reply to Elster." *Political Studies* 28 (1980): 129–35.

———. Review of Melvin Rader's *Marx's Interpretation of History*. *Clio* 10 (1981): 229–33.

———. "Functional Explanation, Consequence Explanation, and Marxism." *Inquiry* 25 (1982): 27–56.

———. "Marx and Locke on Land and Labour." *Proceedings of the British Academy* 71 (1985): 357–88. Reprinted in *Self-Ownership, Freedom, and Equality*. Oxford: Oxford University Press, 1995.

———. *History, Labour, and Freedom*. Oxford: Oxford University Press, 1988.

———. "On the Currency of Egalitarian Justice." *Ethics* 99 (1989): 906–44.

———. "Equality of What? On Welfare, Goods and Capabilities." *Recherches Economiques de Louvain* 56 (1990): 357–82. Reprinted in M. Nussbaum and A. Sen, eds. *The Quality of Life*. Oxford: Oxford University Press, 1993.

———. "Incentives, Inequality, and Community." In Grethe B. Peterson, ed. *The Tanner Lectures on Human Values*. Vol. 13. Salt Lake City: University of Utah Press, 1992.

———. "The Pareto Argument for Inequality." *Social Philosophy and Policy* 12 (1995): 160–85.

———. *Self-Ownership, Freedom, and Equality*. Oxford: Oxford University Press, 1995.

———. "Where the Action Is: On the Site of Distributive Justice." *Philosophy and Public Affairs* 26 (1997): 3–30.

———. "Once More into the Breach of Self-Ownership." *Journal of Ethics* 2 (1998): 57–96.

———. "Expensive Tastes and Multiculturalism." In R. Bhargava, A. K. Bagchi, and R. Sudarshan, eds. *Multiculturalism, Liberalism and Democracy*. New Delhi: Oxford University Press, 1999.

———. *If You're an Egalitarian, How Come You're So Rich?* Cambridge Mass.: Harvard University Press, 2001.

———. "Facts and Principles." *Philosophy and Public Affairs* 31 (2003): 211–45.

———. "Expensive Tastes Rides Again." In J. Burley, ed. *Dworkin and His Critics.* Oxford: Blackwell, 2004.

———. *Rescuing Justice and Equality.* Cambridge Mass.: Harvard University Press, 2008.

———. *Why Not Socialism?* Princeton: Princeton University Press, 2009.

———. "How to Do Political Philosophy." In his *On The Currency of Egalitarian Justice, and Other Essays*, Michael Otsuka, ed. Princeton: Princeton University Press, 2011.

———. *Finding Oneself in the Other.* Michael Otsuka, ed. Princeton: Princeton University Press, 2012.

Cohen, G. A., and W. Kymlicka. "Human Nature and Social Change in the Marxist Conception of History." *Journal of Philosophy* 85 (1988): 171–91. Reprinted in Cohen, *History, Labour, and Freedom.*

Cohen, Joshua. Review of *Karl Marx's Theory of History. Journal of Philosophy* 79 (1982): 253–73.

———. "Structure, Choice and Legitimacy: Locke's Theory of the State." *Philosophy and Public Affairs* 15 (1986): 301–24.

Danto, Arthur. *Nietzsche as Philosopher.* New York: Columbia University Press, 1965.

Dodds, E. R. *The Greeks and the Irrational.* Berkeley: University of California Press, 1951.

———. *The Ancient Concept of Progress.* Oxford: Oxford University Press, 1973.

Dostoyevsky, Fyodor. *Crime and Punishment.* 1866. London: Penguin, 2003.

Dworkin, Ronald. *Taking Rights Seriously.* London: Duckworth, 1977.

———. "What Is Equality? Part 1, Equality of Welfare." *Philosophy and Public Affairs* 10 (1981): 185–246.

———. "What Is Equality? Part 2, Equality of Resources." *Philosophy and Public Affairs* 10 (1981): 283–345.

———. *Sovereign Virtue.* Cambridge, Mass.: Harvard University Press, 2000.

———. "Replies." In J. Burley, ed. *Dworkin and His Critics.* Oxford: Blackwell, 2004.

Elster, Jon. "Exploring Exploitation." *Journal of Peace Research* 15 (1978): 3–17.

———. *Logic and Society.* New York: John Wiley, 1978.

———. *Ulysses and the Sirens.* Cambridge: Cambridge University Press, 1979.

———. "Cohen on Marx's Theory of History." *Political Studies* 28 (1980): 121–28.

———. "Marxism, Functionalism, and Game Theory: The Case for Methodological Individualism." *Theory and Society* 11 (1982): 453–82.

————. *Making Sense of Marx*. Cambridge: Cambridge University Press, 1985.

Engels, Friedrich. *The Conditions of the Working Class in England in 1844*. Florence Kelley Wischnewetzky, trans. London, George Allen & Unwin, Museum Street. Printed by the Riverside Press, Edinburgh, n.d.

Feuerbach, Ludwig. *The Essence of Christianity*. Written 1841, translation first published 1854. 2nd ed. George Elliot, trans. New York: Harper Torchbooks, 1957.

————. *Principles of the Philosophy of the Future*. Written 1843. Indianapolis: Bobbs-Merrill, 1966.

Fodor, Jerry. "Cat's Whiskers." Review of A. W. Moore, *Points of View. London Review of Books*, October 30, 1997.

Foot, Philippa. "Moral Beliefs." *Proceedings of the Aristotelian Society* 59 (1958–59): 83–104.

Frankena, W. "Obligation and Motivation in Recent Moral Philosophy." In A. I. Melden, ed. *Essays in Moral Philosophy*. Seattle: University of Washington Press, 1958.

Frankfurt, Harry. "Freedom of the Will and the Concept of a Person." In *The Importance of What We Care About*. Cambridge: Cambridge University Press, 1988.

Gauthier, David. *The Logic of Leviathan*. Oxford: Oxford University Press, 1969.

————. "David Hume, Contractarian." *Philosophical Review* 88 (1979): 3–38.

Gerth, H., and C. Wright Mills. *Character and Social Structure*. New York: Harcourt Brace, 1953.

Gough, J. W. *The Social Contract: A Critical Study of Its Development*. 2nd ed. Oxford: Oxford University Press, 1957.

Grieg, J.Y.T. *The Letters of David Hume*. Vol. 1. Oxford: Oxford University Press, 1932.

Griffin, James. *Well-Being*. Oxford: Oxford University Press, 1987.

Halévy, Daniel. *The Life of Friedrich Nietzsche*. London: T. Fisher Unwin, 1911.

Hampshire, Stuart. *Spinoza*. London: Penguin, 1951.

————. *Thought and Action*. London: Chatto and Windus, 1959.

————. *Freedom of the Individual*. Princeton.: Princeton University Press, 1965.

Hampton, Jean. *Hobbes and the Social Contract Tradition*. Cambridge: Cambridge University Press, 1986.

Hart, H.L.A. "Prolegomenon to the Principles of Punishment." In his *Punishment and Responsibility: Essays in the Philosophy of Law*. New York: Oxford University Press, 1968.

Hegel, G.W.F. *The German Constitution*. 1802. In *Hegel's Political Writings*. Z. A. Pelczynski and T. M. Knox. eds. Oxford: Oxford University Press, 1964.

————. *The Phenomenology of Mind*. 1807. J. B. Baillie, trans. London George Allen & Unwin. 2nd ed., 1949.

———. *Phenomenology of Spirit*. 1807. A. V. Miller, trans. Oxford: Oxford University Press, 1977.

———. *The Science of Logic*. 1812–16. W. H. Johnson and L. G. Struthers, trans. London: George Allen and Unwin, 1929.

———. *The Logic of Hegel*. 1817. W. Wallace, trans. 2nd ed. Oxford: Oxford University Press, 1892.

———. *The Philosophy of Right*. 1821. T. M. Knox, trans. Oxford: Oxford University Press, 1952.

———. *Introduction to the Philosophy of History*. 1840. Leo Rauch, trans. Indianapolis: Hackett, 1988.

Hobbes, Thomas. *The Elements of Law*. 1640. F. Tönnies, ed. London: Simpkin, Marshall and Co., 1923.

———. *De Cive or The Citizen*. 1642. Sterling Lamprecht, ed. New York: Appleton-Century-Crofts, 1949.

———. *Leviathan*. 1651. C. B. MacPherson, ed. London: Penguin, 1968.

Hodges, Donald Clark. "The Young Marx—A Reappraisal." *Philosophy and Phenomenological Research* 27 (1966): 216–29.

Hollingdale, R. J. *Nietzsche: The Man and His Philosophy*. 2nd ed. Cambridge: Cambridge University Press, 1999.

Hume, David. *A Treatise of Human Nature*. 1739–40. L. A. Selbey Bigge and P. H. Nidditch, eds. Oxford: Oxford University Press, 1976.

———. *Enquiries concerning the Human Understanding and concerning the Principles of Morals*. 1748–57. L. A. Selbey Bigge and P. H. Nidditch, eds.. Oxford: Oxford University Press, 1975.

———. "Of the Original Contract." 1777. In Henry D. Aiken, ed. *Hume's Moral and Political Philosophy*. New York: Hafner, 1948.

———. "The Sceptic." 1777. In Henry D. Aiken, ed. *Hume's Moral and Political Philosophy*. New York: Hafner, 1948.

Husami, Ziyad. "Marx on Distributive Justice." *Philosophy and Public Affairs* 8 (1978): 27–64.

Hussey, Edward. *The Presocratics*. London: Duckworth, 1972.

Irwin, Terence. *Plato's Moral Theory*. Oxford: Oxford University Press, 1977.

———. *Classical Thought*. Oxford: Oxford University Press, 1989.

Kant, Immanuel. *Critique of Pure Reason*. 1781/87. Norman Kemp Smith, trans. 2nd ed. London: Macmillan, 1933.

———. *Foundations of the Metaphysics of Morals*. 1785. Lewis Beck White, trans. New York: Prentice Hall, 1989.

———. *Groundwork of the Metaphysic of Morals*. 1785. In H. J. Paton, *The Moral Law*. London, Hutchinson, 1961 reprint; 1966 paperback reprint.

———. *Fundamental Principles of the Metaphysics of Ethics*. 1785. T. K. Abbott, trans. 10th ed. London: Longmans, 1969.

———. *Critique of Practical Reason*. 1788. Lewis Beck White, trans. New York: Macmillan, 1993.S

————. *Metaphysical Principles of Virtue.* 1797. J. W. Ellington, trans. Indianapolis: Bobbs Merrill, 1964. Reprinted in Immanuel Kant, *Ethical Philosophy.* Indianapolis: Hackett, 1983.

Kaufman, Walter, ed. *Nietzsche: Philosopher, Psychologist, Antichrist.* 1st ed. 1950. 4th ed. Princeton: Princeton University Press, 1974.

————. *The Portable Nietzsche.* New York: Viking Penguin, 1954.

Kavka, Gregory. *Hobbesian Moral and Political Theory.* Princeton: Princeton University Press, 1986.

Korsgaard, Christine. *The Sources of Normativity.* Cambridge: Cambridge University Press, 1996.

Kraut, Richard. "Egoism, Love and Political Office in Plato." *Philosophical Review* 82 (1973): 330–44.

Lea, F. A. *The Tragic Philosopher: Friedrich Nietzsche.* London: Methuen, 1957.

Levine, A., and E. Wright. "Rationality and Class Struggle." *New Left Review* 123 (1980): 47–68.

Lloyd Thomas, David. *Locke on Government.* London: Routledge, 1995.

Locke, John. *Two Treatises of Government.* 1690. Peter Laslett, ed. Cambridge: Cambridge University Press, 1988.

Lukács, Georg. *Geschichte und Klassenbewußtsein.* Berlin: Malik-Verlag, 1923.

————. *History and Class Consciousness.* Rodney Livingstone, trans. London: Merlin Press, 1971.

MacKay, D. M. "On the Logical Indeterminacy of a Free Choice." *Mind* 69 (1960): 31–40.

Mackie, J. L. *Hume's Moral Theory.* London: Routledge, 1980.

Marx Karl. *Economic and Philosophic Manuscripts of 1844.* Martin Milligan, trans. Moscow, 1956.

————. *The Holy Family.* 1845. R. Dixon, trans. Moscow: Foreign Language Publishing House, 1956.

————. *The Poverty of Philosophy.* 1847. Moscow: Progress Press, 1955.

————. *The Poverty of Philosophy.* 1847. In *Marx and Engels, Collected Works.* Vol. 6. London: Lawrence and Wishart, 1976.

————. *The Eighteenth Brumaire of Louis Bonaparte.* 1852. In *Marx-Engels Selected Works.* Vol. 1. Moscow: Foreign Languages Publishing House, 1962.

————. *Grundrisse.* 1857–61. London: Penguin, 1973.

————. *A Contribution to the Critique of Political Economy.* 1859. Chicago: C. H. Kerr, 1904.

————. *Capital.* Vol. 1. 1867. S. Moore and E. Aveling, trans. Vol. 2. 1885. Ernest Untermann, trans. Vol. 3. 1894. Ernest Untermann, trans. Chicago: Charles Kerr, 1909. Reprinted 1921.

————. *Capital.* Vol. 1. 1867. Ben Fowkes, trans. Vol. 2. 1885. David Fernbach, trans. Vol. 3. 1894. David Fernbach, trans. London: Penguin, 1976–81.

———— *Capital.* Vol. 3. 1894. S. Moore and E. Aveling, trans. New York: International Publishers, 1961.

———. *Die Frühschriften*. Siegfried Landshut, ed. Stuttgart: A. Kröner, 1953.

———. *Selected Writings in Sociology and Social Philosophy*. T. B. Bottomore and M. Rubel, eds. London: Watts, 1956.

———. *Early Writings*. T. B. Bottomore, ed. London: Watts, 1963.

———. *Pre-Capitalist Economic Formations*. E. J. Hobsbawm, ed. London: Lawrence and Wishart, 1964.

———. *Early Writings*. L. Colletti, ed. R. Livingstone and G. Bentor, trans. London, Penguin, 1975.

Marx, Karl, and Friedrich Engels. *The German Ideology*. 1845–46. Moscow: Progress Press, 1964.

———. *The German Ideology*. 1845–46. London: Lawrence and Wishart, 1965.

———. *The Communist Manifesto*. 1848. In *Marx-Engels Selected Works*. Vol. 1. Moscow: Foreign Languages Publishing House, 1962.

McLean, Iain. *Public Choice*. London: Wiley-Blackwell, 1978.

Miller, David, *Hume's Political Thought*. Oxford: Oxford University Press, 1981.

Miller, Richard. "Productive Forces and the Forces of Change." Review of *Karl Marx's Theory of History*. *Philosophical Review* 90 (1981): 91–117.

———. *Analyzing Marx*. Princeton: Princeton University Press, 1984.

Morgan, George. *What Nietzsche Means*. New York: Harper & Row, 1965.

Murphy, Mark C. "Was Hobbes a Legal Positivist?" *Ethics* 106 (1995): 846–73.

Nagel, Thomas. *The Last Word*. New York: Oxford University Press, 1997.

Niebuhr, Reinhold. *Moral Men and Immoral Society*. New York: Scribner, 1932.

Nietzsche, Friedrich. *The Birth of Tragedy*. 1872. In *The Complete Works of Friedrich Nietzsche*. Vol. 1. O. Levy, ed. W. A. Haussmann, ed. London: George Allen and Unwin, 1909.

———. *The Birth of Tragedy*. 1872. In *The Birth of Tragedy and The Genealogy of Morals*. Francis Golffing, trans. New York: Doubleday Anchor, 1956.

———. *Human, All Too Human, I*. 1878. Gary Handwerk, trans. Stanford, Calif.: Stanford University Press, 1995.

———. *The Gay Science*. 1882, 1887. Extracts in *The Portable Nietzsche*. Walter Kaufman, ed. New York: Viking Penguin, 1954.

———. *Thus Spoke Zarathustra*. 1883–85. In *The Portable Nietzsche*. Walter Kaufman, ed. New York: Viking Penguin, 1954.

———. *Beyond Good and Evil*. 1886. Marianne Cowan, trans. South Bend, Ind.: Gateway, 1955.

———. *Beyond Good and Evil*. 1886. Walter Kaufman, trans. New York: Vintage, 1966.

———. *The Genealogy of Morals*. 1887. In *The Birth of Tragedy and The Genealogy of Morals*. Francis Golffing, trans. New York: Doubleday Anchor, 1956.

———. *The Antichrist*. 1888. In *The Portable Nietzsche*. Walter Kaufman, ed. New York: Viking Penguin, 1954.

————. *Ecce Homo*. 1888. In *On the Genealogy of Morals and Ecce Homo*. Walter Kaufman, ed. New York, Vintage, 1989.

————. *Twilight of the Idols*. 1888. In *The Portable Nietzsche*. Walter Kaufman, ed. New York: Viking Penguin, 1954.

Nozick, Robert. *Anarchy, State, and Utopia*. New York: Basic Books, 1974.

Oldenquist, Andrew. "Loyalties." *Journal of Philosophy* 79 (1982): 173–93.

Paton, H. J. *The Categorical Imperative*. Chicago: University of Chicago Press, 1948.

Peters, Richard. *The Concept of Motivation*. London: Routledge and Kegan Paul, 1960.

Pindar. *The Odes of Pindar*. Richmond Lattimore, trans. Chicago: University of Chicago Press, 1947.

Pinkard, Terry. *Hegel's Phenomenology*. Cambridge: Cambridge University Press, 1996.

Plato. *Protagoras*. G. Vlastos, ed. Indianapolis: Bobbs-Merrill, 1956.

————. *The Republic*. R. Waterfield, trans. Oxford: World Classics, 1993.

————. *Laws*. In *The Dialogues of Plato in Two Volumes*. Vol. 2. B. Jowett, ed. Oxford: New York: Random House, 1937.

Plekhanov, N. *The Development of the Monist View of History*. Moscow: Progress Press, 1956.

Pound, Ezra. *The Cantos of Ezra Pound*. New York: New Directions, 1996.

Rawls, John. *A Theory of Justice*. Rev. ed. Oxford: Oxford University Press, 1999.

Raz, Joseph. *The Morality of Freedom*. Oxford: Oxford University Press, 1988.

Reid, Thomas. *Essays on the Active Powers of Man*. Edinburgh: printed for John Bell, and G.G.J. & J. Robinson: London, 1788.

Santayana, George. *George Santayana's Marginalia, A Critical Selection: Book Two, McCord–Zeller*. John McCormick, ed. Vol. 6 of *The Works of George Santayana*. Cambridge, Mass.: MIT Press, 2011.

Scanlon, T. M. "Promises and Practices." *Philosophy and Public Affairs* 19 (1990): 199–226.

Schelling, T. C. *The Strategy of Conflict*. Cambridge Mass.: Harvard University Press, 1960, 1980.

Schiller, Friedrich. *On the Aesthetic Education of Man*. R. Snell, trans. New Haven: Yale University Press, 1954.

Schlaifer, Robert. "Greek Theories of Slavery from Homer to Aristotle." *Harvard Studies in Classical Philology* 47 (1936): 165–204.

Schulz, Wilhelm. *Die Bewegung der Produktion. Eine geschichtlich-statistische Abhandlung*. Zurich: Druck und Verlag des literarischen Comptoirs, 1843.

Schumpeter, Joseph. *Capitalism, Socialism and Democracy*. New York: Harper and Rowe, 1950.

————. *A History of Economic Analysis*. London: Allen and Unwin, 1951.

Sellars, Wifrid. "Thought and Action." In *Freedom and Determinism*. Keith Lehrer, ed. New York: Random House, 1966.

Shaver, Rob. "Leviathan, King of the Proud." *Hobbes Studies* 3 (1990): 54–74.

Shklar, Judith. "Hegel's *Phenomenology*: An Elegy for Hellas." In Z. A. Pelczynski, ed. *Hegel's Political Philosophy*. Cambridge: Cambridge University Press, 1971.

Smith, Adam. *The Wealth of Nations*. London: Dutton, Dent, Everyman's Library, 1954.

Soll, Ivan. *Introduction to Hegel's Metaphysics*. Chicago: University of Chicago Press, 1969.

Stevenson, C. L. "Persuasive Definitions." *Mind* 47 (1938): 331–50.

Strauss, Leo. *The Political Philosophy of Hobbes*. 1936. Chicago: University of Chicago Press, 1951.

Strawson, P. F. "Determinism." In D. Pears ed. *Freedom and the Will*. London: Macmillan, 1963.

Taylor, Charles. *Hegel*. Cambridge: Cambridge University Press, 1975.

Tawney, R. H. *Religion and the Rise of Capitalism*. London: Penguin, 1938.

Thompson, E. P. *The Making of the English Working Class*. London: Penguin, 1980.

Thomson, Judith Jarvis. *The Realm of Rights*. Cambridge Mass.: Harvard University Press, 1990.

Tully, James. *A Discourse on Property*. Cambridge: Cambridge University Press, 1980.

Vallentyne, Peter. Review of Jody Kraus, *The Limits of Hobbesian Contractarianism*. *Ethics* 106 (1995): 193–94.

Waldron, Jeremy. "The Advantages and Difficulties of the Humean Theory of Property." *Social Philosophy and Policy* 11 (1994): 85–123.

Warnock, Geoffrey. *The Object of Morality*. London: Methuen, 1971.

Weber, Max, "Politics as a Vocation." In *From Max Weber: Essays in Sociology*. H. H. Gerth and C. W. Mills, eds. Oxford: Routledge, 1991.

Wertheimer, Roger. *The Significance of Sense*. Ithaca N.Y.: Cornell University Press, 1972.

Whelan, Frederick. "Marx and Revolutionary Virtue." In J. R. Pennock and J. W. Chapman, eds. *Marxism*. Nomos XXVI. New York: New York University Press, 1983.

White, Alan. *Attention*. Oxford: Blackwell, 1964.

Whitman, Walt. *Complete Poems*. London: Penguin, 2005.

Williams, Bernard. "The Analogy of Soul and State in Plato." In E. N. Lee, R. M. Rorty, and A.P.D. Mourelatos, eds. *Exegesis and Argument*. New York: Humanities Press, 1973.

———. "Persons, Character, and Morality." In his *Moral Luck*. Cambridge: Cambridge University Press, 1981.

———. *Shame and Necessity*. Berkeley: University of California Press, 1993.

Winch, Peter. *The Idea of a Social Science and Its Relation to Philosophy*. London: Routledge and Kegan Paul, 1958.

————. "The Universalizability of Moral Judgements." *The Monist* 49 (1965): 196–214.

Wittgenstein, Ludwig. *Philosophical Investigations*. G.E.M. Anscombe, trans. Cambridge: Cambridge University Press, 1974.

Wolff, Robert Paul. "Nozick's Derivation of the Minimal State." In J. Paul, ed. *Reading Nozick*. Oxford: Blackwell, 1981.

Wood, Allen W. "The Marxian Critique of Justice." *Philosophy and Public Affairs* 1 (1972): 244–82.

————. *Karl Marx*. London: Routledge and Kegan Paul, 1981.

————. *Hegel's Ethical Thought*. Cambridge: Cambridge University Press, 1990.

Wright Mills, C. *White Collar*. New York: Oxford University Press, 1951.

————. *The Sociological Imagination*. New York: Oxford University Press, 1959.

Young, Gary "Justice and Capitalist Production." *Canadian Journal of Philosophy* 8 (1978): 421–55.

————. "Doing Marx Justice." *Canadian Journal of Philosophy*, Supplementary Volume, 7 (1981): 251–68.

Index